FAST TRACK TO A 5

Preparing for the AP® Chemistry Examination

To Accompany
Chemistry
8th and 9th Editions
by Steven S. Zumdahl and Susan A. Zumdahl

Laura L. Duncan
Boulder High School, Boulder, Colorado

Kara A. Pezzi
Appleton East High School, Appleton, Wisconsin

Sheldon Knoespel
Jackson Community College and Michigan State University, Michigan

CENGAGE
Learning·

Australia • Brazil • Japan • Korea • Mexico • Singapore • Spain • United Kingdom • United States

For product information and technology assistance, contact us at **Cengage Learning Customer & Sales Support, 1-888-915-3276**

For permission to use material from this text or product, submit all requests online at **www.cengage.com/permissions** Further permissions questions can be e-mailed to **permissionrequest@cengage.com**

ISBN-13: 978-1-133-61151-6
ISBN-10: 1-133-61151-6

Cengage Learning
200 First Stamford Place, 4th Floor
Stamford, CT 06902
USA

Cengage Learning is a leading provider of customized learning solutions with office locations around the globe, including Singapore, the United Kingdom, Australia, Mexico, Brazil, and Japan. Locate your local office at **www.cengage.com/global**

Cengage Learning products are represented in Canada by Nelson Education, Ltd.

To learn more about Cengage, visit **www.cengage.com**

To find online supplements and other instructional support, please visit **www.cengagebrain.com**

Printed in the United States of America
5 6 7 8 17 16 15 14

CONTENTS

ABOUT THE AUTHORS

LAURA DUNCAN has been an AP Chemistry teacher at Boulder High School in Colorado since 2002, and an AP exam reader since 2011. She earned a B.A. in chemistry from the University of California, Santa Cruz in 1977, and a Ph.D. in chemical engineering from the University of Notre Dame in 1985. She worked in process and product development and pharmaceutical project management for almost 20 years before daring to reenter the classroom. She has worked for ETS in developing a syllabus for the new curriculum and is certain that her students will continue their stellar record of earning an average score of 4 on the exam.

KARA PEZZI is a former analytical chemist who left private industry in 1992 to pursue her passion for teaching. She has taught chemistry and AP Chemistry at Appleton East and two other high schools in Wisconsin. Kara, a National Board Certified Teacher and a 2011 recipient of the Presidential Award for Excellence in Mathematics and Science Teaching, was a mentor for the United States National Chemistry Olympiad team and currently serves as USNCO Coordinator for Northeast Wisconsin. During her time with ETS, she has worked on question development for the revised course and currently serves as a table leader for the AP Chemistry exam reading.

SHELDON KNOESPEL currently teaches chemistry part time at Jackson Community College in Jackson, Michigan. He also serves as a part time science education instructor at Michigan State University and was the site coordinator for the Michigan Science Olympiad state tournament. Sheldon has also served as one of the committee members for the Laboratory Practical section of the American Chemical Society's United States National Chemistry Olympiad Exam. Previously Sheldon was employed with the MSU Department of Chemistry where he was Chemical Demonstrator for fourteen years. Prior to that he taught at Olivet High School, Olivet, Michigan, where he taught all of the physical sciences, including AP Chemistry, for more than twenty years.

PREFACE

Students, take a minute from your busy schedule of classes and studying and look around you. Everything you see (and some things that you don't) is a product of chemistry. From the paper and ink that this book is made from to the water, flavorings, and stimulants that may be in the beverage you are drinking—all are composed of nanoscopic particles that interact with one another to create the world in which we live. We hope that as you study chemistry, you will gain a deeper appreciation and understanding of how everything in our world is connected at the molecular level.

Several people helped in the creation of this study guide. The critical comments of reviewers Sheila Nguyen of Centennial High School in Corona, California and Murray D. Eicher of Academic Magnet High School in North Charleston, South Carolina helped us to think deeply about how to organize the content of the book and make it meaningful to students. Karen Ettinger of O'Donnell Learn kept us on track and facilitated communication among the authors and reviewers.

On a personal level, this book would not be possible without the support of our family members and especially our students who inspire us each day to tackle new challenges.

Part I

Strategies for the AP Exam

PREPARING FOR THE AP® CHEMISTRY EXAMINATION

Advanced Placement can be exhilarating. Whether you are taking an AP course at your school or you are working on AP independently, the stage is set for a great intellectual experience.

But sometime after New Year's Day, when the examination begins to loom on a very real horizon, Advanced Placement can seem downright intimidating—in fact, offered the opportunity to take the examination just to see what it's like, even adults long out of high school refuse. If you dread taking the test, you are in good company.

The best way to deal with an AP examination is to master it, not let it master you. If you can think of these examinations as a way to show off how much chemistry you know, you have a leg up. Attitude and confidence *do* help. If you are not one of those students, there is still a lot you can do to sideline your anxiety. This book is designed to put you on a fast track. Focused review and practice time will help you master the examination so that you can walk in with confidence and score a 5.

WHAT'S IN THIS BOOK

This book is keyed to *Chemistry* by Steven and Susan Zumdahl, 8th and 9th editions, but because it follows the College Board Concept Outline, it is compatible with all textbooks. It is divided into three sections. Part I offers suggestions for getting yourself ready, from signing up to take the test and sharpening your pencils to organizing a free-response essay. This is followed by the list of AP Chemistry learning objectives from the College Board curriculum. At the end of Part I, you will find a Diagnostic Test that has all of the elements of the AP Chemistry Examination.

Part II is made up of 13 chapters—again following the College Board Concept Outline. These chapters are not a substitute for your textbook and class discussion; they simply review the AP chemistry course. At the end of each chapter, you will find 15 multiple-choice questions and two free-response questions based on the material in that chapter. At the end of each answer, you will find page references directing you to the discussion on that particular point in *Chemistry* and the AP Chemistry learning objective number covering that point.

AP® and Advanced Placement Program® are trademarks registered and/or owned by the College Board, which was not involved in the production of, and does not endorse, this product.

Part III has two complete AP Chemistry examinations. At the end of each test, you will find the answers, explanations, and references to *Chemistry* and the AP Chemistry learning objective for the multiple-choice and the free-response questions.

What's in the *Chemistry* Textbook That Will Help Your Preparation

As you work your way through the textbook there are some features that will assist you in getting the most out of the textbook:

- Make use of the Conceptual Problem Solving Method introduced in Chapter 3 in which you break the problem down into three parts: (1) Where are we going? (2) How do we get there? and (3) Reality Check.
- Make certain you carefully study the Sample Exercises with solutions in each chapter. These will often give you a guide to help develop your problem solving skills.
- Read the For Review section that highlights the material presented in the chapter as a means to double check your understanding before you proceed.
- Answer the Review Questions at the end of each chapter as a measure of your understanding. This will give you instant feedback as to how much of the chapter you may need to study again.
- Perform the multiple-choice AP assessment items at the end of each chapter. They are tied to the Learning Objectives which are part of the AP format. Practice doing computations for these questions without a calculator. You are not allowed to use a calculator in the multiple-choice section of the test, so you need to be good at estimating.
- Working in small groups, answer the Active Learning Questions at the end of each chapter. This is an excellent opportunity to gauge your level of understanding and to receive assistance from your classmates.
- Do as many Challenge and Marathon Problems as you can. These problems are intended to incorporate many different concepts into the solution. Problems like this are particularly good practice for the free-response portion of the AP exam.

Being successful in chemistry usually involves careful reading of the textbook and working as many different types of problems as possible. The successful student is not one who memorizes a bunch of facts but one who is able to synthesize and analyze the problem. Chemistry is like a lot of subjects in that an understanding of new material often depends on an understanding of previous concepts.

Setting Up a Review Schedule

If you have been doing your homework steadily and keeping up with the course work, you are in good shape. Organize your notes, homework, and handouts from class by topic. Reference these materials as well as your textbook and this study guide when you have difficulty in a specific section. But even if you have done all that—or if it is too late to do all that—there are some more ways to get it all together.

To begin, read Part I of this book. You will be much more comfortable going into the exam if you understand how the exam questions are designed and how best to approach them. Then take the Diagnostic Test and see where you are right now.

Take out a calendar and set up a schedule for yourself. If you begin studying early, you can chip away at the review chapters in Part II. You will be surprised—and pleased—by how much material you can cover in half an hour a day of study for a month or so before the test. Look carefully at the sections of the Diagnostic Test; if you missed a number of questions in one particular area, allow more time for the chapters that cover that area of the course. The practice tests in Part III will give you more experience with different kinds of multiple-choice questions and the wide range of free-response questions.

If time is short, skip reading the review chapters (although you might read through the chapter subheadings) and work on the multiple-choice and free-response questions at the end of each review. This will give you a good idea of your understanding of that particular topic. Then take the tests in Part III.

If time is *really* short, go straight from Part I to Part III. Taking practice tests over and over again is the fastest, most practical way to prepare. You cannot study chemistry by reading it like a novel. You must actively do problems to gain understanding and excel in your performance. Athletes do not perform well just by reading books about their sport or by watching others. They must get up and practice. So, you too, just like athletes, must practice, practice, practice if you want to do your best!

BEFORE THE EXAMINATION

By February, long before the exam, you need to make sure that you are registered to take the test. Many schools take care of the paperwork and handle the fees for their AP students, but check with your teacher or the AP coordinator to make sure that you are on the list. This is especially important if you have a documented disability and need test accommodations. If you are studying AP independently, call AP Services at the College Board for the name of the local AP coordinator, who will help you through the registration process.

The evening before the exam is not a great time for partying. Nor is it a great time for cramming. If you like, look over class notes or drift through your textbook, concentrating on the broad outlines, not the small details, of the course. You might also want to skim through this book and read the AP tips.

The evening before the exam *is* a great time to get your things together for the next day. Sharpen a fistful of no. 2 pencils with good erasers; bring a scientific calculator with fresh batteries. Certain types of calculators are not allowed, so be sure to verify with your teacher or the College Board that your model is acceptable. For example, you cannot use a calculator with a typewriter-style keyboard or a cell phone. Cell phones are not even allowed in the testing room, so you will need a watch and be certain to turn off the alarm if it has one. Bring a piece of fruit or a power bar and a bottle of water for the break. Make sure you have your Social Security number and whatever photo identification and admission ticket are required. Then relax. And get a good night's sleep.

On the day of the examination, plan to arrive early. It is wise not to skip breakfast—studies show that students who eat a hot breakfast before testing get higher grades. Be careful not to drink a lot of liquids, necessitating a trip to the bathroom during the exam. Breakfast will give you the energy you need to power you through the exam—and more. You will spend some time waiting while everyone is seated in the right room for the right exam before the test has even begun. With a short break between Section I and Section II, the AP Chemistry exam lasts for more than two and a half hours. So be prepared for a long morning. You do not want to be distracted by a growling stomach or hunger pangs.

Be sure to wear comfortable clothes, taking along a sweater in case the heating or air-conditioning is erratic. Be sure, too, to wear clothes you like—everyone performs better when they think they look better—and by all means wear your lucky socks.

You have been on the fast track. Now go get a 5!

TAKING THE AP® CHEMISTRY EXAMINATION

The AP Chemistry curriculum emphasizes the importance of inquiry and reasoning in science, and requires depth of understanding more than the memorization of facts. On the exam you may be asked to do a range of tasks, such as interpreting lab data or making predictions based on your knowledge of chemical principles.

Some content in your text will not be tested in the examination, although your teacher may choose to include that material in your course.

The AP Chemistry exam will consist of two sections. The sections are described below.

Section I: The main features of the multiple-choice sections are given in the following table.

	Format
Number of questions	60
Time to complete	90 minutes
Number of choices	4
Calculator	No
Weighting	50%

The questions will generally refer to "real world" situations and may contain several parts. Some sample questions are given in the "Strategies for the Multiple-Choice Section" that follows.

Section II: After Section I is collected, you will have a short break. The main features of the free-response sections are given in the following table.

	Format
Number of questions	7 total. The questions are made up of 3 long questions (parts a–d or parts a–e) and 4 short questions (parts a–b).

	Format
Point value	This section is worth up to 46 points. Each long question is worth up to 10 points. Each short question is worth up to 4 points.
Types of long and short questions (at least one question from each type)	Lab I Lab II Representation I Representation II Quantitative
Time to complete	90 minutes
Calculator	Yes
Weighting	50%

In this section, you will be asked to:

■ Design an experiment to test a hypothesis, given a specific set of laboratory equipment (Lab I)
■ Interpret and draw conclusions from data (Lab II)
■ Use models to describe physical phenomena (Representations I and II)
■ Follow a logical or analytical pathway to solve a problem (Quantitative)

When answering these questions, you will need to be able to explain, say, what is happening at the atomic or molecular level when a substance changes from a solid, to a liquid, to a gas; but in addition, you may be asked to draw diagrams of the three phases to demonstrate that you can make models of systems.

The focus on laboratory work as a tool of scientific inquiry means that you will need to practice writing laboratory procedures, understand the correct use of laboratory equipment to gather data, and incorporate safe practices. Some example questions are given in the "Strategies for Answering Free-Response Questions" that follows.

STRATEGIES FOR THE MULTIPLE-CHOICE SECTION

Each question in the multiple-choice section is worth one point, and since there is no penalty for guessing, you want to make the most educated guess! Here are some rules of thumb to help you:

■ **Read the question carefully** Pressured for time, many students make the mistake of reading the questions too quickly or merely skimming them. By reading a question carefully, you may already have some idea about the correct answer. You can then look for it in the responses.

■ **Eliminate any answer you know is wrong** You can write on the multiple-choice questions in the test book. As you read through the responses, draw a line through any answer you know is wrong.

■ **Read all of the possible answers, then choose the most accurate response** AP examinations are written to test your precise knowledge of a subject. Some of the responses may be partially correct but there will only be one response that is completely true.

■ **Avoid absolute responses** These answers often include the words "always" or "never." For example, the statement "all chlorides are always soluble in water" is incorrect because compounds such as silver chloride and lead (II) chloride are insoluble in water.

■ **Mark tough questions** If you are hung up on a question, make an educated guess, but mark it in the margin of the question book and come back to review it later if you have time.

TYPES OF MULTIPLE-CHOICE QUESTIONS

The exam will include short and long questions. The latter will ask several questions about the same set of data. Here are some suggestions for approaching each of the various kinds of multiple-choice questions:

CLASSIC/BEST ANSWER QUESTIONS This is the most common type of multiple-choice question. It simply requires you to read the question and select the most correct answer. The example below is a short question.

1. Given the following reduction potentials, which metal would be best for a pipeline carrying dilute hydrochloric acid?

Reaction	E°, V
$Ti^{+3} + 3e^- \rightarrow Ti$	+0.72
$Zn^{+2} + 2e^- \rightarrow Zn$	−0.76
$Cu^{+2} + 2e^- \rightarrow Cu$	+0.34
$Fe^{+2} + 2e^- \rightarrow Fe$	−0.44

(A) Ti
(B) Zn
(C) Cu
(D) Fe

ANSWER: A. You are looking for the metal that is least likely to be oxidized by the protons in a solution of the strong acid. The higher (most positive) the reduction potential, the less likely the metal will be oxidized. Eliminate (B) and (D) because their reduction potentials are negative, indicating that they are more likely to be oxidized. Of the two remaining, (A) has the largest positive value. (Learning Objective 3.12: The student can make qualitative or quantitative predictions about galvanic or electrolytic reactions based on half-cell reactions and potentials and/ or Faraday's laws.)

NONCALCULATOR COMPUTATIONS These questions require computation without the use of a calculator. Simple mathematics or the choice of the correct algebraic setup will be involved.

1. A weak acid, HA, has a K_a value of 1.0×10^{-6}. A student adds 10.0 mL of 0.200 M NaOH to 40.0 mL of 0.100 M HA and the two react completely. Calculate the final pH.
    (A) 2.0
    (B) 6.0
    (C) 7.0
    (D) 8.0

ANSWER: **B**. To answer this question, you must consider at what point in the titration the question is referring to. Because the base, NaOH, is twice as concentrated as the acid, HA, it will take half as much NaOH to reach the equivalence point, or 20.0 mL. We are not at the equivalence point. Half the amount of the NaOH, 10.0 mL, needed to reach the equivalence point has been added. Halfway to the equivalence point, the pH equals the pK_a which equals $-\log (K_a)$ or 6.0. (Learning Objective 6.13: The student can interpret titration data for monoprotic or polyprotic acids involving titration of a weak or strong acid by a strong base (or a weak or strong base by a strong acid) to determine the concentration of the titrant and the pK_a for a weak acid, or the pK_b for a weak base.)

2. $2 \text{ C}(s) + \text{O}_2(g) \rightarrow 2 \text{ CO}(g)$

    Into a 3.0-L container at 25°C are placed 1.2 g of carbon (graphite), and 3.2 g of oxygen gas.

    If the carbon and the oxygen react completely to form $\text{CO}(g)$, what will be the final pressure in the container at 25°C?
    (A) $\dfrac{0.05(0.082)(298)}{3.0}$ atm
    (B) $\dfrac{0.10(0.082)(25)}{3.0}$ atm
    (C) $\dfrac{0.15(0.082)(298)}{3.0}$ atm
    (D) $\dfrac{0.10(0.082)(298)}{3.0}$ atm

ANSWER: **C**. To answer this question, 1.2 g of carbon is 0.10 mol of carbon (1 mole of carbon equals 12 g). Similarly, 3.2 g of O_2 is 0.10 mol of O_2. The limiting reactant is carbon producing 0.10 mol of CO. O_2 is present in excess. (0.10 mol of CO requires 0.05 mol of O_2 leaving 0.05 mol of O_2.) When the reaction is complete, there is 0.10 mol CO + 0.05 mol O_2 left which equals 0.15 mol total. (Learning Objective 2.6: The student can apply mathematical relationships or estimation to determine macroscopic variables for ideal gases. Learning Objective 3.4: The student is able to relate quantities (measured mass of substances, volumes of solutions, or volumes and pressures of gases) to identify stoichiometric relationships for a reaction, including situations involving limiting reactants and situations in which the reaction has not gone to completion.)

Long Question

Questions 1 and 2 refer to the following data.

A student performing an experiment to determine the relative intermolecular forces of various liquids immerses a thermocouple covered with filter paper in a specific liquid, and monitors the resulting temperature change over a 3-minute interval. The data she obtains are:

Liquid	ΔT (°C)
Ethanol	8.0
1-Propanol	7.5
2-Propanol	8.0
Water	3.5

1. Based on these data, which substance has the strongest intermolecular forces?
   (A) Ethanol
   (B) 1-Propanol
   (C) 2-Propanol
   (D) Water

ANSWER: D. Substances with strong intermolecular forces do not readily change phase from liquid to gas. Temperature change, specifically cooling, is related to the amount of substance that evaporates, so a low temperature change indicates less evaporation and higher intermolecular forces. Water exhibits the smallest temperature change so water must have the strongest intermolecular forces. (Learning Objective 2.13: The student is able to describe the relationships between the structural features of polar molecules and the forces of attraction between the particles.)

2. Why does 2-propanol have a greater temperature change than 1-propanol?
   (A) 1-Propanol has more London dispersion forces because it has a longer carbon chain.
   (B) 2-Propanol has more London dispersion forces because it has a longer carbon chain.
   (C) The hydrogen bonds are stronger in 1-propanol than in 2-propanol.
   (D) The hydrogen bonds are stronger in 2-propanol than in 1-propanol.

ANSWER: A. Both substances are able to form the same number of hydrogen bonds per molecule, so this does not explain the difference in temperature change and eliminates choices (C) and (D). 1-Propanol has a straight three-carbon chain so it has more contact points available for London dispersion forces than the branched chain of 2-propanol. (Learning Objective 2.16: The student is able to explain the properties (phase, vapor pressure, viscosity, etc.) of small and large molecular compounds in terms of the strengths and types of intermolecular forces.)

STRATEGIES FOR THE FREE-RESPONSE SECTION

Section II of the AP exam comes with a periodic table and a table of equations and constants. The needed portions of the standard reduction potentials, $E°_{red}$, will be provided within the questions.

- Scan all of the questions in the section you are working in and mark those that you know you can answer correctly. Do these problems first.
- Show all of your work and use units where requested. Partial credit will be awarded for problems if the correct work is shown but the answer is not present or is incorrect. In problems involving calculations, circle your final answer.
- Cross out incorrect answers with an "X" rather than spending time erasing.
- Be clear, neat, and organized in your work. If a grader cannot clearly understand your work, you may not receive full credit.
- Three of the questions will have several parts. Attempt to solve each part. Even if your answer to the first part is incorrect, you still may be awarded points for the remaining parts of the question if the work is correct for those parts.
- Units are important in your answer. Keeping track of your units throughout calculations, and performing unit cancellation where possible, will help guide you to your answer. Points will be deducted for missing or incorrect units in the answer. However, if the question does not specify the requirement of units, points will not be deducted for missing units, although they can be deducted for incorrect units.
- You do not need to work the questions in order. Make sure you put the number of the question in the corner of each page of your essay booklet. In addition, questions are sometimes broken into parts, such as (a) and (b). When this is the case, label each part of your response.

STRATEGIES FOR ANSWERING FREE-RESPONSE QUESTIONS

Free-response questions will ask you to explain, compare, and predict. Minor calculations, showing mathematical relationships, or drawing graphs or structures, may also be involved. Usually these are not traditional essay questions. Most free-response questions do not require an introduction or conclusion. Most do not even require a thesis. Many of these questions may be written in a bulleted or short-answer format. Although this may sound easier than writing a traditional essay, it is important that you know the material very well because these are targeted questions. Examination readers want specifics. They are looking for accurate information presented in clear, concise prose. You cannot mask vague information with elegant prose. The use of appropriate vocabulary terms is strongly suggested as this may make the difference between the awarding of a point or not.

To be successful in writing free-response answers for the AP Chemistry exam, be sure to get straight to the answer and use key terms in your explanations. Sometimes, if you ramble on and on, you might accidentally state an incorrect fact. Points will be deducted for incorrect or extraneous information.

Techniques to write free-response questions include chart format, bullet format, and outline format. None of these styles requires that you write complete sentences. In each of these styles, restate the question in simple terms, using your own words. Restate each part (a, b, and so on) separately, not together. In your restatement and response, underline key words or concepts.

■ **Fill in a chart to answer the question.** This style is helpful in answering questions about electronic and molecular structure. This method is also used in the example on identification of the set of four quantum numbers for each electron in an element in this chapter.

■ **In bullet or number format, make a list,** using a bullet (■) or number for each new concept. Leave room between concepts because you may want to come back later to fill them in.

■ **Outline format** is more traditional, using Roman numerals, letters, etc. This takes more time to organize ideas, but it does show progression of ideas in a logical sequence. As in the bulleted format, leave room between concepts because you may want to come back later to fill them in.

■ Lastly, **the freestyle method,** but this sometimes results in rambling and incomplete answers. Also, writing in paragraphs does not allow room for additional ideas to be added.

TYPES OF FREE-RESPONSE QUESTIONS

The free-response questions may be long or short. The long questions typically include four or five parts and are worth up to 10 points. The short questions include one or two parts and are worth up to 4 points. Samples and descriptions of the main categories of questions follow.

SAMPLE PROBLEM, LAB I: In this type of question, you will be asked to demonstrate your ability to plan and write a laboratory procedure based on your knowledge of chemical principles. The graders will also be looking for your knowledge of safe practices. These can be long or short questions, but will often be long questions, as in the example below.

You are given a set of four clear liquids. One is ethanol, one is a dilute solution of acetic acid, one is water, and one is a dilute solution of sodium hydroxide. Design an experiment to identify the liquids. Describe the steps, the data you would collect, and how the data support the identifications. Laboratory equipment for your experiment should be taken from the list below. (You may not need all of the equipment.)

50-mL beakers	fume hood
hot plate	stirring rods
0.1 M NaHCO$_3$	phenolphthalein indicator
conductivity meter	safety glasses
thermometer	beaker tongs

Answer:

1. Work under a fume hood, because several of the liquids are volatile.
2. Wear safety glasses to protect your eyes from the acid, base, and alcohol.
3. Put approximately 5 mL of each liquid in each of 4 50-mL beakers.
4. First test: Of the liquids, only sodium hydroxide will turn pink in the presence of phenolphthalein indicator. Add a drop of indicator to each solution and stir gently. The one that turns pink is sodium hydroxide solution. Clean off the stirring rods with distilled water so they will not cause contamination in subsequent tests. (Learning Objective 6.15: The student can identify a given solution as containing a mixture of strong acids and/or bases and calculate or estimate the pH—and concentrations of all chemical species—in the resulting solution.)
5. Second test: Of the remaining liquids, only acetic acid will react with sodium hydrogen carbonate to release carbon dioxide gas. The phenolphthalein indicator will not interfere with the test, so the same beakers can be used. Add approximately 5 mL of sodium hydrogen carbonate solution to the three remaining solutions and stir gently. The one that bubbles is the acetic acid being neutralized by the weak base to form water, carbon dioxide gas, and aqueous sodium acetate. (Learning Objective 6.16: The student can identify a given solution as being the solution of a monoprotic weak acid or base (including salts in which one ion is a weak acid or base), calculate the pH and concentration of all species in the solution, and/or infer the relative strengths of the weak acids or bases from given equilibrium concentrations.)
6. Third test: Of the remaining liquids, ethanol has a much lower boiling temperature than water because it has weaker intermolecular forces (it can only make one hydrogen bond per molecule, and water can make two). Put approximately 10 mL of each in two separate 50-mL beakers and put on a hot plate set at medium temperature. Check the temperatures of the liquids when they boil by placing a thermometer in the liquid, but not touching the bottom or sides of the beaker. The water should boil at around 90–100°C; the ethanol will boil at a much lower temperature. Use the beaker tongs to remove the beakers from the hot plate as soon as you are done making measurements. (Learning Objective 2.16: The student is able to explain the properties (phase, vapor pressure, viscosity, etc.) of small and large molecular compounds in terms of the strengths and types of intermolecular forces.)
7. Dispose of all liquids in the designated liquid waste containers in your lab.

Solving this problem also involves the use of Science Practice 4: The student can plan and implement data collection strategies in relation to a particular scientific question. [Note: Data can be collected from many different sources, e.g., investigations, scientific observations, the findings of others, historic reconstruction, and/or archived data.] The problem also involves the use of Science Practice 5: The student can perform data analysis and evaluation of evidence.

Problem, Lab II: Here you will be given data and asked to draw conclusions based on these data. Your answers must demonstrate your knowledge of the specific chemical principles that relate to the observations. Using proper vocabulary is critical. These questions may be long or short. The example is a long question.

You are given a set of four vials of clear liquids, designated A, B, C, and D. One is ethanol, one is a dilute solution of acetic acid, one is mineral oil, and one is a dilute solution of sodium hydroxide. In a series of experiments, you collect the following data:

- Only A and B are strongly conductive.
- Only B turns pink when phenolphthalein indicator is added.
- When equal portions of each liquid are placed on thermocouples and the amount of cooling tracked over a 5-minute period, C shows the greatest change.
- When small portions of the liquids are mixed with water, all form homogeneous solutions except D, which forms a separate layer on the top.

Use this information to identify the contents of each vial. Explain clearly how you used the data to come to your conclusions.

Answer:
1. Compounds that ionize when dissolved in water form conductive solutions. Of the four liquids, only the sodium hydroxide solution (a base) and the acetic acid solution (an acid) consist of ions. A and B must be the acid and base. Since B turns pink when phenolphthalein is added, and phenolphthalein is only pink in basic solutions, B must be sodium hydroxide and A must be acetic acid. (Learning Objective 2.15: The student is able to explain observations regarding the solubility of ionic solids and molecules in water and other solvents on the basis of particle views that include intermolecular interactions and entropic effects. Learning Objective 2.16: The student is able to explain the properties (phase, vapor pressure, viscosity, etc.) of small and large molecular compounds in terms of the strengths and types of intermolecular forces.)
2. Ethanol is completely soluble in water because it can form hydrogen bonds with water. Mineral oil is nonpolar and will not dissolve in water. D must be mineral oil because it forms a layer on the top of water. (Learning Objective 2.15: The student is able to explain observations regarding the solubility of ionic solids and molecules in water and other solvents on the basis of particle views that include intermolecular interactions and entropic effects.)
3. Although ethanol forms hydrogen bonds with itself, it can only make one hydrogen bond per molecule and water can make two. With fewer intermolecular forces per molecule, ethanol will be more volatile than water and the aqueous acid and base solutions. Mineral oil is nonpolar but as a linear molecule has

many contact points for London dispersion forces; it is also relatively nonvolatile. Ethanol will evaporate the most in a set period of time and therefore cool the thermocouple the most. C must be ethanol. (Learning Objective 2.16: The student is able to explain the properties (phase, vapor pressure, viscosity, etc.) of small and large molecular compounds in terms of the strengths and types of intermolecular forces.)

Solving this problem also demonstrates Science Practice 5: The student can perform data analysis and evaluation of evidence.

Scientists, chemists in particular, create models of atomic/molecular behavior that explain what is observed at "large" scale. In Representation problems, you are asked to talk about the strengths and weaknesses of key models. There are two types of Representation questions.

SAMPLE PROBLEM, REPRESENTATION I: For Representation I questions you are asked to discuss how a model of particles behave on the microscopic (particulate) level and explain macroscopic observations. You will need to understand the strengths and the weaknesses of various models. These can be long or short questions. The example below is a short question.

In the kinetic-molecular theory (KMT), gas atoms/molecules are depicted as particles with no appreciable volume, in constant random motion, that collide elastically with one another and do not interact with each other. What aspect(s) of this model break(s) down when a system's temperature decreases and pressure increases?

Answer:
1. In KMT, the number and size of molecules are so small relative to the size of the container that their volume can be neglected, and the system volume is essentially that of the "empty" container. The main way to increase pressure is to decrease the system volume. If the system volume decreases enough, the volume of the molecules themselves is no longer negligible and must be taken into account. Also, the molecules may get close enough for intermolecular forces to come into play, so the molecules now are able to interact with each other.
2. Temperature is a measure of molecular motion, so a lower temperature indicates that the molecules are moving more slowly. When they move more slowly, they can spend enough time near each other for intermolecular forces to become significant. (Learning Objective 2.4: The student is able to use KMT and concepts of intermolecular forces to make predictions about the macroscopic properties of gases, including both ideal and nonideal behaviors.)

SAMPLE PROBLEM, REPRESENTATION II: This kind of problem is similar to Representation I, except that your answer will contain diagrams as well as explanations. These can be long or short questions. This example is a short question.

Water is a liquid at room temperature, but hydrogen chloride and hydrogen are gases under the same conditions. Draw a particulate representation of each substance, clearly indicating the intermolecular forces that account for these observations, and name the primary intermolecular force for each.

Answer:

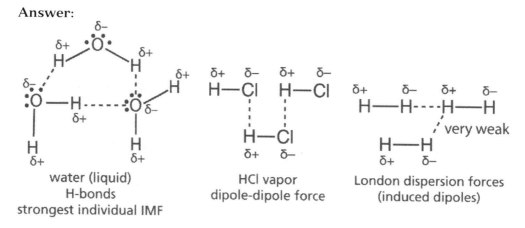

water (liquid)
H-bonds
strongest individual IMF

HCl vapor
dipole-dipole force

London dispersion forces
(induced dipoles)

(Learning Objective 2.1: Students can predict properties of substances based on their chemical formulas, and provide explanations of their properties based on particle views. Learning Objective 2.4: The student is able to use KMT and concepts of intermolecular forces to make predictions about the macroscopic properties of gases, including both ideal and nonideal behaviors.)

SAMPLE PROBLEM, QUANTITATIVE: This type of question will ask you to follow a logical, analytical pathway to solve a problem. These can be long or short questions. The example given is a long question.

$$C_2H_4(g) \ + \ 3\,O_2(g) \ \rightarrow \ 2\,CO_2(g) \ + \ 2\,H_2O(g)$$

Information about the substances involved in the reaction presented above is tabulated below.

Substance	$S°$(J/mol·K)	$G°_f$(kJ/mol)
$C_2H_4(g)$	?	68
$O_2(g)$	205	0
$CO_2(g)$	213.6	−394
$H_2O(g)$	189	−229

Bond	Bond Energy (kJ/mol)
O – H	467
O – O	146
O = O	495
C – H	413
C – C	347
C = C	614
C ≡ C	839
C – O	358
C = O	799

(a) Calculate the value for the standard free energy change, $\Delta G°$, at 25°C for the reaction. What does the sign of $\Delta G°$ indicate about the reaction?

(b) Calculate the value for the standard enthalpy change, $\Delta H°$, at 25°C for the reaction. What does the sign of $\Delta H°$ indicate about the reaction?

(c) Calculate the value for the standard entropy change, $\Delta S°$, at 25°C for the reaction. What does the sign of $\Delta S°$ indicate about the reaction?

(d) Calculate the value for the absolute entropy of $C_2H_4(g)$ at 25°C.

ANSWER

(A) $\Delta G° = 2(-394) + 2(-229) - 68 = -1314$ kJ/mol

(B)

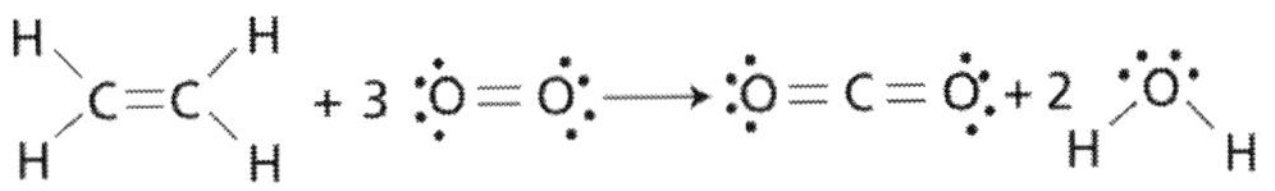

Bonds Broken		Bonds Formed	
4 C–H	4(413)	4 C=O	4(799)
1 C=C	1(614)	4 O–H	4(467)
3 O=O	3(495)		−5064 kJ
	+3751 kJ		

$\Delta H° = 3751$ kJ + $(-5064$ kJ$) = -1313$ kJ

The reaction is exothermic since $\Delta H°$ is negative.

(C) $\Delta G° = \Delta H° - T\Delta S°$; $\Delta S° = (\Delta H° - \Delta G°) / T$

$\Delta S° = -1313 - (-1314$ kJ$) / 298$ K $= 0.0034$ kJ/K

A positive sign of change in entropy indicates that entropy is increasing in the reaction.

Here, it barely changes.

(D) $\Delta S° = 2\, S°_{CO_2} + 2\, S°_{H_2O} - (S°_{C_2H_4} + 3\, S°_{O_2})$

$S°_{C_2H_4} = 2\, S°_{CO_2} + 2\, S°_{H_2O} - 3\, S°_{O_2} - \Delta S°$

$= 2(213.6) + 2(189) - 3(205) - 3.4 = 187$ J/K

Learning Objective 5.8: The student is able to draw qualitative and quantitative connections between the reaction enthalpy and the energies involved in the breaking and formation of chemical bonds.

Learning Objective 5.13: The student is able to predict whether or not a physical or chemical process is thermodynamically favored by determination of (either quantitatively or qualitatively) the signs of both $\Delta H°$ and $\Delta S°$, and calculation or estimation of $\Delta G°$ when needed.

Learning Objective 5.14: The student is able to determine whether a chemical or physical process is thermodynamically favorable by calculating the change in standard Gibbs free energy.

AP CHEMISTRY LEARNING OBJECTIVES

The following is the list of learning objectives from the College Board curriculum.

LEARNING OBJECTIVE 1.1 The student can justify the observation that the ratio of the masses of the constituent elements in any pure sample of that compound is always identical on the basis of the atomic molecular theory.

LEARNING OBJECTIVE 1.2 The student is able to select and apply mathematical routines to mass data to identify or infer the composition of pure substances and/or mixtures.

LEARNING OBJECTIVE 1.3 The student is able to select and apply mathematical relationships to mass data in order to justify a claim regarding the identity and/or estimated purity of a substance.

LEARNING OBJECTIVE 1.4 The student is able to connect the number of particles, moles, mass, and volume of substances to one another, both qualitatively and quantitatively.

LEARNING OBJECTIVE 1.5 The student is able to explain the distribution of electrons in an atom or ion based upon data.

LEARNING OBJECTIVE 1.6 The student is able to analyze data relating to electron energies for patterns and relationships.

LEARNING OBJECTIVE 1.7 The student is able to describe the electronic structure of the atom, using PES data, ionization energy data, and/or Coulomb's law to construct explanations of how the energies of electrons within shells in atoms vary.

LEARNING OBJECTIVE 1.8 The student is able to explain the distribution of electrons using Coulomb's law to analyze measured energies.

LEARNING OBJECTIVE 1.9 The student is able to predict and/or justify trends in atomic properties based on location on the periodic table and/or the shell model.

LEARNING OBJECTIVE 1.10 Students can justify with evidence the arrangement of the periodic table and can apply periodic properties to chemical reactivity.

LEARNING OBJECTIVE 1.11 The student can analyze data, based on periodicity and the properties of binary compounds, to identify patterns and generate hypotheses related to the molecular design of compounds for which data are not supplied.

LEARNING OBJECTIVE 1.12 The student is able to explain why a given set of data suggests, or does not suggest, the need to refine the atomic model from a classical shell model with the quantum mechanical model.

LEARNING OBJECTIVE 1.13 Given information about a particular model of the atom, the student is able to determine if the model is consistent with specified evidence.

LEARNING OBJECTIVE 1.14 The student is able to use data from mass spectrometry to identify the elements and the masses of individual atoms of a specific element.

LEARNING OBJECTIVE 1.15 The student can justify the selection of a particular type of spectroscopy to measure properties associated with vibrational or electronic motions of molecules.

LEARNING OBJECTIVE 1.16 The student can design and/or interpret the results of an experiment regarding the absorption of light to determine the concentration of an absorbing species in a solution.

LEARNING OBJECTIVE 1.17 The student is able to express the law of conservation of mass quantitatively and qualitatively using symbolic representations and particulate drawings.

LEARNING OBJECTIVE 1.18 The student is able to apply conservation of atoms to the rearrangement of atoms in various processes.

LEARNING OBJECTIVE 1.19 The student can design, and/or interpret data from, an experiment that uses gravimetric analysis to determine the concentration of an analyte in a solution.

LEARNING OBJECTIVE 1.20 The student can design, and/or interpret data from, an experiment that uses titration to determine the concentration of an analyte in a solution.

LEARNING OBJECTIVE 2.1 Students can predict properties of substances based on their chemical formulas, and provide explanations of their properties based on particle views.

LEARNING OBJECTIVE 2.2 The student is able to explain the relative strengths of acids and bases based on molecular structure, interparticle forces, and solution equilibrium.

LEARNING OBJECTIVE 2.3 The student is able to use aspects of particulate models (i.e., particle spacing, motion, and forces of attraction) to reason about observed differences between solid and liquid phases and among solid and liquid materials.

LEARNING OBJECTIVE 2.4 The student is able to use KMT and concepts of intermolecular forces to make predictions about the macroscopic properties of gases, including both ideal and nonideal behaviors.

LEARNING OBJECTIVE 2.5 The student is able to refine multiple representations of a sample of matter in the gas phase to accurately represent the effect of changes in macroscopic properties on the sample.

LEARNING OBJECTIVE 2.6 The student can apply mathematical relationships or estimation to determine macroscopic variables for ideal gases.

LEARNING OBJECTIVE 2.7 The student is able to explain how solutes can be separated by chromatography based on intermolecular interactions.

LEARNING OBJECTIVE 2.8 The student can draw and/or interpret representations of solutions that show the interactions between the solute and solvent.

LEARNING OBJECTIVE 2.9 The student is able to create or interpret representations that link the concept of molarity with particle views of solutions.

LEARNING OBJECTIVE 2.10 The student can design and/or interpret the results of a separation experiment (filtration, paper chromatography, column chromatography, or distillation) in terms of the relative strength of interactions among and between the components.

LEARNING OBJECTIVE 2.11 The student is able to explain the trends in properties and/or predict properties of samples consisting of particles with no permanent dipole on the basis of London dispersion forces.

LEARNING OBJECTIVE 2.12 The student can qualitatively analyze data regarding real gases to identify deviations from ideal behavior and relate these to molecular interactions.

LEARNING OBJECTIVE 2.13 The student is able to describe the relationships between the structural features of polar molecules and the forces of attraction between the particles.

LEARNING OBJECTIVE 2.14 The student is able to apply Coulomb's law qualitatively (including using representations) to describe the interactions of ions, and the attractions between ions and solvents to explain the factors that contribute to the solubility of ionic compounds.

LEARNING OBJECTIVE 2.15 The student is able to explain observations regarding the solubility of ionic solids and molecules in water and other solvents on the basis of particle views that include intermolecular interactions and entropic effects.

LEARNING OBJECTIVE 2.16 The student is able to explain the properties (phase, vapor pressure, viscosity, etc.) of small and large molecular compounds in terms of the strengths and types of intermolecular forces.

LEARNING OBJECTIVE 2.17 The student can predict the type of bonding present between two atoms in a binary compound based on position in the periodic table and the electronegativity of the elements.

LEARNING OBJECTIVE 2.18 The student is able to rank and justify the ranking of bond polarity on the basis of the locations of the bonded atoms in the periodic table.

LEARNING OBJECTIVE 2.19 The student can create visual representations of ionic substances that connect the microscopic structure to macroscopic properties, and/or use representations to connect the microscopic structure to macroscopic properties (e.g., boiling point, solubility, hardness, brittleness, low volatility, lack of malleability, ductility, or conductivity).

LEARNING OBJECTIVE 2.20 The student is able to explain how a bonding model involving delocalized electrons is consistent with macroscopic properties of metals (e.g., conductivity, malleability, ductility, and low volatility) and the shell model of the atom.

LEARNING OBJECTIVE 2.21 The student is able to use Lewis diagrams and VSEPR to predict the geometry of molecules, identify hybridization, and make predictions about polarity.

LEARNING OBJECTIVE 2.22 The student is able to design or evaluate a plan to collect and/or interpret data needed to deduce the type of bonding in a sample of a solid.

LEARNING OBJECTIVE 2.23 The student can create a representation of an ionic solid that shows essential characteristics of the structure and interactions present in the substance.

LEARNING OBJECTIVE 2.24 The student is able to explain a representation that connects properties of an ionic solid to its structural attributes and to the interactions present at the atomic level.

LEARNING OBJECTIVE 2.25 The student is able to compare the properties of metal alloys with their constituent elements to determine if an alloy has formed, identify the type of alloy formed, and explain the differences in properties using particulate level reasoning.

LEARNING OBJECTIVE 2.26 Students can use the electron sea model of metallic bonding to predict or make claims about the macroscopic properties of metals or alloys.

LEARNING OBJECTIVE 2.27 The student can create a representation of a metallic solid that shows essential characteristics of the structure and interactions present in the substance.

LEARNING OBJECTIVE 2.28 The student is able to explain a representation that connects properties of a metallic solid to its structural attributes and to the interactions present at the atomic level.

LEARNING OBJECTIVE 2.29 The student can create a representation of a covalent solid that shows essential characteristics of the structure and interactions present in the substance.

LEARNING OBJECTIVE 2.30 The student is able to explain a representation that connects properties of a covalent solid to its structural attributes and to the interactions present at the atomic level.

LEARNING OBJECTIVE 2.31 The student can create a representation of a molecular solid that shows essential characteristics of the structure and interactions present in the substance.

LEARNING OBJECTIVE 2.32 The student is able to explain a representation that connects properties of a molecular solid to its structural attributes and to the interactions present at the atomic level.

LEARNING OBJECTIVE 3.1 Students can translate among macroscopic observations of change, chemical equations, and particle views.

LEARNING OBJECTIVE 3.2 The student can translate an observed chemical change into a balanced chemical equation and justify the choice of equation type (molecular, ionic, or net ionic) in terms of utility for the given circumstances.

LEARNING OBJECTIVE 3.3 The student is able to use stoichiometric calculations to predict the results of performing a reaction in the laboratory and/or to analyze deviations from the expected results.

LEARNING OBJECTIVE 3.4 The student is able to relate quantities (measured mass of substances, volumes of solutions, or volumes and pressures of gases) to identify stoichiometric relationships for a reaction, including situations involving limiting reactants and situations in which the reaction has not gone to completion.

LEARNING OBJECTIVE 3.5 The student is able to design a plan in order to collect data on the synthesis or decomposition of a compound to confirm the conservation of matter and the law of definite proportions.

LEARNING OBJECTIVE 3.6 The student is able to use data from synthesis or decomposition of a compound to confirm the conservation of matter and the law of definite proportions.

LEARNING OBJECTIVE 3.7 The student is able to identify compounds as Bronsted-Lowry acids, bases, and/or conjugate acid-base pairs, using proton-transfer reactions to justify the identification.

LEARNING OBJECTIVE 3.8 The student is able to identify redox reactions and justify the identification in terms of electron transfer.

LEARNING OBJECTIVE 3.9 The student is able to design and/or interpret the results of an experiment involving a redox titration.

LEARNING OBJECTIVE 3.10 The student is able to evaluate the classification of a process as a physical change, chemical change, or ambiguous change based on both macroscopic observations and the distinction between rearrangement of covalent interactions and noncovalent interactions.

LEARNING OBJECTIVE 3.11 The student is able to interpret observations regarding macroscopic energy changes associated with a reaction or process to generate a relevant symbolic and/or graphical representation of the energy changes.

LEARNING OBJECTIVE 3.12 The student can make qualitative or quantitative predictions about galvanic or electrolytic reactions based on half-cell reactions and potentials and/or Faraday's laws.

LEARNING OBJECTIVE 3.13 The student can analyze data regarding galvanic or electrolytic cells to identify properties of the underlying redox reactions.

LEARNING OBJECTIVE 4.1 The student is able to design and/or interpret the results of an experiment regarding the factors (i.e., temperature, concentration, surface area) that may influence the rate of a reaction.

LEARNING OBJECTIVE 4.2 The student is able to analyze concentration vs. time data to determine the rate law for a zeroth-, first-, or second-order reaction.

LEARNING OBJECTIVE 4.3 The student is able to connect the half-life of a reaction to the rate constant of a first-order reaction and justify the use of this relation in terms of the reaction being a first-order reaction.

LEARNING OBJECTIVE 4.4 The student is able to connect the rate law for an elementary reaction to the frequency and success of molecular collisions, including connecting the frequency and success to the order and rate constant, respectively.

LEARNING OBJECTIVE 4.5 The student is able to explain the difference between collisions that convert reactants to products and those that do not in terms of energy distributions and molecular orientation.

LEARNING OBJECTIVE 4.6 The student is able to use representations of the energy profile for an elementary reaction (from the reactants, through the transition state, to the products) to make qualitative predictions regarding the relative temperature dependence of the reaction rate.

LEARNING OBJECTIVE 4.7 The student is able to evaluate alternative explanations, as expressed by reaction mechanisms, to determine which are consistent with data regarding the overall rate of a reaction, and data that can be used to infer the presence of a reaction intermediate.

LEARNING OBJECTIVE 4.8 The student can translate among reaction energy profile representations, particulate representations, and symbolic representations (chemical equations) of a chemical reaction occurring in the presence and absence of a catalyst.

LEARNING OBJECTIVE 4.9 The student is able to explain changes in reaction rates arising from the use of acid-base catalysts, surface catalysts, or enzyme catalysts, including selecting appropriate mechanisms with or without the catalyst present.

LEARNING OBJECTIVE 5.1 The student is able to create or use graphical representations in order to connect the dependence of potential energy to the distance between atoms and factors, such as bond order (for covalent interactions) and polarity (for intermolecular interactions), which influence the interaction strength.

LEARNING OBJECTIVE 5.2 The student is able to relate temperature to the motions of particles, either via particulate representations, such as drawings of particles with arrows indicating velocities, and/or via representations of average kinetic energy and distribution of kinetic energies of the particles, such as plots of the Maxwell-Boltzmann distribution.

LEARNING OBJECTIVE 5.3 The student can generate explanations or make predictions about the transfer of thermal energy between systems based on this transfer being due to a kinetic energy transfer between systems arising from molecular collisions.

LEARNING OBJECTIVE 5.4 The student is able to use conservation of energy to relate the magnitudes of the energy changes occurring in two or more interacting systems, including identification of the systems, the type (heat versus work), or the direction of energy flow.

LEARNING OBJECTIVE 5.5 The student is able to use conservation of energy to relate the magnitudes of the energy changes when two nonreacting substances are mixed or brought into contact with one another.

LEARNING OBJECTIVE 5.6 The student is able to use calculations or estimations to relate energy changes associated with heating/cooling a substance to the heat capacity, relate energy changes associated with a phase transition to the enthalpy of fusion/vaporization, relate energy changes associated with a chemical reaction to the enthalpy of the reaction, and relate energy changes to $P\Delta V$ work.

LEARNING OBJECTIVE 5.7 The student is able to design and/or interpret the results of an experiment in which calorimetry is used to determine the change in enthalpy of a chemical process (heating/cooling, phase transition, or chemical reaction) at constant pressure.

LEARNING OBJECTIVE 5.8 The student is able to draw qualitative and quantitative connections between the reaction enthalpy and the energies involved in the breaking and formation of chemical bonds.

LEARNING OBJECTIVE 5.9 The student is able to make claims and/or predictions regarding relative magnitudes of the forces acting within collections of interacting molecules based on the distribution of electrons within the molecules and the types of intermolecular forces through which the molecules interact.

LEARNING OBJECTIVE 5.10 The student can support the claim about whether a process is a chemical or physical change (or may be classified as both) based on whether the process involves changes in intramolecular versus intermolecular interactions.

LEARNING OBJECTIVE 5.11 The student is able to identify the noncovalent interactions within and between large molecules, and/or connect the shape and function of the large molecule to the presence and magnitude of these interactions.

LEARNING OBJECTIVE 5.12 The student is able to use representations and models to predict the sign and relative magnitude of the entropy change associated with chemical or physical processes.

LEARNING OBJECTIVE 5.13 The student is able to predict whether or not a physical or chemical process is thermodynamically favored by determination of (either quantitatively or qualitatively) the signs of both $\Delta H°$ and $\Delta S°$, and calculation or estimation of $\Delta G°$ when needed.

LEARNING OBJECTIVE 5.14 The student is able to determine whether a chemical or physical process is thermodynamically favorable by calculating the change in standard Gibbs free energy.

LEARNING OBJECTIVE 5.15 The student is able to explain how the application of external energy sources or the coupling of favorable with unfavorable reactions can be used to cause processes that are not thermodynamically favorable to become favorable.

LEARNING OBJECTIVE 5.16 The student can use LeChâtelier's principle to make qualitative predictions for systems in which coupled reactions that share a common intermediate drive formation of a product.

LEARNING OBJECTIVE 5.17 The student can make quantitative predictions for systems involving coupled reactions that share a common intermediate, based on the equilibrium constant for the combined reaction.

LEARNING OBJECTIVE 5.18 The student can explain why a thermodynamically favored chemical reaction may not produce large amounts of product (based on consideration of both initial conditions and kinetic effects), or why a thermodynamically unfavored chemical reaction can produce large amounts of product for certain sets of initial conditions.

LEARNING OBJECTIVE 6.1 The student is able to, given a set of experimental observations regarding physical, chemical, biological, or environmental processes that are reversible, construct an explanation that connects the observations to the reversibility of the underlying chemical reactions or processes.

LEARNING OBJECTIVE 6.2 The student can, given a manipulation of a chemical reaction or set of reactions (e.g., reversal of reaction or addition of two reactions), determine the effects of that manipulation on Q or K.

LEARNING OBJECTIVE 6.3 The student can connect kinetics to equilibrium by using reasoning about equilibrium, such as LeChâtelier's principle, to infer the relative rates of the forward and reverse reactions.

LEARNING OBJECTIVE 6.4 The student can, given a set of initial conditions (concentrations or partial pressures) and the equilibrium constant, K, use the tendency of Q to approach K to predict and justify the prediction as to whether the reaction will proceed toward products or reactants as equilibrium is approached.

LEARNING OBJECTIVE 6.5 The student can, given data (tabular, graphical, etc.) from which the state of a system at equilibrium can be obtained, calculate the equilibrium constant, K.

LEARNING OBJECTIVE 6.6 The student can, given a set of initial conditions (concentrations or partial pressures) and the equilibrium constant, K, use stoichiometric relationships and the law of mass action (Q equals K at equilibrium) to determine qualitatively and/or quantitatively the conditions at equilibrium for a system involving a single reversible reaction.

LEARNING OBJECTIVE 6.7 The student is able, for a reversible reaction that has a large or small K, to determine which chemical species will have very large versus very small concentrations at equilibrium.

LEARNING OBJECTIVE 6.8 The student is able to use LeChâtelier's principle to predict the direction of the shift resulting from various possible stresses on a system at chemical equilibrium.

LEARNING OBJECTIVE 6.9 The student is able to use LeChâtelier's principle to design a set of conditions that will optimize a desired outcome, such as product yield.

LEARNING OBJECTIVE **6.10** The student is able to connect LeChâtelier's principle to the comparison of Q to K by explaining the effects of the stress on Q and K.

LEARNING OBJECTIVE **6.11** The student can generate or use a particulate representation of an acid (strong or weak or polyprotic) and a strong base to explain the species that will have large versus small concentrations at equilibrium.

LEARNING OBJECTIVE **6.12** The student can reason about the distinction between strong and weak acid solutions with similar values of pH, including the percent ionization of the acids, the concentrations needed to achieve the same pH, and the amount of base needed to reach the equivalence point in a titration.

LEARNING OBJECTIVE **6.13** The student can interpret titration data for monoprotic or polyprotic acids involving titration of a weak or strong acid by a strong base (or a weak or strong base by a strong acid) to determine the concentration of the titrant and the pK_a for a weak acid, or the pK_b for a weak base.

LEARNING OBJECTIVE **6.14** The student can, based on the dependence of K_w on temperature, reason that neutrality requires $[H^+] = [OH^-]$ as opposed to requiring pH = 7, including especially the applications to biological systems.

LEARNING OBJECTIVE **6.15** The student can identify a given solution as containing a mixture of strong acids and/or bases and calculate or estimate the pH (and concentrations of all chemical species) in the resulting solution.

LEARNING OBJECTIVE **6.16** The student can identify a given solution as being the solution of a monoprotic weak acid or base (including salts in which one ion is a weak acid or base), calculate the pH and concentration of all species in the solution, and/or infer the relative strengths of the weak acids or bases from given equilibrium concentrations.

LEARNING OBJECTIVE **6.17** The student can, given an arbitrary mixture of weak and strong acids and bases (including polyprotic systems), determine which species will react strongly with one another (i.e., with $K > 1$) and what species will be present in large concentrations at equilibrium.

LEARNING OBJECTIVE **6.18** The student can design a buffer solution with a target pH and buffer capacity by selecting an appropriate conjugate acid-base pair and estimating the concentrations needed to achieve the desired capacity.

LEARNING OBJECTIVE **6.19** The student can relate the predominant form of a chemical species involving a labile proton (i.e., protonated/deprotonated form of a weak acid) to the pH of a solution and the pK_a associated with the labile proton.

LEARNING OBJECTIVE **6.20** The student can identify a solution as being a buffer solution and explain the buffer mechanism in terms of the reactions that would occur on addition of acid or base.

LEARNING OBJECTIVE 6.21 The student can predict the solubility of a salt, or rank the solubility of salts, given the relevant K_{sp} values.

LEARNING OBJECTIVE 6.22 The student can interpret data regarding solubility of salts to determine, or rank, the relevant K_{sp} values.

LEARNING OBJECTIVE 6.23 The student can interpret data regarding the relative solubility of salts in terms of factors (common ions, pH) that influence the solubility.

LEARNING OBJECTIVE 6.24 The student can analyze the enthalpic and entropic changes associated with the dissolution of a salt, using particulate level interactions and representations.

LEARNING OBJECTIVE 6.25 The student is able to express the equilibrium constant in terms of $\Delta G°$ and RT and use this relationship to estimate the magnitude of K and, consequently, the thermodynamic favorability of the process.

A Diagnostic Test

The purpose of this test is to give you an indication of how well you will perform on the AP Chemistry exam. These questions are representative of the AP Chemistry examination, but bear in mind it is impossible to predict exactly how well you will do on the actual exam. Calculators may not be used for answering questions in the first section of this test. The first section is 50% of your total test grade. Time yourself to finish this part in 90 minutes. There are two types of multiple-choice questions used in this examination. One type consists of a data set that will be used to answer 3–5 multiple-choice questions. The other type of multiple-choice question consists of a question or incomplete statements followed by four possible answers. Select the one that is best in each case.

AP CHEMISTRY EXAMINATION
Section I: Multiple-Choice Questions
Time: 90 minutes
Number of Questions: 60

No calculators can be used in this section. A periodic table and a formula chart with constants is provided.

Directions: Each of the questions or incomplete statements below is followed by four suggested answers or completions. Select the one that is best in each case.

Questions 1–3 refer to the following:

Various masses of calcium chloride were dissolved in water and added to 6.00 mL of 1.7 M sodium carbonate. The graph of the data is below.

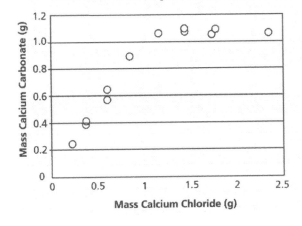

1. What technique would separate calcium carbonate precipitate from the rest of the substances in the reaction?
   (A) column chromatography
   (B) distillation
   (C) evaporation
   (D) filtration

2. Which chemical was NOT present in the reaction vessel after 0.5 grams of calcium chloride reacted?
   (A) calcium chloride
   (B) sodium carbonate
   (C) calcium carbonate
   (D) sodium chloride

29

Periodic Table of Elements

1 H 1.008																		2 He 4.003
3 Li 6.941	4 Be 9.012											5 B 10.81	6 C 12.01	7 N 14.01	8 O 16.00	9 F 19.00	10 Ne 20.18	
11 Na 22.99	12 Mg 24.31											13 Al 26.98	14 Si 28.09	15 P 30.97	16 S 32.07	17 Cl 35.45	18 Ar 39.95	
19 K 39.10	20 Ca 40.08	21 Sc 44.96	22 Ti 47.88	23 V 50.94	24 Cr 52.00	25 Mn 54.94	26 Fe 55.85	27 Co 58.93	28 Ni 58.69	29 Cu 63.55	30 Zn 65.38	31 Ga 69.72	32 Ge 72.59	33 As 74.92	34 Se 78.96	35 Br 79.90	36 Kr 83.80	
37 Rb 85.47	38 Sr 87.62	39 Y 88.91	40 Zr 91.22	41 Nb 92.91	42 Mo 95.94	43 Tc (98)	44 Ru 101.1	45 Rh 102.9	46 Pd 106.4	47 Ag 107.9	48 Cd 112.4	49 In 114.8	50 Sn 118.7	51 Sb 121.8	52 Te 127.6	53 I 126.9	54 Xe 131.3	
55 Cs 132.9	56 Ba 137.3	57 La* 138.9	72 Hf 178.5	73 Ta 180.9	74 W 183.9	75 Re 186.2	76 Os 190.2	77 Ir 192.2	78 Pt 195.1	79 Au 197.0	80 Hg 200.6	81 Tl 204.4	82 Pb 207.2	83 Bi 209.0	84 Po (209)	85 At (210)	86 Rn (222)	
87 Fr (223)	88 Ra 226	89 Ac† (227)	104 Rf (227)	105 Db	106 Sg	107 Bh	108 Hs	109 Mt	110 Ds	111 Rg (272)								

*Lanthanides

58 Ce 140.1	59 Pr 140.9	60 Nd 144.2	61 Pm (145)	62 Sm 150.4	63 Eu 152.0	64 Gd 157.3	65 Tb 158.9	66 Dy 162.5	67 Ho 164.9	68 Er 167.3	69 Tm 168.9	70 Yb 173.0	71 Lu 175.0

†Actinides

90 Th 232.0	91 Pa (231)	92 U 238.0	93 Np (237)	94 Pu (244)	95 Am (243)	96 Cm (247)	97 Bk (247)	98 Cf (251)	99 Es (252)	100 Fm (257)	101 Md (258)	102 No (259)	103 Lr (260)

3. Explain the relatively horizontal portion of the graph from about 1.2 g to 2.4 g of $CaCl_2$.
   (A) Calcium chloride was the limiting reagent.
   (B) Sodium carbonate was the limiting reagent.
   (C) Calcium carbonate was no longer being produced.
   (D) Calcium chloride and sodium carbonate reached equilibrium.

Questions 4–7 refer to the following:

Photoelectron spectra of 2 elements are shown below. The units of energy are MJ.

Element A

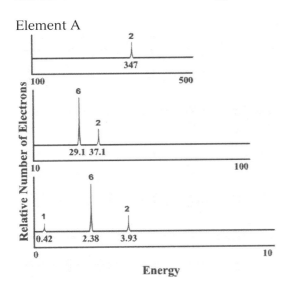

Element B

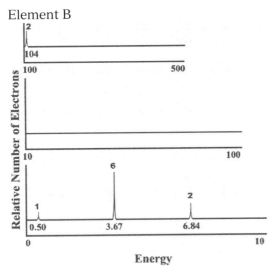

4. How many shells or energy levels are occupied in Element A?
   (A) 3
   (B) 4
   (C) 5
   (D) 6

5. Which electron is in the valence shell of Element A?
   (A) 0.42
   (B) 3.93
   (C) 37.1
   (D) 347

6. Propose a reason why the peak of highest energy for Element A has a higher energy (347 MJ) than the peak of highest energy in Element B (104 MJ).
   (A) The electrons in Element A are farther from the nucleus than the electrons in Element B.
   (B) The electrons in Element A are closer to the nucleus than the electrons in Element B.
   (C) Element A has more electrons than Element B.
   (D) Element A has greater shielding than Element B.

7. Which element would be more reactive with water?
   (A) Element A because the least attracted electron is 0.42 MJ.
   (B) Element A because the most attracted electron is 347 MJ.
   (C) Element B because the least attracted electron is 0.50 MJ.
   (D) Element B because the most attracted electron is 104 MJ.

GO ON TO NEXT PAGE

For questions 8–9, consider the electrochemical cell:

$$Cu|Cu^{2+}\,(1\ M)\ \|\ Ag^+\,(1\ M)|Ag$$

The cell reaction is
$$2\ Ag^+(aq) + Cu(s) \rightarrow Cu^{2+}(aq) + 2\ Ag(s).$$

The measured voltage is +0.46 V.

8. Increasing the concentration of silver ions will
   (A) cause a decrease in blue color in the cell
   (B) increase the cell voltage above +0.46 V
   (C) decrease the concentration of copper(II) ions
   (D) cause no change in the cell voltage

9. The reaction at the anode is
   (A) $Ag^+(aq) + e^- \rightarrow Ag(s)$
   (B) $Ag(s) \rightarrow Ag^+(aq)$
   (C) $Cu(s) \rightarrow Cu^{2+}(aq) + 2\ e^-$
   (D) $Cu^{2+}(aq) + 2\ e^- \rightarrow Cu(s)$

10. The diagram below shows how the potential energy of N–C–O bond is related to bond angle. At 300 K, the atoms vibrate and deviate approximately +/– 4° from the average bond angle. How does an increase in temperature affect the deviation in the bond angle?

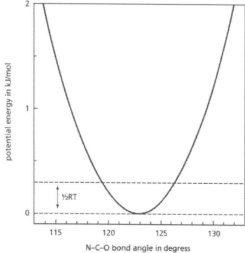

© O.S. Smart, 1995

(A) No change because temperature does not affect bond angle.
(B) Increase because molecules are moving faster.
(C) Increase because atoms have more kinetic energy.
(D) Increase because as the degrees of temperature increase, the degrees of angle increase.

11. The amount of silver which will be formed when 0.00200 mol of Ag_2S reacts completely with excess zinc is
    (A) 0.00100 mol
    (B) 0.00200 mol
    (C) 0.00400 mol
    (D) 0.00800 mol

12. The solubility of $Zn(OH)_2$ is $2.0 \times 10^{-6}\ M$ at a certain temperature. Determine the value of the K_{sp} at this same temperature.
    (A) 4.0×10^{-6}
    (B) 8.0×10^{-6}
    (C) 1.6×10^{-17}
    (D) 3.2×10^{-17}

13. The K_c for $A + B \rightleftharpoons C$ is 4.0. The K_c for $2\ C \rightleftharpoons 2\ A + 2\ B$ is
    (A) 1/16
    (B) 1/4
    (C) 8
    (D) 16

14. Calculate $\triangle G°$ for the reaction C (*diamond*) → C (*graphite*) and predict spontaneity given the following information.
    C (*diamond*) + $O_2(g) \rightarrow CO_2(g)$
    $\qquad \triangle G° = -397\ kJ/mol$
    C (*graphite*) + $O_2(g) \rightarrow CO_2(g)$
    $\qquad \triangle G° = -394\ kJ/mol$
    (A) +3 kJ/mol; spontaneous
    (B) –3 kJ/mol; spontaneous
    (C) +3 kJ/mol; nonspontaneous
    (D) –3 kJ/mol; nonspontaneous

Calcium Oxide   Magnesium Oxide

15. Calcium oxide, CaO, has a lower melting temperature than magnesium oxide, MgO, due to the
    (A) higher charge density of Mg^{2+} than of Ca^{2+}
    (B) higher charge density of Ca^{2+} than of O^{2-}
    (C) greater atomic volume of Mg^{2+} than of O^{2-}
    (D) greater atomic volume of Mg^{2+} than of Ca^{2+}

16. The equilibrium system not affected by the pressure change which results from a volume change at constant temperature is
    (A) $2 O_3(g) \rightleftharpoons 3 O_2(g)$
    (B) $PCl_5(g) \rightleftharpoons PCl_3(g) + Cl_2(g)$
    (C) $H_2(g) + I_2(g) \rightleftharpoons 2 HI(g)$
    (D) $2 NO_2(g) \rightleftharpoons N_2O_4(g)$

17. A solution of 50.0 mL of 0.0010 M $Ba(OH)_2$ is slowly titrated with 50.0 mL of 0.0030 M H_2SO_4. The conductivity of this solution will
    (A) decrease to near zero, then increase
    (B) decrease to near zero and remain very low
    (C) increase as the acid is added then become constant at a high value
    (D) increase as the acid is added and then slowly become very low

18. Which of the following pairs illustrates the law of multiple proportions?
    (A) SO_2, SO_3
    (B) CO_2, CCl_4
    (C) NaCl, NaBr
    (D) NH_4Cl, NH_4Br

19. Determine the pH of a 0.10 M solution of a base, B, with a K_b of 1.0×10^{-5}.
    (A) 3.00
    (B) 6.00
    (C) 8.00
    (D) 11.00

20. Isotopic forms of the same element
    (A) differ in the number of neutrons
    (B) are formed by gaining electrons
    (C) always have a positive charge
    (D) have the same number of neutrons

21. The number of moles of oxygen atoms in one mole of iron(II) phosphate is
    (A) 2
    (B) 3
    (C) 4
    (D) 8

22. Magnesium fluoride, a salt of low solubility in water, has a K_{sp} of 6.4×10^{-9}. The concentration of Mg^{2+} ions in this solution would be
    (A) $\sqrt{6.4 \times 10^{-9}}\, M$
    (B) $\sqrt{(6.4 \times 10^{-9}/2)}\, M$
    (C) $\sqrt[3]{(6.4 \times 10^{-9}/3)}\, M$
    (D) $\sqrt[3]{(6.4 \times 10^{-9}/4)}\, M$

GO ON TO NEXT PAGE

Questions 23 and 24 refer to this pH curve for the titration of 50.0 mL of 0.100 M acid with 0.100 M base.

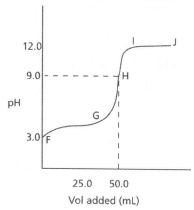

23. What type of titration does this curve represent?
    (A) strong acid/strong base
    (B) strong acid/weak base
    (C) weak acid/strong base
    (D) either a strong acid/strong base or a weak acid/strong base

24. Buffering is most effective
    (A) between points F and G
    (B) between points G and H
    (C) at point H between points I and J
    (D) between both F and G and between I and J

25. a. ∧   b. ∧OH   c. ∧O∧

    H-C-C-H (with H H above, H H H H)   H-C-C-O-H H_3C O CH_3

    Arrange the above liquids in order of increasing vapor pressure:
    (A) b < c < a
    (B) b < a < c
    (C) a < c < b
    (D) a < b < c

26. Bond angle data shows the following angles for three compounds:

    CH_4 109.5°
    NH_3 107°
    H_2O 104.5°

    This trend is basically because
    (A) lone pairs of electrons require more room than bonding pairs
    (B) hydrogen atoms repel each other more in water than in CH_4 or NH_3
    (C) oxygen has a higher electronegativity than does N, and C has even less
    (D) of the attempt of all central atoms to achieve the tetrahedral shape

27. Which of the following are in order of increasing boiling points?
    (A) $RbCl$ < CH_3Cl < CH_3OH < CH_4
    (B) CH_4 < CH_3Cl < CH_3OH < $RbCl$
    (C) CH_4 < CH_3OH < CH_3Cl < $RbCl$
    (D) $RbCl$ < CH_3OH < CH_3Cl < CH_4

28. When 100.0 mL of 2.0 M NH_3 and 100.0 mL of 1.0 M $AgNO_3$ are mixed, but before any reaction occurs, the major species in solution are
    (A) Ag^+, NO_3^-, NH_3, and H_2O
    (B) Ag^+, NO_3^-, NH_4^+, and OH^-
    (C) NH_3 and $Ag(NH_3)_2^+$
    (D) NH_3, $Ag(NH_3)_2^+$, and H_2O

29. The geometry of a PH_3 molecule is described by the VSEPR model as
    (A) trigonal planar
    (B) tetrahedral
    (C) bent or angular
    (D) trigonal pyramidal

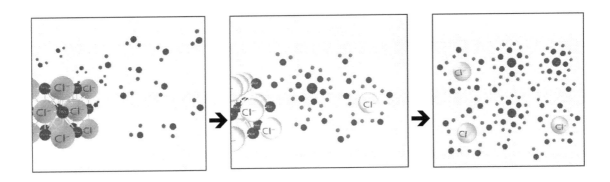

30. The dissolution of sodium chloride shown in the diagram above may be considered either a chemical or a physical change. Justify this statement.

	Chemical Change	**Physical Change**
(A)	Na^+ and Cl^- bonds are broken.	H–O–H bonds are broken.
(B)	Na^+ and Cl^- form ion-dipole attractions to water.	Hydrogen bonds between water molecules are broken.
(C)	H–O–H bonds are broken.	Na^+ and Cl^- bonds are broken.
(D)	Hydrogen bonds between water molecules are broken.	Na^+ and Cl^- form ion–dipole attractions to water.

31. The molecule whose Lewis structure requires resonance structures to best explain its bonding is
    (A) CO_2
    (B) PCl_5
    (C) OF_5
    (D) SO_2

32. $A + B \rightleftharpoons 2\,C$
    The equilibrium concentrations of reactants and products for the reaction above are

Substance	Concentration (M)
A	0.25
B	0.25
C	0.050

What is the value of the equilibrium constant, K?
(A) 0.040
(B) 0.16
(C) 0.80
(D) 25

33. The K_a for a weak acid is 5.0×10^{-10} at 25°C. Determine the value of K_b for the conjugate base of this weak acid.
    (A) 0.50×10^{-5}
    (B) 1.5×10^{-5}
    (C) 2.0×10^{-5}
    (D) 5.0×10^{-5}

34. The species with the most polar bond is
    (A) F–F
    (B) Sc–Ti
    (C) Cr–Br
    (D) P–Cl

GO ON TO NEXT PAGE

35. When equal volumes of 0.150 M NaOH and 0.150 M HC₂H₃O₂ are mixed, the resulting solution has a pH of about 9. This is due to
(A) an unequal number of moles of OH⁻ (from the NaOH) and H⁺ (from the HC₂H₃O₂)
(B) the C₂H₃O₂⁻ reacting with water to provide more OH⁻
(C) the cation of the acid, which remains in solution at the equivalent point, and is a base
(D) both the C₂H₃O₂⁻ reacting with water and the acidic nature of the anion of the acid

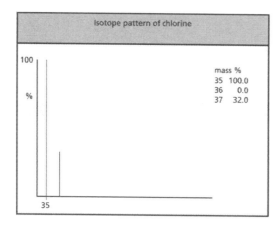

36. According to the mass spectrum above, the isotopic composition of ³⁵Cl:³⁷Cl is closest to
(A) 35:37
(B) 100:32
(C) 50:50
(D) 75:25

37. Of the following, the species that has the largest radius is
(A) Cl⁻
(B) Br⁻
(C) K⁺
(D) Sr²⁺

38. The pH of a 0.001 M HBr solution is
(A) 3.0
(B) 7.0
(C) 11.0
(D) impossible to determine without more data

39. Aqueous solutions of lead(II) nitrate and potassium chromate are allowed to react and produce a yellow solid. The results show
(A) both lead(II) chromate and potassium nitrate have low K_{sp} values
(B) lead(II) chromate has a low K_{sp} value
(C) potassium nitrate has a low K_{sp} value
(D) potassium chromate has a low K_{sp} value

40. A rigid cylinder contains CO₂ gas at a constant temperature. Some of the carbon dioxide is allowed to escape. Which of the following applies to the CO₂?
(A) The pressure of the gas increases.
(B) The volume of the gas decreases.
(C) The average molecular speed decreases.
(D) The distance between CO₂ molecules is increased.

41. Which of the following is most likely to be a brittle compound with low conductivity as a solid, and have a high melting point?
(A) RbF
(B) CCl₄
(C) ICl
(D) SF₆

42. $2 NH_3(g) \rightarrow N_2(g) + 3 H_2(g)$

The above reaction occurs in a closed system of constant volume and temperature. What is the resultant pressure of the hydrogen if the partial pressure of the ammonia decreases by 0.40 atm?
(A) increases by 0.20 atm
(B) increases by 0.40 atm
(C) increases by 0.60 atm
(D) decreases by 0.60 atm

43. Air is pumped into a rigid steel cylinder at constant temperature. The increase in pressure is due to
    (A) increased molecular collisions
    (B) the greater kinetic energy of the gas particles
    (C) increase in the size of the individual molecules
    (D) the greater force of attraction between gas molecules at high pressure

44. Which of the following gases would depart the most from ideal behavior?
    (A) H_2
    (B) Xe
    (C) He
    (D) N_2

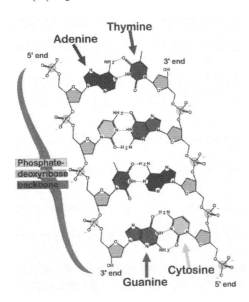

45. The double helix structure of deoxyribonucleic acid (DNA) is shown above. When DNA replicates, the two strands must "unzip." Which statement describes the energy requirements and forces involved?
    (A) Energy must be added to break the covalent bonds.
    (B) Energy must be added to break the hydrogen bonds.
    (C) Energy is released when the covalent bonds break.
    (D) Energy is released when the hydrogen bonds break.

46. $2\ KClO_3(s) \rightarrow KCl(s) + 3\ O_2(g)$

    According to the above equation, 0.40 mol of solid $KClO_3$ completely decomposes, forming KCl and O_2. The dry gas is collected at STP. The volume of this oxygen gas would be most nearly
    (A) 1.4 L
    (B) 14 L
    (C) 140 L
    (D) 1400 L

47. A hollow steel cylinder of volume 24 L contains 1.0 mole of N_2 and 2.0 mol of Ar. The partial pressure of the N_2 is
    (A) 1/2 the total pressure
    (B) 1/3 the total pressure
    (C) 2 times that of the Ar
    (D) equal to that of the Ar

48. As the atomic number increases from lithium to fluorine, the atomic radii
    (A) do not change because the electrons are being added to the same energy level
    (B) increase due to greater electron repulsion
    (C) decrease because the increased the greater nuclear charge exerts a larger attraction on the electrons
    (D) decrease because two orbitals (s and p) are filling

49. Assume that $2\ A + B \rightarrow C$ is the rate determining step. 3.0 moles of A and 2.0 moles of B are placed in a 1.0-L flask; after five minutes the concentration of C reaches $1.0\ M$ and the rate will have
    (A) decreased by a factor of 6
    (B) decreased by a factor of 9
    (C) decreased by a factor of 10
    (D) decreased by a factor of 18

GO ON TO NEXT PAGE

50. For a given reaction at a temperature of 27°C, the rate law is Rate = k [X][Y]. If the concentration of X and of Y are both 0.40 M, the rate is 4.0×10^{-6} mol L⁻¹ min⁻¹. Determine the value of k (the rate constant) at this temperature.
    (A) 2.5×10^{-5} L mol⁻¹ min⁻¹
    (B) 2.5×10^{-3} L mol⁻¹ min⁻¹
    (C) 2.5×10^{-5} mol L⁻¹ min⁻¹
    (D) 1.0×10^{-6} L mol⁻¹ min⁻¹

51. The major reason an increase in temperature causes an increase in reaction rate is that
    (A) the activation energy changes with temperature
    (B) the fraction of high energy molecules increases
    (C) molecules collide with greater frequency
    (D) catalysts become more effective

52. Catalysts effectively increase reaction rate by
    (A) increasing the K_{eq}
    (B) increasing the concentration of the reactant
    (C) decreasing the concentration of the products
    (D) lowering the activation energy requirements

53. For all zero-order reactions,
    (A) the reaction rate is independent of time
    (B) the rate constant equals zero
    (C) the concentration of reactants does not change over time
    (D) activation energy is very low

54. The first-order rate constant for nuclear decay of ⁶⁰Co is 0.13 yr⁻¹, and for ⁹⁰Sr it is 0.24 yr⁻¹.
    (A) The half-life of Sr is longer than that of Co.
    (B) The half-life of Sr is shorter than that of Co.
    (C) The half-lives of Sr and Co are equal.
    (D) The half-lives of Sr and Co cannot be compared from these data.

55. To determine the order with respect to Br⁻ in the reaction

    $$BrO_3^-(aq) + 5\ Br^-(aq) + 6\ H^+(aq) \rightarrow$$
    $$3\ H_2O(l) + 3\ Br_2(g)$$

    solutions should be prepared which differ in
    (A) [BrO₃⁻]
    (B) [Br⁻]
    (C) [H⁺]
    (D) [BrO₃⁻] and [Br⁻] and [H⁺]

56. Identify the process that produces the greatest change in entropy per mole of substance.
    (A) $H_2O(l) \rightarrow H_2O(g)$
    (B) $CH_3OH(l) \rightarrow CH_3OH(aq)$
    (C) $C_{10}H_8(s) \rightarrow C_{10}H_8(l)$
    (D) C (graphite) → C (diamond)

Questions 57–58 refer to the following.

10 g each of substances X and Y at −25°C were heated on the same hot plate.

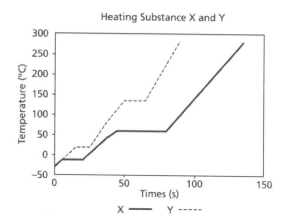

57. Identify and justify the substance with the higher specific heat capacity.
    (A) X; lower melting and boiling points
    (B) X; more energy needed to melt and boil
    (C) Y; higher melting and boiling points
    (D) Y; less energy needed to melt and boil

58. After 50 s, which substance gained more heat?
    (A) Y because the temperature is higher
    (B) X because it is boiling
    (C) Y because its temperature is still changing
    (D) They both absorbed the same amount of heat because the hot plate is the same

Questions 59–60 refer to the following.

The enthalpy of reaction of HCl and NaOH is to be calculated. The solutions are combined in an insulated container that is isolated from the environment.

59. Which data must be collected to calculate the enthalpy of reaction?
    (A) volume, pressure, initial and final temperature
    (B) conductivity, concentration, pH
    (C) initial and final temperature, absorbance, concentration
    (D) concentration, volume, initial and final temperature

60. How does the temperature change and why does it occur?
    (A) The temperature increases because potential energy of the chemical bonds is transformed into thermal energy.
    (B) The temperature increases due to the friction of mixing.
    (C) The temperature decreases because water formed in the reaction has a high specific heat capacity.
    (D) The temperature decreases due to decrease in entropy from the formation of a salt.

Advanced Placement Chemistry Equations and Constants

Throughout the test the following symbols have the definitions specified unless otherwise noted.

L, mL	=	liter(s), milliliter(s)	mm Hg	=	millimeters of mercury
g	=	gram(s)	J, kJ	=	joule(s), kilojoule(s)
nm	=	nanometer(s)	V	=	volt(s)
atm	=	atmosphere(s)	mol	=	mole(s)

ATOMIC STRUCTURE

$$E = h\nu$$
$$c = \lambda\nu$$

E = energy
ν = frequency
λ = wavelength

Planck's constant, $h = 6.626 \times 10^{-34}$ J s

Speed of light, $c = 2.998 \times 10^8$ m s^{-1}

Avogadro's number $= 6.022 \times 10^{23}$ mol^{-1}

Electron charge, $e = -1.602 \times 10^{-19}$ coulomb

EQUILIBRIUM

$$K_c = \frac{[C]^c[D]^d}{[A]^a[B]^b}, \text{ where } a\,A + b\,B \rightleftarrows c\,C + d\,D$$

$$K_p = \frac{(P_C)^c(P_D)^d}{(P_A)^a(P_B)^b}$$

$$K_a = \frac{[H^+][A^-]}{[HA]}$$

$$K_b = \frac{[OH^-][HB^+]}{[B]}$$

$K_w = [H^+][OH^-] = 1.0 \times 10^{-14}$ at 25°C

$\quad = K_a \times K_b$

$pH = -\log[H^+], pOH = -\log[OH^-]$

$14 = pH + pOH$

$$pH = pK_a + \log\frac{[A^-]}{[HA]}$$

$pK_a = -\log K_a, pK_b = -\log K_b$

Equilibrium Constants

K_c (molar concentrations)

K_p (gas pressures)

K_a (weak acid)

K_b (weak base)

K_w (water)

KINETICS

$$\ln[A]_t - \ln[A]_0 = -kt$$

$$\frac{1}{[A]_t} - \frac{1}{[A]_0} = kt$$

$$t_{1/2} = \frac{0.693}{k}$$

k = rate constant
t = time
$t_{1/2}$ = half-life

GASES, LIQUIDS, AND SOLUTIONS

$$PV = nRT$$

$$P_A = P_{total} \times X_A, \text{ where } X_A = \frac{\text{moles A}}{\text{total moles}}$$

$$P_{total} = P_A + P_B + P_C + \ldots$$

$$n = \frac{m}{M}$$

$$K = {}°C + 273$$

$$D = \frac{m}{V}$$

$$KE \text{ per molecule} = \frac{1}{2}mv^2$$

Molarity, M = moles of solute per liter of solution

$$A = abc$$

P = pressure
V = volume
T = temperature
n = number of moles
m = mass
M = molar mass
D = density
KE = kinetic energy
v = velocity
A = absorbance
a = molar absorptivity
b = path length
c = concentration

Gas constant, R = 8.314 J mol^{-1} K^{-1}
$\qquad\qquad\quad$ = 0.08206 L atm mol^{-1} K^{-1}
$\qquad\qquad\quad$ = 62.36 L torr mol^{-1} K^{-1}
1 atm = 760 mm Hg
$\qquad\;\;$ = 760 torr
STP = 0.00 °C and 1.000 atm

THERMOCHEMISTRY/ ELECTROCHEMISTRY

$$q = mc\Delta T$$

$$\Delta S° = \sum S° \text{ products} - \sum S° \text{ reactants}$$

$$\Delta H° = \sum \Delta H_f° \text{ products} - \sum \Delta H_f° \text{ reactants}$$

$$\Delta G° = \sum \Delta G_f° \text{ products} - \sum \Delta G_f° \text{ reactants}$$

$$\Delta G° = \Delta H° - T\Delta S°$$

$$= -RT \ln K$$

$$= -nFE°$$

$$I = \frac{q}{t}$$

q = heat
m = mass
c = specific heat capacity
T = temperature
$S°$ = standard entropy
$H°$ = standard enthalpy
$G°$ = standard free energy
n = number of moles
$E°$ = standard reduction potential
I = current (amperes)
q = charge (coulombs)
t = time (seconds)

Faraday's constant, F = 96,485 coulombs per mole
$\qquad\qquad\qquad\qquad$ of electrons
$$1 \text{ volt} = \frac{1 \text{ joule}}{1 \text{ coulomb}}$$

GO ON TO NEXT PAGE

Introduction to Section II: Free-Response Questions

Section II of the AP Chemistry Examination counts for 50% of the total test grade and involves several parts. Answering these questions gives you an opportunity to demonstrate your ability to present your material in clear, orderly, and convincing language. Your answers will be graded on the basis of accuracy, the kinds of information you include to support your responses, and the importance of the descriptive material used. Be specific; general, all-encompassing answers will not be graded as well as detailed answers with examples and equations. CLEARLY SHOW THE METHOD USED AND THE STEPS INVOLVED IN ARRIVING AT YOUR ANSWERS. It is to your advantage to do this, since you may obtain partial credit if you do and you will receive little or no credit if you do not. Attention should be paid to significant figures. On the AP exam, be sure to write all your answers to the questions on the lined pages following each question in the test booklet. Do not write your answers in the white space between questions.

Section II: Free-Response Questions
Time: 90 minutes
Number of Questions: 7

Allow yourself no more than 90 minutes to answer these questions. You may use a calculator, the equations sheet, and the periodic table throughout this section. All questions must be answered.

1. $2\ SO_3(g) \rightleftharpoons O_2(g) + 2\ SO_2(g)$ $\qquad \Delta H° = +791.44\ kJ\ mol^{-1}$

    A 3.21-g sample of sulfur trioxide is placed in a 2.25-L cylinder and allowed to reach equilibrium at a constant temperature of 500. K, as shown in the above equation. Analysis shows 1.23×10^{-2} mol of sulfur dioxide at equilibrium.

    (a) Sketch the reaction profile (or progress) on the axes given.

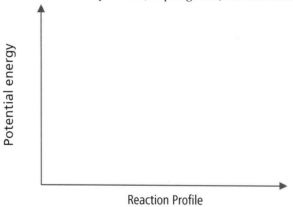

    (b) Write the equilibrium constant expression (K_c) for this system.
    (c) Calculate the concentration of all three gases at equilibrium.
    (d) Calculate the K_c value for this system.
    (e) Draw a particulate model with 10 particles to show the chemical species present in the cylinder at equilibrium. Clearly identify each chemical species in the model.

(f) In a separate experiment, all of the variables remained the same except the temperature was raised to 750. K
  (i) Predict how the equilibrium concentrations of the reactants and products will change.
  (ii) Use bonding and collision theories to explain why the concentrations changed.

2. Perbromic acid, $HBrO_4$, can react with sulfuric acid, H_2SO_4, in the following manner: $HBrO_4 + H_2SO_4 \rightarrow H_3SO_4^+ + BrO_4^-$.
  (a) This reaction occurs in a nonaqueous medium.
    (i) Indicate the two conjugate acid–base pairs in this reaction and label the acids in each pair.
    (ii) Identify the stronger acid.
    (iii) Use principles of bonding and/or atomic structure to explain why that acid is stronger.
  (b) In the SO_4^{2-} ion, sulfur is surrounded by four oxygen atoms in a tetrahedral structure. Draw a Lewis structure for the $H_3SO_4^+$ ion.

3. Analysis of an iron(II) ion solution by titration with a standardized potassium permanganate solution leads to the determination of the percent of iron in the original solution. The purple color of permanganate ion also acts as an indicator. The endpoint of the titration occurs when a very faint pink or colorless solution of manganese(II) ion is present. When performing this laboratory work, the solid of known mass and containing iron(II) is dissolved in 25.0 mL of water.
  (a) Explain how each of the following affects the reported percentage of iron in the unknown solid:
    (i) The student fills the buret with $KMnO_4$ after rinsing with only deionized water.
    (ii) An air bubble appears in the buret tip before titration begins.
    (iii) More than 25.0 mL of water is used to dissolve the solid.
    (iv) Each time the volume of fluid is measured in the buret, measurement is made to the top of the meniscus, rather than the bottom of the meniscus.
  (b) Assuming that the accepted value for the percentage of iron in the original sample was 7.77% and that your experiment gave a result of 6.896%, determine the percentage error in your work.
  (c) Write a balanced net ionic equation for the reaction which occurs between iron(II) ions and the permanganate ion in acidic solution.

GO ON TO NEXT PAGE

4. The melting points of carboxylic acids found in milk are in the graph below. Saturated means all carbon-carbon bonds in the molecule are single bonds.

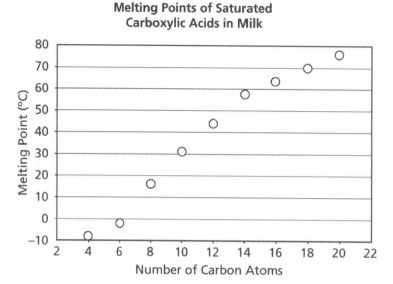

Melting Points of Saturated Carboxylic Acids in Milk

(a) Identify and explain the relationship between the number of carbon atoms and the melting point of the acid in terms of the intermolecular forces present.

(b) Predict and explain the trend in solubility of carboxylic acids in water which makes up 87% of milk.

There are several unsaturated carboxylic acids present in milk. Unsaturated means at least one carbon-carbon double bond is present. Data for three C_{18} carboxylic acids are listed below.

Acid Name	Number of Double Bonds	Melting Point (°C)	
Oleic	1	13	
Linoleic	2	−5	
Linolenic	3	−11	

(c) Identify and explain the relationship between the number of double bonds and the melting point of the acid in terms of the intermolecular forces and molecular shape.

5. Explain the following observations:
    (a) When a solid is heated at its melting point, the temperature does not increase.
    (b) When alcohol (ethanol) is poured over your arm, your skin feels cold.

6. For a given reaction, a proposed rate law is Rate = k[X][Y].
   (a) Explain how the value of the rate constant, k, may be changed.
   (b) Compare the rate of a first-order reaction with the rate of a zero-order reaction.
   (c) Explain why knowing the rate law expression is essential when proposing a reaction mechanism.

7. Effervescent cold tablets are composed of 1.000 g of citric acid ($H_3C_6H_5O_7$) and 1.916 g of sodium bicarbonate. When placed into water, the two solids dissolve and react.
   (a) Write the balanced net ionic equation for this reaction assuming that the acid is fully deprotonated in this reaction.
   (b) Determine the theoretical volume of gas produced at STP.

   In a calorimetry experiment, two tablets placed into 25.0 g of water at 21.2°C lowers the temperature of the water to 13.6°C. Assume no heat exchange with the surroundings.
   (c) The reaction is spontaneous at room temperature. Predict the sign of $\Delta H°$, $\Delta S°$, and $\Delta G°$. Justify your answers.
   (d) Calculate the energy absorbed by the water (specific heat capacity of H_2O = 4.18 J g^{-1} °C^{-1}).
   (e) Calculate $\Delta H°$ for the balanced chemical equation.

END OF EXAMINATION

Answers to Diagnostic Test

Section I: Multiple-Choice Questions

Score your test using the table below.

Determine how many questions you answered correctly. You will find explanations of the answers on the following pages.

1. D	2. A	3. B	4. B	5. A
6. B	7. A	8. B	9. C	10. C
11. C	12. D	13. A	14. B	15. A
16. C	17. A	18. A	19. D	20. A
21. D	22. D	23. C	24. A	25. A
26. A	27. B	28. A	29. D	30. B
31. D	32. A	33. C	34. C	35. B
36. D	37. B	38. A	39. B	40. D
41. A	42. C	43. A	44. B	45. B
46. B	47. B	48. C	49. D	50. A
51. B	52. D	53. A	54. B	55. B
56. A	57. B	58. D	59. D	60. A

Calculate your score:

Number answered correctly: _____

What your score means:

Each year, since the test is different, the scoring is a little different. But generally, if you scored 20 or more on the multiple-choice questions, you'll most likely get a 3 or better on the test. If you scored 28 or more, you'll probably score a 4 or better. And if you scored 40 or more, you'll most likely get a 5. Keep in mind that the multiple-choice section is worth 50% of your final grade, and the free-response section is worth 50% of your final grade. To learn more about the scoring for the free-response questions, turn to the last page of this section.

Answers and Explanations

Section I: Multiple-Choice Questions

1. **Answer: D** Filtration can be used to separate a heterogeneous mixture while the other techniques can be used to separate homogeneous mixtures (*Chemistry* 8th ed. pages 26–28/9th ed. pages 27–31). LO 1.19

2. **ANSWER: A** The positive slope at the left part of the graph indicates a direct relationship between the mass of calcium chloride and the mass of calcium carbonate. This means that $CaCl_2$ is the limiting reagent and is determining the mass of $CaCO_3$ produced (*Chemistry* 8th ed. pages 107–115/9th ed. pages 114–123). LO 3.4

3. **ANSWER: B** In the horizontal portion of the graph, the mass of $CaCl_2$ is not related to the mass of $CaCO_3$ produced. Therefore, the constant amount of Na_2CO_3 (6.00 mL of 1.7 *M* solution must be responsible for the horizontal portion of the graph and must be the limiting reagent (*Chemistry* 8th ed. pages 107–115/9th ed. pages 114–123). LO 3.4

4. **ANSWER: B** The spectrum shows 3 completely filled energy levels. The peak at 347 MJ (2 electrons) is energy level 1. The 2 peaks at 29.1 and 37.1 MJ (8 electrons) is energy level 2. The 2 peaks at 2.38 and 3.93 MJ (8 electrons) is energy level 3. The last peak at 0.42 MJ is 1 electron in energy level 4. LO 1.5

5. **ANSWER: A** 0.42 MJ means that electron requires the least amount of energy to be removed from the atom. It has the lowest attraction to the nucleus, therefore it must be in a valence shell. LO 1.7

6. **ANSWER: B** The electrons in Element A are closer to the nucleus because there must be more protons exerting a greater nuclear attraction. Larger energy values indicate the electrons are more tightly held to the nucleus. LO 1.6

7. **ANSWER: A** The electron with 0.42 MJ of energy needed for its removal is a valence electron that is farther from the nucleus. It experiences less of an effective nuclear charge and can more easily be removed by water. LO 1.10

8. **ANSWER: B** Increasing the [Ag⁺] will cause a shift toward products, causing an increase in the potential difference of this cell. This would, over time, cause an increase in the concentration of copper(II) ions, making the blue of the copper(II) ions darker (*Chemistry* 8th ed. pages 836–842/9th ed. pages 852–858). LO 3.12

9. **ANSWER: C** By definition the anode is the site of oxidation. Oxidation is the loss of electrons. Copper must lose two electrons to become copper(II) ions. Half-reactions involving a decrease in positive charge, like responses (B) and (D), require a gain of electrons (*Chemistry* 8th ed. pages 823–833/9th ed. pages 839–849). LO 3.13

10. **ANSWER: C** Higher temperature causes atoms in the molecule to vibrate with increased energy which leads to greater deviation from the equilibrium bond angle. LO 5.1

11. **ANSWER: C** This is a very straightforward use of the chemical formula and your understanding of moles. Since there are two moles of silver atoms per formula unit of silver sulfide, there are twice as many moles of silver atoms as moles of formula units of the

silver sulfide (*Chemistry* 8th ed. pages 81–84/9th ed. pages 85–90). LO 3.3

12. **Answer: D** From the equation $Zn(OH)_2(s) \rightarrow Zn^{2+}(aq) + 2\ OH^-(aq)$ you can see that if 2.0×10^{-6} mol/L of the zinc hydroxide dissolves, that will result in the same concentration of zinc ions (2.0×10^{-6} mol/L) and twice that much of hydroxide ions (2.0×10^{-6} mol/L × 2 = 4.0×10^{-6} mol/L). Then: $K_{sp} = [Zn^{2+}][OH^-]^2 = (2.0 \times 10^{-6})(4.0 \times 10^{-6})^2 = 3.2 \times 10^{-17}$ (*Chemistry* 8th ed. pages 744–752/9th ed. pages 759–768). LO 6.21

13. **Answer: A** Note that the second equation is the reverse of the first, and has been doubled. Therefore the K_c for the second equation will be the reciprocal of the first squared: $(1/4)^2 = 1/16$ (*Chemistry* 8th ed. pages 597–601 esp. Example 13.2 and "Conclusions About the Equilibrium Expression"/9th ed. pages 610–614 esp. Example 13.2 and "Conclusions About the Equilibrium Expression"). LO 6.2

14. **Answer: B** To calculate $\Delta G°$ for C (*diamond*) → C (*graphite*), you must flip the second equation and then add the equations together.

C (*diamond*) + ~~$O_2(g)$~~ → ~~$CO_2(g)$~~ $\Delta G° = -397$ kJ/mol
~~$CO_2(g)$~~ → C (*graphite*) + ~~$O_2(g)$~~ $\Delta G° = +394$ kJ/mol
C (*diamond*) → C (*graphite*) $\Delta G° = -3$ kJ/mol

Negative values for $\Delta G°$ indicate spontaneous reactions. The high E_a makes this a kinetically slow reaction (*Chemistry* 8th ed. pages 790–794/9th ed. pages 805–810). LO 5.18

15. **Answer: A** Both CaO and MgO are ionically bonded. Both involve oxygen; therefore the difference in melting temperatures must be due to the difference in attraction developed by Mg compared to that of Ca. Both are 2+ ions, but magnesium ions are smaller, meaning that the charge is more concentrated in the Mg^{2+} ion. The combination of charge and size factors, called the charge density, affects the force of attraction that the ion has; ionic charge / ionic radius = charge density (*Chemistry* 8th ed. pages 318–327/9th ed. pages 329–339). LO 2.24

16. **Answer: C** Equilibrium tends to shift to the side with the least number of moles to relieve pressure. When the number of gaseous moles is equal, there will be no change to the system. This effect of a change in pressure on an equilibrium system is described by LeChâtelier's principle (*Chemistry* 8th ed. pages 620–626 esp. Sample Exercise 13.14/9th ed. pages 633–639 esp. Sample Exercise 13.14). LO 6.8

17. **Answer: A** The reaction forms $BaSO_4(s)$ which means that ions are removed from solution, thereby making the solution less conductive. However, continued addition of the acid causes the conductivity to increase again with the excess of ions (*Chemistry* 8th ed. pages 144–150/9th ed. pages 153–158). LO 2.8

18. **ANSWER: A** The law of multiple proportions is illustrated by two elements which form at least two compounds. It then compares the ratios of the masses of one element with a constant mass of the other element in the two (or more) compounds. These ratios always reduce to simple whole numbers (*Chemistry* 8th ed. pages 41–44/9th ed. pages 44–47). LO 1.1

19. **ANSWER: D** Using the general equation B + HOH ⇌ HB$^+$ + OH$^-$,
    $K_b = [HB^+][OH^-]/[B]$
    $1.0 \times 10^{-5} = x^2/0.10$
    $x^2 = 1.0 \times 10^{-6}$
    $[OH^-] = 1.0 \times 10^{-3}\ M$ pOH = 3.00
    pH = 14.00 – 3.00 = 11.00
    (*Chemistry* 8th ed. pages 665–666/9th ed. pages 679–680). LO 6.16

20. **ANSWER: A** Isotopes are found for every element and differ from each other in mass for the same element due only to a different number of neutrons in the nucleus (*Chemistry* 8th ed. pages 50–52, 77–80/9th ed. pages 54–55, 82–85). LO 1.14

21. **ANSWER: D** Begin by determining the formula for iron(II) phosphate: $Fe_3(PO_4)_2$. From this you can see that there are two phosphate ions with four oxygens in each, for a total of 8 moles of oxygen for each mole of $Fe_3(PO_4)_2$ (*Chemistry* 8th ed. pages 56–67/9th ed. pages 59–70). LO 1.4

22. **ANSWER: D** When solving K_{sp} problems, first write the equation with the solid on the left and the ions on the right: $MgF_2(s) \rightleftharpoons Mg^{2+}(aq) + 2\ F^-(aq)$. If s represents the mol/L of the solid that goes into solution, $[Mg^{2+}]$ also equals s, and $2s$ represents the $[F^-]$. Next write the K_{sp} expression in terms of s: $K_{sp} = (s)(2s)^2 = 4s^3 = 6.4 \times 10^{-9}$. $s = \sqrt[3]{(6.4 \times 10^{-9}/4)}\ M$ (*Chemistry* 8th ed. pages 743–747/9th ed. pages 759–763). LO 6.21

23. **ANSWER: C** A good clue as to the type of titration curve is the position of the equivalence point, which is the center of the vertical section of the graph showing the very rapid change of pH. In this case, that is in the basic region (above 9). At this point, the amount of added OH$^-$ equals the original amount of acid. The pH exceeds 7 (neutral) due to the hydrolysis of the anion from the acid (*Chemistry* 8th ed. pages 713–715, 717–725/9th ed. pages 727–729, 731–739). LO 6.13

24. **ANSWER: A** The leveling-off shown between F and G is caused by buffering. Optimal buffering occurs when $[HA] = [A^-]$, which would be at a volume of 25 mL of base in this case (*Chemistry* 8th ed. pages 710–712, 717–725/9th ed. pages 724–726, 731–739). LO 6.20

25. Answer: A

	name	formula	IMF Present
a.	propane	$CH_3CH_2CH_3$	London dispersion
b.	ethanol	CH_3CH_2OH	London dispersion, dipole-dipole, hydrogen bonding
c.	dimethyl ether	CH_3OCH_3	London dispersion, dipole-dipole

The more easily a substance can attain the vapor state, the more molecules will be available to exert vapor pressure. Propane molecules only have to overcome relatively weak London dispersion forces to go into the gas phase. The other molecules have stronger IMF to overcome (*Chemistry* 8th ed. pages 440–443, 471–479/9th ed. pages 455–458, 483–491). LO 2.16

26. Answer: A Lone pairs of electrons (unbonded pairs) are less associated with the attractive forces of positive nuclei, therefore will occupy more space than bonded pairs (*Chemistry* 8th ed. pages 380–382/9th ed. pages 391–393). LO 2.17

27. Answer: B

formula	IMF Present
CH_4	London dispersion
CH_3Cl	London dispersion, dipole-dipole
CH_3OH	London dispersion, dipole-dipole, hydrogen bonding
RbCl	Ion-ion

The temperature at which substances boil is a function of the forces between the molecules of that substance (intermolecular forces). Small, nonpolar molecules boil at the lowest temperatures since they have the weakest IMF to overcome (London dispersion). As polarity increases, so does the boiling temperature, Ionic substances have the highest attraction which means the boiling temperature is the highest (*Chemistry* 8th ed. pages 440–443/9th ed. pages 455–458). LO 2.16

28. Answer: A Before reaction, no combination of NH_3 and Ag^+ has formed; the silver nitrate is found as ions, the ammonia is molecular, and water is also present (*Chemistry* 8th ed. pages 759–762/9th ed. pages 774–777). LO 3.2

29. Answer: D The VSEPR model is very helpful in describing almost all molecular shapes. Note that in PH_3 the shape may, at first, seem to be tetrahedral (4 electron domains) or trigonal planar (due to the formula), but it does not have a hydrogen in one of the four apex positions, so it is a trigonal pyramid. Molecular shape is determined by the position of the nuclei and not by the position of just electrons, either pairs or single electrons (*Chemistry* 8th ed. pages 378–390, esp. Figure 8.16/9th ed. pages 389–402, esp. Figure 8.16). LO 2.21

30. **ANSWER: B** Ionic bonds between Na^+ and Cl^- are broken when NaCl dissolves. Hydrogen bonds between some water molecules are broken and the ions forms ion–dipole bonds with water. The ion–dipole bonds are comparable in strength to covalent bonds (*Chemistry* 8th ed. pages 130–132, 501–504/9th ed. pages 139–141, 514–517). LO 5.10

31. **ANSWER: D** The need for resonance structures seems to be greatest for molecules in which the same two elements are bonded with different type bonds (e.g., one single, one double bond) in the same molecule. The usual Lewis structure for sulfur dioxide shows that the sulfur and oxygen are bonded with one single bond and, in the other sulfur–oxygen bond, doubly bonded. (Be sure you can draw this Lewis structure.) (*Chemistry* 8th ed. pages 374–378/9th ed. pages 385–389). LO 2.21

32. **ANSWER: A**

$$K = \frac{[C]^2}{[A][B]}$$

$$K = \frac{(0.05)^2}{(0.25)(0.25)}$$

This math can be simply calculated by changing the decimals into fractions and using mathematical manipulation to put all numbers in the numerator for ease of multiplication.

$$K = \left(\frac{1}{20}\right)\left(\frac{1}{20}\right)\left(\frac{4}{1}\right)\left(\frac{4}{1}\right) = \frac{16}{400} \quad \text{which reduces to 4/100 or 0.040}$$

(*Chemistry* 8th ed. pages 597–601/9th ed. pages 610–614). LO 6.5

33. **ANSWER: C**
    $K_a \times K_b = K_w$
    $K_b = 1.0 \times 10^{-14}/5.0 \times 10^{-10} = 2.0 \times 10^{-5}$ (*Chemistry* 8th ed. pages 671–677/9th ed. pages 686–691). LO 6.16

34. **ANSWER: C** While using actual electronegativities would be helpful for this question, a good generalization is that the further apart the elements are on the periodic table the greater the difference in control they have over the shared electron pair, and the more polar the bond. Note also that this is a question dealing with the polarity of an individual bond and not with the polarity of an entire molecule (*Chemistry* 8th ed. pages 344–346/9th ed. pages 356–358). LO 2.18

35. **ANSWER: B** The conjugate base of a weak acid is reacting with water (this is hydrolysis): $C_2H_3O_2^- + HOH \rightleftharpoons HC_2H_3O_2 + OH^-$. OH^- raises the pH (*Chemistry* 8th ed. pages 717–725/9th ed. pages 731–739). LO 6.13

36. **ANSWER: D** Mass spectra assign the largest peak (most abundant isotope) a value of 100%, but that does not mean that isotope has 100% abundance. Assume abundance of ^{37}Cl is x. Examining the relationship between the lines shows that ^{35}Cl is 3 times larger than ^{37}Cl or $3x$. $x + 3x = 100$ since the total abundance must equal

100%. Therefore ^{37}Cl is 25% and ^{35}Cl is 75% (*Chemistry* 8th ed. pages 49–52, 77–80/9th ed. pages 54–55, 82–85). LO 1.14

37. **ANSWER: B** Ions with negative charges have gained an electron and are therefore larger than their parent atoms. Between the chloride ions and the bromide ion you have outermost electrons in the third energy level versus the fourth energy level, hence we would expect Br⁻ to be larger (*Chemistry* 8th ed. pages 349–353, esp. Figure 8.8/9th ed. pages 361–365, esp. Figure 8.8). LO 1.9

38. **ANSWER: A** Since HBr is a strong acid (completely dissociated), the [H⁺] would be 0.001 *M* which gives a pH = –log 0.001 = 3.0 (*Chemistry* 8th ed. pages 642–651/9th ed. pages 656–666). LO 6.15

39. **ANSWER: B** The substances you might expect to form solids due to low solubility might be lead(II) chromate and potassium nitrate. There are two rules which suggest the latter is not going to precipitate: "most 1A compounds are soluble," and "most nitrate salts are soluble" (*Chemistry* 8th ed. pages 144–149/9th ed. pages 153–157). LO 6.22

40. **ANSWER: D** If gas is allowed to escape, then there are fewer molecules left within the cylinder; these fewer molecules exert less pressure (gas pressure is due to the collision of gas particles with the sides of the container). These remaining gas molecules occupy the entire container, so there must be more room between the individual molecules (*Chemistry* 8th ed. pages 181–183, 205–212/9th ed. pages 190–192, 214–222). LO 2.6

41. **ANSWER: A** Compounds with these properties are ionically bonded. This suggests elements from the far left side of the periodic table (1A or 2A) with elements from the far right side (6A or 7A) (*Chemistry* 8th ed. pages 357–358, 468–471/9th ed. pages 369–370, 480–483). LO 2.19

42. **ANSWER: C** While this may appear to be an equilibrium question, it is actually just asking you to show an understanding of the stoichiometry between ammonia and hydrogen gases as this reaction proceeds. If enough ammonia reacts to cause a decrease of 0.40 atm in pressure, then enough hydrogen is formed to cause an increase in pressure of 0.60 atm, (0.40 atm × 3 mol H_2/2 mol NH_3) (*Chemistry* 8th ed. pages 101–107/9th ed. pages 108–114). LO 2.6

43. **ANSWER: A** Go back to first principles: What is pressure? The basic kinetic-molecular theory of gases indicates that gas pressure is due to molecular collisions and more collisions mean greater pressure (*Chemistry* 8th ed. pages 205–212/9th ed. pages 214–222). LO 2.4

44. **ANSWER: B** Nonideal (real) gases differ from ideal gases because of two factors: attractions between real gas molecules and the molecular volume of real gases. Xe has 54 electrons which make the atom very polarizable so it has significant IMF. It also has the

largest atomic volume of the gases listed (*Chemistry* 8th ed. pages 214–216/9th ed. pages 224–226). LO 2.4

45. **Answer: B** Hydrogen bonds exist between the nitrogenous bases in DNA. This relatively strong IMF must absorb energy to overcome the attraction between the atoms of the different strands of DNA (*Chemistry* 8th ed. pages 441–442/9th ed. pages 456–457). LO 5.9

46. **Answer: B** This stoichiometry problem may cause you to reach for your calculator, but that tool is not needed; note the widely differing answers for the volume of the gas. 0.40 mol of $KClO_3$ will form 0.60 mol of oxygen gas. The molar volume of gases at STP is 22.4 L/mol, so the volume is around 14 L (0.60 mol × 22 L/mol) (*Chemistry* 8th ed. pages 101–107, 194–199/9th ed. pages 108–114, 203–208). LO 3.4

47. **Answer: B** The part of the pressure (partial pressure) due to a gas in a mixture of gases is the same as the mole ratio of that gas to the total, which is the same as the ratio of the number of molecules of that gas to the total number of molecules. In this case there are 3 moles of gas total of which Ne is 1 part, hence 1/3 of the total pressure is due to the Ne (*Chemistry* 8th ed. pages 199–205/9th ed. pages 208–214). LO 2.6

48. **Answer: C** The atomic volume decreases due to an increase in nuclear charge; note that the "added" electrons are going into the same principal energy level as you go from left to right across the same period (*Chemistry* 8th ed. pages 318–323 esp. Figure 7.34, 908–912 esp. Figure 19.2/9th ed. pages 329–334 esp. Figure 7.34, 927–932 esp. Figure 19.2). LO 1.9

49. **Answer: D** Since this occurs as a one step reaction, we can write that the rate = $k[A]^2[B]$. Initially the rate will be proportional to $(3)^2(2) = 18$. Later, [A] becomes 3 – 2 = 1, and [B] becomes 2 – 1 = 1, so the rate is then proportional to $(1)^2(1) = 1$. That means a change in the rate by a factor of 18 to 1, or that the rate is now 1/18 as large as it was originally (*Chemistry* 8th ed. pages 547–565/9th ed. pages 559–577). LO 4.2

50. **Answer: A** This time you need to use the form $k = \text{rate}/[X][Y]$ to determine the value of the rate constant, k.

    $k = 4.0 \times 10^{-6} \, \text{mol L}^{-1} \, \text{min}^{-1}/(4.0 \times 10^{-1} \, \text{mol L}^{-1})(4.0 \times 10^{-1} \, \text{mol L}^{-1})$

    $= 1/4 \times 10^{-4} \, \text{L mol}^{-1} \, \text{min}^{-1} = 0.25 \times 10^{-4} \, \text{L mol}^{-1} \, \text{min}^{-1}$

    $= 2.5 \times 10^{-5} \, \text{L mol}^{-1} \, \text{min}^{-1}$

    (Note that if set up in this way, the mathematics become rather easy to handle.) Do watch units for rate constants, which, unlike equilibrium constants, traditionally have units assigned (*Chemistry* 8th ed. pages 547–565/9th ed. pages 559–577). LO 4.2

51. **Answer: B** There is almost always a question on kinetics like this on a test. Note that it is not just the greater number of molecular collisions that cause the reaction to occur faster but an increase in

the fraction of high-energy molecules which can then obtain the activation energy requirement and reaction that cause this rate increase (*Chemistry* 8th ed. pages 565–575, esp. Figure 12.12/9th ed. pages 577–588, esp. Figure 12.12). LO 4.6

52. **ANSWER: D** Catalysts lower the activation energy barrier by forming a different activated complex (*Chemistry* 8th ed. pages 570–575, esp. Figures 12.15 and 12.16/9th ed. pages 583–588, esp. Figures 12.15 and 12.16). LO 4.8

53. **ANSWER: A** For a zero-order rate law, rate = $k[A]^0$ (i.e., n = zero). Since any number taken to the zero power is equal to 1, rate = k (the rate constant). This has the physical meaning that the rate does not speed up or slow down over time (like most reactions do); it either takes place at a constant rate or does not take place at all (*Chemistry* 8th ed. pages 551–560, Table 12.6 on page 561, 576–577/9th ed. pages 563–572, Table 12.6 on page 574, 588–589). LO 4.2

54. **ANSWER: B** This is an application of the half-life expression for first-order rate laws, $t_{1/2} = 0.693/k$. Note that half-life (time) and the rate constant are inversely related; hence the element with the lower rate constant will have the longer half-life (*Chemistry* 8th ed. pages 551–560/9th ed. pages 563–572). LO 4.3

55. **ANSWER: B** If you wish to determine how order is affected by a given concentration, then a series of reactions should be run with changes in only the concentration of that substance, with all other concentrations held constant (as well as all other conditions like temperature held constant) (*Chemistry* 8th ed. pages 551–560 esp. Sample Exercise 12.5/9th ed. pages 563–572 esp. Sample Exercise 12.5). LO 4.1

56. **ANSWER: A** Gases have the most random organization and have the most microstates available. Gas formation is a driving force in chemical and physical processes due to the increase in entropy (*Chemistry* 8th ed. pages 773–779/9th ed. pages 788–794). LO 5.12

57. **ANSWER: B** Substances with larger IMF must absorb more energy to change phase. The longer horizontal portions of substance X indicate energy is being used to overcome IMF (*Chemistry* 8th ed. pages 471–478/9th ed. pages 483–490). LO 5.6

58. **ANSWER: D** Both substances were on the same hot plate so both were receiving the same amount of energy. The substances heated at different rates due to differences in specific heat capacity (*Chemistry* 8th ed. pages 471–478/9th ed. pages 483–490). LO 5.5

59. **ANSWER: D** This is an example of a calorimetry lab. To determine the energy gained or released (q), you will use $q = s \times m \times \Delta T$ where s is the specific heat capacity, m is the mass of the system, and ΔT is the temperature change. In order to calculate for one mole, you will need volume and molarity of the solutions (*Chemistry* 8th ed. pages 243–251/9th ed. pages 252–260). LO 5.7

60. **ANSWER: A** This is a reaction between a strong acid and a strong base and it is exothermic so the temperature will increase. The increase is due to the large amount of energy released when H^+ and OH^- bond to form H_2O (*Chemistry* 8th ed. pages 243–251/9th ed. pages 252–260). LO 5.8

SECTION II: FREE-RESPONSE QUESTIONS

Question 1: Answers

(a)

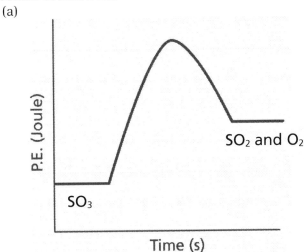

(b) $K_C = \dfrac{[O_2][SO_2]^2}{[SO_3]^2}$

This question could have asked you to calculate K_p instead. If that were the case, partial pressures would be shown in parentheses and the equation would have been

$K_p = \dfrac{(O_2)(SO_2)^2}{(SO_3)^2}$.

(c) $[SO_2] = 1.23 \times 10^{-2}$ mol/2.25 L = 0.00547 M

$[O_2]$ = (one-half as much as above) = 0.00273 M

initial mole SO_3 = 3.21 g/80.1 g/mol = 0.0401 mol

$[SO_3]$ = (0.0401 mol – 0.0123 mol)/2.25 L = 0.0124 M

(d) $K_C = (0.00273)(0.00547)^2/(0.0124)^2 = 5.31 \times 10^{-4}$ Recall that units are not shown on equilibrium constants.

(e) To represent the equilibrium mixture, one model will represent approximately 0.002 M. 3 particles of SO_2, 1 particle of O_2, and 6 particles of SO_3.

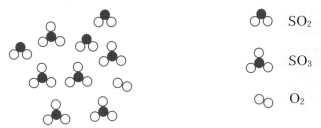

(f) (i) $[SO_3]$ will decrease and $[SO_2]$ and $[O_2]$ will increase.

(ii) Since the reaction is endothermic, a higher temperature will force the reaction to products to relieve the stress according to Le Chatelier's principle. The higher temperature means that more particles will have sufficient energy to overcome the activation energy and produce products.

(*Chemistry* 8th ed. pages 602–604, 609–614/9th ed. pages 615–616, 621–627)

Question 2: Answers

(a) (i) The pairs are $HBrO_4$ (acid)/BrO_4^- (conjugate base) and H_2SO_4 (base)/$H_3SO_4^+$ (conjugate acid). Note that acid form always has one more H^+ than its conjugate base.

(ii) $HBrO_4$ is the stronger acid because it was the one to donate a proton to H_2SO_4.

(iii) The electronegativity of the elements in question can be arranged as $O > Br > S > H$. Br is more electronegative than S, and therefore Br has a stronger attraction for electrons than S. This stronger attraction increases the polarity of the O–H bond in $HBrO_4$ and will cause the molecule to dissociate into H^+ and BrO_4^-. The H^+ will be attracted to H_2SO_4 and will form the $H_3SO_4^+$ ion.

(b)

(*Chemistry* 8th ed. pages 640–642, 645, 679–682/9th ed. pages 654–656, 659, 693–695)

Question 3: Answers

(a) (i) The $KMnO_4$ is actually less concentrated than you believe it to be since it has been diluted with the water left in the buret. That means that more of the standardized solution will be needed to react with the iron(II) solution leading you to report that the iron concentration is higher than it actually is.

(ii) If the air bubble stays in the buret during the entire titration, then there is no effect. However, if it is replaced by the $KMnO_4$ solution during the titration, then less solution leaves the buret than you are reporting, leading to a higher than correct percentage of the iron(II).

(iii) If more water is added to the flask that contains the iron salt, it will not affect the number of moles of iron(II) and therefore not affect the reported result.

(iv) If the same point on the meniscus is used as a reference, there will not be any effect on the percentage of iron reported.

(b) $$\% \text{ Error} = \frac{(\text{your lab results} - \text{accepted value})}{\text{accepted value}} \times 100\%$$

$$\frac{(6.896 - 7.77)}{7.77} \times 100\% = -11\%$$

Note that the answer is known only to two significant figures.

(c) $5 Fe^{2+}(aq) + MnO_4^-(aq) + 8 H^+(aq) \rightarrow 5 Fe^{3+}(aq) + Mn^{2+}(aq) + 4 H_2O(l)$.
(*Chemistry* 8th ed. pages 156–158, 165–168/9th ed. pages 165–169, 175–177)

Question 4: Answers
(a) Carboxylic acids have a nonpolar chain that has London dispersion forces as the main IMF and the functional group has a polar C=O (carbonyl group) that has dipole–dipole forces and an O–H (hydroxyl group) that can form hydrogen bonds. When the number of carbons is low, the polar end of the molecule with dipole-dipole and hydrogen bonding predominates. As the number of carbon atoms increases, the proportion of London dispersion forces also increases. As the strength of the London dispersion forces increases, the molecules will experience greater attractions. More energy is needed to overcome these attractions so the melting point is higher.
(b) The solubility of the carboxylic acids in water decreases as the number of carbon atoms increases. The predominant IMF in water is hydrogen bonding. Water is able to interact with other molecules whose predominant IMFs are dipole-dipole or hydrogen bonding. As the number of carbon atoms increases, the London dispersion forces become predominant and water cannot interact with those molecules.
(c) As the number of double bonds increases, the melting point of unsaturated carboxylic acid decreases. Even though the molecules are approximately equal in terms of number of electrons and therefore in terms of London dispersion forces, the shape of the molecules limits the locations of interactions between the molecules. The mono-unsaturated oleic acid has a greater chance of stacking and having many locations where electrons from each molecule can interact. The di- and tri-unsaturated acids have shapes that do not allow close packing and therefore they have fewer interactions and lower melting points. The more interactions molecules can form, the more energy must be added to overcome attractions, which leads to higher melting points.

Question 5: Answers
(a) Temperature is directly related to average kinetic energy. At the melting point, the thermal energy being added to the system is overcoming the attractive forces (potential energy) between the particles. Once all of the attractive forces (IMF) are broken, the temperature increases due to an increase in the average kinetic energy of the particles.
(b) An endothermic process causes this. The alcohol evaporates. This requires energy which is lost by your skin, so the temperature of your skin decreases.
(*Chemistry* 8th ed. pages 238–244, 475–477/9th ed. pages 248–253, 487–489)

Question 6: Answers
(a) The rate constant may be changed by changing the temperature (but not by changing the concentration of X or of Y). Recall the Arrhenius equation.
(b) For zero-order reactions, the rate is constant {Rate = $k[A]^0 = k(1) = k$}. This means that the rate does not change with concentration as it does with a first-order reaction {Rate = $k[A]^1$}.
(c) All reactants in the rate determining step must be part of the rate law expression because each of those reactants controls the reaction rate.
(*Chemistry* 8th ed. pages 547–565, Table 12.6 on page 562/9th ed. pages 559–577, Table 12.6 on page 574)

Question 7: Answers

(a) $H_3C_6H_5O_7(aq) + 3\ HCO_3^-(aq) \rightarrow C_6H_5O_7^{3-}(aq) + 3\ CO_2(g) + 3\ H_2O(l)$

(b) $\dfrac{1.000\ g\ H_3C_6H_5O_7}{192.12\ g/mol} = 0.005205\ mol$

$\dfrac{1.916\ g\ NaHCO_3}{84.01\ g/mol} = 0.02281\ mol$

	$H_3C_6H_5O_7$ +	$3\ HCO_3^-$ →	$C_6H_5O_7^{3-}$ +	$3\ CO_2$ +	$3\ H_2O$
initial mol	0.005205	0.02281	0	0	0
change mol	–x	–3x	+x	+3x	+3x
final mol	0	0.0072	0.005205	0.01561	0.01561

Since one of the reactants must be used up $x = 0.005205$ or $x = 0.02281/3 = 0.007603$. $x \neq 0.007603$ because neither reactant can have a negative number of moles at the end of the reaction. Therefore $H_3C_6H_5O_7$ is the limiting reactant.

$0.01561\ mol\ CO_2 \times 22.414\ L\ mol^{-1} = 0.3499\ L$

(c) $\Delta H° = +$; the reaction is endothermic since the temperature of the water decreased; energy flowed from surroundings into system

$\Delta S° = +$; the reaction began with 2 solids (or aqueous solutions) and formed a gas which has more microstates than other states of matter

$\Delta G° = -$; since the reaction was spontaneous, $\Delta G°$ must be negative (definition of a spontaneous process)

(d) $q = m \times c \times \Delta T$

$= (25.0\ g)(4.18\ J\ g^{-1}\ °C^{-1})(-7.6°C) = -790\ J$

(e) qH_2O, 2 tablets after each $q = -790\ J$ so $q2$ tablets $= +790\ J$. 2 tablets $= 2 \times 0.005205$ mol $H_3C_6H_5O_7 = 0.01041$ mol

$790\ J/0.01041\ mol = 76000\ J/mol = 76\ kJ/mol$ (Note: This was real data collected by students; the assumption about no interaction with surroundings may not be valid.)

SCORING THE FREE-RESPONSE QUESTIONS

It is difficult to come up with an exact score for this section of test. However, if you compare your answers to the answers in this book, remembering that each part of the test you answer correctly is worth points even if the other parts of the answer are incorrect (see the section titled "Types of Free-Response Questions" on page 12 of this book), you can get a general idea of the percentage of the questions for which you would get credit. If you believe that you got at least one-third of the possible credit, you would probably receive a 3 on this part of the test. If you believe that you would receive close to half or more of the available credit, your score would more likely be a 4 or a 5.

Part II

A Review of AP Chemistry

NON-TESTABLE CHEMISTRY CONCEPTS

The following topics, which have long been part of the AP Chemistry curriculum, have been eliminated because they are comprised of knowledge you are expected to have acquired in a prior class. You will not be assessed specifically on this content, but knowing the information may make it easier to answer some exam questions.

- Memorizing exceptions to the Aufbau principle, but you should be able to explain why a specific configuration is an exception
- Interpreting phase diagrams
- Knowledge of colligative properties
- Calculation of molality
- Knowing the definition of Lewis acids, but you are still responsible for understanding the formation of complex ions and their qualitative effect on solubility

1

CHEMICAL FOUNDATIONS

In this chapter, you will perform the basic calculations used in chemistry. Chemists use equipment with varying degrees of precision. The measurements recorded in an experiment must reflect the precision of the equipment used. The results of the calculations in an experiment also must reflect the precision of the equipment.

Many of the problems in chemistry use dimensional analysis to convert from one unit to another or to solve stoichiometry problems. Other basic calculations that will be discussed are density and temperature conversions.

You should be able to

- Identify the number of significant figures in a given measurement.
- Perform calculations involving significant figures.
  - Memorize the rules for counting and performing operations with significant figures.
- Differentiate between accuracy and precision as they apply to measurement.
- Determine the density of solids and liquids and calculate volumes or masses using the given density.
- Convert between units of temperature: degrees Celsius and Kelvin.
- Identify the characteristics of the states of matter: solids, liquids, and gases.
- Identify changes as being physical or chemical.
- Name compounds and write formulas for binary compounds, ternary compounds (those with polyatomic ions), and acids.
- Memorize the chemical formulas and charges of the polyatomic ions and the most common transition metal ions.

AP Tips

Significant figures are important in calculations. A maximum of one point in the free-response sections will be deducted for errors in significant figures that are off by ±1 significant figure.

Units are the key to problem solving. Include units in your calculated work to ensure that your answer has units that agree with the problem. Every measured number or number calculated from measurements has a unit except for equilibrium constants, which by convention are reported without units. When a calculation specifically asks for units to be included, you can be assured that the lack of units or incorrect units will result in a point deduction.

UNCERTAINTY IN MEASUREMENT

(*Chemistry* 8th ed. pages 11–14/9th ed. pages 11–14)

SIGNIFICANT FIGURES

The significant figures of a measurement are all of the certain digits in a measurement, those that represent actual marks on the measuring instrument, and the first uncertain digit (estimated number). Students should be able to read measurements to the proper number of significant figures.

> EXAMPLE: Figure 1.7 on page 11 in the 8th edition and Figure 1.7 on page 12 in the 9th edition shows the measurement of a volume of liquid using a buret. The *certain digits* in the measurement are the three digits 20.1. The digit to the right of the one must be estimated by interpolating between the 0.1-mL marks. The measurement with *uncertainty* can be reported as 20.15 mL.

PRECISION AND ACCURACY

Accuracy refers to the agreement of a particular value with a true value. Precision refers to the degree of agreement among several measurements of the same quantity. The degree of precision refers to the number of digits that a measuring device permits one to measure. In a measuring device, all except the last digit, which is estimated, are certain. For example, a balance which measures to the nearest 0.0001 g is more precise than one that measures to the nearest 0.01 g.

$$\text{Percent Error} = \frac{\text{Experimental Value} - \text{Actual Value}}{\text{Actual Value}} \times 100\%$$

> EXAMPLE: In an experiment, the density of aluminum is to be determined. Two students perform the experiment three times and obtain the following results.

Trial	Student A	Student B
1	2.45 g/mL	2.69 g/mL
2	2.43 g/mL	2.70 g/mL
3	2.44 g/mL	2.71 g/mL

Describe the accuracy and precision of each student's results. For Student A, calculate the average density and the percent error if the actual value is 2.70 g/mL.

SOLUTION: Student A's average density is 2.44 g/mL while Student B's average density is 2.70 g/mL. The values for Student A are precise, but inaccurate. The values are precise because they are consistent, but inaccurate because they are not close to the accepted value. The percent error for Student A is

$$\text{Percent Error} = \frac{\text{Experimental Value} - \text{Actual Value}}{\text{Actual Value}} \times 100\%$$

$$= \frac{2.44 \text{ g/mL} - 2.70 \text{ g/mL}}{2.70 \text{ g/mL}} \times 100\%$$

$$= \frac{0.26 \text{ g/mL}}{2.70 \text{ g/mL}} \times 100\%$$

$$= -9.6\%$$

Significant figure rules are described below.

The values for Student B are both precise and accurate.

Random error (indeterminate error) means that a measurement has an equal probability of being high or low.

Systematic error (determinate error) occurs in the same direction each time; it is either always high or always low.

EXAMPLE: A balance could have a defect causing it to give a result that is consistently 1.000 g too high. What type of error is this?

SOLUTION: A consistently high error is a systematic error. This type of error could be due to miscalibration.

SIGNIFICANT FIGURES AND CALCULATIONS

It is important to know the uncertainty in the final result in an experiment. The final reported result cannot have more certainty than the least precise measurement. The number of significant figures in a single value will be determined. Memorize the rules below and use them to answer the examples that follow.

Rules for Counting Significant Figures

1. Nonzero integers always count as significant figures.

2. Zeros: There are three classes of zeros.

   a. Leading zeros precede all the nonzero digits and do not count as significant figures. Example: 0.0025 has 2 significant figures.

   b. Captive zeros are zeros between nonzero numbers. These always count as significant figures. Example: 1.008 has 4 significant figures.

   c. Trailing zeros are zeros at the right end of the number.

   Trailing zeros are only significant if the number contains a decimal point. Example: 1.00×10^2 has 3 significant figures.

   Trailing zeros are not significant if the number does not contain a decimal point. Example: 100 has 1 significant figure.

3. Exact numbers, which can arise from counting or definitions such as 1000 mm = 1 m never limit the number of significant figures in a calculation.

EXAMPLE: How many significant figures are in each of the following?

100 L

SOLUTION: There is 1 significant figure. Trailing zeros do not count. Only the "1" is significant.

0.001010 L

SOLUTION: There are 4 significant figures. Leading zeros do not count. The numbers "1010" are significant because one zero is captive and the other zero is trailing, but a decimal is present.

Rules for Significant Figures in Calculations

1. For multiplication and division, the number of significant figures in the result is the same as the measurement with the fewest number of significant figures in the calculation.

2. For addition and subtraction, the result has the same number of decimal places as the measurement with the fewest number of decimal places in the calculation.

3. Rules for rounding:

   In a series of calculations, carry the extra digits to the final result, then round.

   If the digit to be removed

   is less than 5, the preceding digit stays the same. For example, 2.44 rounds to 2.4.

   is greater than or equal to 5, the preceding digit is increased by 1. For example, 2.45 rounds to 2.5.

It is important to calculate the results of mathematical expressions to the proper number of significant figures. Memorize the rules above and apply them to the examples that follow.

> EXAMPLE: Perform the following calculations to the correct number of significant figures.
>
> 1) 16.8 g + 3.2557 g
>
> SOLUTION: The calculator answer is 20.0557. The correct answer is 20.1 g. The answer should have one decimal place.
>
> 2) 27 g/4.148 mL
>
> SOLUTION: The calculator answer is 6.509161041. The correct answer is 6.5 g/mL. The answer should have 2 significant figures.

DIMENSIONAL ANALYSIS

(*Chemistry* 8th ed. pages 17–20/9th ed. pages 18–22)

Dimensional analysis is used to convert from one unit to another. It is the single most valuable mathematical technique that you will use in general chemistry. The method involves conversion factors to cancel units until you have the proper unit in the proper place. When you are setting up problems using dimensional analysis, you should be more concerned with units than numbers.

> EXAMPLE: The density of mercury is 13.6 g/cm³. How many liters is 1500 kg?

$$L = 1500 \text{ kg} \times \left(\frac{1000 \text{ g}}{1 \text{ kg}} \right) \times \left(\frac{1 \text{ cm}^3}{13.6 \text{ g}} \right) \times \left(\frac{1 \text{ mL}}{1 \text{ cm}^3} \right) \times \left(\frac{1 \text{ L}}{1000 \text{ mL}} \right)$$

SOLUTION:

$$= 110 \text{ L}$$

Double check that all of your units cancel properly. If they do, your numerical answer is probably correct. If they don't, your answer is definitely wrong.

DENSITY

(*Chemistry* 8th ed. pages 24–26/9th ed. pages 26–27)

> Density is the mass of substance per unit volume of substance.
> Density = mass/volume
> D = m/V

The density of regular shaped objects can be determined by using equations for determining volume such as $l \times w \times h$ for a cube or $\pi r^2 h$ for a cylinder. The density of an object can be determined through the *water displacement method*. The object is massed and then submerged in a measured amount of water in a graduated cylinder. The final volume in the graduated cylinder is read. The volume of water displaced by the object is the volume of the object.

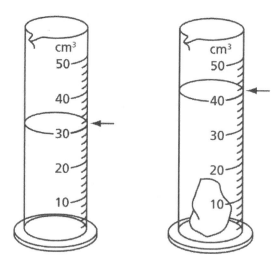

EXAMPLE: A sample containing 33.42 g of metal pellets is poured into a graduated cylinder containing 12.7 mL of water, causing the water level in the cylinder to rise to 21.6 mL. Calculate the density of the metal.

SOLUTION:

Volume of metal = (Volume H_2O metal) – Volume H_2O

$\qquad$ = 21.6 mL – 12.7 mL = 8.9 mL

Density of metal $= \dfrac{33.42 \text{ g}}{8.9 \text{ mL}} = 3.8$ g/mL

Note: The answer has 2 significant figures.

TEMPERATURE

(*Chemistry* 8th ed. pages 21–24/9th ed. pages 22–26)

You should be able to interconvert between Celsius and Kelvin. You should also know the freezing and boiling points of water on each scale.

$$T_K = T_C + 273.15$$

EXAMPLE: The boiling point of water on top of Long's Peak in Colorado (14,255 feet above sea level) is about 86.0°C. What is the boiling point in Kelvin?

SOLUTION:

$T_K = T_C + 273.15 = 86.0°C + 273.15 = 359.2$ K (one place after the decimal according to significant figure rules)

CLASSIFICATION OF MATTER

(*Chemistry* 8th ed. pages 26–29/9th ed. pages 27–31)

Matter exists in three states: solid, liquid, and gas. Properties of these three states of matter are listed below.

State of Matter	Shape	Volume
Solid	Fixed	Fixed
Liquid	Not definite	Fixed
Gas	Not fixed; takes shape of container	Not fixed; takes volume of container

CHANGES IN MATTER

Matter can undergo physical or chemical changes.

Physical changes in matter do not change the original composition of the substance. Changes in state such as boiling or melting are physical changes. Changes involving an alteration in the form of the substance such as grinding or tearing are physical. Physical properties are properties of a substance that can be observed without changing the composition of the substance. During a physical change, intramolecular bonds are not broken and no reaction between atoms occurs. For example, density, color, and boiling point are physical properties.

Chemical changes in matter change the composition of the original substance by breaking and making bonds between atoms. A new substance is produced when a chemical change occurs. Evidence that a chemical change has occurred includes change in color or odor; the production of a gas or a solid (precipitate); and the absorption or release of energy as seen by a temperature change or light given off. Some examples of chemical properties include flammability and reactivity to air.

COMPOUNDS

Elements combine in various ways to form compounds. Chemists generally divide compounds into two classes: ionic (formed by the transfer of electrons) and covalent (formed by the sharing of electrons) and each class has a unique nomenclature system that is used.

IONS

(*Chemistry* 8th ed. pages 52–53, 56–57, 61–62/9th ed. pages 55–57, 57–59, 65–66)

An ion is an atom that has lost or gained electrons and therefore has a positive or negative charge due to an imbalance of protons and electrons. A polyatomic ion is a group of atoms bonded together as a single unit that carries a net charge.

EXAMPLE: Aluminum forms a cation, a positive ion, by losing three electrons:

$$Al \rightarrow Al^{3+} + 3\ e^-$$

Oxygen forms an anion, a negative ion, by gaining two electrons:

$$O + 2\ e^- \rightarrow O^{2-}$$

An ammonium cation is formed when ammonia, a neutral compound, gains a hydrogen ion.

$$NH_3 + H^+ \rightarrow NH_4^+$$

NOMENCLATURE

(*Chemistry* 8th ed. pages 56–67/9th ed. pages 60–70)

When you finish this section you will be able to name, or give formulas for, the following classes of compounds: binary salts, salts with polyatomic ions, binary covalent compounds and acids.

Use the flowcharts that follow to answer the questions below.

Naming Compounds from the Given Formula

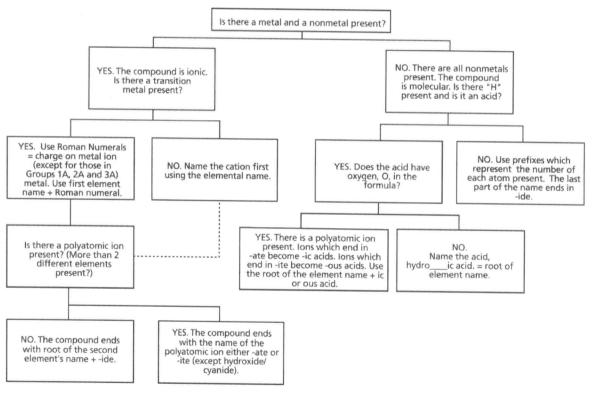

EXAMPLE:

Name each of the following compounds.

a. CaF_2 d. KIO_3

b. Cl_2O_7 e. $HF(aq)$

c. CuO f. $HNO_2(aq)$

SOLUTION:

a. calcium fluoride

b. dichlorine heptoxide

c. copper(II) oxide

d. potassium iodate

e. hydrofluoric acid

f. nitrous acid

Writing Formulas from the Given Name

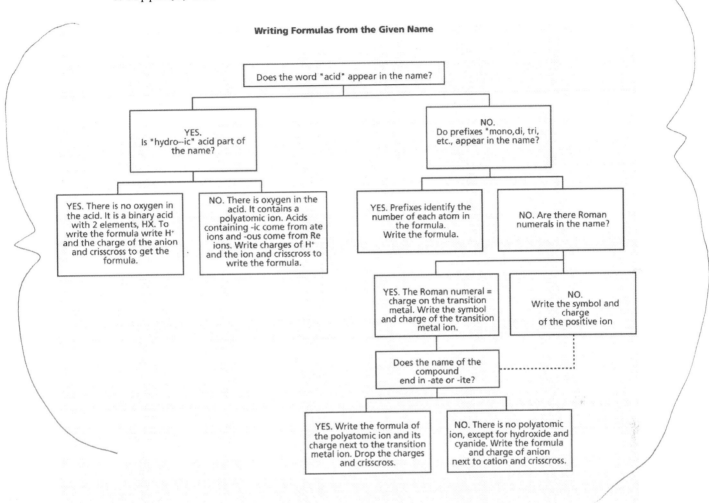

EXAMPLE:

Write the formulas for each of the following compounds.

a. tin(IV) oxide

b. hydrosulfuric acid

c. nickel(II) nitrate

d. sulfurous acid

e. potassium chloride

f. iodine pentafluoride

SOLUTION:

a. SnO_2

b. $H_2S(aq)$

c. $Ni(NO_3)_2$

d. $H_2SO_3(aq)$

e. KCl

f. IF_5

MULTIPLE-CHOICE QUESTIONS

Since this chapter is a review of chemistry, most of the questions below are not at the level seen on the AP Chemistry exam. No calculators are to be used in this section.

When choosing your answers, it is helpful to make the general observation that numerical answers tend to fall into one of two areas. Quite often the answers will vary greatly from each other. For example, you usually know if an answer of 3.0 grams or 300. grams is more reasonable. Secondly, consider how many significant figures an answer should have when examining all of the answers.

1. Measurements indicate a charge of 0.400 coulombs (C) passes a point in 0.20 seconds. The current (i.e., the rate of charge flow, in C/s) is best expressed as
   (A) 0.080 C/s
   (B) 0.0800 C/s
   (C) 2.0 C/s
   (D) 2.00 C/s

2. A given sample contains 2.4 g of hydrogen, 30.5 g of sulfur, and 75.09 g of oxygen. What is the total mass of the sample?
   (A) 107.99 g
   (B) 108.0 g
   (C) 108 g
   (D) 1.1×10^2 g

3. What is the percent mass of sulfur in the above mixture (see number 2)?
   (A) 2.82%
   (B) 2.8%
   (C) 28.2%
   (D) 28%

4. The correct name for B_2O_3 is
   (A) boron oxide
   (B) diboron trioxide
   (C) boron(II) oxide(III)
   (D) beryllium oxide

5. The correct name for $Mg(OH)_2$ is
   (A) magnesium hydroxide
   (B) magnesium(I) hydroxide
   (C) magnesium(II) hydroxide(I)
   (D) magnesium hydrogen oxide

6. The correct formula for iodine monobromide is
   (A) $I_2(Br_2)_2$
   (B) IBr
   (C) I_2Br
   (D) I_2Br_2

7. The correct formula for copper(II) phosphate is
    (A) $CuPO_4$
    (B) Cu_3P_2
    (C) $Cu_3(PO_4)_2$
    (D) Cu_2PO_4

8. A student was trying to find the density of an unknown substance by measuring the mass of specific volumes of liquid. She used 3 different volumetric pipets and an electronic balance to obtain the data below. The actual density is 1.50 g/mL. Which of the following would account for her results?

Volume (mL)	Mass (g)	Density (g/mL)
10.00	16.091	1.609
20.00	32.106	1.605
15.00	24.072	1.605

    (A) Random error; the pipets were poor quality.
    (B) Random error; the balance was dirty.
    (C) Systematic error; the pipets delivered too much volume.
    (D) Systematic error; the mass indicated on the balance was too large.

9. The density of copper is approximately 9.0 g/cm³. What is the mass of 20.0 cm³ of pure copper?
    (A) 2.2 g
    (B) 200 g
    (C) 180. g
    (D) 180 g

10. An experiment that tested the effect of temperature on pressure was performed and data indicated a direct relationship between pressure and temperature. The student forgot to convert his temperatures from Celsius to Kelvin when he graphed temperature vs. pressure, however. How would this affect his results?

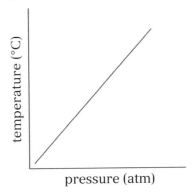

    (A) The slope of the line is 273 times too large.
    (B) The slope of the line is 273 times too small.
    (C) The y-intercept of the line is 273 units too high.
    (D) The y-intercept of the line is 273 units too low.

11. Which of the following processes represents a chemical change?
    (A) water boiling
    (B) iodine subliming
    (C) sugar dissolving in water
    (D) natural gas burning

12. What physical process is represented in the particulate model below?

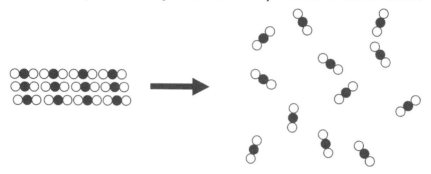

    (A) $CO_2(s) \rightarrow CO_2(l)$
    (B) $CO_2(s) \rightarrow CO_2(g)$
    (C) $CO_2(l) \rightarrow CO_2(g)$
    (D) $(CO_2)_{12} \rightarrow 12\ CO_2$

13. What is the formula of hydrosulfuric acid?
    (A) HS
    (B) H_2S
    (C) H_2SO_3
    (D) H_2SO_4

14. A pure solid is heated and it decomposes into two substances, one a liquid and the other a gas. One can conclude with certainty that:
    (A) the two products are elements
    (B) one of the products is an element
    (C) the original solid is not an element
    (D) both products are compounds

15. A student measures the mass of silver in a sample and does four determinations. The results are 1.75 g, 1.71 g, 1.85 g, and 1.93 g. The true value is 1.81 g. Which statement concerning the results is correct?
    (A) high precision and accurate results
    (B) high precision and poor accuracy
    (C) poor precision and poor accuracy
    (D) poor precision and accurate results

FREE-RESPONSE QUESTIONS

1. (a) Describe how, in the laboratory, you might determine experimentally the density of a solid, such as a sugar cube, which is water soluble. Indicate what equipment you might best use in the process.
   (b) Then describe a second experimental method for determining the density of this same object, so that you might verify the results of the first method.

2. Standard deviation is a measure of reproducibility of data. Low standard deviation means the data are precise. Percent error measures accuracy. Low percent error means accurate data. Use the data below to make a claim about why appropriate graduated cylinders should be used for accurate and precise volume measurements. Support your claim with evidence.

Glassware Used	Approximate Volume Measured (mL)	% Error	Standard Deviation
10-mL graduated cylinder	9	–1.80	0.0110
100-mL graduated cylinder	45	–2.43	0.0347
1000-mL graduated cylinder	45	–19.09	0.1357
50-mL Erlenmeyer flask	45	–3.83	0.0306
50-mL beaker	45	–4.13	0.0754
100-mL beaker	45	–7.12	0.0250
2000-mL beaker	50	–12.62	0.1921

Answers

MULTIPLE-CHOICE QUESTIONS

1. **C** Even if you do not understand what is meant by a term (in this case, current) you can often successfully attack a problem by careful attention to units. In the problem, you are seeking an answer in C/s, so divide the 0.400 C by 0.20 s (and keep your answer to 2 significant figures) (*Chemistry* 8th ed. pages 14–15/9th ed. pages 14–15).

2. **B** Each of these values is known to one-tenth of a gram (0.1 g) or more, so the total may be known to no more than the nearest 0.1 g.

   2.4 g + 30.5 g + 75.09 g = 107.99 g = 108.0 g

   Remember, when adding or subtracting, you do not count the number of significant figures but instead look at the position of the decimal point in each of the data used in the calculation (*Chemistry* 8th ed. pages 14–15/9th ed. pages 14–15).

3. **C** Remember that no calculators are allowed on the multiple-choice portion of the AP exam. You should be able to do "mental math" to solve the problem.

$$\frac{30.5 \text{ g}}{108.0 \text{ g}} \times 100 \approx \frac{30}{100} \times 100 \approx 30\%$$

Now you are dividing, so the answer is known to the number of significant figures which is the least number of significant figures in data used to obtain the answer (here, 3 significant figures in the mass of sulfur limits the answer to 3 significant figures even though you know the total mass to 4). Also note that the 100% is known by definition, that is, it is considered an "exact number" (*Chemistry* 8th ed. pages 14–15/9th ed. pages 14–15).

4. **B** Prefixes are used when naming covalent (nonmetal–nonmetal) compounds (*Chemistry* 8th ed. pages 63–64/9th ed. pages 66–67).

5. **A** Roman numerals are used with transition metal compounds to indicate the charge or oxidation number of the metal ion in this compound. Since transition metal ions can often have more than one charge (oxidation number), this identification is necessary. There is no need for such nomenclature when the magnesium ion used for it can have only a 2+ charge. Note also that even the transition metal ions Ag^+, Zn^{2+}, and Cd^{2+} generally are found with only the oxidation number indicated, and since there is only one form of ion, Roman numerals are not used with these three transition metal ions (*Chemistry* 8th ed. pages 56–61, esp. Table 2.4/9th ed. pages 59–64, esp. Table 2.4).

6. **B** As indicated in the discussion for question #4, prefixes in covalently bonded compounds are used to correctly write the formula (*Chemistry* 8th ed. pages 63–64/9th ed. pages 66–67).

7. **C** Both copper with a 2+ and a 1+ charge are common ions. It is necessary to assign copper the 2+ charge in this case and then determine the ratio of Cu^{2+} and PO_4^{3-} to make the unit neutral; hence $Cu_3(PO_4)_2$ (*Chemistry* 8th ed. pages 61–62, esp. Table 2.5/9th ed. pages 64–65, esp. Table 2.5).

8. **D** The calculated densities were all precise but too large. This means that systematic error was present. It is very unlikely that 3 different volumetric pipets would have the same error so the error is most likely in the balance (*Chemistry* 8th ed. pages 12–14/9th ed. pages 12–14).

9. **D** From density = m/v, solving for mass and using mass = $(d) \times (v)$ = 9.0 g/cm³ × 20.0 cm³. The answer can only have 2 significant figures, 180 g (*Chemistry* 8th ed. pages 24–26/9th ed. pages 26–27).

10. **D** Since the relationship between Celsius and Kelvin is K = °C + 273.15, graphing the temperature in Celsius will cause the intercept to be –273°C instead of 0 K (*Chemistry* 8th ed. pages 21–23/9th ed. pages 22–25).

11. **D** When natural gas burns, at least two new substances are produced, CO_2 and H_2O. Choices (A), (B), and (E) are all examples of phase

changes or changes of state, which are physical changes. Choice (C) is an example of a mixture, which can be separated by physical means back into the original substances (*Chemistry* 8th ed. pages 25–29/9th ed. pages 27–31).

12. **B** The model represents solid carbon dioxide subliming into gaseous carbon dioxide (*Chemistry* 8th ed. page 27/9th ed. page 29).

13. **B** Acids that are made from nonoxygen-containing anions are named as *hydro- -ic* (*Chemistry* 8th ed. pages 66–67, and Appendix 6/9th ed. pages 69–70).

14. **C** The original solid is pure and therefore it must be a compound because it can be chemically decomposed into simpler substances. You are not given specific information about the composition of the products and thus you can not make any definite conclusions about them (*Chemistry* 8th ed. pages 28–29/9th ed. pages 30–31).

15. **D** The average of the measurements is 1.81 g, which is the same as the true value. Therefore, the accuracy is high. The range of measured values is 1.75 g to 1.93 g, which is a difference of 0.18 g, or 10% of the average value, which is poor precision. Precision is a measure of how close the measurements are to each other (*Chemistry* 8th ed. pages 13–14/9th ed. pages 13–14).

FREE-RESPONSE QUESTIONS

1 (a) Since density is a ratio of the mass of the object compared to the volume of the object, you might first determine the mass of the sugar cube using a balance. Greater precision is possible with an analytical balance. Then determine the volume of this regular cube by measuring its length, width, and depth (they should all be the same, of course!) and calculating the volume [$V = (l) \times (w) \times (d) = $ (side)^3]. It is then a simple step to divide the mass by the volume just calculated (*Chemistry* 8th ed. pages 24–25/9th ed. pages 26–27).

   (b) The second method suggests a liquid displacement method for determining volume. However the liquid used may not be water since the object is water soluble. Select a nonpolar liquid to keep this polar solid from dissolving, perhaps, 1,1,1-trichloroethane (*Chemistry* 8th ed. pages 24–25 and 130–132/9th ed. pages 26–27 and 139–141).

2. The 10-mL graduated cylinder is both accurate and precise for volumes of less than 10 mL. The evidence for this is the low percent error (–1.80%) and the low standard deviation. These values indicate measured values that are close to theoretical and values that are reproducible. The 100-mL graduated cylinder is the second most accurate measuring device with a percent error of –2.43%, but the precision is actually not as good as the 100-mL beaker or 50-mL Erlenmeyer flask. The graduated cylinder has a standard deviation of 0.0347, which is higher than the beaker (0.0250) and the flask (0.0306) (*Chemistry* 8th ed. pages 12–14 and A10–12/9th ed. pages 12–14 and A10–A12).

BIG IDEA 1:
ATOMIC STRUCTURE
AND PERIODICITY

2

Big Idea 1

The chemical elements are fundamental building materials of matter, and all matter can be understood in terms of arrangements of atoms. These atoms retain their identity in chemical reactions.

Atoms are the fundamental building blocks of the elements which comprise all matter. Big Idea 1 relates to 3 main topics in this chapter: atomic structure, periodicity, and macroscale matter. The structure of the atom is the basis for the organization of the elements on the periodic table. Physical and chemical changes that we see on the macroscopic scale are the result of how atoms interact with other atoms and with electromagnetic radiation. Because atoms are so incredibly small we use moles as a unit of measurement when describing quantities of atoms.

You should be able to
- Use evidence to explain why atomic models have changed throughout history.
- Calculate the average atomic mass of an atom from mass spectrometry and isotopic data.
- Use photoelectron spectroscopy as evidence to show that electrons exist in quantized shells.
- Justify the arrangement of the periodic table based on the quantum mechanical model of the atom.

- Convert between mass, moles, and numbers of representative particles (atoms, molecules, formula units) of a substance.
- Calculate the molar mass of a compound and the percent composition of an element in a compound.
- Express the law of conservation of mass using symbolic representations and particulate models.

AP Tip

Writing coherent answers to the free-response questions is essential. You need to differentiate between restating facts and explaining the concepts and evidence that supports the facts. Questions that involve mathematical problem solving should clearly show your work and answer. Partial credit may be awarded for some questions.

PART 1: ATOMIC STRUCTURE

EVIDENCE FOR ATOMS

MODELS CHANGE OVER TIME

Atomic models have been around since Democritus first thought about dividing matter by continually cutting it into smaller and smaller pieces until it could no longer be cut: *atomos*. The idea of atoms was opposed by Aristotle and it took about 2500 years until scientific evidence was used to revive the idea of atoms.

HISTORY OF THE ATOM

(*Chemistry* 8th ed. pages 42–50/9th ed. pages 44–54)

JOHN DALTON

Dalton's model of the atom was based on the work of many scientists. He used the law of definite proportion and the law of multiple proportions to provide evidence for his model.
 Dalton's model has 4 parts:

1. Each element is made of atoms.

2. Atoms of a given element are identical; atoms of different atoms are different in some fundamental ways.

3. Atoms can combine to form compounds and a given compound always has the same relative number and types of atoms.

4. Chemical reactions involve rearrangement of the ways the atoms are bonded together. The atoms themselves are not changed.

(*Chemistry* 8th ed. pages 41–44/9th ed. pages 44–47)

THE LAW OF DEFINITE PROPORTION

The law of definite proportion states that a given compound always contains exactly the same proportions of elements by mass.

> EXAMPLE: A sample of H_2SO_4 contains 2.02 g hydrogen, 32.07 g sulfur, and 64.00 g oxygen. How many grams of sulfur and grams of oxygen are present in a second sample of H_2SO_4 containing 7.27 g of hydrogen?
>
> SOLUTION: Hydrogen is increased by a factor of 3.60 (7.27/2.02). Therefore
>
> g sulfur = 32.07 × 3.60 = 115.45 g sulfur = 115 g sulfur
>
> g oxygen = 64.00 g × 3.60 = 230.4 g oxygen = 230 g oxygen

THE LAW OF MULTIPLE PROPORTIONS

The law of multiple proportions: When two elements form a series of compounds, the ratio of masses of the second element that combine with 1 gram of the first element can always be reduced to the smallest whole numbers.

> EXAMPLE: Sulfur and oxygen can react to form both sulfur dioxide and sulfur trioxide. In sulfur dioxide there are 32.06 g sulfur and 32.00 g oxygen. In sulfur trioxide there are 32.06 g sulfur combined with 48.00 g oxygen. What is the ratio of the weights of oxygen that combine with 32.06 g sulfur?
>
> SOLUTION: 48.00/32.00 = 1.5 or 3:2, demonstrating the law of multiple proportions.

DISCOVERY OF THE NUCLEUS

Dalton's model of hard spheres that were identical for each element was quickly challenged because the model could not account for the way electricity interacted with matter and also did not account for the fact that most elements were composed of isotopes.

ISOTOPES

(*Chemistry* 8th ed. pages 78–81/9th ed. pages 83–85)

Isotopes are atoms of the same element with different numbers of neutrons and therefore different atomic masses.

MASS SPECTROMETRY

(*Chemistry* 8th ed. pages 78–80/9th ed. pages 83–85)

Mass spectrometry is an analytical technique that is used to determine the mass spectrum of an element. Most elements exist as isotopes of different mass, and the mass spectrometer can determine the ratio of the masses.

An element sample is ionized and the resulting fragments are passed through a magnetic field that deflects the ions based on mass and charge. The deflection separates the ions and a unique spectrum is created. The relative heights of peaks on the spectrum provide evidence for the isotopic ratio of the element.

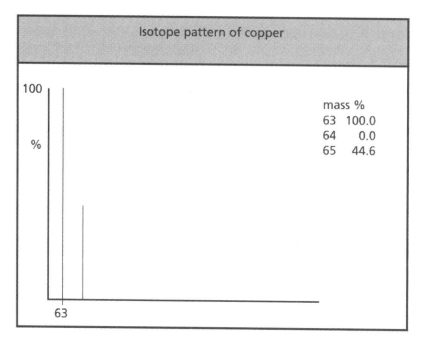

Isotope	Atomic Mass (amu)
^{63}Cu	62.9
^{65}Cu	64.9

The mass spectrum of copper is shown above. The highest peak is often set to 100%, but that is just an arbitrary scale. The relationship between the peaks is what is important. If you had 1446 atoms of copper, the data show that 1000 of those atoms would be copper-63 and 446 atoms would be copper-65. An average atomic mass could be calculated from these data.

$$\frac{\left[(1000 \text{ atoms})\left(62.9 \, \tfrac{amu}{atom}\right) + \left(446 \text{ atoms}\right)\left(64.9 \, \tfrac{amu}{atom}\right)\right]}{1446 \text{ atoms}} = 63.5 \text{ amu}$$

You are probably more familiar with calculating average atomic mass from percent abundance data, but the percent composition data originally came from mass spectrometry experiments. In this case, 69.16% of the sample (1000/1446 atoms) was copper-63 and the remaining 30.84% of the sample (446/1446 atoms) was copper-65.

CALCULATION OF AVERAGE ATOMIC MASS FROM ISOTOPIC DATA

(*Chemistry* 8th ed. pages 78–81/9th ed. pages 83–85)

The average atomic mass of an element can be calculated from the percent abundance and mass of each isotope for that element.

Avg Atomic Mass = (percent abundance of isotope × mass number)

EXAMPLE: Element "E" is present with the following mass values and natural abundances.

Isotope	Mass Number (amu)	Percent Abundance (%)
^{10}E	10.01	19.78
^{11}E	11.01	80.22

What is the average atomic mass of the element, E? What is the element?

SOLUTION: (0.1978)(10.01) + (0.8022)(11.01) = 10.812 amu.

The element is boron.

NIELS BOHR

(*Chemistry* 8th ed. page 295–300/9th ed. pages 306–310)

Niels Bohr used the line spectrum of hydrogen to develop his atomic model. Bohr proposed that the electron in the hydrogen atom moves around the nucleus only in certain allowed circular orbits and the line spectra of elements are the result of electrons moving between these allowed orbits. Bohr's model has often been described as a solar system model. Since a moving electron radiates energy, this model was unstable using classical mechanics and the model was shown to be incorrect. Furthermore, the model only worked for hydrogen and could not predict the spectra of other elements. An understanding of the electromagnetic spectrum is necessary to understand Bohr's model and subsequent atomic models.

why do they teach us about the failed and incorrect models? What's the point?

ELECTROMAGNETIC RADIATION

(*Chemistry* 8th ed. pages 285–286/9th ed. pages 296–298)

Electromagnetic radiation provides an important means of energy transfer. Light from the sun reaches the earth in the form of radiation that includes ultraviolet and visible radiation. Electromagnetic radiation, from the shortest to the longest wavelength, includes gamma rays, x-rays, ultraviolet, visible, infrared, microwaves, and radio waves. All types of electromagnetic radiation exhibit both wave-like and particle-like behavior and travel at the speed of light in a vacuum.

Chemists have used the interaction of light with matter to study the structure of the atom.

CHARACTERISTICS OF WAVES

(*Chemistry* 8th ed. pages 285–286/9th ed. pages 296–298)

Wavelength, λ, is the distance between two consecutive peaks or troughs in a wave.

Frequency, υ, is the number of waves (cycles) per second that passes a given point in space.

Wavelength and frequency are related by the equation:

$$\upsilon = c / \lambda$$

in which c is the speed of light in a vacuum, 2.9979×10^8 m/s. Wavelength is measured in meters, and frequency is measured in 1/s, or hertz (Hz).

ENERGY OF ELECTROMAGNETIC RADIATION

(*Chemistry* 8th ed. pages 285–287/9th ed. pages 296–298)

Energy is quantized and can occur only in whole number multiples of $h\upsilon$. Each small packet of energy is called a quantum. A system can transfer energy only in discrete quanta. The change in energy for a system can be represented by

$$\Delta E = nh\upsilon$$

where n is an integer (1,2,3,...), h is Planck's constant which equals 6.626×10^{-34} Js, and υ is the frequency.

Einstein viewed electromagnetic energy as a stream of particles called photons. And the energy of each photon can be given by

$$E_{photon} = hc/\lambda$$

EXAMPLE: The laser in an audio compact disc player uses light with a wavelength of 7.80×10^2 nm. Calculate the frequency of this radiation. What is the energy of this radiation per photon?

SOLUTION: 1 nm $= 10^{-9}$ m

$(7.80 \times 10^2 \text{ nm})(1 \times 10^{-9} \text{ m/1 nm}) = 7.80 \times 10^{-7}$ m

$$\upsilon = \frac{c}{\lambda} = \frac{2.998 \times 10^8 \text{ m/s}}{7.80 \times 10^{-7} \text{ m}} = 3.84 \times 10^{14} \text{ s}^{-1}$$

$E_{photon} = hc/\lambda$

$= (6.626 \times 10^{-34} \text{ Js})(2.998 \times 10^8 \text{ m/s}) / 7.80 \times 10^{-7} \text{ m}$
$= 2.55 \times 10^{-19}$ J

ATOMIC SPECTRUM

(*Chemistry* 8th ed. pages 294–295/9th ed. pages 305–306)

A continuous spectrum contains all wavelengths of visible light. A line spectrum contains only a few lines, each corresponding to a discrete wavelength. When atoms are excited by adding energy, electrons move to higher energy levels as they absorb the energy. When the electrons return to their ground-state energies, the excess energy is given off by emitting light of various wavelengths to produce an emission spectrum or line spectrum.

The Emission lines for the element Hydrogen which correspond to the absorption lines for the same element

QUANTUM MECHANICAL MODEL

(*Chemistry* 8th ed. pages 300–303/9th ed. pages 310–313)

Our current model of the atom is the quantum mechanical model. In this model, we treat the electrons as a wave and do not believe it is possible to describe the path of an electron. An orbital is a three-dimensional electron density map in which there is a very high probability of finding the electron. The Heisenberg uncertainty principle is an important part of the model. It states that we cannot know both the momentum and location of an electron. The quantum mechanical (QM) model is an improvement over the Bohr model because the QM model supports evidence of energy levels and sublevels within atoms. The QM model can be approximated using computers and is the basis for software that predicts molecular shape and reactivity.

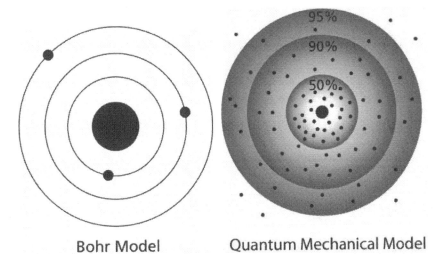

Bohr Model   Quantum Mechanical Model

ELECTROSTATIC FORCES HOLD THE ATOM TOGETHER

A neutral atom is composed of protons and neutrons in the nucleus and electrons in energy levels or "shells" outside of the nucleus. Coulomb's law states that the force between the two particles is proportional to the magnitude and inversely proportional to the square of the distance between them.

$$|F| = k_e \frac{|q_1 q_2|}{r^2}$$

where F = force, k_e = proportionality constant, q = charges on each particle and r is the distance between the particles.

If the charges are of opposite signs, the force is attractive and if the charges are of the same sign, the force is repulsive. As the distance between the charges increases, the attractive force between the charges decreases. When comparing two atoms that have electrons approximately the same distance from the nucleus (such as nitrogen and oxygen), the nucleus with the higher nuclear charge (oxygen) will have a higher attractive force for the electrons.

PHOTOELECTRON SPECTROSCOPY

Photoelectron spectroscopy (PES) is a technique that can be used to provide evidence for electron shells in an atom. Light is shined on an atom and the minimum frequency needed to remove an electron is determined. If the frequency of light is greater than the threshold needed to remove an electron, the extra energy is retained by the ionized atom as kinetic energy. Because energy is conserved, the energy of light that hits the atom (h) must equal the energy required to remove the electron (IE) and the kinetic energy (KE) of the removed electron.

h = KE + IE

Since the frequency of the light hitting the atom is known and the kinetic energy of the removed electron can be measured, the ionization energy of the electron can be calculated. Electrons that are farther away from the nucleus require less ionization energy and therefore have higher kinetic energy when removed. Electrons that are farther from the nucleus experience a smaller effective nuclear charge due to shielding from electrons in lower energy levels. Inner electrons have a higher electrostatic attraction to the nucleus and require a higher ionization energy to remove them. This results in electrons with lower kinetic energy. Electrons that are closer to the nucleus experience a greater effective nuclear charge due to less shielding.

The ionization energies of the first twenty elements are listed in the table below.

Element	Ionization Energy (MJ/mol)					
H	1.31					
He	2.37					
Li	6.26	0.52				
Be	11.5	0.90				
B	19.3	1.36	0.80			
C	28.6	1.72	1.09			
N	39.6	2.45	1.40			
O	52.6	3.12	1.31			
F	67.2	3.88	1.68			
Ne	84.0	4.68	2.08			
Na	104	6.84	3.67	0.50		
Mg	126	9.07	5.31	0.74		
Al	151	12.1	7.79	1.09	0.58	
Si	178	15.1	10.3	1.46	0.79	
P	208	18.7	13.5	1.95	1.01	
S	239	22.7	16.5	2.05	1.00	
Cl	273	26.8	20.2	2.44	1.25	
Ar	309	31.5	24.1	2.82	1.52	
K	347	37.1	29.1	3.93	2.38	0.42
Ca	390	42.7	34.0	4.65	2.9	0.59

Both hydrogen and helium have a single ionization energy that corresponds to the $n = 1$ energy level electrons. Even though helium has 2 electrons, they are both approximately equally distant from the nucleus and therefore have the same ionization energy.

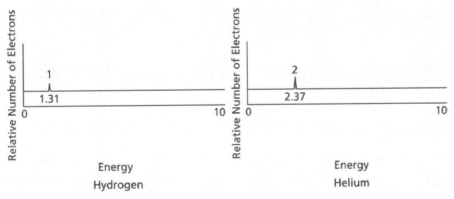

Lithium has 2 ionization energies that correspond to n = 1 and n = 2 energy levels. Boron's ionization energies, however, do not seem to follow the pattern at first. The IE for n = 1 (19.3 MJ/mol) is about 14 times greater than n = 2 (1.36 MJ/mol). There is less than 2 times difference between the two sets of outermost electrons (1.36 MJ/mol and 0.80 MJ/mol). This evidence supports the idea of 2 subshells in n = 2. The subshell closer to the nucleus is called 2s and the one farther away is called 2p.

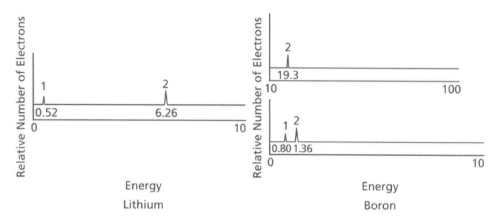

EXAMPLE: How do the data in the table above support the claim that calcium's electrons are in 4 shells?

SOLUTION: The first ionization energy of calcium is about 9 times larger than the second indicating that electrons are in n = 1. The second and third ionization energies are about 1.25 times different indicating that those electrons are probably in the same shell (n = 2). The 3rd and 4th energy level are approximately 7 times different indicating the existence of another shell (n = 3). IE$_4$ is about 1.6 times larger than IE$_5$ indicating 2 subshells in n = 3. Finally, IE$_5$ is about 5 times larger than IE$_4$ indicating another energy level, n = 4.

The core electrons effectively shield the valence electrons from the positive charge of the nucleus due to the repulsion of like charges. Less energy is required to remove electrons and overcome the attractive forces of the nucleus. This phenomenon also explains the differences in ionization energy in subshells of the same energy level.

QUANTUM NUMBERS

(*Chemistry* 8th ed. pages 303–304/9th ed. pages 313–314)

Quantum numbers characterize various properties of the orbitals. There are four quantum numbers. The Pauli exclusion principle states that no two electrons can have the same set of four quantum numbers.

The principal quantum number, *n*, is related to the size and energy of the orbital. As *n* increases, the orbital becomes larger, which also means it is higher in energy.

The angular momentum quantum number, ℓ, is related to the shape of atomic orbitals.

The magnetic quantum number, m_ℓ is related to the orientation of the orbital in space relative to the other orbitals in the atom.

The electron spin quantum number, m_s, has only two values: +1/2 and –1/2. This quantum number is necessary to describe the fact that the electron has two possible orientations, or spins, when placed in an external magnetic field. Because electrons can only adopt two different spins, each orbital can hold a maximum of two electrons.

The four quantum numbers are summarized in the following table.

Quantum Numbers

Name	Designation	Property of the Orbital
Principal quantum number	n	Related to size and energy of the orbital
Angular momentum quantum number	ℓ	Related to the shape of the orbital
Magnetic quantum number	m_ℓ	Related to the position of the orbital in space in relation to other orbitals
Electron spin quantum number	m_s	Related to the spin of the electron, which can be only one of two values

The principal quantum number, n, is the number which appears in front of the types of orbital s, p, d, or f. In general, for periods (rows) 1, 2, and 3, the principal quantum number, n, is the same as the row number. For periods 3, 4, 5, 6, and 7, the principal quantum number written before s and p orbitals is the same as the row number for the main group of elements, those in columns 1–2 and 13–18 (1A through 8A). For the transition elements, the value of n which is written in front of the d orbital is 1 number less than the row number. For example, scandium, in period 4, has a value of n equal to 3 for its d electron. In the sixth row of the periodic table, the f-transition elements occur after lanthanum. For these elements, the value of n which is placed before the f is 2 less than the row in which they occur.

ORBITAL SHAPES AND ENERGIES

(Chemistry 8th ed. pages 305–308/9th ed. pages 314–318)

s ORBITALS

The *s* orbitals have a spherical distribution of electron density. The *s* orbitals become larger as the value of *n* increases.

Nodes are areas in which there is zero probability of finding an electron. The 2*s* has one node which separates areas of high probability, the 3*s* has two nodes, and so forth.

p ORBITALS

There are three *p* orbitals which first appear in *n* = 2. The *p* orbitals have two lobes which are separated by a node at the nucleus. The *p* orbitals are labeled n_{px}, n_{py}, and n_{pz}, according to the axis along which the lobe lies.

Degenerate orbitals are orbitals with the same value of *n* which have the same energy. The three *p* orbitals in the same energy level are degenerate or equal in energy.

d AND f ORBITALS

The *d* orbitals first occur when *n* = 3 but in the fourth period of the periodic table. The *f* orbitals first occur when *n* = 4 and in the sixth period.

> EXAMPLE: Which of the following orbital designations is incorrect: 1*s*, 1*p*, 2*d*, 4*f*?

> SOLUTION: 1*p* is incorrect: *p* orbitals do not exist in energy level 1; *n* = 2 is the first energy level that has *p* orbitals

> 2*d* is incorrect: *d* orbitals do not exist in energy level 2; the first energy level with *d* orbitals is energy level 3

> EXAMPLE: Give the maximum number of electrons in an atom that can have the quantum number *n* = 3.

> SOLUTION: Energy level 3 is comprised of 3 types of orbitals: *s*, *p*, and *d*. Two electrons can exist in an *s* orbital, 6 in a *p* orbital, and 10 in a *d* orbital. Therefore, 18 electrons can exist in level 3. For any energy level, $2n^2$ = max number of electrons for any energy level.

> EXAMPLE: Give the maximum number of electrons in an atom that can exist in 2*p* orbitals.

> SOLUTION: Each 2*p* orbital can hold 2 electrons with spins in opposite directions. Since three orientations of *p* orbitals exist, a total of 6 electrons can be in 2*p*.

PART 2: PERIODICITY

ARRANGING THE ELEMENTS

ELECTRONIC STRUCTURE AND PERIODIC TABLE

(*Chemistry* 8th ed. pages 317–318/9th ed. pages 328–329)

The current arrangement of the periodic table is a result of the repeating pattern of electron arrangement as the atomic number of the elements increases.

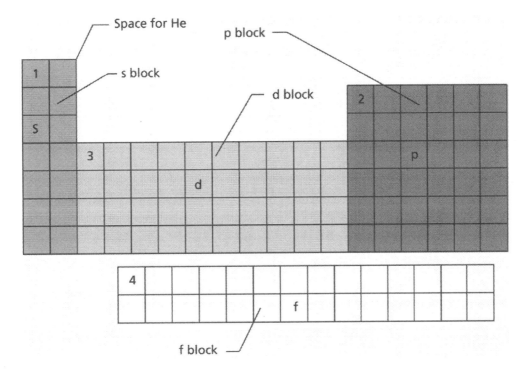

AUFBAU PRINCIPLE AND ELECTRON CONFIGURATIONS

(*Chemistry* 8th ed. pages 312–318/9th ed. pages 322–329)

The aufbau principle is a scheme used to reproduce the electron configuration of the ground states of atoms by successively filling sublevels with electrons in a specific order that is directly related to the amount of energy within each orbital.

The electron configuration for an atom of an element represents all of the electrons in the atom and it shows in which energy levels and orbitals the electrons reside.

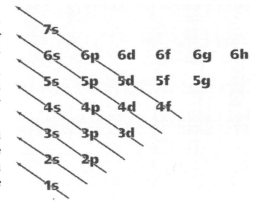

EXAMPLE: Write an electron configuration for oxygen.

SOLUTION: The electron configuration for oxygen is $1s^2 2s^2 2p^4$.

To write an electron configuration for an atom of an element, follow the aufbau principle and add electrons to the lowest energy orbital, the 1s. Using the Pauli exclusion principle, each orbital holds two electrons, we fill up the 1s with two electrons of opposite spin, then the 2s, to get $1s^2 2s^2$. We have used four electrons so far and oxygen has eight total electrons. The remaining four electrons go into the three 2p orbitals. Hund's rule requires that we place one electron in each separate p orbital with parallel spin before pairing electrons. Write the electron configuration as $1s^2 2s^2 2p^4$.

EXAMPLE: Write the abbreviated electron configuration for oxygen.

SOLUTION: The abbreviated electron configuration for oxygen is $[He]2s^2 2p^4$.

To write the abbreviated electron configuration, write the noble gas symbol which comes before the element in brackets followed by the remaining electrons.

ORBITAL DIAGRAMS

(*Chemistry* 8th ed. pages 312–313/9th ed. pages 322–323)

The orbital diagram displays the same information as the electron configuration. In addition, the spin of the electron is also represented.

EXAMPLE: Give the orbital diagram for oxygen.

SOLUTION:

$$\underset{1s}{\uparrow\downarrow} \quad \underset{2s}{\uparrow\downarrow} \quad \underset{2p}{\underline{\uparrow\downarrow \; \uparrow \; \uparrow}}$$

The first arrow in the 1s orbital represents an electron spinning in a particular direction. The second electron occupying the same orbital must spin in the opposite direction since, according to the Pauli exclusion principle, only two electrons with opposite spin can occupy the same orbital. When the 1s orbital is filled, the 2s orbital fills in the same manner as the 1s. There are three degenerate 2p orbitals, so one electron must go into each of the 2p orbitals according to Hund's rule. The fourth 2p electron becomes paired with the first 2p electron.

The orbital diagram for oxygen shows unpaired electrons in 2p. Unpaired electrons in atoms or molecules make particles paramagnetic. This means that the substance is attracted to a magnet. The attraction is relatively weak in most instances.

VALENCE ELECTRONS

(*Chemistry* 8th ed. page 313/9th ed. page 323)

Valence electrons are the electrons in the outermost principal quantum level of an atom. In the example with oxygen, the valence electrons are in the second quantum (energy) level. In the second energy level, there are six valence electrons, two in the 2s and four in the 2p. Coincidentally, the valence electrons of a main group element are the same as the group number in the old A-B group system, except for helium which has two valence electrons. All of the electrons that are not in the highest energy level are known as core electrons. The $1s$ electrons in oxygen are core electrons. Pages 315 and 316 of the 8th edition and pages 326 and 327 of the 9th edition of *Chemistry* display helpful diagrams which show how the orbitals are filled in various parts of the periodic table.

PERIODIC TRENDS IN ATOMIC PROPERTIES

(*Chemistry* 8th ed. pages 318–323/9th ed. pages 329–334)

ATOMIC RADII

(*Chemistry* 8th ed. pages 322–323/9th ed. pages 333–334)

Atomic radii decrease in going from left to right across a period from the alkali metals to the halogens. This can be explained by an increasing effective nuclear charge, which causes the electrons to be drawn closer to the nucleus.

Atomic radius increases down a group because of the increases in the orbital sizes in successive principal quantum levels. Also, there is an increase in the shielding of the nucleus by the core electrons, which decreases the effective nuclear charge felt by the valence electrons.

> **EXAMPLE:** Arrange the following atoms in order of increasing atomic radius.
>
> C, Al, F, Si
>
> **SOLUTION:** F < C < Si < Al; F and C are in the second period, which means that they have two shells or energy levels. Within a period, the radius decreases as the atomic number increases because the higher nuclear charge that results from added protons increases the attraction between the electrons and the nucleus. This means F will be smaller than C. Al and Si are in the third period and have one more energy level, so they will have a larger radius than atoms in period two. Since Si has more protons than Al, it has a smaller radius.

IONIZATION ENERGY

(*Chemistry* 8th ed. pages 318–321/9th ed. pages 329–332)

Ionization energy is the energy required to remove an electron from a gaseous atom or ion.

The first ionization energy is the energy required to remove the highest energy electron (the one bound least tightly) which is one of the valence electrons.

$$X(g) + \text{energy} \rightarrow X^{1+}(g) + e^-$$

For lithium, the first ionization energy is the energy required to remove an electron from the 2s orbital. The configuration for lithium is $1s^2 2s^1$ and the valence electron is the 2s electron.

In general, the first ionization energy increases across a period from left to right. This trend can be related to the trend in atomic radii. The smaller the atom, the greater is its first ionization energy. In going across a period from left to right, atomic radii decrease as the charge on the nucleus increases. There are irregularities in this trend in ionization energy. The first ionization energy decreases from beryllium to boron because the electrons in the 2s orbital are much more effective at shielding the electrons in the 2p orbital than they are at shielding each other. In all atoms except for hydrogen, the np orbital is slightly higher in energy than the ns orbital. The higher energy 2p electron of boron is easier to remove than one of the 2s electrons of beryllium.

The first ionization energy decreases from nitrogen to oxygen due to repulsion of paired electrons in the p^4 configuration of oxygen. Nitrogen has a valence electron configuration $[He]2s^2 2p^3$ and oxygen has a valence electron configuration of $[He]2s^2 2p^4$.

The first ionization energy decreases down a group with increasing atomic number because the valence electrons become easier to remove as the atoms become larger going down a group. Shielding due to electron repulsion in core energy levels reduces the effective nuclear charge of the atoms. This lowers the attraction between the nucleus and the valence electrons which means less energy is needed to remove an electron.

The second ionization energy is the energy required to remove the second outermost electron. This value is larger than the first ionization energy. The first ionization energy removes an electron from a neutral atom. The second ionization energy removes an electron from a positive ion.

$$X^{1+}(g) + energy \rightarrow X^{2+}(g) + e^-$$

The increase in positive charge binds the electrons more tightly, and the ionization energy increases as each successive electron is removed. Also, a slightly larger increase in ionization energy occurs when removing an electron from a higher orbital. such as a 3p orbital vs. a 3s orbital. For example, the difference between the first and second ionization energies in magnesium is 709 kJ. Both of these electrons are 3s. The difference between the first and second ionization energy of aluminum, however, is 1238 kJ. The first electron removed is 3p which is effectively shielded by 3s. The second electron removed is 3s which has less shielding and therefore a stronger attraction to the nucleus. Note a large increase occurs in ionization energy when a core electron from a full energy level is removed.

General increase

Successive Ionization Energies for Period 3 Elements						
Element	IE$_1$	IE$_2$	IE$_3$	IE$_4$	IE$_5$	IE$_6$	IE$_7$
Na	498	4560	6910	9540	13 400	16 600	20 100
Mg	736	1445	7730	10 600	13 600	18 000	21 700
Al	577	1815	2740	11 600	15 000	18 310	23 290
Si	787	1575	3220	4350	16 100	19 800	23 800
P	1063	1890	2905	4950	6270	21 200	25 400
S	1000	2260	3375	4565	6950	8490	27 000
Cl	1255	2295	3850	5160	6560	9360	11 000
Ar	1519	2665	3945	5770	7230	8780	12 000

General decrease (left vertical label)

EXAMPLE: Explain why the difference between the third ionization energy and fourth ionization energy for aluminum is so large in comparison with the first and second and second and third ionization energies.

SOLUTION: Aluminum has the valence electron configuration [Ne]$3s^2 3p^1$. The first electron removed is the $3p$, the second electron removed is a $3s$, and the third electron removed is the remaining $3s$ electron. The fourth electron, a core electron (a $2p$), requires much more energy for removal than the valence electrons, the $3s$ and the $3p$ electrons, because it is more tightly bound due to a higher effective nuclear charge.

EXAMPLE: Arrange the following atoms in order of increasing first ionization energy. I, Rb, Na

SOLUTION: Na will have the smaller radius. Rb < I < Na. Na has the largest IE$_1$ because the electron is removed from the $2s$ sublevel. Both Rb and I have valence electrons in the 5th energy level, but I has 53 protons and a smaller radius than Rb with only 37 protons which makes I smaller than Rb. The smaller the atom, the more energy required to remove the valence electron.

ELECTRON AFFINITY

(*Chemistry* 8th ed. pages 321–322/9th ed. pages 332–333)

Electron affinity is the energy change associated with the addition of an electron to a gaseous atom.

$$X(g) + e^- \rightarrow X^-(g)$$

In general, electron affinity becomes increasingly negative or exothermic as we proceed across a period with increasing atomic number. The greater the charge on the nucleus of the atom, the greater is the affinity for electrons. The addition to a noble gas, however, would require the added electron to reside in a new, higher energy level which is energetically unfavorable, so that stable, isolated X⁻ ions do not exist. Electron affinities are not measured for noble gases.

Electron affinities become slightly more positive, less exothermic, going down a group. The electron–nucleus attraction decreases down a group due to increasing atomic size and shielding. But the added electron experiences less electron–electron repulsion, since the orbital to which the electron is being added, is increasingly spread out. One exception to this trend is fluorine. The value of electron affinity for F is more positive than that of Cl due to the small size of the F atom and the greater electron–electron repulsion in the smaller $2p$ sublevel.

> EXAMPLE: Arrange the following elements from the least to the most exothermic electron affinity. Cl, Al, P and justify your answer.

> SOLUTION: From the least to the most exothermic is Al, P, Cl. In general, the greater the effective nuclear charge on the atom, the more exothermic the electron affinity. Higher effective nuclear charges will have greater attraction between the positive nucleus and the negative electrons. Since all attractions release energy, a greater attraction will release more energy.

IONIC RADII

(*Chemistry* 8th ed. pages 352–353/9th ed. pages 363–365)

Cations are smaller than their parent atoms and anions are larger than their parent atoms. The size of an ion depends on its nuclear charge, the number of electrons it contains, and the outer energy level of the atom. Positive ions are always smaller than neutral parent atoms because the nuclear charge is the same but the number of electrons has decreased, increasing the effective nuclear charge felt by each remaining electron. When all the valence electrons are lost, the change in volume is greater because as n decreases, the radial probability is smaller so the radius is smaller.

Anions are larger than their parent atoms because the electrons gained cause the proton to electron ratio to decrease, and the effective nuclear charge felt by each electron decreases. Electron–electron repulsions also increase. The electrons spread out more to accommodate the additional electrons.

In an isoelectronic series, ions contain the same number of electrons.

> EXAMPLE: Arrange the following ions in order of increasing size: Ca^{2+}, S^{2-}, K^+, Cl^-.

> SOLUTION: All of the ions mentioned above are isoelectronic with argon, containing 18 electrons each. In order of increasing size $Ca^{2+} < K^+ < Cl^- < S^{2-}$. Ca^{2+} is the smallest because it contains the greatest number of protons. The greater the positive charge on the nucleus, the stronger the attraction for electrons.

PART 3: MATTER ON THE MACRO SCALE

THE MOLE

(*Chemistry* 8th ed. pages 81–84/9th ed. pages 85–90)

The mole is defined as the number of atoms in exactly 12 g of carbon-12. Calculations involving moles utilize the conversions in the table below.

1 mol of …	is …
monoatomic element	6.022×10^{23} atoms
molecular compound or diatomic element	6.022×10^{23} molecules
ionic compound	6.022×10^{23} formula units

MOLAR MASS

(*Chemistry* 8th ed. pages 84–87/9th ed. pages 90–92)

Molar mass is the mass of 1 mole of an element or compound.

EXAMPLE: The principal ore in the production of aluminum cans has a molecular formula of $Al_2O_3 \bullet 2H_2O$. What is the mass in grams of 2.10×10^{24} formula units (f.u.) of $Al_2O_3 \bullet 2H_2O$?

SOLUTION: The molar mass of $Al_2O_3 \bullet 2H_2O$ is approximately 138 g/mol. Since this is an ionic compound, 1 mol contains 6.022×10^{23} formula units.

$$2.10 \times 10^{24} \text{ formula units} \times \frac{1 \text{ mol } Al_2O_3 \bullet 2H_2O}{6.022 \times 10^{23} \text{ f.u.}} \times \frac{138 \text{ g}}{1 \text{ mol } Al_2O_3 \bullet 2H_2O} = 481 \text{ g}$$

PERCENT COMPOSITION

(*Chemistry* 8th ed. pages 88–90/9th ed. pages 94–96)

The mass percentages of elements in a compound can be obtained by comparing the mass of each element present in 1 mole of the compound to the total mass of 1 mole of compound.

$$\frac{\text{Mass of element in 1 mol of compound}}{\text{Mass of 1 mol of compound}} \times 100\%$$

EXAMPLE: Calculate the percent of oxygen in $Mg(NO_3)_2$.

SOLUTION: The molar mass of $Mg(NO_3)_2$ is approximately 164 g/mol. There are 6 moles of oxygen in each mole of $Mg(NO_3)_2$ so the molar mass of oxygen must be multiplied by 6.

$$\frac{\left(\dfrac{16 \text{ g O}}{\text{mol O}} \right)\left(\dfrac{6 \text{ mol O}}{\text{mol } Mg(NO_3)_2} \right)}{148 \text{ g mol}^{-1} Mg(NO_3)_2} \times 100 = \mathbf{65\%}$$

CHANGES IN MATTER

Matter exists as pure substances or mixtures and can undergo physical or chemical changes.

Physical changes in matter do not change the original composition of the substance. Changes in state such as boiling or melting are physical changes. Changes involving an alteration in the form of the substance such as grinding or tearing are physical. Physical properties are properties of a substance that can be observed without changing the composition of the substance. During a physical change, bonds are not broken and no reaction between atoms occurs. For example, density, color, and boiling point are physical properties.

Chemical changes in matter change the composition of the original substance by breaking and making bonds between atoms. A new substance is produced when a chemical change occurs. Evidence that a chemical change has occurred includes change in color or odor or the production of a gas or a solid (precipitate). Some examples of chemical properties include flammability and reactivity to air.

MIXTURES AND PURE SUBSTANCES

(*Chemistry* 8th ed. pages 28–29/9th ed. pages 28–31)

Pure substances, such as elements or compounds, make up mixtures. The following chart summarizes mixtures and the methods for separating them.

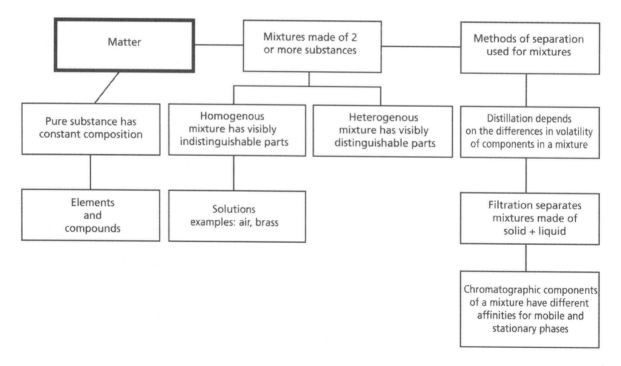

CONSERVATION OF ATOMS

Matter cannot be created nor destroyed in any physical or chemical change. All changes of matter involve the same basic steps: energy is added to overcome attractions between the particles, the particles rearrange, and energy is released as new attractions are formed. Conservation of atoms is represented in particulate models and in symbolic representations that may include mathematical and/or chemical equations. Key examples of the recycling of matter include biogeochemical cycles such as the nitrogen cycle, carbon cycle, and water cycle.

The physical changes that occur as water goes through its phase changes are shown below.

PARTICULATE MODEL

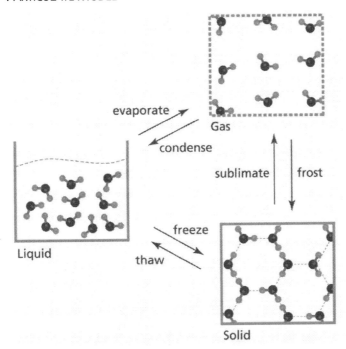

SYMBOLIC REPRESENTATION

$$H_2O(s) \rightleftharpoons H_2O(l) \rightleftharpoons H_2O(g)$$

CONSERVATION OF MASS

(*Chemistry* 8th ed. page 41/9th ed. page 44)

The number of particles (atoms, formula units, molecules) in a given mass of a substance can be calculated by knowing the chemical formula of the substance and applying the mole concept. The coefficients in a balanced chemical equation indicate the relative number of particles involved in the reaction. Since the number of atoms is constant, the total mass of reactants and products must also be constant.

IDENTIFYING AND MEASURING MATTER

(*Chemistry* 8th ed. pages A16–A19/9th ed. pages A16–A19)

Atoms and molecules interact with electromagnetic radiation in a variety of ways. The most commonly used types of spectral analysis include infrared spectroscopy (IR) and ultraviolet/visible spectroscopy (UV-Vis).

INFRARED SPECTROSCOPY

IR spectroscopy involves measuring the radiation absorbed by molecules as they stretch, bend, and twist. Certain functional groups such as –OH and –C=O have distinctive absorbance bands on IR spectra. Each molecule produces a unique spectrum that can be used for identification purposes.

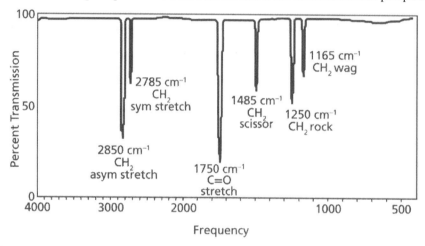

UV-VIS SPECTROSCOPY

(*Chemistry* 8th ed. pages A16–A17/9th ed. pages A16–A17)

UV-Vis spectroscopy utilizes the transition of electrons and produces diffuse bands that are generally used for quantification, not identification, of particular molecules.

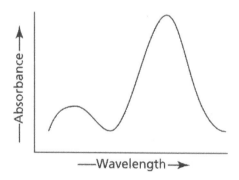

BEER'S LAW

(Chemistry 8th ed. pages A17–A19/9th ed. pages A17–A19)

The amount of chemical can be quantified using Beer's law (Beer-Lambert law). The absorbance of an analyte at a given wavelength is directly proportional to the analyte concentration.

$$A = \varepsilon \ell c$$

where A is the absorbance at the given wavelength, ε is the molar absorptivity, ℓ is the pathlength of the cell containing the chemical, and c is the concentration. Since ε and ℓ are constant, if the absorbance of a known concentration is measured, the concentration of an unknown substance can be determined from measuring the absorbance of the unknown.

GRAVIMETRIC ANALYSIS AND TITRATION

(Chemistry 8th ed. pages 151–152, 157/9th ed. pages 160–161, 166)

Analytical techniques such as gravimetric analysis and titration use conservation of mass to determine the quantity of an analyte in a solution. In gravimetric analysis the substance of interest is selectively precipitated from a solution and the mass of the precipitate is used to determine the mass of the analyte. A titration involves the use of an indicator to determine the stoichiometric equivalence point of a reaction. A common indicator is a color change. The point at which the change occurs is called the end point.

MULTIPLE-CHOICE QUESTIONS

No calculators are to be used in this section.

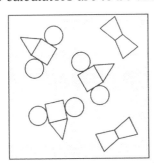

1. The particulate model above is a representation of a mixture of
   (A) an element and a compound
   (B) atoms and molecules
   (C) four different atoms
   (D) two different compounds

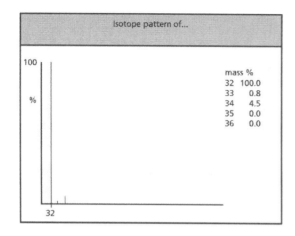

2. Name the element whose mass spectrum is shown above.
   (A) germanium
   (B) selenium
   (C) sulfur
   (D) fermium

3. The formation of an aluminum ion occurs when 3 electrons are removed. Which electron would require the most energy to remove?
   (A) 3s because it is filled before 3p
   (B) 3p because it is farther from the nucleus
   (C) 3p because it only has 1 electron in the orbital
   (D) 3s because it experiences higher attractive forces

4. The concentration of a red-colored solution of cobalt(II) ions needs to be determined. What spectroscopic technique would be the best choice?
   (A) photoelectron spectroscopy because the electron arrangement is responsible for the color
   (B) UV-Vis spectrometry because the solution has a color
   (C) infrared spectrometry because the solution is red
   (D) mass spectrometry because knowing the mass can allow for calculation of concentration

5. The correct orbital diagram for the valence electrons of silicon is
   (A) _↑↓_ _↑↓_ ____ ____
       3s   3p   3p   3p

   (B) _↑_ _↑_ _↑_ _↑_
       3s   3p   3p   3p

   (C) _↑↓_ _↑_ _↓_ ____
       3s   3p   3p   3p

   (D) _↑↓_ _↑_ _↑_ ____
       3s   3p   3p   3p

6. Glass for electronic devices needs to be more durable than typical window glass. Sodium ions on the glass surface are replaced by larger ions when the glass is dipped into a molten salt. Which type of salt would give the toughest glass?
   (A) lithium
   (B) magnesium
   (C) potassium
   (D) calcium

7. The chemical reaction $Br_2 + 2\,Na \rightarrow 2\,NaBr$ is best represented by which model?

   (A)
   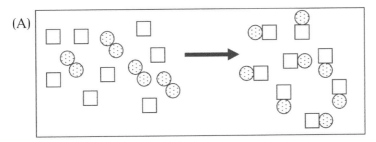

   (B)
   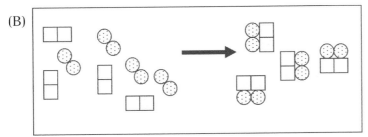

   (C)
   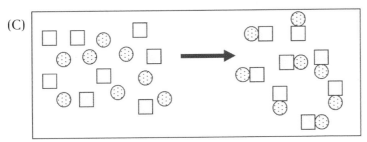

   (D)
   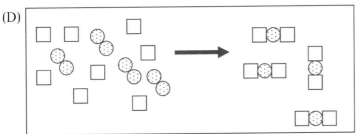

8. Sucrose, $C_{12}H_{22}O_{11}$, has a molar mass of 342 g/mol. How many atoms of carbon are there in 684 g of sucrose?
   (A) 6.02×10^{23} atoms
   (B) 1.45×10^{25} atoms
   (C) 1.20×10^{24} atoms
   (D) 3.01×10^{23} atoms

9. The quantum mechanical atomic model replaced the Bohr atomic model because
   (A) Bohr's model did not account for neutrons
   (B) the quantum mechanical model was based on mathematics
   (C) electrons act as waves as well as particles
   (D) Bohr's model could not predict the spectra for elements other than hydrogen

10. 1 gram of mercury is sealed in a glass tube. The tube is heated slightly and all of the mercury vaporizes. What mass of mercury remains in the tube?
    (A) less than 1 gram because the vapor has less mass than the liquid
    (B) 1 gram because the number of atoms has not changed
    (C) more than 1 gram because the vapor occupies more space than the liquid
    (D) the mass cannot be determined because it depends on the volume of the tube

Isotope	Atomic Mass (amu)	Percent Abundance
^{48}X	48.0	10.0
^{50}X	50.0	90.0

11. What is the average atomic mass of element X based on the data above?
    (A) 49.0 amu
    (B) 49.5 amu
    (C) 49.8 amu
    (D) 50.0 amu

12. Why does chlorine gain an electron to become a chloride ion?
    (A) Atoms become stable when they achieve a full octet.
    (B) Less shielding means there is room for another electron.
    (C) Adding an electron completely fills the s and p orbitals of energy level 3.
    (D) An electron is attracted to the large effective nuclear charge.

13. Nitrogen and oxygen can combine in many different proportions to create different compounds. Which compound has a N:O mass ratio of 7:20?
    (A) dinitrogen monoxide
    (B) dinitrogen pentoxide
    (C) nitrogen monoxide
    (D) nitrogen dioxide

14. Which particulate model represents copper(II) carbonate?

(A)

(B)

(C)

(D)

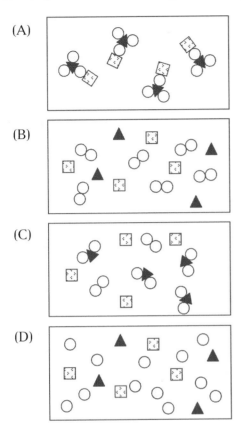

15. How many moles of sulfuric acid would completely react with 0.30 moles potassium hydroxide in a titration?
(A) 0.15
(B) 0.30
(C) 0.60
(D) 1.0

FREE-RESPONSE QUESTIONS

1. A 1956 dime is made of a silver-copper alloy and has a mass of 2.490 g. The dime was dissolved in nitric acid and a blue solution remained. The solution was quantitatively transferred to a 100-mL volumetric flask and brought to volume with water.

(a) A 50.00-mL aliquot of the solution was reacted with excess sodium chloride solution. The precipitate, AgCl, was filtered, washed, and dried. The mass of the precipitate was 1.375 g. What is the percent silver in the dime?

(b) A 1.5-mL aliquot of the original sample was analyzed with a UV-Vis spectrophotometer at 740 nm and the absorbance was 0.420. Calculate the copper(II) ion concentration and the percent silver in the dime. Calibration curve data are presented below.

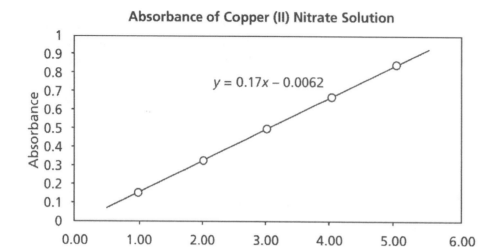

Absorbance of Copper (II) Nitrate Solution

$y = 0.17x - 0.0062$

Copper(II) Nitrate Standard Curve	
concentration (mg/mL)	Absorbance
5.00	0.843
4.00	0.672
3.00	0.507
2.00	0.336
1.00	0.161

(c) The 1956 dime is known to be 90% silver.
(i) Which method produced more accurate results?
(ii) Comment on potential sources of error for the less accurate method.

2. A mysterious element was analyzed by photoelectron spectroscopy (PES) and mass spectroscopy (MS). The spectrograms are below.
   (a) Identify the mysterious element from the spectral data.
   (b) Explain how the MS supports your identification.
   (c) Explain how the PES supports your identification.

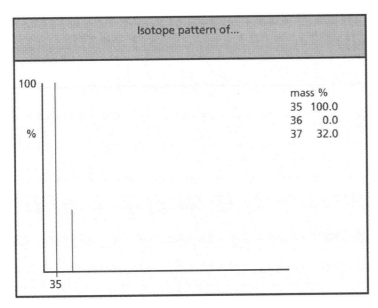

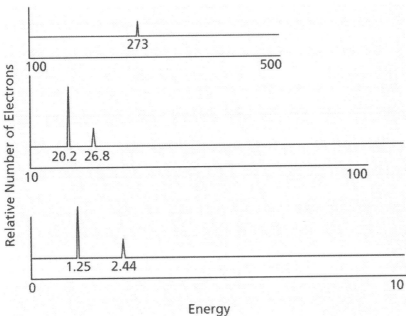

Answers

MULTIPLE-CHOICE QUESTIONS

1. **A** Each shape in the particulate model represents a different element. The two trapezoids bonded together represent a diatomic element and the triangle-square-circles represent a compound (*Chemistry* 8th ed. pages 28–29/9th ed. pages 28–31). LO 1.1

2. **C** The element is sulfur because the peak with the highest intensity has a mass of 32 (*Chemistry* 8th ed. pages 78–80/9th ed. pages 83–85). LO 1.14

3. **D** Electrons that are closer to the nucleus experience greater Coulombic forces of attraction and therefore require more energy to be removed (*Chemistry* 8th ed. pages 318–321/9th ed. pages 329–332). LO 1.9

4. **B** UV-Vis spectrometry provides for quantification of analytes that absorb energy in the visible and ultraviolet range (*Chemistry* 8th ed. pages A16–A17/9th ed. pages A16–A17). LO 1.15

5. **D** Silicon has 4 valence electrons. 3s is filled with opposite spinning electrons and 3p has 2 filled subshells with parallel electron spins (*Chemistry* 8th ed. pages 312–313/9th ed. pages 322–323). LO 1.12

6. **C** Atomic radii increase down a group due to an increase in the volume of higher energy levels and increase shielding of valence electrons (*Chemistry* 8th ed. pages 322–323/9th ed. pages 333–334). LO 1.11

7. **A** Bromine is a diatomic element that reacts with a 1:2 ratio with sodium (*Chemistry* 8th ed. page 161/9th ed. page 170). LO 1.18

8. **B** It takes 342 g to make one mole of the compound and you have twice that amount. Therefore you have 2.00 mole of this substance (684 g / 342 g/mol). Each mole of the substance contains 12 moles of carbon, for a total of 12 moles of carbon. Multiply this by Avogadro's number to obtain the atoms of carbon (*Chemistry* 8th ed. pages 81–87/9th ed. pages 85–92). LO 1.4

9. **D** A model that only works for 1 element is not a good model (*Chemistry* 8th ed. pages 295–300/9th ed. pages 306–310). LO 1.12

10. **B** Phase changes only rearrange particles; no matter is created nor destroyed (*Chemistry* 8th ed. page 41/9th ed. page 44). LO 1.18

11. **C** (48.0 amu)(0.100) + (50.0 amu)(0.900) = 49.8 amu (*Chemistry* 8th ed. pages 78–81/9th ed. pages 83–85). LO 1.1

12. **D** "A" group number = number of valence electrons (*Chemistry* 8th ed. page 316/9th ed. page 328). LO 1.9

13. B N_2O_5; 28 g nitrogen and 80 g oxygen in 1 mole give a ratio of 7:20 (*Chemistry* 8th ed. page 43/9th ed. page 46). LO 1.1

14. A The particulate model shows only 1 kind of particle (*Chemistry* 8th ed. pages 28–29/9th ed. pages 28–31). LO 1.1

15. A The ratio of H_2SO_4 to KOH in the balanced equation is 1 : 2 so half as many moles of acid are needed (*Chemistry* 8th ed. pages 158–159/9th ed. pages 167–168). LO 1.20

FREE-RESPONSE QUESTIONS

1. (a) g Ag^+ = (1.375 g AgCl)(1 mol AgCl/143.35 g AgCl)(1 mol Ag^+/1 mol AgCl) (107.2 g Ag^+/1 mol Ag^+)
    = 1.305 g Ag^+
    1.305 g Ag^+ in the 50.00-mL aliquot means 2.070 g Ag^+ in the 100.00-mL sample and 2.070 g Ag in the dime.

    (2.070 g Ag/2.490 g dime) × 100 = 83.13% Ag
    (*Chemistry* 8th ed. pages 88–90/9th ed. pages 94-96). LO 1.19

   (b) The equation of best fit, y = 0.17x – 0.0062, shows the relationship between absorbance and concentration of Cu^{2+}.
    x = (0.420 + 0.0062)/0.17
    x = 2.51 mg/mL
    x = 0.251 g Cu^{2+}/100 mL solution; 0.251 g Cu in the dime
    (0.251 g Cu/2.490 g dime) × 100 = 10.1% Cu and 89.9% Ag
    (*Chemistry* 8th ed. pages A17–A19/9th ed. pages A17–A19).
    LO 1.16

   (c) (i) The spectrometric method was more accurate with a percent error of –0.1% compared to –7.6% error in the gravimetric analysis.

    (ii) Potential sources of error include loss of analyte during transfer for the reaction or loss of precipitate during filtration (*Chemistry* 8th ed. page A10/9th ed. page A10). LO 5.1

2. (a) The element is chlorine.

   (b) MS shows a prominent peak at 35 amu. Chlorine's average atomic mass of 35.45 amu means the majority of the isotopes are ^{35}Cl (*Chemistry* 8th ed. pages 78–80/9th ed. pages 83–85). LO 1.14

   (c) PES shows 3 occupied energy levels. The electrons closest to the nucleus have the highest ionization energy and must be 1*s*. The height of the top peak (energy 273 MJ) must correspond to 2 electrons in 1*s*. The other short peaks in the spectrum (26.8 MJ and 2.44 MJ must also correspond to 2 electrons in *s* orbitals. The peak at 20.2 MJ is 3 times the height of the nearby peak meaning that peak must represent 6 electrons in 2*p*. The peak at 1.25 MJ is 2.5 times the height of the peak at 3*s* so that must represent 5 electrons in 3*p*. The electron configuration must be $1s^22s^22p^63s^23p^5$. LO 1.7

3

BIG IDEA 2:
BONDING AND STRUCTURE

Big Idea 2

Chemical and physical properties of materials can be explained by the structure and the arrangement of atoms, ions, or molecules and the forces between them.

The chemical and physical properties you observe can be explained by the structure and arrangement of atoms, ions or molecules and the forces between them. Big Idea 2 is divided into four chapters, Chapters 3, 4, 5, and 6. In Chapter 3, you will learn about the different types of bonds that form, the nature of those bonds, a model that is used to predict the three-dimensional structure of covalently-bonded molecules. These are *intra*molecular forces, attractions *between* atoms *within* a molecule. You will also learn about *inter*molecular forces, the attractions *between* molecules that arise as a result of these bonds. You will apply these ideas as you learn about gases (Chapter 4), liquids and solids (Chapter 5), and solutions (Chapter 6).

You should be able to
- Identify the characteristics of ionic and covalent bonding.
- Identify the relative sizes of ions.
- Identify the effect of lattice energy on melting points of ionic compounds.
- Use electronegativity to predict the polarity of covalent bonds.
- Draw Lewis symbols for atoms and Lewis structures for molecular compounds and polyatomic ions.

■ Assign molecular shapes using the VSEPR model for molecules, polyatomic ions, and multi-centered molecules and polyatomic ions, from linear through the octahedral shape.

■ Assign hybrid orbitals to central atoms of molecules and polyatomic ions.

■ Compare bond lengths and bond strengths in molecules.

■ Identify the intermolecular forces in a substance.

■ Know the difference between intramolecular forces (chemical bonds) and intermolecular forces (forces of attraction).

■ Predict and explain the properties of substances based on their chemical formulas, and to provide explanations based on drawing representations of the substances and their intermolecular forces.

IONIC BONDING

(*Chemistry* 8th ed. pages 341–342/9th ed. pages 352–353)

Ionic bonding is the result of electrostatic attraction of oppositely charged ions. Ionic compounds form when an atom which loses electrons easily (atoms with low electron affinity) reacts with an atom that has a high affinity for electrons. Most of the time, an ionic compound is formed when a metal reacts with a nonmetal.

COULOMB'S LAW

(*Chemistry* 8th ed. pages 341–342/9th ed. pages 352–353)

Coulomb's law expresses the energy of interaction between a pair of ions. This is directly proportional to the charge on each ion and inversely proportional to the distance between the ions. The greater the charge on the ions, the stronger the ionic bond, and if the charges are equal, then we expect a smaller ion to have a stronger ionic bond. Note that the energy will always be negative because one ion is a cation (positive) and the other an anion (negative).

$$E = (2.31 \times 10^{-19} \text{ J} \bullet \text{nm}) \left(\frac{Q_1 Q_2}{r} \right).$$

E is the energy of interaction between a pair of ions, in joules.

r is the distance in nanometers between ion centers.

Q_1 and Q_2 are the charges of the ions.

IONS: ELECTRON CONFIGURATION AND SIZES

(*Chemistry* 8th ed. pages 350–353/9th ed. pages 361–365)

PREDICTING FORMULAS OF IONIC COMPOUNDS; FORMATION OF IONIC COMPOUNDS

When a metal and a nonmetal react, each forms an ion with a noble gas configuration in its valence shell. The metal loses all of its outermost electrons while the nonmetal gains electrons to complete its valence shell.

EXAMPLE: Explain how atoms of sodium and oxygen form an ionic compound.

SOLUTION: Sodium and oxygen have the following valence electron configurations:

Na: $[Ne]3s^1$

O: $[He]2s^22p^4$

The electronegativity of oxygen is much greater than that of sodium, so electrons are transferred from sodium to oxygen. Oxygen needs two electrons to fill its $2p$ valence orbitals and to achieve the configuration of neon. Sodium loses one electron to achieve the electron configuration of neon. Two sodium atoms are needed to give one oxygen atom the two electrons necessary to fill its valence orbitals. The oxide ion has an electron configuration like that of neon.

$$2\,Na \rightarrow 2\,Na^+ + 2\,e^-$$
$$O + 2\,e^- \rightarrow O^{2-}$$

Using electron configurations:

$$Na \rightarrow Na^+ + e^- \qquad O + 2\,e^- \rightarrow O^{2-}$$

$$1s^22s^22p^63s^1 = [Ne]3s^1 \rightarrow [Ne] + e^- \quad [He]2s^22p^4 + 2\,e^- \rightarrow [He]2s^22p^6 = [Ne]$$

LATTICE ENERGY

(*Chemistry* 8th ed. pages 355–357/9th ed. pages 367–369)

Lattice energy is the energy release that occurs when separated gaseous ions are packed together to form an ionic solid.

$$X^{x+}(g) + Y^{y-}(g) \rightarrow X_yY_x(s) + energy$$

$$\text{Lattice energy} = k\left(\frac{Q_1Q_2}{r}\right)$$

k is a proportionality constant dependent on the structure of the solid and the electron configuration of the ions.

r is the distance in nanometers between the ion centers.

Q_1 and Q_2 are the charges of the ions.

EXAMPLE: Which has the more exothermic lattice energy, NaCl or KCl?

SOLUTION: NaCl has the more exothermic lattice energy. The product $Q_1 \times Q_2$ is the same for both substances so the denominator must be considered. Na^+ is smaller than K^+, so the distance between the centers of the sodium and chloride ions is less than the distance between the potassium and chloride ions. For identical numerators, a smaller denominator gives a more exothermic lattice energy.

Covalent Bonding

(*Chemistry* 8th ed. page 342/9th ed. page 353)

Covalent bonding involves sharing valence electrons between nuclei with similar electronegativities. A covalent or molecular compound is usually formed by bonding two or more nonmetals. There are some metallic compounds that have covalent bonds, such as beryllium chloride, $BeCl_2$, because the electronegativities of the atoms are similar.

Electronegativity

(*Chemistry* 8th ed. pages 344–346/9th ed. pages 356–358)

Electronegativity measures the ability of an atom in a molecule to attract shared electrons to itself. The two factors affecting electronegativity are effective nuclear charge (Z_{eff}) and electron shielding. Going from left to right across a period, there are more protons pulling on electrons (higher Z_{eff}), so the electron shells are pulled closer into the nucleus, the atomic size decreases, and the electronegativity increases. Going down a column, more electron shells are added, shielding the valence electrons from the positively charged nucleus, so the atomic size increases and the electronegativity decreases.

> EXAMPLE: Place the following atoms in order of increasing electronegativity: Cs, Rb, S, Al, Sr, O.
>
> SOLUTION: In order of increasing electronegativity: Cs < Rb < Sr < Al < S < O.
>
> Electronegativity increases from the lower left to the upper right of the periodic table.

Polar Bond

(*Chemistry* 8th ed. pages 343–349/9th ed. pages 355–360)

The type of bond formed between two atoms is related to the difference in electronegativity between the two atoms. For identical atoms, such as a molecule of hydrogen, the electronegativity difference is zero. There is an equal sharing of electrons between the atoms, and the bond formed is a nonpolar covalent bond. When the difference in electronegativities is very small (less than 0.4), the bond is described as nonpolar. An important nonpolar covalent bond is the C–H bond in organic compounds.

When two atoms have a very large difference (greater than 1.7) in electronegativity, an ionic bond forms. For example, atoms of lithium and chlorine have a large difference in electronegativity and form an ionic compound.

A polar covalent bond results when there is an unequal sharing of electrons. The difference in the electronegativities of atoms in the polar covalent bond is between that of the ionic and nonpolar bonds (greater than 0.3 but less than 1.7). In general, the farther apart two atoms are on the periodic table, the more polar the bond. Fluorine is the most electronegative atom, so the closer an atom is to fluorine, the more electronegative it is. An example of a polar covalent bond is HF, which has the following charge distribution.

$$H–F$$
$$\delta^+ \; \delta^-$$

EXAMPLE: Which of the following three bonds will be most polar? O–F, N–F, C–F

SOLUTION: The most polar bond will be the bond in which the difference in electronegativities is the greatest. Since you are not given electronegativities in this question, you must estimate the differences by looking at how far apart the atoms are on the periodic table. C is further from F than N or O, so the C–F bond is most polar, followed by N–F and O–F .

BOND POLARITY AND DIPOLE MOMENTS

Fluorine is the most electronegative element in the periodic table. When HF is placed in an electric field, the molecules tend to orient themselves with the fluoride end toward the positive pole and the hydrogen end toward the negative pole. HF is said to have a dipole moment, having two poles. An arrow points to the negative charge center and the tail of the arrow indicates the positive center of charge.

$$\delta+ \qquad\qquad \delta-$$

A diatomic molecule with a polar bond has a dipole moment. Molecules with more than two atoms can also have dipolar behavior. This is addressed in the section on molecular shapes where we look at the distribution of charge in the molecule.

LOCALIZED ELECTRON BONDING MODEL

(*Chemistry* 8th ed. page 364/9th ed. page 376)

The localized electron model assumes that a molecule is composed of atoms that are bound together by sharing pairs of electrons using the atomic orbitals of the bound atoms. Lone pairs are pairs of electrons which are localized in an area around one atom. Bonding pairs occupy the space between atoms.

LEWIS STRUCTURES

(*Chemistry* 8th ed. pages 365–372/9th ed. pages 376–383)

The Lewis structure shows how the valence electrons are arranged among atoms in a molecule.

Steps for writing Lewis structures:

1. Sum the total valence electrons from each atom. For a polyatomic ion, add one electron for each negative charge on the anion, or take away one electron for each positive charge on the cation.

2. Place the least electronegative element in the middle. (Hydrogen can never be in the middle because it can form only one bond.) Draw the outer atoms around the central atom. Chemical formulas are often written in the order in which they are connected, such as HCN. The central atom is sometimes written first in a formula, when a central atom has a group of other atoms bonded to it, as in $SO_4{}^{2-}$.

3. Connect the central atom to the outer atoms using a line to indicate each pair of bonding electrons.

4. Count the valence electrons used in the bonds in step 3 and subtract these from the total valence electrons in step 1 to determine how many valence electrons remain.

    Valence electrons left =

    Total valence electrons (step 1) – Valence electrons used (step 3).

5. Arrange the remaining electrons around the atoms to follow the octet rule for families 4A–7A outer atoms to satisfy the duet rule for hydrogen (hydrogen needs only two electrons to have a filled orbital) and the octet rule for second-row elements and the periods following.

6. Determine the number of valence electrons remaining as in step 4. Place the remaining electrons on the central atom to satisfy the octet rule for elements in the second row and after.

    a. If there are no electrons remaining to satisfy the central atom, then add a double bond for every pair of electrons you are "short" and readjust the number of electrons on each surrounding atom.

    b. Elements in periods higher than the second can have more than eight electrons. If $n > 2$, then d orbitals exist and the number of electrons that can surround the element can exceed eight.

7. Check that the valence electrons drawn = the total valence electrons in step 1.

    EXAMPLE: Draw the Lewis Structure for NF_3.

    SOLUTION: Step 1: Total valence electrons = $[1 \times N(5\ e^-) + 3 \times F(7\ e^-)]$ =

    $5\ e^-$ + $21\ e^-$ = 26 valence electrons.

    Steps 2 and 3: Place nitrogen in the middle and connect the fluorine atoms to nitrogen using a line to represent a single bond which is a pair of electrons.

Step 4: Count the valence electrons used. Count two electrons for each single bond (2 × 3 single bonds = 6 electrons used). Count the electrons left. 26 – 6 = 20 electrons left.

Step 5: Satisfy the octet rule for each of the outer fluorine, F, atoms. Each F atom needs six more to complete the octet.

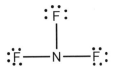

Step 6: Count electrons remaining after satisfying the outer atoms. 20 – 6(3) used = 2 electrons left. Place remaining electrons on central atom, nitrogen, and its octet is completed.

Step 7: Check that electrons drawn, 26, equals the total valence electrons in step 1.

RESONANCE

(*Chemistry* 8th ed. pages 373–374/9th ed. pages 384–385)

Resonance occurs when more than one correct Lewis structure can be drawn for a molecule or ion.

EXAMPLE: Draw the Lewis structure for the nitrate ion, NO_3^-.

SOLUTION: Step 1: Total valence electrons: 5 from N and 6 from each O and 1 from the negative charge on the ion = 5 + 3(6) + 1 = 24.

Step 2: Place nitrogen in the middle and connect the oxygen atoms to nitrogen.

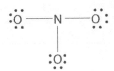

Step 4: Count valence electrons used, 2 for each single bond (2 × 3 single bonds = 6 electrons used). Count the electrons left. 24 – 6 = 18 electrons left.

Step 5: Satisfy the octet rule for each of the outer atoms of oxygen. Each O atom needs six more to complete the octet.

Step 6: Count electrons remaining after satisfying the outer atoms. 18 – 6(3) used = 0 electrons left. The central atom, N, still needs two more electrons to satisfy the octet rule. You can add a double bond for every pair of electrons you are "short."

One double bond forms between the N and the O. A double bond is made of two pairs of electrons. However, the nitrate ion does not have one double bond and two single bonds. All of the three bonds are the same length, somewhere intermediate between a single bond and a double bond. The nitrate ion exists as an average of three resonance structures as pictured below.

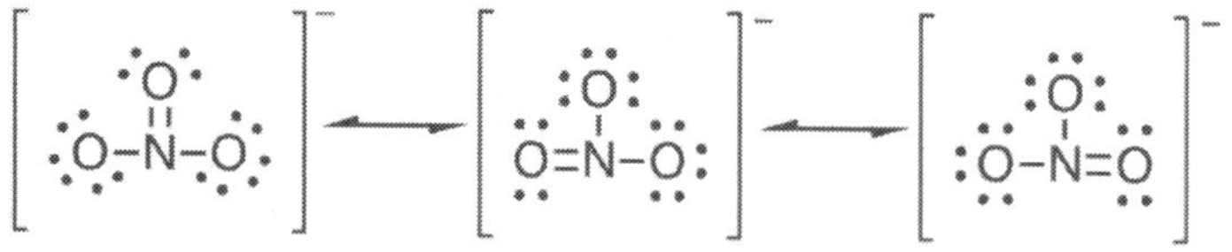

Step 7: Check that electrons drawn, 26, equals the total valence electrons in step 1.

EXCEPTIONS TO THE OCTET RULE

Elements with a Z value less than 6 often do not follow the octet rule. For example, boron tends to form compounds in which boron can have fewer than eight electrons, such as boron trifluoride, BF_3. Boron can have six electrons around it.

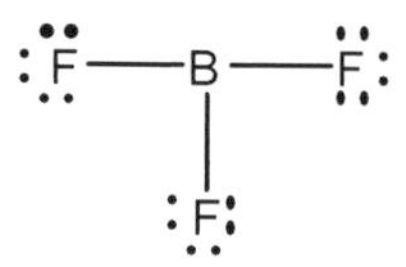

Some elements in period 3 of the periodic table and beyond can exceed the octet rule. For example, ClF_3, has 10 electrons around the central atom.

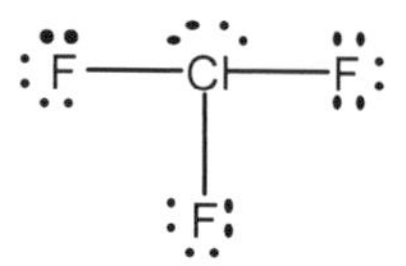

Elements in the third period have $3s$, $3p$, and $3d$ valence orbitals. The valence electrons in chlorine occupy the $3s$ and $3p$ orbitals. The $3d$ orbital is empty and can hold extra electrons. Elements in the second period have only $2s$ and $2p$ orbitals. These elements cannot have more than eight electrons in their valence orbitals because they do not have d orbitals available.

MOLECULAR STRUCTURE: THE VSEPR MODEL

(*Chemistry* 8th ed. pages 378–389/9th ed. pages 389–402)

The valence shell electron-pair repulsion (VSEPR) model predicts the geometries of molecules and polyatomic ions. The structure around the central atom is determined by minimizing electron-pair repulsions. Bonding and nonbonding pairs of electron are positioned as far apart as possible. Nonbonding or lone pairs of electrons require more room than bonding pairs and tend to compress the angle between bonding pairs.

Steps to apply the VSEPR model:

1. Draw the Lewis structure of the molecule.

2. Count the bonding and nonbonding electron pairs around the central atom. (For structures with multiple bonds, count the multiple bond as one effective pair of electrons.)

3. Count the number of atoms attached to the central atom. Look in the chart below to find the arrangement that minimizes that repulsion, placing the electrons as far apart as possible. For example, BeH_2, another exception to the octet rule, has two electron pairs and two atoms attached to the central atom. If the two bonded pairs of electrons are placed 180° apart, the resulting linear geometry has minimal repulsion.

Molecular Shapes and Bond Angles

No. of Electron Pairs	Electron Pair Geometry (Bond Angle)	No. of Bonding Electron Pairs	No. of Lone Electron Pairs	Molecular Geometry	Formula	2D Structure	Hybrid Orbital
2	Linear (180°)	2	0	Linear	BeH_2	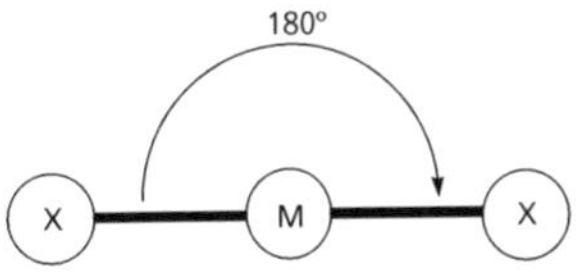	sp
3	Trigonal planar (120°)	3	0	Trigonal planar	CO_3^{2-}	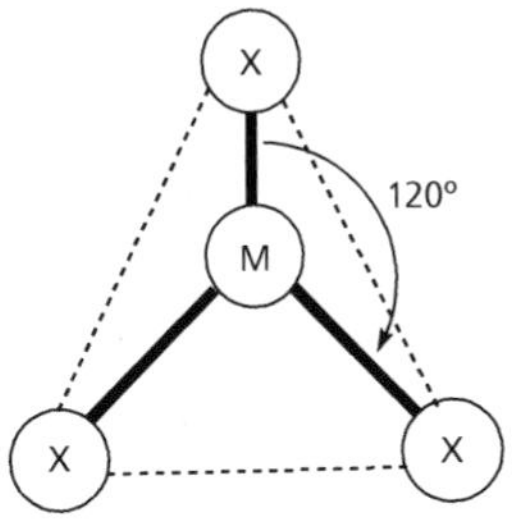	sp^2
3	Trigonal planar (120°)	3	1	Bent	NO_2^-	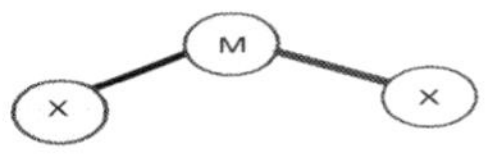	sp^2

No. of Electron Pairs	Electron Pair Geometry (Bond Angle)	No. of Bonding Electron Pairs	No. of Lone Electron Pairs	Molecular Geometry	Formula	2D Structure	Hybrid Orbital
4	Tetrahedral (109.5°)	4	0	Tetrahedral	CH_4		sp^3
4	Tetrahedral (>109.5°)	3	1	Trigonal pyramidal	NH_3		sp^3
4	Tetrahedral (>>109.5°)	2	2	Bent	H_2O		sp^3
5	Trigonal bipyramidal (90°, 120°)	5	0	Trigonal bipyramidal	PCl_5		sp^3d

Hybridization beyond sp^3 is beyond scope of course but is included here for completeness and clarity.

No. of Electron Pairs	Electron Pair Geometry (Bond Angle)	No. of Bonding Electron Pairs	No. of Lone Electron Pairs	Molecular Geometry	Formula	2D Structure	Hybrid Orbital
5	Trigonal bipyramidal (90° and >120°)	4	1	Seesaw unsymmetrical tetrahedron	SF_4		sp^3d
5	Trigonal bipyramidal (90° and 180°)	3	2	T-shaped	BrF_3		sp^3d
5	Trigonal bipyramidal (180°)	2	3	Linear	ICl_2^-		sp^3d
6	Octahedral (90°)	6	6	Octahedral	SF_6		sp^3d^2

No. of Electron Pairs	Electron Pair Geometry (Bond Angle)	No. of Bonding Electron Pairs	No. of Lone Electron Pairs	Molecular Geometry	Formula	2D Structure	Hybrid Orbital
6	Octahedral (90°)	5	1	Square pyramidal	BrF_5		sp^3d^2
6	Octahedral (90°)	4	2	Square planar	ICl_4^-		sp^3d^2

EXAMPLE: Predict the molecular structure of the carbon dioxide molecule. Is this molecule expected to have a dipole moment?

SOLUTION: First we must draw the Lewis structure for the CO_2 molecule.

$$\ddot{O}=C=\ddot{O}$$

In this structure for CO_2, there are two effective pairs around the central atom (each double bond is counted as one effective pair). There are two atoms attached to the central atom.

According to the table, a linear arrangement is required.

Each C–O bond is polar, but, since the molecule is linear, the dipoles cancel out and the molecule is nonpolar.

EXAMPLE: Draw the Lewis structure for PF_5 and identify the molecular geometry.

SOLUTION: PF_5 has 40 valence electrons. Connecting 5 F atoms to P, the central atom, uses 10 electrons in five single bonds. The 30 remaining electrons can be used to satisfy the octet rule for each F atom. There are 5 electron pairs around P and 5 atoms attached to P, resulting in a trigonal bipyramidal shape.

EXAMPLE: Draw the Lewis structure for CH_3OH.

$$H-\overset{\overset{\displaystyle H}{|}}{\underset{\underset{\displaystyle H}{|}}{C}}-\overset{\cdot\cdot}{\underset{\underset{\displaystyle H}{}}{O}}:$$

SOLUTION: This molecule has more than one central atom, the carbon and the oxygen. Hydrogen cannot be in the middle since it can form only one bond. Draw the correct Lewis structure and then using the rules for VSEPR, assign the molecular geometry around each central atom. The carbon atom has four electron pairs around it and four atoms attached resulting in tetrahedral geometry. Oxygen also has four electron pairs around it, but only has two atoms attached. This leads to bent geometry around oxygen.

EXAMPLE: Arrange the following molecules in order of increasing bond angles: H_2S, CCl_4, NF_3.

SOLUTION: First, draw the correct Lewis structure for each molecule and then assign an approximate bond angle for each.

Each of the four molecules has four electron pairs around the central atom, resulting in a tetrahedral arrangement of the electron pairs about the central atom and approximately a $109.5°$ bond angle. H_2S has two lone pairs on the central atom; NF_3 has one lone pair on the central atom. These lone pairs repel more than the bonded electron pairs and will cause the bond angle to be smaller than the expected $109.5°$. The more lone pairs, the smaller the bond angle.

In order of increasing bond angles, the answer is $H_2S < NF_3 < CCl_4$.

HYBRIDIZATION

Hybridization describes the mixing of atomic orbitals to form molecular orbitals of equal energies that share electrons during bond formation. For example, in methane (CH_4), the $2s$ orbital and three $2p$ orbitals of carbon mix together to form four sp^3 hybrid orbitals, each with the same energy. The sp^3 orbital of carbon overlaps the $1s$ orbital of hydrogen, creating a region of high electron density between the two nuclei. These overlapping orbitals form a single bond, also known as a sigma (σ) bond, similar to the one shown here.

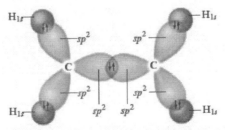

In general, the sum of the superscripts on the hybrid orbitals equals the number of electron groups (multiple bonds count as one group)

around the central atom. The carbon atom in CH_4 has 4 electron groups around the central atom. The sum of the superscripts in sp^3 equals 4.

Multiple bonds are formed by sharing electrons in unhybridized orbitals above and below the σ bond The carbon atom in carbon dioxide is sp hybridized. There are 2 electron groups around the C atom. The sum of the superscripts in sp is 2. The $2s$ orbital and one of the $2p$ orbitals of carbon mix to form sp, leaving two $2p$ orbitals unused. There are three electron groups around each oxygen atom (one bonding group and two lone pairs), so the oxygen atoms are sp^2 hybridized. The carbon atom has two unhybridized p orbitals perpendicular to the sp^2 orbital; the oxygen atoms have one unhybridized p orbital each. The parallel p orbitals can share a pair of electrons above and below the carbon-oxygen bonds, forming a pi (π) bond.

A double bond, such as the one in carbon dioxide, consists of one sigma bond because of the head-on overlap of sp^2 orbitals of each carbon atom and one pi bond due to the parallel p orbitals. A triple bond consists of one sigma bond and two pi bonds.

The hybrid orbitals are oriented in space according to the VSEPR model. For example, the four sp^3 orbitals have a tetrahedral arrangement (there are 4 electron groups around the central atom).

BOND LENGTH

(*Chemistry* 8th ed. page 363/9th ed. page 375)

As the number of bonds between two atoms increases, the bond grows shorter and stronger.

> **EXAMPLE:** Arrange the following molecules in order of decreasing C–C bond length: C_2H_4, C_2H_2, C_2H_6.

> **SOLUTION:** In order of decreasing C–C bond length: C_2H_6, C_2H_4, C_2H_2.

First, draw the Lewis structure for each molecule.

The C–C triple bond is the shortest, followed by the double bond, and the single bond.

INTERMOLECULAR FORCES

(*Chemistry* 8th ed. pages 440–443/9th ed. pages 455–458)

Intermolecular forces are attractions *between* molecules, unlike intramolecular bonds which are attractions *within* a molecule. Molecules with strong intermolecular forces require more energy to separate from each other, so they will tend to have relatively high melting points, boiling points, and heats of vaporization. When in liquid phase, they will generally have higher viscosity and higher surface tension.

DIPOLE–DIPOLE ATTRACTIONS

Polar molecules attract each other, lining up so that their positive and negative poles are close to each other. Polar molecules generally have higher boiling points than nonpolar molecules of similar molar mass because they have dipole–dipole attractions in addition to London forces. An example of a polar molecule is SO_2.

HYDROGEN BONDING

Hydrogen bonding is an unusually strong dipole–dipole force among molecules in which hydrogen is bound to a highly electronegative atom such as nitrogen, oxygen, or fluorine. The hydrogen bond occurs between the hydrogen on one of these electronegative atoms and an O, F, or N on another molecule. This is the strongest type of intermolecular force, and results in molecules with higher boiling points than molecules attracted to each other by dipole–dipole forces. Examples of molecules which exhibit H-bonding include H_2O, NH_3, and HF.

LONDON DISPERSION FORCES

London dispersion forces exist between all molecules and account for the boiling points of the noble gases. If there were no attractions at all between molecules, then they would never liquefy. The electron cloud can experience temporary shifts that result in one side of the molecule becoming more negative than the other, causing a temporary dipole. This instantaneous dipole can induce a similar dipole on a neighboring atom.

It follows that the greater the charge on the nucleus and the larger the number of electrons in the molecule, the greater the induced dipole. As the atomic number increases down a group, atoms become more polarizable, that is, the electron cloud can become polarized due to the instantaneous dipole. For example, the halogens all experience London dispersion forces, but the force becomes stronger toward the bottom of the group. F_2 and Cl_2 are found as gases in nature, Br_2 is a liquid, and I_2 is a solid due to increasing London forces as the atomic number and size of the electron cloud increases in the group.

It is important to recognize that, particularly for organic compounds such as hydrocarbons, strength of London dispersion forces depends on the length or surface area of the molecule as much as on the molar mass. A straight chain has more potential contact points than a branched structure with the same formula, therefore has more contact points and stronger London dispersion forces.

EXAMPLE: Arrange C_2H_6, CH_4, C_4H_{10} in order of increasing boiling point.

SOLUTION: In order of increasing boiling point $CH_4 < C_2H_6 < C_4H_{10}$. None of these molecules is polar, so they only exhibit London dispersion forces. The higher the molar mass and the longer the molecule, the more polarizable the molecule becomes. C_4H_{10} has the greatest molar mass and longest straight chain of carbons, followed by C_2H_6, and has the strongest London dispersion forces.

MULTIPLE-CHOICE QUESTIONS

No calculators are to be used in this section.

1. The compound most likely to be ionic is
   (A) KF
   (B) CCl_4
   (C) CO_2
   (D) ICl

2. Which of the following substances contains both ionic and covalent bonds?
   (A) NH_3
   (B) CH_4
   (C) NaOH
   (D) ICl

3. The type of bonding within a water molecule is
   (A) ionic bonding
   (B) polar covalent bonding
   (C) nonpolar covalent bonding
   (D) hydrogen bonding

4. Dinitrogen oxide, N_2O, has two double bonds. The general structure is N=N=O. The formal charge on the oxygen atom in this molecule is
   (A) zero
   (B) positive one (+1)
   (C) positive two (+2)
   (D) negative one (–1)

5. The Lewis structure of which molecule requires resonance structures?
   (A) $MgCl_2$
   (B) SiO_2
   (C) SO_2
   (D) OCl_2

6. The predicted geometry (shape) of PH_3, according to the VSEPR theory, is
   (A) bent or angular
   (B) trigonal pyramidal
   (C) tetrahedral
   (D) trigonal planar

7. Rank the following from lowest to highest boiling temperature:
C_2H_6 C_2H_5OH C_2H_5Cl
(A) $C_2H_6 < C_2H_5OH < C_2H_5Cl$
(B) $C_2H_5OH < C_2H_5Cl < C_2H_6$
(C) $C_2H_5Cl < C_2H_6 < C_2H_5OH$
(D) $C_2H_6 < C_2H_5Cl < C_2H_5OH$

8. The total number of lone pairs in PCl_3 is
(A) 1
(B) 8
(C) 10
(D) 12

9. The Lewis structure for carbon dioxide is
(A) :C̈=O–O:
(B) :C̈–Ö–Ö
(C) :Ö=C=Ö:
(D) :Ö=C=Ö:

10. Which of the following molecules has a dipole moment?
SO_3 CCl_4 PF_3
(A) SO_3 and CCl_4 only
(B) CCl_4 only
(C) PF_3 only
(D) SO_3, CCl_4, and PF_3

11. A triple bond is comprised of
(A) three σ (sigma) bonds
(B) two σ (sigma) bonds and one π (pi) bond
(C) one σ (sigma) bond and two π (pi) bonds
(D) three π (pi) bonds

12. A substance with strong intermolecular forces of attraction would be expected to have
(A) a low boiling point
(B) a high vapor pressure
(C) a high heat of vaporization
(D) a low melting point

13. What is the ELECTRON PAIR (or ELECTRON REGION) arrangement around the central atom in the molecule IF_5?
(A) trigonal pyramidal
(B) square planar
(C) octahedral
(D) square pyramidal

14. In which bond does the oxygen atom possess a partial positive charge?
(A) O–H
(B) O–F
(C) N–O
(D) O–C

15. The effect of lone pairs on molecular geometry is
    (A) to push other atoms closer together because lone pairs are localized on only one nucleus, so they spread out more
    (B) to allow the other atoms to be further apart because lone pairs take up less space than bonding pairs
    (C) to destabilize the molecule by creating a dipole
    (D) none, because they are just another pair of electrons

FREE-RESPONSE QUESTIONS

1.

1-propanol   2-propanol

1-propanol boils at 97°C, while 2-propanol boils at 87.5°C. Account for this difference in boiling points.

2.

This polypeptide is both hydrophilic and hydrophobic. Explain what will happen when it is added to water.

Answers

MULTIPLE-CHOICE QUESTIONS

1. **A** Bonds formed from elements with greater differences in electronegativity are most likely ionic in nature. (Electronegativity increases for elements as you move up and to the right on the periodic table.) (*Chemistry* 8th ed. pages 350–351/9th ed. pages 361–362). LO 2.17

2. **C** NaOH is an ionic substance (metal to nonmetal). In this case, the anion is a covalently-bonded polyatomic, OH⁻ (*Chemistry* 8th ed. pages 341–343/9th ed. pages 352–356). LO 2.17.

3. **B** This question is asking you to consider the nature of the bonding between hydrogen and oxygen in water (note the term *within* in the question!). With an electronegativity difference (H = 2.1 and

O = 3.5) of 1.4, this suggests a bond of a very polar covalent nature due to the uneven sharing of the pair of electrons between hydrogen and oxygen (Note: The force *between* one water molecule and another water molecule is known as a hydrogen bond.) (*Chemistry* 8th ed. pages 346–350/9th ed. pages 358–361). LO 2.13

4. **A** To determine the formal charge on an atom you need to determine the difference in the number of electrons assigned to the atom in the molecule and the number of outermost (valence) electrons on the free atom. In this case, the double bond between nitrogen and oxygen allows oxygen to "own" two (one-half of the four) electrons in the bond, plus totally own the other four electrons. (If this is not clear to you, draw the Lewis structure for this molecule.) Since the number of electrons assigned to oxygen in the molecule and as a free atom is the same, the formal charge is zero. Note that you are not required to use formal charge calculations to explain why certain atoms do not obey the octet rule (*Chemistry* 8th ed. pages 374–378/9th ed. pages 385–389). LO 2.21

5. **C** Watch for *resonance* when it is possible to draw more than one valid Lewis structure. This tends to occur when the same kind of atoms are bonded once as a single bond and again with a multiple bond holding the same kind of atoms together. In this case there is a single bond between sulfur and one of the oxygen atoms, and a double bond between sulfur and the other oxygen atom (*Chemistry* 8th ed. pages 373–374/9th ed. pages 384–385). LO 2.21

$$:\!\overset{..}{\underset{..}{O}}\!-\!\overset{..}{S}\!=\!\overset{..}{\underset{..}{O}} \longleftrightarrow :\!\overset{..}{\underset{..}{O}}\!=\!\overset{..}{S}\!-\!\overset{..}{\underset{..}{O}}\!:$$

6. **B** It is the position of the nuclei upon which we base the shape of a molecule. From the Lewis structure, you can see an unshared pair of electrons on the P; it is this unshared pair which repels the bonded pairs (between P and H) down toward the corners of a tetrahedron. However, the top pair does not contribute to the shape; hence the geometry is a trigonal pyramid (*Chemistry* 8th ed. pages 378–389/9th ed. pages 389–401). LO 2.21

$$\overset{..}{H\!-\!P\!-\!H}\atop{\underset{H}{|}}$$

7. **D** Consider the IMF (intermolecular forces) between molecules. C_2H_6, with the lowest boiling temperature is nonpolar and hence has a low IMF. C_2H_5OH has hydrogen bonding between molecules. Watch for these high IMF when hydrogen is bonded to O, N, or F. C_2H_5Cl is polar covalent and has intermediate strength IMF between molecules (Measured boiling temperatures are as follows: for C_2H_6 it is –88.3°C, for C_2H_5OH it is +78.5°C, and for C_2H_5Cl it is +12.3°C.) (*Chemistry* 8th ed. page 443/9th ed. page 458). LO 2.16

8. **C** A sketch of the Lewis structure will show three lone pairs on each of the chlorine atoms and one more lone pair on the phosphorus atom, for a total of 10 lone pairs (*Chemistry* 8th ed. pages 349–351/9th ed. pages 360–362). LO 2.21

9. **C** First count the number of total outermost (valence) electrons. Each oxygen has six and the carbon has four, for a total of sixteen. Only response C, with two double bonds, has sixteen valence electrons (*Chemistry* 8th ed. pages 364–372/9th ed. pages 376–383). LO 2.21

10. **C** In order to have a dipole moment there must be polar covalent bonds present and an asymetrical distribution of charge. In order to determine this, you must consider both the nature of the bonding (extent of polarity) and the arrangement of these bonds (the molecular shape). If all the vectors, resulting from polar bonds, cancel each other, then there is zero dipole moment. In the case of PF_3, the shape is that of a trigonal pyramid, the vectors do not cancel each other, and the molecule is polar (*Chemistry* 8th ed. pages 346–350/9th ed. pages 358–361). LO 2.21

11. **C** All bonds between atoms start with sharing a pair of electrons in overlapping orbitals. This is called a sigma bond. Multiple bonds occur when electrons in unhybridized orbitals above and below the sigma bond are shared. Each multiple bond is a pi bond, so a triple bond contains one sigma and two pi bonds (*Chemistry* 8th ed. pages 408–410/9th ed. pages 420–422). LO 2.21

12. **C** A great deal of energy would be required to overcome strong intermolecular forces between the molecules within the substance in order for them to move from liquid to gaseous state (*Chemistry* 8th ed. pages 440–444/9th ed. pages 455–459). LO 2.16

13. **C** Iodine has 7 valence electrons and each fluorine atom has 7 valence electrons; so 7 + 5(7) = 42 electrons. Thus there are five bonding pairs and one lone pair around the central atom. The six pairs or regions of electrons assume an octahedral arrangement (*Chemistry* 8th ed. pages 378–387/9th ed. pages 389–398). LO 2.21

14. **B** Since fluorine is the most electronegative element in the periodic table, the oxygen atom, when covalently bonded to the fluorine atom, will have a partial positive charge (*Chemistry* 8th ed. pages 344–349/9th ed. pages 356–360). LO 2.17

15. **A** Lone pairs are only localized around one nucleus, so they spread out close to that nucleus and take up more room (*Chemistry* 8th ed. page 382/9th ed. pages 356–360). LO 2.21

FREE-RESPONSE QUESTIONS

1. Both molecules are able to make hydrogen bonds with their OH groups, so their boiling points are relatively high. Because 1-propanol's OH group is at the end of the carbon chain, the molecule has more contact points available for London dispersion forces of attraction and its boiling point is higher (Chemistry 8th ed. pages 343–349, 353–359, 440–443, 466–471, 474/9th ed. pages 355–360, 365–371, 455–458, 479–483, 486). LO 2.13

2.

these regions will repel water

The lone pairs on the nitrogen and oxygen atoms will be attracted to the slightly positive hydrogen atoms of water, forming dipole–dipole attractions (specifically, hydrogen bonds). The nonpolar CH_3 (methyl) groups will repel the polar water molecules. The molecule may float on the water's surface, with the hydrophobic portion facing up out of the water and the hydrophilic portion facing down. Or it may organize in layers, with the nonpolar portions facing each other, away from the water, and the polar portions facing the water (*Chemistry* 8th ed. pages 504–505/9th ed. pages 517–518). LO 2.8

4

Big Idea 2: Gases

Big Idea 2

Chemical and physical properties of materials can be explained by the structure and the arrangement of atoms, ions, or molecules and the forces between them.

In this section, the laws describing gas behavior are explored. Mathematical laws relating the properties of pressure, volume, temperature, and moles of gas are considered. Densities and molar masses of ideal gases will be determined from the ideal gas law. Stoichiometric calculations will be performed for reactions involving gases. Pressures of gases in a mixture will be examined. The behavior of ideal gases will be explained by the kinetic molecular theory. Real gases will be compared to ideal gases.

Questions about gas behavior and gas laws can be either qualitative or quantitative in the multiple-choice section.

The free-response portion of the exam can include questions about an experiment involving gases such as the determination of the molar mass or molar volume of a gas. Essay questions about ideal or real gas behavior or the kinetic-molecular theory may also appear.

You should be able to
- Perform calculations with gas laws: Boyle's, Charles', Avogadro's, and ideal.
- Perform calculations with the ideal gas law to find the density or molar mass of the gas.

- Interpret or draw graphical relationships between gas variables.
- Perform stoichiometric calculations for reactions which involve gases as reactants, products, or both.
- Perform calculations with molar volume.
- Perform calculations with Dalton's law of partial pressures for a mixture of gases.
- Perform calculations for gases collected over water.
- Use kinetic-molecular theory (KMT) and knowledge of intermolecular forces to predict ideal and nonideal gas properties
- Draw representations of gas-phase materials that illustrate the intermolecular forces and the effects of changing physical conditions on the materials.
- Use data regarding real gases to identify deviations from ideal gas behavior and identify the molecular interactions leading to these deviations.

AP Tip

Mathematical equations will be provided in the free-response section of the exam, but not for the multiple-choice part. It is best to memorize the equations or know how to derive the equations from one equation.

GAS LAWS

(*Chemistry* 8th ed. pages 183–194/9th ed. pages 192–203)

The table below summarizes the gas laws that can be derived from the ideal gas law. A typical problem involves solving for the missing variable when given a set of initial and final conditions for a gas sample. **Be sure to perform all gas calculations involving temperature using the Kelvin scale, not degrees Celsius.** Temperature (K) = °C + 273.15.

Gas Law	Equations	Definition
Boyle's law	$P = (nRT)\,1/V$ $$\boxed{P_1V_1 = P_2 2}$$	The product of the pressure and the volume is a constant, k, for a trapped sample of gas at constant temperature.
Charles' law	$V = (nR/P)T$ $$\boxed{\frac{V_1}{T_1} = \frac{V_2}{T_2}}$$	The volume of a gas at constant pressure increases linearly with the temperature of the gas.

Gas Law	Equations	Definition
Avogadro's law	$V = (RT/P)n$ $\dfrac{V_1}{n_1} = \dfrac{V_2}{n_2}$	Equal volumes of gases at the same temperature and pressure contain the same number of moles of gas.
Ideal gas law	$PV = nRT$ R = universal gas constant $= 0.08206 \text{ L} \times \text{atm}/(\text{K} \times \text{mol})$	An equation of state for a gas, where the state of a gas is its condition at a given time.
Dalton's law	$P_{total} = P_1 + P_2 + P_3 + \ldots$ $P_{total} = n_{tot}RT/V$	For a mixture of gases, the sum of the pressures of the individual gases is equal to the total pressure. The total pressure depends on the total moles of gas present.

GRAPHICAL RELATIONSHIPS FOR GAS LAWS

(*Chemistry* 8th ed. pages 183–187/9th ed. pages 192–196)

BOYLE'S LAW Pressure is inversely related to volume. A graph of P vs. $1/V$ is a straight line.

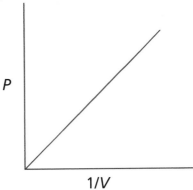

CHARLES' LAW Volume is directly proportional to temperature. A graph of V vs. T is linear. Extrapolation of this graph for all gases to zero volume results in the same temperature, $-273.15°C$ (0 K), which is absolute zero.

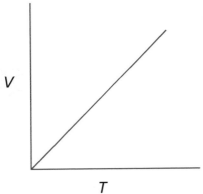

EXAMPLE: A sample tube containing 103.6 mL of CO gas at 20.6 torr is connected to an evacuated 1.13-L flask. What will the pressure be when the CO is allowed into the flask?

SOLUTION: $P_1V_1 = P_2V_2$; $P_2 = \dfrac{P_1V_1}{V_2} = \dfrac{(20.6 \text{ torr})(0.1036 \text{ L})}{1.47 \text{ L}} = 1.45$ torr

Note: Units of volume must cancel out. Remember to convert to the same units for all volume measurements.

EXAMPLE: A quantity of gas at 27.0°C is heated in a closed vessel until the pressure is doubled. To what temperature is the gas heated?

SOLUTION: Pressure is directly proportional to temperature in Kelvin units, so before you do any computations, convert the temperature to Kelvin. If the pressure is doubled, the temperature will also double. 27.0°C + 273.15 = 300.2 K. The answer is 600.4 K (or 327.2°C).

GAS STOICHIOMETRY

(*Chemistry* 8th ed. pages 194–199/9th ed. pages 203–208)

If the pressure, volume, and temperature of ideal gases are known, stoichiometric calculations can be performed. This is discussed in more detail in Big Idea 3.

MOLAR VOLUME

(*Chemistry* 8th ed. pages 194–195/9th ed. pages 203–204)

One mole of an ideal gas at 0°C and 1 atm occupies 22.4 L. Standard temperature and pressure (STP) are the conditions 0°C and 1 atm.

EXAMPLE: What mass of helium is required to fill a 1.5-L balloon at STP?

SOLUTION: $1.5 \text{ L} \times \dfrac{1 \text{ mol He}}{22.4 \text{ L}} \times \dfrac{4.0 \text{ g He}}{1 \text{ mol}} = 0.27 \text{ g He}$

MOLAR MASS OF A GAS

(*Chemistry* 8th ed. pages 198–199/9th ed. pages 207–208)

The molar mass of a gas can be calculated from its measured density, d. The density of a gas can also be calculated from the molar mass of the gas.

The equation relating density and molar mass can be derived from $PV = nRT$. Since n = grams/molar mass, PV = (grams /molar mass) RT.

$$\text{Molar Mass} = \frac{dRT}{P} = \frac{(\text{mass})RT}{V \times P}$$

EXAMPLE: A sample of gas weighing 0.800 g occupies a 256-mL flask at 100°C and 750.0 torr. Determine the molar mass of the gas.

SOLUTION: First, convert pressure from torr to atm.

$$750.0 \text{ torr} \times \frac{1.00 \text{ atm}}{760.0 \text{ torr}} = 0.986 \text{ atm}$$

$$\text{Molar mass} = \frac{0.800 \text{ g} \times \dfrac{0.08206 \text{ L atm}}{\text{mol K}} \times 373 \text{ K}}{0.256 \text{ L} \times 0.986 \text{ atm}} = 97.0 \text{ g/mol}$$

DALTON'S LAW

(*Chemistry* 8th ed. pages 199–205/9th ed. pages 208–214)

For a mixture of gases in a container, the total pressure is the sum of the pressures that each gas would exert if it were alone.

$$P_{total} = P_1 + P_2 + P_3 + \ldots$$

The partial pressure of a gas, P_{gas}, is the pressure that a particular gas would exert if it were alone in the container. The subscripts refer to the individual gases (gas₁, gas₂, and so on). The partial pressure of each gas can be calculated from the ideal gas law:

$$P_1 = n_1 RT/V$$

The total pressure of the mixture, P, can be represented as

$$P_{total} = n_{tot} RT/V$$

The mole fraction is the ratio of the number of moles of a given component in a mixture to the total number of moles in the mixture.

$$X_1 = n_1/n_{tot}$$

EXAMPLE: A mixture of 1.00 g of H_2 and 1.00 g of He is placed in a 1.00-L container at 27°C. Calculate the mole fraction and partial pressure of each gas. Calculate the total pressure in the container.

SOLUTION: $n_{H_2} = 1.00 \text{ g } H_2 \times \dfrac{1 \text{ mol } H_2}{2.02 \text{ g } H_2} = 0.496 \text{ mol } H_2$

$n_{He} = 1.00 \text{ g He} \times \dfrac{1 \text{ mol He}}{4.00 \text{ g}} = 0.250 \text{ mol He}$

$X_{H2} = \dfrac{0.496 \text{ mol}}{0.496 \text{ mol} + 0.250 \text{ mol}} = 0.665;$ $X_{He} = \dfrac{0.250 \text{ mol}}{0.496 \text{ mol} + 0.250 \text{ mol}} = 0.335$

$$P_{H_2} = \frac{n_{H_2}RT}{V} = \frac{0.496 \text{ mol} \times \dfrac{0.08206 \text{ L} \times \text{atm}}{\text{mol} \times \text{K}} \times 300 \text{ K}}{1.00 \text{ l}} = 12.2 \text{ atm}$$

$$P_{He} = \frac{n_{He}RT}{V} = \frac{0.250 \text{ mol} \times \dfrac{0.08206 \text{ L} \times \text{atm}}{\text{mol} \times \text{K}} \times 300 \text{ K}}{1.0 \text{ L}} = 6.15 \text{ atm}$$

$P_{total} = P_{He} + P_{H_2} = 12.2 \text{ atm} + 6.15 \text{ atm} = 18.4 \text{ atm}$

GAS COLLECTION OVER WATER

(*Chemistry* 8th ed. pages 202–205/9th ed. pages 211–214)

A gas can be collected by displacement of water. A mixture of gases results due to a mixture of water vapor and the gas being collected. Refer to Figure 5.13 on page 204 of the 8th edition and page 213 of the 9th edition of *Chemistry*.

EXAMPLE: A sample weighing 0.986 g contains zinc and some impurities. Excess hydrochloric acid is added and reacts with the zinc but not the impurities. Determine the percentage of zinc in the sample if 240.0 mL of hydrogen gas is collected over water at 30.0°C and 1.032 atm. The vapor pressure of water at this temperature is 0.042 atm.

SOLUTION: Beginning with the balanced equation:

$Zn + 2 HCl \rightarrow ZnCl_2 + H_2$

One mole of zinc will produce one mole of hydrogen gas.

Using Dalton's law and the vapor pressure of water at the specified temperature:

$P_{total} = P_{atm} = P_{H_2} + P_{H_2O}; \quad P_{H_2} = P_{atm} - P_{H_2O}$

$P_{H_2} = 1.032 \text{ atm} - 0.042 \text{ atm} = 0.990 \text{ atm}$

$$n_{H_2} = \frac{P_{H_2} \times V}{RT} = \frac{0.990 \text{ atm} \times 0.240 \text{ L}}{0.08206 \text{ L atm mol}^{-1} \text{ K}^{-1} \times 303.2 \text{ K}} = 0.00955 \text{ mol H}_2$$

$$0.00955 \text{ mol H}_2 \times \frac{1 \text{ mol Zn}}{1 \text{ mol H}_2} \times \frac{65.4 \text{ g Zn}}{1 \text{ mol Zn}} = 0.625 \text{ g Zn}$$

$$\%Zn = \frac{\text{g Zn} \times 100\%}{\text{g sample}} = \frac{0.625 \text{ g}}{0.986 \text{ g}} \times 100\% = 63.3\% \text{ Zn}$$

Note that the vapor pressure of water at various temperatures can be found in tables of known physical constants. When you solve this kind of problem, the vapor pressure of water will be provided.

KINETIC-MOLECULAR THEORY

(*Chemistry* 8th ed. pages 205–213/9th ed. pages 214–223)

The kinetic-molecular theory is a model that attempts to explain the properties of an ideal gas. The postulates of the kinetic-molecular theory are

1. The volume of the individual particles of a gas can be assumed to be negligible.
2. The gas particles are in constant motion. The pressure exerted by the gas is due to the collisions of the gases with the walls of the container.
3. The gases are not attracted to one another.
4. The average kinetic energy of a gas is directly proportional to the Kelvin temperature.

$$(KE)_{average} = 3/2\ RT = \frac{1}{2}\ mv^2_{avg}$$

Note that the value of R here is 8.31 J mol^{-1} K^{-1}. The other values of R do not have the correct units for energy calculations.

EXAMPLE: Three identical flasks are filled with three different gases.

Flask A: CO at 760 torr and 0°C

Flask B: N_2 at 250 torr and 0°C

Flask C: H_2 at 100 torr and 0°C

In which flask will the molecules have the greatest average kinetic energy? In which flask will the molecules have the greatest average velocity?

SOLUTION: All molecules will have the same average kinetic energy since they are all at the same temperature. Flask C will have the greatest average velocity since hydrogen has the lowest molar mass. At constant T, the lightest molecules are fastest, on average.

REAL GASES

(*Chemistry* 8th ed. pages 214–217/9th ed. pages 224–227)

The ideal gas model fails at high pressure and low temperature. Real gas molecules take up space and experience attractive forces between molecules. At high pressure there is less empty space between molecules, and the volume of molecules becomes more significant. An ideal gas could be compressed to zero volume, but for a real gas, as the pressure doubles, the volume of empty space cannot continue to be halved. As the temperature decreases, the molecules have less kinetic energy to overcome the attractive forces between gas molecules; these attractive forces may cause the gas to condense.

The van der Waals equation modifies the assumptions of the kinetic-molecular theory to fit the behavior of real gases. The van der Waals constant a adjusts for the presence of intermolecular attractions; the van der Waals constant b adjusts for the size of the atom or molecule.

$$[P_{obs} + a(n/V)^2] \times (V - nb) = nRT$$

EXAMPLE: Which of the following gases would you expect to have the largest value of the van der Waals constant, b: H_2, N_2, CH_4, C_2H_6, or C_3H_8?

SOLUTION: Since the van der Waals constant, b, is a measure of the size of the molecule. C_3H_8 has the largest molar volume and should have the largest value of b.

EXAMPLE: Which of the following gases would you expect to have the largest value of the van der Waals constant, a: H_2, CO_2, CH_4, or N_2?

SOLUTION: CO_2 has the largest value for a, which measures intermolecular attractions. All the molecules are nonpolar so the only force present is an induced dipole or London force which increases as the number of electrons and protons in the molecule increases.

MULTIPLE-CHOICE QUESTIONS

No calculators are to be used in this section.

1. Under what conditions does a gas behave more like a real gas than an ideal gas?
   (A) high temperature and low pressure
   (B) high temperature and high pressure
   (C) low temperature and low pressure
   (D) low temperature and high pressure

2. What is the volume of 3.00 mol of gas at STP?
   (A) 22.4 L
   (B) 3 × 22.4 L
   (C) 3 × 22.4 L × 273/760
   (D) It cannot be determined without knowing which gas is involved.

3. An ideal gas of volume 189. mL is collected over water at 30°C and 777 torr. The vapor pressure of water is 32 torr at 30°C. What pressure is exerted by the dry gas under these conditions?
   (A) 320 torr
   (B) 745 torr
   (C) 777 torr
   (D) 32/777 torr

4. A 14.0-L cylinder contains 5.60 g N_2, 40.0 g Ar, and 6.40 g O_2. What is the total pressure in atm at 27°C? (R = the ideal gas constant.)
   (A) 26 R
   (B) 30 R
   (C) 60 R
   (D) 120 R

5. In a closed rigid system, 7.0 mol CO_2, 7.0 mol Ar, 7.0 mol N_2, and 4.0 mol Ne are trapped, with a total pressure of 10.0 atm. What is the partial pressure exerted by the neon gas?
   (A) 1.6 atm
   (B) 4.0 atm
   (C) 10.0 atm
   (D) 21.0 atm

6. Consider the reaction:

   $C_2H_6(g) + 7/2\ O_2(g) \rightarrow 2\ CO_2(g) + 3\ H_2O(g)$

   If 6.00 g ethane, $C_2H_6(g)$ burn, what volume of $CO_2(g)$ will be formed at STP?
   (A) 0.200 L
   (B) 2.20 L
   (C) 9.00 L
   (D) 22.4 L

7. Cl_2 and F_2 combine to form a gaseous product; one volume of Cl_2 reacts with three volumes of F_2 yielding two volumes of product. Assuming constant conditions of temperature and pressure, what is the formula of the product?
   (A) Cl_2F_2
   (B) ClF_2
   (C) Cl_2F
   (D) ClF_3

8. Decreasing the temperature of an ideal gas from 80°C to 40°C causes the average kinetic energy to
   (A) decrease by a factor of two
   (B) increase by a factor of two
   (C) increase by a factor of four
   (D) decrease by less than a factor of two

9. The average speed of the molecules of a gas is proportional to the
   (A) reciprocal of absolute temperature, $(1/T)$
   (B) absolute temperature
   (C) square root of the absolute temperature
   (D) square of the absolute temperature

10. A 5.00-L vessel contains 2.00 moles of helium and 3.00 moles of hydrogen at a pressure of 10.0 atm. Maintaining a constant temperature, an additional 3.00 moles of hydrogen are added. What is the partial pressure of hydrogen gas in the vessel at the end? (Assume that the gases behave ideally.)
    (A) 6.00 atm
    (B) 10.0 atm
    (C) 12.0 atm
    (D) 20.0 atm

Questions 11–13 refer to Figure 1 and Figure 2 below. On the right is a key to identify the gases in the problems.

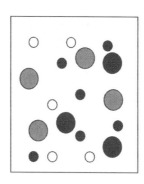

| **Figure 1** | **Figure 2** | **Key to Gas Symbols** |

11. In Figure 1 there are three gases present, Gas A, B, and C. The number of spheres represents the number of moles of each gas present. If the total pressure within the vessel is 5.00 atm, what is the partial pressure of Gas B?
    (A) 1.00 atm
    (B) 1.33 atm
    (C) 1.50 atm
    (D) 1.67 atm

12. Suppose that another gas D is added to the vessel in Figure 1, keeping the temperature and the volume constant. This is represented by Figure 2 above. What happens to the partial pressure of Gas B?
    (A) increases
    (B) decreases
    (C) stays the same
    (D) cannot be predicted

13. What happens to the total pressure for the system described in Question 12? (In other words, compare the total pressure in Figure 1 versus Figure 2.)
    (A) increases
    (B) decreases
    (C) remains the same
    (D) cannot be predicted

14. Increasing the pressure on a gas in a rigid container at constant temperature will
    (A) increase the average kinetic energy of the gas molecules
    (B) increase the influence of intermolecular attractions, because the molecules will be closer together
    (C) increase the influence of intermolecular attractions, because the molecules will be moving more slowly
    (D) decrease the average kinetic energy of the gas molecules

15. Consider two samples of a gas in identical rigid containers, Sample A at 273 K and Sample B at 300 K. Which of the following statements is true?
   (A) The average kinetic energy of Sample A is less than that of Sample B.
   (B) The samples have the same average velocity.
   (C) The samples must contain the same number of moles of gas.
   (D) The pressure of Sample A is more than the pressure of Sample B.

FREE-RESPONSE QUESTIONS

Calculators may be used for this section.

1. (a) Compare the temperature of freshly made coffee made at lower altitudes to coffee made at higher altitudes. Cite the relevant intermolecular forces in your explanation.
   (b) Under what conditions are gases most "ideal"? Explain why, in terms of KMT and intermolecular forces of attraction.
   (c) One mole of water and one mole of propane are placed in separate, closed, 1-L containers and heated to 110°C. The pressure in the water vapor container is less than the pressure in the propane container. Explain this observation.
   (d) How does gaseous pressure relate to changes in volume? Explain.

2. Assume that two cylinders at 27°C are connected by a closed stopcock (valve) system. The right-hand cylinder contains 2.40 L of hydrogen at 0.600 atm; the left cylinder is larger and contains 6.80 L of helium at 1.40 atm.

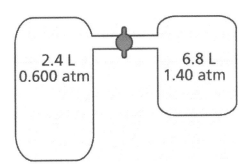

   (a) How many moles of each gas are present?
   (b) What is the total pressure when the valve is open?
   (c) Determine the partial pressure of these two gases at 27.0°C when the stopcock is opened.

Answers

MULTIPLE-CHOICE QUESTIONS

1. **D** At low temperature and high pressure, the molecules are closer together and therefore the forces between molecules become more important as they are stronger. The actual (finite) volume of individual molecules also becomes more important

as more of the total space is actually occupied by finite molecular volume (*Chemistry* 8th ed. pages 214–217/9th ed. pages 224–227). LO 2.4

2. **B** The molar volume of all gases at STP is 22.4 L, so three moles would occupy 22.4 L/mol × 3 moles (*Chemistry* 8th ed. pages 214–217/9th ed. pages 224–227). LO 2.6

3. **B** The total pressure = 777 torr. Of this, 32 torr is due to the water vapor, hence 777 – 32 = 745 torr of pressure are allocated to the dry gas (*Chemistry* 8th ed. pages 199–205, 471–478/9th ed. pages 208–214, 483–490). LO 2.6

4. **B** Use $P_{Total} = N_{Total}RT/V$ to determine the pressure. From the mass of each of the gases you can find 0.200 mol of N_2, 1.00 mol of Ar, and 0.200 mol of O_2 to give a total number of moles (*n*) of 1.4 mol. Therefore $P_{Total} = R \times 1.40$ mol × 300 K / 14.0 L = 30 *R*. Note: You do not need a calculator to divide 1.4 by 14 and then multiply by 300! (*Chemistry* 8th ed. pages 188–194/9th ed. pages 197–203). LO 2.6

5. **A** The total number of moles is 25.0 (7.0 + 7.0 + 7.0 + 4.0 = 25.0), hence the Ne is 4.0/25.0 of the total amount of gas and exerts 4.0/25.0 of the total pressure, or 4.0/25.0 × 10.0 atm = 1.6 atm (*Chemistry* 8th ed. pages 199–205/9th ed. pages 208–214). LO 2.6

6. **C** 6.0 g of ethane / 30. g/mol yields 0.20 mol of ethane, which forms twice that number of moles of carbon dioxide. Since one mol of gas occupies 22.4 L at STP, 22.4 L/mol × 0.20 mol × 2 CO_2/C_2H_6 = 8.96 L of carbon dioxide (rounded to two significant figures = 9.0 L) (*Chemistry* 8th ed. pages 194–199/9th ed. pages 203–208). LO 2.6

7. **D** This problem assumes you understand Avogadro's Law, "At constant temperature and pressure, the volume of a gas is directly proportional to the number of moles of the gas." To apply that to this problem, 1 volume Cl_2 + 3 volumes $F_2 \rightarrow$ 2 volumes Cl_xF_{3x}. The simplest formula for the product becomes ClF_3 (*Chemistry* 8th ed. pages 183–188/9th ed. pages 192–197). LO 2.6

8. **D** Be careful here to note the difference between the kinds of temperature scales and what they mean. Even though the Celsius temperature is half as much, the average kinetic energy is proportional to the Kelvin temperature. In this case that ratio is only 353/313 = 1.13 so the average kinetic energy decreases only by a factor of 1.13 (*Chemistry* 8th ed. pages 203–212/9th ed. pages 212–222). LO 2.6

9. **C** In this case the question is about the average speed (not the energy) of the molecules. Review root-mean-square velocity (*Chemistry* 8th ed. pages 211–212/9th ed. pages 221–222). LO 2.6

10. **D** The initial partial pressure of the hydrogen = 10 atm × (3.0/5.0) = 6.0 atm. The amount of hydrogen present is doubled from 3.0 moles to 6.0 moles, therefore the partial pressure will increase proportionally to 12.0 atm. According to KMT, the volume of the particles is negligible and the particles do not interact with each other, so it does not matter what other gases are added or what other gases are present (*Chemistry* 8th ed. pages 199–203/9th ed. pages 208–212). LO 2.4

11. **B** The partial pressure = mole fraction × total pressure. In this case, partial pressure of Gas B = (4/15)(5.00 atm) = 1.33 atm (*Chemistry* 8th ed. pages 199–203/9th ed. pages 208–212). LO 2.4

12. **C** Since the amount of Gas B remains the same, there would be no change in the partial pressure of this gas (*Chemistry* 8th ed. pages 199–203/9th ed. pages 208–212). LO 2.4

13. **A** Since the total number of moles of gas in the vessel has now increased, the total pressure will also increase (*Chemistry* 8th ed. pages 199–203/9th ed. pages 208–212). LO 2.4

14. **B** Intermolecular forces are more significant when molecules are closer together (*Chemistry* 8th ed. pages 214–216/9th ed. pages 224–226). LO 2.4

15. **A** According to KMT, temperature is a measure of the kinetic energy of the gas, which in turn is related to the average velocity. A higher temperature means higher average velocity (*Chemistry* 8th ed. page 210/9th ed. page 220). LO 2.4

FREE-RESPONSE QUESTIONS

1. (a) At low altitudes, the amount of air above the surface of the earth, and therefore the total atmospheric pressure, would be greater. Water boils at a higher temperature under such conditions since a higher vapor pressure is required for the liquid to become a gas. The coffee made at higher altitude will not be as hot (*Chemistry* 8th ed. pages 481–482/9th ed. pages 493–494). LO 2.16

   (b) In this question, be careful not to confuse "conditions" with "physical properties" or "characteristics of the gaseous molecules." The conditions under which real gases are most ideal are those of low pressure and high temperature. "Low pressure" implies that the gas molecules are far apart from each other, so the forces of attraction between the molecules are weak. The finite volume of individual molecules is also, therefore, a small part of the total volume occupied by the gas, as required by KMT. Finally, at higher temperatures the molecules are moving so rapidly that the effect of intermolecular attractions is negligible (*Chemistry* 8th ed. pages 188–194, 214–217/9th ed. pages 197–203, 224–227). LO 2.4

(c) Water molecules are polar and attracted to each other by hydrogen bonding. At temperatures just above water's boiling point, these attractions will be more important. Because of this attraction, the molecules will hit the container walls less frequently and the pressure will be less than predicted by the ideal gas law. Nonpolar propane molecules only experience London dispersion forces of attraction which are weak and easily overcome (*Chemistry* 8th ed. pages 214–217/9th ed. pages 224–227). LO 2.4

(d) Gaseous pressure is inversely proportional to the volume of the container. If only the volume of the container is less, for example, the molecules have less room to move around before striking the sides and therefore strike the sides of the container more often. This assumes that the temperature is held constant (*Chemistry* 8th ed. pages 183–186/9th ed. pages 192–195). LO 2.4

Note: What assumption is made in your answer to D?

2. Solving this problem has three steps. (1) To determine the pressure exerted by each gas, first calculate the number of moles of each ($n = PV / RT$), (2) and then use the total number of moles of gas and $p = nRT/V$ to calculate the total pressure when the total volume is 9.20 L. (3) Finally, the partial pressure of each gas is the total pressure × the mol fraction of that gas (*Chemistry* 8th ed. pages 188–194 and 199–200/9th ed. pages 197–203 and 208–209). LO 2.6

For hydrogen: $(0.600 \text{ atm} \times 2.40 \text{ L}) / (R \times 300. \text{ K}) = 0.0585 \text{ mol of } H_2$

For helium: $(1.40 \text{ atm} \times 6.80 \text{ L}) / (R \times 300. \text{ K}) = 0.397 \text{ mol of He}$

Total number of moles = 0.0585 + 0.397 mol = 0.456 mol

Total pressure is then $(0.456 \text{ mol} \times R \times 300. \text{ K}) / (9.20 \text{ L}) = 1.22 \text{ atm}$

Use the mol fractions: $(0.0585/0.456) \times 1.22 \text{ atm} = 0.157 \text{ atm } H_2$

$(0.397/0.456) \times 1.22 \text{ atm} = 1.06 \text{ atm He}$

5

BIG IDEA 2:
LIQUIDS AND SOLIDS

Big Idea 2

Chemical and physical properties of materials can be explained by the structure and the arrangement of atoms, ions, or molecules and the forces between them.

The forces that hold together solids and liquids, the condensed states of matter, are similar. The effect of these forces on properties such as surface tension and vapor pressure will be reviewed. The bonding models, structure, and properties of liquids and solids will be discussed. Changes in state from solid to liquid to gas will also be considered.

You should be able to
  ■ Describe the intermolecular forces that account for observed properties of liquids such as surface tension, capillary action, viscosity, vapor pressure, and boiling point.
  ■ Draw pictures that illustrate the observed differences between solids and liquids, and identify the interparticle forces (also known as intermolecular forces) that account for those differences.
  ■ Draw pictures of or explain atomic level representations that illustrate the observed differences in physical properties between solids of a specific type or solids of different types, and identify the interparticle forces that account for those differences.
  ■ Use your understanding of the type of bonding present in solids to draw pictures that illustrate the observed differences

between solids and liquids, and identify the interparticle forces that account for those differences.

> ## AP Tip
>
> In essay questions about this topic, you may be asked to draw pictures illustrating interactions between molecules.

INTERMOLECULAR FORCES

(*Chemistry* 8th ed. pages 440–443/9th ed. pages 455–458)

Intermolecular forces were introduced in Chapter 3. In this chapter, you will see the effect of intermolecular forces on properties of liquids such as boiling point, surface tension, and vapor pressure.

When molecular compounds such as water undergo changes in state, a disruption of forces that attract molecules to each other, the intermolecular forces, is involved. The covalent bonds in the molecules are not broken. When ionic compounds such as sodium chloride change state, ionic bonds are broken.

PROPERTIES OF LIQUIDS

SURFACE TENSION

(*Chemistry* 8th ed. page 443/9th ed. page 458)

Molecules at the surface of a liquid are pulled inward by the molecules beneath them. The surface tension of a liquid is the resistance of a liquid to increasing its surface area. Liquids with strong intermolecular forces tend to have high surface tensions.

> EXAMPLE: Equal-sized drops of Hg, Br_2, or H_2O are placed onto the same glass surface. Which of the three liquids will have the most spherical shape?
>
> SOLUTION: Hg will have the most spherical shape due to the metallic bonding which occurs between mercury atoms. Metallic bonding is stronger than both the hydrogen bonding in water and the London dispersion forces of bromine.

CAPILLARY ACTION

(*Chemistry* 8th ed. page 443/9th ed. page 458)

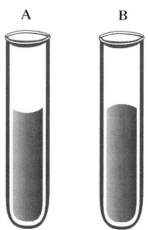

A   B

The rise of liquids up very narrow tubes is called capillary action. Water and dissolved nutrients move upward through plants via capillary action.

Adhesive forces, the attractions between a liquid and its container, cause the liquid to creep up the walls of the container. Adhesive forces are opposed by cohesive forces, the intermolecular forces in the liquid that try to decrease the liquid's surface area. Molecules with strong intermolecular attractions will have stronger cohesive forces than adhesive forces.

> EXAMPLE: Two different liquids are placed in separate glass tubes. Liquid A forms a concave meniscus. Liquid B forms a convex meniscus. Why do the meniscuses of Liquids A and B have two different shapes? Suggest a possible identity for each liquid.

> SOLUTION: Liquid A's adhesive forces are stronger than its cohesive forces, as in water. Liquid B's cohesive forces are stronger than its adhesive forces, as in mercury.

VISCOSITY

(*Chemistry* 8th ed. pages 443–444/9th ed. pages 458–459)

Viscosity is a measure of a liquid's resistance to flow. The greater its resistance, the more slowly it will flow. Molasses, motor oil, and glycerol are viscous liquids. Highly viscous liquids have large intermolecular forces or are very complex molecules with large molar masses and many electrons, such as polymers. For example, grease is viscous because it contains long hydrocarbon chains which can get tangled. Gasoline consists of shorter carbon chains three to eight carbons long and is therefore a nonviscous liquid. Viscosity decreases with increasing temperature because more molecules will have greater average kinetic energy to overcome the intermolecular forces of the liquid.

VAPOR PRESSURE

(*Chemistry* 8th ed. pages 471–475/9th ed. pages 483–487)

In the process of vaporization (evaporation), liquid molecules leave the surface and form a vapor. The heat of vaporization (enthalpy of vaporization, ΔH_{vap}) is the energy required to vaporize 1 mole of a liquid at its normal boiling point (1 atm). This quantity is endothermic because energy is required to overcome the intermolecular forces. In the reverse process, condensation, energy is released as the IMFs form between the particles when the gas molecules get close enough to interact with each other.

In a closed container, a liquid and its vapor are at equilibrium when the rate of evaporation equals the rate of condensation. The equilibrium vapor pressure is the pressure above the liquid from the molecules of the liquid in the gas phase.

Volatile liquids are liquids with high vapor pressures. The vapor pressure at a given temperature is determined by the intermolecular forces of the liquid. Strong intermolecular forces result in lower vapor pressure. Weak intermolecular forces result in higher vapor pressure because the liquid molecules are not held together as strongly and readily escape from the surface.

The vapor pressure of a liquid increases with increasing temperature. At higher temperatures, more molecules will have sufficient kinetic energy to overcome intermolecular forces and break free from the surface of the liquid.

The dependence of vapor pressure on temperature is represented in the figure.

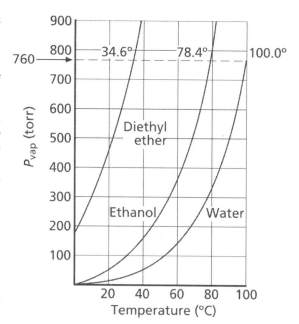

EXAMPLE: Explain why diethyl ether, $CH_3CH_2OCH_2CH_3$, is more volatile than ethanol, CH_3CH_2OH, at 25°C.

SOLUTION: The dipole forces in diethyl ether are weaker than the hydrogen bonding in ethanol. The weaker the intermolecular forces, the higher the liquid's vapor pressure and volatility.

BOILING

(*Chemistry* 8th ed. page 478/9th ed. page 490)

The boiling of a liquid occurs in a container open to the atmosphere when the vapor pressure of the liquid equals atmospheric pressure. Bubbles containing the vapor form within the liquid and rise to the surface due to their reduced density. During boiling, the temperature remains constant until all of the liquid vaporizes. The normal boiling point of a liquid is the temperature at which the vapor pressure of a liquid is equal to standard atmospheric pressure (1 atm = 760 mm Hg). To determine the normal boiling point of a liquid, interpolate the vapor pressure curve for the liquid at 1 atmosphere.

EXAMPLE: What are the normal boiling points of diethyl ether and ethanol?

SOLUTION: The normal boiling points for diethyl ether and ethanol are approximately 34.6°C and 78.4°C, respectively. The normal boiling point occurs at 1 atm and can be found by interpolating the vapor pressure curves above.

EXAMPLE: At a location 19,340 ft above sea level, the atmospheric pressure is 350 torr. At what temperature will water boil? Will it take more or less time to cook an egg at this location than at sea level or 1 atm?

SOLUTION: Using the vapor pressure curve above, at 350 torr, water will boil at about 80°C. It will take more time to hard-boil an egg at this elevation because water boils at a temperature lower than that at sea level, and therefore contains less kinetic energy.

EXAMPLE: Pressure cookers heat a small amount of water under high constant pressure. What effect does using a pressure cooker have on cooking time?

SOLUTION: Food in a pressure cooker will take less time to prepare because it will cook at a higher temperature. When the pressure is increased, the boiling point will increase until the vapor pressure of the liquid equals the pressure above the liquid. Once the boiling point is reached, the temperature will not change as long as there is liquid present. Vapor pressure is directly proportional to temperature.

STRUCTURE AND TYPES OF SOLIDS

(*Chemistry* 8th ed. pages 444–446, 449–451/9th ed. pages 459–460, 463–465)

CRYSTALLINE SOLIDS

Crystalline solids are classified according to the type of particle that occupies the lattice points: atoms, molecules, or ions. The four types of crystalline solids are molecular, ionic, metallic, and network covalent. The table below describes each of these solids.

Type of Solid	Molecular	Ionic	Atomic	Metallic	Network Covalent
Examples	$C_6H_{12}O_6$	NaCl	Ar	Cu	C (diamond)
Particles occupying lattice points	Molecule	Ions	Atoms	Atoms	Atoms
Bonds or forces between lattice points	Dispersion forces	Ionic	Dispersion forces	Delocalized nondirectional metallic	Covalent
Melting points	Low	High	Low	High (1083°C)	Very high (3500°C)
Electrical conductivity as solid	None	None	None	Yes	None
Electrical conductivity when melted	None	Yes	None	Yes	None
Other properties		Brittle		Malleable and ductile	Insulator very hard

A lattice is a three-dimensional system of points designating the points of the components (atoms, molecules, or ions) that make up the substance. A unit cell is the smallest repeating unit of a lattice.

AMORPHOUS SOLIDS

Amorphous solids, such as rubber and glass, have particles with no orderly structure.

STRUCTURE AND BONDING IN METALS

Metallic bonding is characterized as an array of positively charged nuclei surrounded by a "sea" of mobile electrons. It is said that the bonding is nondirectional; the metallic atoms can easily slide over each other because the environment will be the same. This model explains the observed properties of metals: they are malleable, conductive, can be formed into thin sheets and pulled into wires (ductile).

ALLOYS

Alloys are mixtures of metallic elements and have metallic properties. Substitutional alloys, like brass and sterling silver, have host metal atoms replaced by atoms of similar size. Brass is a substitutional alloy made of copper and zinc. Interstitial alloys have smaller atoms occupying the empty spaces between the metal atoms within the structure. The presence of the smaller atoms changes the properties of the host making it harder and stronger. Steel is an interstitial alloy containing iron and carbon.

CHANGES IN STATE

HEATING CURVES

(*Chemistry* 8th ed. pages 473–478/9th ed. pages 485–490)

Chapter 11 (Big Idea 5) includes a discussion of the quantitative aspects of the heating curve. Energy is added at a constant rate to a solid and a plot of temperature vs. time is drawn. The first plateau on the heating curve represents the melting point of the substance. The second plateau on the heating curve represents the boiling point of the substance. The temperature does not change during melting or boiling because the energy added is used to overcome intermolecular forces.

Usually, the plateau for the boiling point is longer in duration than the melting plateau because it takes more energy to separate the molecules from a liquid into a gaseous state than from a solid into a liquid state. This greater energy is related to the greater forces that must be overcome.

MULTIPLE-CHOICE QUESTIONS

No calculators are to be used in this section.

1. Water has a higher capillary action than mercury due to
   (A) higher dipole–dipole forces between the water molecules
   (B) strong cohesive forces within water
   (C) weak adhesive forces in water
   (D) strong cohesive forces in water which work with strong adhesive forces

2. Small drops of water tend to bead up because of
   (A) high capillary action
   (B) the shape of the meniscus
   (C) the resistance to increased surface area
   (D) low London dispersion forces

3. The vapor pressure increases in a predictable order as shown as
   (A) $CH_4 < C_2H_5OH < C_2H_5–O–C_2H_5 < Ne$
   (B) $Ne < CH_4 < C_2H_5–O–C_2H_5 < C_2H_5–OH$
   (C) $C_2H_5–OH < C_2H_5–O–C_2H_5 < CH_4 < Ne$
   (D) $C_2H_5–O–C_2H_5 < C_2H_5–OH < Ne < CH_4$

4. Several liquids are compared by adding them to a series of 50-mL graduated cylinders, then dropping a steel ball of uniform size and mass into each. The time required for the ball to reach the bottom of the cylinder is noted. This is a method used to compare the differences in a property of liquids known as
   (A) surface tension
   (B) buoyancy
   (C) capillary action
   (D) viscosity

5. The properties of solids vary with their bonding. An example of this is shown by
   (A) ionic solids with strong electrostatic attractions called ionic bonds, which have high melting temperatures
   (B) molecular solids with high intermolecular forces which have high melting temperatures
   (C) ionic solids with highly mobile ions which have high conductance
   (D) amorphous solids with strong London dispersion forces and high vapor pressure

6. As you go down the noble gas family on the periodic table, the boiling temperature increases. This trend is due mainly to
   (A) an increase in hydrogen bonding
   (B) a decrease in dipole–dipole forces
   (C) the lower atomic masses as you go down the family
   (D) an increase in London dispersion forces

7. Graphite and diamond are network solids, but graphite is slippery, black, and a conductor, while diamond is hard, colorless, and an insulator. This is because
   (A) graphite and diamond are made of different elements
   (B) diamond is made up of tetrahedrally bonded carbon atoms, while graphite is made up of fused six-membered rings arranged in sheets
   (C) graphite contains impurities that result in a less dense solid
   (D) diamond contains covalent bonds, while graphite contains ionic bonds

8. Which of the following properties of water is/are due to the intermolecular hydrogen bonding between the water molecules?
   (A) Ice floats on water.
   (B) Water has a high heat of vaporization.
   (C) The specific heat of water (4.184 J/°C·g) is much higher than that of lead (0.128 J/°C·g).
   (D) All of the above.

9. The substances neon, sodium fluoride, carbon monoxide, and methylamine all have low molar masses. Order these substances in increasing boiling points or melting points.
   (A) Ne   <   CO   < CH_3NH_2 <   NaF
   (B) NaF   <   CO   < CH_3NH_2 <   Ne
   (C) Ne   < CH_3NH_2 <   CO   <   NaF
   (D) CH_3NH_2 <   CO   <   NaF   <   Ne

10. A substance with strong intermolecular forces of attraction would be expected to have
    (A) a low boiling point
    (B) a high vapor pressure
    (C) a high heat of vaporization
    (D) a high solubility in water

11. Consider a closed flask containing a liquid and its vapor. Which statement is *incorrect*?
    (A) The vapor exerts a pressure called the vapor pressure.
    (B) Increasing the temperature of the liquid would lead to a greater vapor pressure.
    (C) Evaporation and condensation will eventually cease after a constant pressure has been attained.
    (D) Increasing the volume of the container at constant temperature would cause increased condensation until the pressure of the vapor was once again the same as it had been.

12. 1-Butanol ($CH_3CH_2CH_2CH_2OH$) would be expected to have a higher boiling temperature than 1-propanol ($CH_3CH_2CH_2OH$) because
    (A) it has a higher molar mass
    (B) its longer carbon chain and greater number of electrons result in more London dispersion forces
    (C) its hydrogen bonding is stronger
    (D) it is a less polar molecule

13. A substance is found to be nonconductive, to have a relatively low melting point, and to be insoluble in water. This is most likely
    (A) a metal
    (B) an ionic solid
    (C) a molecular solid
    (D) a network covalent solid

14. The fact that metals are conductive is best explained by which of the following statements?
    (A) The metal nuclei reside in a "sea" of delocalized electrons.
    (B) The metals form anions and cations which allow electrons to travel.
    (C) The metals have extra electrons which can carry a charge.
    (D) all of these

15. The type of bonding in a solid can be tested by placing the substance in water because
    (A) soluble ionic substances form conductive aqueous solutions
    (B) soluble covalently bonded substances form aqueous solutions that are not conductive
    (C) most network solids are not soluble in water
    (D) all of the above are true

FREE-RESPONSE QUESTIONS

Calculators and equation tables may be used.

1. Four solids are tested for conductivity as solids, solubility in water, and conductivity in aqueous solution if soluble. The results are listed below.

	A	B	C	D
Conducts as solid?	Y	N	N	N
Soluble in water?	N	Y	N	Y
Forms conductive solution?	N	Y	N	N

Identify the type of bonding present in each solid based on these data. Describe explicitly how the data lead to your conclusions.

2. Stearic acid is a primary component of animal fat, which is solid at room temperature. Oleic acid is a component of olive oil, which is liquid at room temperature. What intermolecular forces account for these observations?

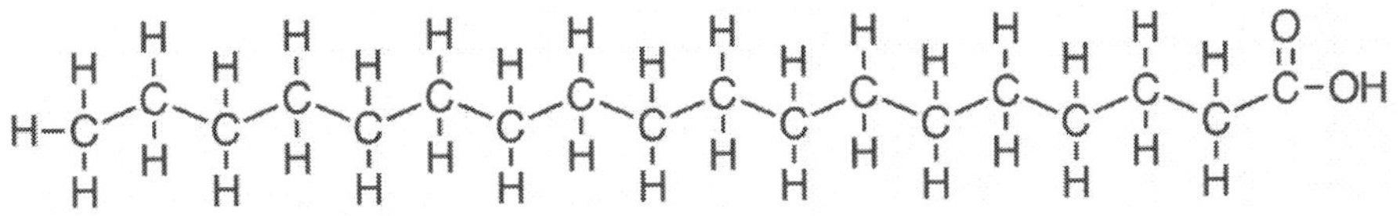

Stearic acid

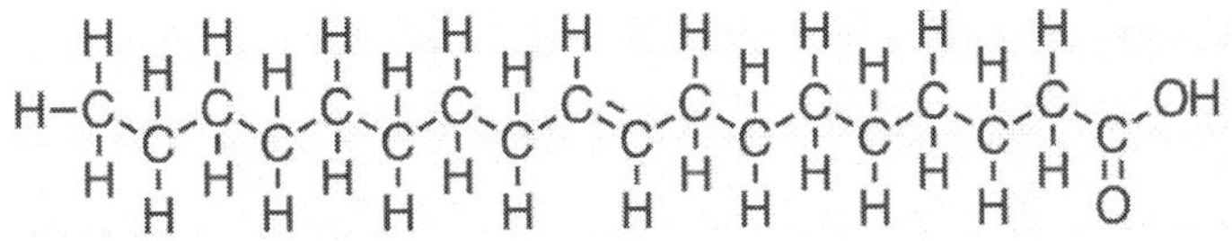

Oleic acid

Answers

MULTIPLE-CHOICE QUESTIONS

1. **D** The strong adhesive forces lead to a creeping effect as water moves up the narrow tubing and the strong cohesive forces attempt to minimize the surface area (*Chemistry* 8th ed. pages 443–444/9th ed. pages 458–459). LO 2.3

2. **C** This is a description of surface tension, which is a result of high dipole–dipole forces between water molecules. These intermolecular forces are also called hydrogen bonds (*Chemistry* 8th ed. pages 443–444/9th ed. pages 458–459). LO 2.3

3. **C** Examining the IMF will suggest that only the alcohol (C_2H_5–OH) has an exposed –OH, suggesting strong hydrogen bonding. The other three are essentially controlled by weaker London dispersion

forces, which are greater in the larger, more massive compound. Realize also that the higher the IMF, the lower the vapor pressure (*Chemistry* 8th ed. pages 471–473/9th ed. pages 483–485). LO 2.16

4. **D** The resistance to flow of any fluid is called viscosity. As you would predict, liquids with high viscosity (e.g., maple syrup) have large intermolecular forces (*Chemistry* 8th ed. pages 443–444/9th ed. pages 458–459). LO 2.3

5. **A** Ionic bonds are unusually strong, requiring high temperatures to melt ionic substances. Table salt, for example, which is Na^+Cl^-, melts at 804°C (*Chemistry* 8th ed. pages 466–471, esp. Table 10.7/9th ed. pages 479–483, esp. Table 10.7). LO 2.19, LO 2.26, LO 2.32

6. **D** These very symmetrical atoms are nonpolar; except for the induced dispersion forces, they would all boil at 0 K. As it is, He boils at 4 K and Ne at 25 K (*Chemistry* 8th ed. pages 440–443/9th ed. pages 455–458). LO 2.11

7. **B** Both graphite and diamond are made up of the same element, carbon, and in both cases the atoms are covalently bonded to each other. The sheets of graphite can slip over each other, giving it a slippery quality, and electrons in unhybridized orbitals allow conductivity. Diamond has no unhybridized electrons and does not conduct electricity (*Chemistry* 8th ed. pages 457–468, esp. Figure 10.22/9th ed. pages 471–480, esp. Figure 10.26). LO 2.30

8. **D** All of the anomalous properties of water are due to the exceptionally effective intermolecular hydrogen bonding (*Chemistry* 8th ed. pages 439–444, 450, 467–468/9th ed. pages 455–459, 464, 479–480). LO 2.16

9. **A** The intermolecular forces in order are London dispersion forces, the weakest, then dipole-dipole, then hydrogen bonding, and lastly the strongest being ionic forces holding the lattice of NaF together (*Chemistry* 8th ed. pages 440–443/9th ed. pages 455–458). LO 2.16

10. **C** A high heat of vaporization would be expected of a substance with strong intermolecular forces because a significant amount of energy would be required to liberate the molecules from the liquid to gaseous state. Low boiling point, low melting point, high solubility in water, and a high vapor pressure would indicate that the forces holding the molecules together are relatively weak; therefore, the molecules are able to be separated more easily by added energy or outside forces of attraction, as is the case with the solvent in its ability to act on the solute (*Chemistry* 8th ed. pages 440–443/9th ed. pages 455–458). LO 2.16

11. **C** Once an equilibrium vapor pressure has been reached at a given temperature within the container, the rate of condensation and rate of evaporation become equal but neither one ceases (*Chemistry* 8th ed. pages 471–478/9th ed. pages 483–490). LO 2.16

12. **B** The longer carbon chain, rather than the molar mass per se, leads to greater London dispersion forces holding the molecules together (*Chemistry* 8th ed. pages 440–443, 471–474/9th ed. pages 455–458, 483–486). LO 2.16

13. **C** In network solids, atoms or molecules bond together with strong directional covalent bonds. Two important network solids are diamond and silica (*Chemistry* 8th ed. pages 449–451, 457–462/9th ed. pages 463–465, 471–476). LO 2.22

14. **A** The "electron sea" model was developed to explain metal conductivity. Although metals do form cations, this does not explain why elemental metals are conductive. Anions are substances with "extra" electrons, and metals generally do not form anions (*Chemistry* 8th ed. pages 454–455/9th ed. pages 468–469). LO 2.26

15. **D** (*Chemistry* 8th ed. pages 440–443, 471–474/9th ed. pages 455–458, 483–486). LO 2.22

FREE-RESPONSE QUESTIONS

1. Solid A is most likely metallic. The delocalized "sea of electrons" results in high conductivity. Lack of solubility in water indicates that the intermolecular forces are very strong (*Chemistry* 8th ed. pages 454–455/9th ed. pages 468–469). LO 2.22

   Solid B is most likely ionic. Ionic solids are not conductive because their electrons are localized around their respective nuclei. Many ionic solids are soluble in water, and when they dissolve they split up into cations and anions which are attracted to the polar water molecules. The separation of charges leads to formation of a conductive solution (*Chemistry* 8th ed. pages 132–136, 341–343/9th ed. pages 141–145, 352–355). LO 2.22

   Solid C is most likely network covalent, such as sand or diamond. These solids are not particularly conductive because the electrons are localized in the covalent bonds between the atoms. They are also not soluble in polar solvents because the molecules themselves are covalently bonded to each other (*Chemistry* 8th ed. pages 444–446, 449–451/9th ed. pages 458–460, 463–465). LO 2.22

   Solid D is most likely molecular. Like network covalent solids, the electrons are localized in the covalent bonds between the atoms. However, many are soluble in water because they are attracted to each other primarily by London dispersion forces, which can be overcome by the attraction of polar parts of the molecules to polar water (*Chemistry* 8th ed. pages 444–446, 449–451/9th ed. pages 458–460, 463–465). LO 2.22

2. Both molecules are essentially nonpolar because of their very long carbon chains. The primary intermolecular attraction is London dispersion forces. Stearic acid is solid because it has a straight chain so its molecules have many contact points and strong London dispersion forces overall. The double bond in oleic acid creates a kink so there are fewer contact points and weaker London dispersion forces. Therefore, oleic acid is a liquid (*Chemistry* 8th ed. pages 442–443/9th ed. pages 457–458). LO 2.16

6

BIG IDEA 2: SOLUTIONS

Big Idea 2

Chemical and physical properties of materials can be explained by the structure and the arrangement of atoms, ions, or molecules and the forces between them.

In this section, the properties of liquid solutions will be reviewed. Solution composition and factors affecting solubility will be covered.

You should be able to
- Perform calculations with different solution concentrations such as molarity and dilution (note that these are described in more detail in Big Idea 3).
- Explain how the attractions between ions and solvents affect factors determining the solubility of ionic solids and molecules in water and other solvents.
- Draw pictures of or explain representations of solutions that illustrate the interactions between solute and solvent.
- Design or explain the results of separation experiments (chromatography, filtration, distillation) based on the relative strengths of interactions among and between the components. Draw pictures of or explain representations of solutions that illustrate the interactions.

SOLUTIONS AND THEIR COMPOSITIONS

(*Chemistry* 8th ed. pages 498–500/9th ed. pages 511–513)

TYPES OF SOLUTIONS

(*Chemistry* 8th ed. page 498/9th ed. page 511)

A solution is a homogeneous mixture. The table below summarizes the different types of solutions that can exist. In this chapter, the focus will be on liquid solutions.

Various Types of Solutions

Example	State of Solution	State of Solute	State of Solvent
Air, natural gas	Gas	Gas	Gas
Alcohol in water, antifreeze	Liquid	Liquid	Liquid
Brass (copper and zinc)	Solid	Solid	Solid
Carbonated water (soda)	Liquid	Gas	Liquid
Seawater, sugar solution	Liquid	Solid	Liquid
Hydrogen in platinum	Solid	Gas	Solid

The substance being dissolved is the *solute*. When referring to a liquid-liquid or gas-gas solution, the *solvent* is the substance present in the largest amount.

COMPOSITION

(*Chemistry* 8th ed. pages 498–500/9th ed. pages 511–513)

MOLARITY   The molarity, *M*, of a solution (its concentration) is the number of moles of solute per liter of solution.

EXAMPLE: A solution is prepared by mixing 30.0 mL of butane (C_4H_{10}, $d = 0.600$ g/mL) with 65.0 mL of octane (C_8H_{18}, $d = 0.700$ g/mL). Assuming that the volumes add in mixing, calculate concentration of butane in the solution.

SOLUTION:

Butane is the solute because less of it is used. First find the moles of butane.

$$30.0 \text{ mL} \times \frac{0.600 \text{ g}}{1 \text{ mL}} \times \frac{1 \text{ mol}}{58.1 \text{ g}} = 0.310 \text{ mol C}_4\text{H}_{10}$$

The new solution volume is 95.0 mL, or 0.0950 L. Use this to find the molarity.

$$\frac{0.310 \text{ mol C}_4\text{H}_{10}}{0.0950 \text{ L}} = 3.26 \ M$$

FACTORS AFFECTING SOLUBILITY

(*Chemistry* 8th ed. pages 504–507/9th ed. pages 517–520)

The formation of a liquid solution begins by separating the solute into its individual components. Next, the solvent's intermolecular forces must be overcome to make room for the solute. The solute and solvent then interact to form the solution.

STRUCTURAL EFFECTS

Solubility is favored if the solute and solvent have similar intermolecular forces, as determined by their structure. The table below summarizes the solubility of different types of solutes in different types of solvents.

Type of Solute	Type of Solvent	Solubility	Example
Ionic	Polar	Usually soluble	LiCl in H_2O
Polar	Polar	Soluble (miscible)	CH_3OH in H_2O
Nonpolar	Polar	Insoluble (immiscible)	C_6H_{14} in H_2O
Nonpolar	Nonpolar	Soluble (miscible)	C_6H_{14} in CCl_4

EXAMPLE: Discuss the solubility of each of the following solutes in carbon tetrachloride (CCl_4): ammonium nitrate (NH_4NO_3), 1-pentanol ($CH_3CH_2CH_2CH_2CH_2OH$), and pentane ($CH_3CH_2CH_2CH_2CH_3$). Explain why each solute will or will not dissolve.

SOLUTION: First decide which substances are polar. CCl_4 has a central C covalently bonded to identical Cl atoms, so it is nonpolar and nonpolar solutes will dissolve in it. Ammonium nitrate is an ionic compound so it will dissolve in a polar solvent like water; it will not dissolve in a nonpolar solvent. 1-Propanol contains a polar hydroxyl group and will not be soluble in CCl_4. Pentane is a chain of carbons covalently bonded to each other and to hydrogen atoms, so it is nonpolar. It will be miscible (will form a homogeneous mixture) with CCl_4.

MULTIPLE-CHOICE QUESTIONS

No calculators may be used on this part of the exam.

1. The number of moles of $Al(NO_3)_3$ which must be added to water to form 2.00 L of 0.30 M NO_3^- ions is
   (A) 0.60 mol
   (B) 0.20 mol
   (C) 2.4 mol
   (D) 8.0 mol

2. When an ionic salt dissolves in water, the solute–solvent interaction is
   (A) hydrogen bonding
   (B) London forces
   (C) ion–ion forces
   (D) ion–dipole forces

3. When a polar molecule dissolves in water, the solute–solvent interaction is
   (A) hydrogen bonding
   (B) London forces
   (C) dipole–dipole forces
   (D) either (A) or (C)

4. Distillation separates molecules based on differences in
   (A) solubility
   (B) boiling points
   (C) freezing points
   (D) conductivity

5. Why do mineral deposits accumulate on the heating coil of a water distiller?
   (A) The minerals are attracted to the metal surface.
   (B) The water contains solids that are not visible.
   (C) Heating water reduces salt solubility.
   (D) When the water vaporizes, soluble salts precipitate out.

6. How much 12.0 M hydrochloric acid must be used to prepare 2.00 L of a 3.00 M hydrochloric acid solution?
   (A) 250.0 mL
   (B) 50.0 mL
   (C) 500.0 mL
   (D) 100.0 mL

7. In column chromatography, the first substance eluted
   (A) has a high affinity for the mobile phase
   (B) is insoluble in the mobile phase
   (C) precipitates out of the mobile phase
   (D) moves more slowly through the stationary phase than other substances in solution

8. Which of the following pairs of compounds will not form a homogeneous solution?
   (A) sodium chloride and water
   (B) sodium chloride and mineral oil
   (C) water and ethanol
   (D) water and sucrose

9. Over time, a solution of ethanol in water left open to the atmosphere
   (A) does not change concentration because the hydrogen bonds between OH groups of ethanol and OH groups of water are strong
   (B) becomes more concentrated because water is more volatile than ethanol
   (C) becomes less concentrated because ethanol is more volatile than water
   (D) changes in volume, but not concentration, because the hydrogen bonds between OH groups of ethanol and OH groups of water are strong

10. A small amount of copper is added to silver to form sterling silver. This is
    (A) a chemical reaction because the metal atoms bond with each other
    (B) a solution formation, with copper as the solvent and silver as the solute
    (C) a solution formation, with silver as the solvent and copper as the solute
    (D) a chemical reaction because the metals will exchange electrons

11. When a mixture of oil and water sits undisturbed, two distinct layers will form. This is because
    (A) oil molecules are attracted to each other by London dispersion forces and water molecules are attracted to each other by hydrogen bonding, so the two substances separate
    (B) oil and water react to form a new substance that rises to the top
    (C) the less dense substance will rise to the top
    (D) (A) and (C) are true

12. Which equation for dissolving a salt in water is written correctly?
    (A) $Na_2SO_4 \rightarrow Na_2^{2+} + SO_4^{2-}$
    (B) $Na_2SO_4 \rightarrow 2\ Na^+ + SO_4^{2-}$
    (C) $Na_2SO_4 \rightarrow 2\ Na^+ + S^{2-} + 4\ O^{2-}$
    (D) $Na_2SO_4 \rightarrow Na_2^{2+} + S^{2-} + 4\ O^{2-}$

13. Which solute would dissolve in carbon tetrachloride, CCl_4?
    (A) SrF_2
    (B) CH_3OH
    (C) CH_2O
    (D) NaCl

14. Order the following solvents from least polar to most polar:

    C_6H_{14} H_2O CH_3OH $CHCl_3$

    (A) H_2O < CH_3OH < $CHCl_3$ < C_6H_{14}
    (B) C_6H_{14} < CH_3OH < $CHCl_3$ < H_2O
    (C) $CHCl_3$ < C_6H_{14} < CH_3OH < H_2O
    (D) C_6H_{14} < $CHCl_3$ < CH_3OH < H_2O

15. What is the sodium ion concentration when 70.0 mL of 3.0 M Na_2CO_3 is added to 30.0 mL of 1.0 M $NaHCO_3$?
    (A) 0.45 M
    (B) 4.5 M
    (C) 2.4 M
    (D) 5.1 M

FREE-RESPONSE QUESTIONS

1. You are given a sample of seawater contaminated by an oil spill. Describe how you would separate the various components of this mixture to determine the mass of each present (dissolved solids, water, oil). Indicate which mass measurement will be least accurate. The oil may contain some volatile nonpolar substances that are slightly soluble in water. The following equipment is available for you to use:

   Safety goggles   Hot plate
   Wash bottle of distilled water   Ring stand
   Beakers of various sizes   Watch glass
   Filter paper and funnel   Evaporating dish   Desiccator
   Distillation apparatus   Wash bottle of acetone
   Electronic balance with accuracy of ± 0.001 g

2. Sodium chloride is soluble in water but only slightly soluble in ethanol. Use illustrations labeled with the relevant intermolecular forces to explain these observations.

Answers

MULTIPLE-CHOICE QUESTIONS

1. **B** Since every $Al(NO_3)_3$ unit contains 3 units of NO_3^- ions, you need 1/3 as many $Al(NO_3)_3$ units as NO_3^- units. Needed are 0.30 mol/L of NO_3^- × 2.00 L = 0.60 mol NO_3^-. Hence 1/3 × 0.60 mol = 0.20 mol $Al(NO_3)_3$ required (*Chemistry* 8th ed. page 499/9th ed. page 512). LO 2.9

2. **D** Water has a dipole which can either be attracted to the negative anion within the crystal lattice or the positive cation (*Chemistry* 8th ed. pages 130–132, 501–505/9th ed. pages 139–141, 514–518). LO 2.15

3. **D** Water has a dipole which can either be attracted to the positive or negative end of a polar molecule. Water can also form hydrogen bonds with molecules that can also form hydrogen bonds

(*Chemistry* 8th ed. pages 130–132, 501–505/9th ed. pages 139–141, 514–518). LO 2.13

4. **B** In distillation, solutions are heated so that components are separated based on their boiling temperatures, with the most volatile substances evaporating first (*Chemistry* 8th ed. page 27/9th ed. page 29). LO 2.10

5. **D** When the water vaporizes, dissolved salts do not. The concentration of ions increases until precipitation occurs (*Chemistry* 8th ed. page 508/9th ed. page 520). LO 2.10

6. **C** Use the expression $M_1V_1 = M_2V_2$. Remember that the volume unit you are solving for will be the same as the volume unit you know, in this case liters, so you will have to convert from L to mL

$$2.00\ \text{L} \times \frac{3.00\ M}{12.0\ M} = 0.500\ \text{L}$$

(*Chemistry* 8th ed. pages 141–144/9th ed. pages 150–153). LO 2.9

7. **A** The component with the highest affinity for the mobile phase will elute first (*Chemistry* 8th ed. pages 28, 440–443/9th ed. pages 30, 455–458). LO 2.7

8. **B** Mineral oil only has London dispersion forces and cannot dissolve charged substances to any great extent. Water has dipole–dipole forces which strongly attract ions (*Chemistry* 8th ed. pages 440–443/9th ed. pages 455–458). LO 2.13

9. **C** Both liquids will evaporate, but ethanol will evaporate more. Water can make two hydrogen bonds per molecule, but ethanol can only make one. Because ethanol has fewer intermolecular forces of attraction, it will evaporate more quickly than water, lowering the solution concentration (*Chemistry* 8th ed. pages 471–474/9th ed. pages 483–486). LO 2.16

10. **C** The two metals combine to form an alloy. Copper is present in the smallest amount, so it is the solute, and silver is the solvent (*Chemistry* 8th ed. pages 455–457/9th ed. pages 469–471). LO 2.25

11. **D** Polar and nonpolar liquids will separate from each other. Oil is less dense than water, so it will form the top layer (*Chemistry* 8th ed. pages 440–443/9th ed. pages 455–458). LO 2.13

12. **B** The cation is Na^+, and the anion is the polyatomic sulfate, SO_4^{2-} (*Chemistry* 8th ed. page 28/9th ed. page 30). LO 2.23

13. **C** Draw Lewis structures to determine the polarity of the various substances. CH_2O is only slightly polar, so it will dissolve in CCl_4, which is nonpolar

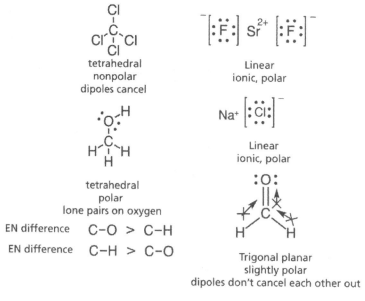

tetrahedral
nonpolar
dipoles cancel

Linear
ionic, polar

Linear
ionic, polar

tetrahedral
polar
lone pairs on oxygen

EN difference   C–O > C–H

EN difference   C–H > C–O

Trigonal planar
slightly polar
dipoles don't cancel each other out

EN difference   C–O > C–H

(*Chemistry* 8th ed. pages 346–349, 365–371, 440–443/9th ed. pages 358–361, 376–382, 455–458). LO 2.21

14. **D**

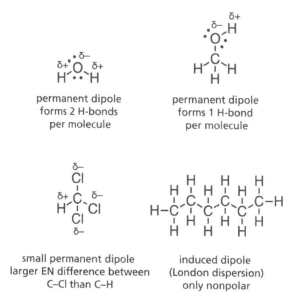

permanent dipole
forms 2 H-bonds
per molecule

permanent dipole
forms 1 H-bond
per molecule

small permanent dipole
larger EN difference between
C–Cl than C–H

induced dipole
(London dispersion)
only nonpolar

(*Chemistry* 8th ed. pages 346–349, 365–371, 440–443/9th ed. pages 358–361, 376–382, 455–458). LO 2.21

15. **B** First, find the moles of Na^+ each solution contributes.

Note that there are 2 moles of Na^+ per mole of Na_2CO_3, so the effective $[Na^+]$ is 6.0 M in Na_2CO_3:

$$70.0 \text{ mL} \times \frac{6.0 \text{ mol}}{1000 \text{ mL}} = 0.420 \text{ mol Na}^+$$

The moles of Na^+ from $NaHCO_3$ are:

$$30.0 \text{ mL} \times \frac{1.0 \text{ mol}}{1000 \text{ mL}} = 0.030 \text{ mol Na}^+$$

The total Na^+ is 0.420 + 0.030 = 0.450 moles.
The total volume is 70.0 + 30.0 = 100. mL.

The concentration is 4.5 M (*Chemistry* 8th ed. page 499/9th ed. page 512). LO 2.9

FREE-RESPONSE QUESTIONS

1. (a) Think about how to approach this problem. The oil is nonpolar and should float on top of the water. The polar salts are dissolved in the water and must be isolated by removing the water.
    (b) Put on your safety goggles and pour the sample into a tared beaker large enough to hold all the material. Record the initial mass.
    (c) Allow the solution to settle until most of the oil appears to have risen to the top. Decant the oil into a tared beaker and record its mass.
    (d) Place the remaining liquid into a distillation apparatus and heat gently at first to remove any volatile nonpolar material. Collect this material in a tared beaker and record its mass.
    (e) Raise the temperature until the water in the pot distills. At this point, the temperature of the solution will be constant. When the temperature begins going up again, indicating that most of the water has been removed, stop distillation. The material remaining in the pot will probably not be completely dry. Use a wash bottle of distilled water to transfer the mass to a tared evaporating dish.
    (f) Heat the remainder gently on a hot plate under the hood to remove any remaining water. If the solids appear gummy, indicating the presence of oil residue, wash with acetone, decanting the wash solution to an appropriate waste container, and continue heating until the solids are dry. Let cool in a desiccator to room temperature and find the mass.
    (g) The masses of oil, of volatile nonpolar material, and of dissolved solids can be found directly. The mass of water should be determined by subtraction from the original mass, since some water remained in the solids at the end of distillation. The amount of oil will be underestimated because it is difficult to remove all the oil by decanting, and whatever was not decanted remained on the salts and was washed off in step f (*Chemistry* 8th ed. pages 26–29/9th ed. pages 27–31). LO 2.10

2. Ionic substances dissolve if the forces of attraction between the cations and anions are less than the forces of attraction between the ions and the solvent. Water is very polar so the attraction between its negative oxygen and Na^+, and between its positive hydrogens and Cl^-, is greater than the attraction between Na^+ and Cl^-. Ethanol has a nonpolar end and a polar end, and is overall less polar than water. Therefore, it is not able to separate as many NaCl molecules as water can, and NaCl is less soluble in ethanol.

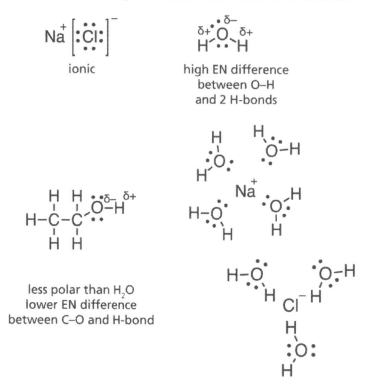

(*Chemistry* 8th ed. pages 440–443/9th ed. pages 455–458). LO 2.8

Big Idea 3:
Chemical Reactions

Big Idea 3

Changes in matter involve the rearrangement and/or reorganization of atoms and/or the transfer of electrons.

The two main kinds of changes studied in chemistry are phase changes (melting, evaporating, freezing) and rearrangement of atoms. Both processes are accompanied either by the release or absorption of energy. In Chapter 7 you learn about the types of reactions, balancing equations, predicting products of chemical reactions, and writing complete and net ionic equations. In Chapter 8 you learn about stoichiometry—calculations relating amounts of reactants and products. Chapter 9 focuses on electrochemistry, a specific application of oxidation–reduction processes. You need to have a qualitative understanding of the energy changes associated with a reaction or process, but specific calculations are covered in Big Idea 5.

You should be able to
- Classify reactions by type.
- Write balanced molecular equations, complete ionic equations, and net ionic equations.
- Predict if a precipitate will form (the only solubility rule you need to memorize is that all Na^+, K^+, NH_4^+, and NO_3^- salts are soluble).
- Identify compounds as Brønsted–Lowry acids and bases based on evidence of proton transfer in the balanced reaction equation.

■ Identify a reaction as oxidation-reduction based on evidence of electron transfer, and balance the reaction equation.

■ Predict products of reactions, given the chemical names of the reactants.

AP Tip

Be sure to know the most common charges of transition metal ions and the physical states of elements at room temperature (i.e., if calcium is placed into water, write as Ca not Ca^{2+}). Write solids, liquids, and gases in molecular form (i.e., write hydrogen chloride gas as HCl, not as separate ions).

EVIDENCE OF A CHEMICAL REACTION

You should be able to recognize macroscopic evidence that a chemical reaction has occurred, including:

Releasing heat or light (exothermic) or cooling off (endothermic)
(*Chemistry* 8th ed. page 238/9th ed. page 248)

Formation of a solid when two aqueous solutions are combined (precipitation)
(*Chemistry* 8th ed. page 145/9th ed. page 153)

Color change, usually because of an indicator in an acid–base reaction or of the formation of products differently colored than the reactants
(*Chemistry* 8th ed. pages 157–158, 728–733/9th ed. pages 166–167, 742–747)

Gas formation, usually in acid–base reactions and in oxidation–reduction reactions

    EXAMPLE: $2\ HCl(aq) + CaCO_3(s) \rightarrow H_2O(l) + CaCl_2(aq) + CO_2(g)$

    EXAMPLE: $2\ H_2O(l) \rightarrow 2\ H_2(g) + O_2(g)$

DESCRIBING REACTIONS IN AQUEOUS SOLUTION

(*Chemistry* 8th ed. pages 150–151/9th ed. pages 158–160)

MOLECULAR EQUATION

A molecular equation gives the overall reaction. It gives information on stoichiometry, and you can deduce whether or not the compounds exist as ions in solution by looking at the phases of matter. For example, in the following equation, both reactants [$KCl(aq)$, $Pb(NO_3)_2(aq)$] are ions, and one product $KNO_3(aq)$ exists as ions: $2\ KCl(aq) + Pb(NO_3)_2(aq) \rightarrow PbCl_2(s) + 2\ KNO_3(aq)$.

COMPLETE IONIC EQUATION

The complete ionic equation gives the equation including all the ions in solution. For example, $2 K^+ + 2 Cl^- + Pb^{2+} + 2 NO_3^- \rightarrow PbCl_2(s) + 2 K^+ + 2 NO_3^-$. The states are aqueous, unless otherwise indicated. Writing species as ions implies that they are in aqueous solution.

NET IONIC EQUATION

When writing a net ionic equation, eliminate the ions that are the same on both reactant and product side; these are called "spectator ions." Only those species that undergo a chemical change are included. The equation must still be balanced!

$$Pb^{2+}(aq) + 2 Cl^-(aq) \rightarrow PbCl_2(s)$$

TYPES OF REACTIONS

Classification of chemical reactions by type allows the prediction of products if given the reactants.

Main Reaction Types
Precipitation
Acid-base
Redox (oxidation-reduction), including Combustion
Synthesis/Decomposition (may also be Redox)

PRECIPITATION REACTIONS

(Chemistry 8th ed. pages 154–165/9th ed. pages 163–174)

Precipitation reactions involve the formation of a solid when two solutions are mixed.

PREDICTING PRECIPITATES

When two solutions of ionic compounds are mixed, exchange anions to form products, remembering that each product formed must be neutral. If no solid is formed, there is no chemical reaction! The only solubility rule you must memorize is that all Na^+, K^+, NH_4^+, and NO_3^- salts are soluble. You can deduce other rules from the context of the question.

EXAMPLE: Write the molecular, complete ionic, and net ionic equations when solutions of potassium chloride and lead(II) nitrate are mixed and a solid product is formed.

SOLUTION:
MOLECULAR EQUATION:

$$2 KCl(aq) + Pb(NO_3)_2(aq) \rightarrow PbCl_2(s) + 2 KNO_3(aq)$$

Lead(II) chloride must be the solid because all nitrates are soluble.

COMPLETE IONIC EQUATION:

$$\cancel{2\ K^+} + 2\ Cl^- + Pb^{2+} + \cancel{2\ NO_3^-} \rightarrow PbCl_2(s) + \cancel{2\ K^+} + \cancel{2\ NO_3^-}$$

NET IONIC EQUATION: $Pb^{2+} + 2\ Cl^- \rightarrow PbCl_2(s)$

Be sure to write the equation in whatever form is requested by the AP exam. When in doubt, write the molecular equation.

ACID–BASE THEORIES: ARRHENIUS AND BRØNSTED–LOWRY

(*Chemistry* 8th ed. pages 639–642/9th ed. pages 653–656)

To work with acid–base reactions, you must be able to identify acids and bases.

The first definition of acids and bases was the Arrhenius theory which states that, in aqueous solution (water), acids produce hydrogen ions and bases produce hydroxide ions.

The Brønsted–Lowry theory says that an acid is a proton (H^+) donor and a base is a proton acceptor. It is more general than the Arrhenius theory, in which only hydroxide bases are considered.

ACID–BASE REACTIONS

(*Chemistry* 8th ed. pages 154–161/9th ed. pages 163–170)

Acid + Base → Salt + H_2O

Memorize the list of strong acids and strong bases below. All others are weak acids or bases.

Strong Acids	Strong Bases
HCl, HBr, HI	Group I Hydroxides, (LiOH, NaOH . . .)
H_2SO_4 ($HSO_4^- =$ weak)	
HNO_3	
$HClO_4$	

STRONG ACID–STRONG BASE REACTIONS

(*Chemistry* 8th ed. page 154/9th ed. page 163)

Strong acids and bases are assumed to be 100% ionized in aqueous solution; write all reactants in ionic form. After combining the proton and the proton acceptor, the remaining cation(s) and anion(s) make up the salt, which in most cases will be soluble.

For the examples that follow, all states are aqueous, unless otherwise indicated.

EXAMPLE: Equimolar solutions of hydrochloric acid and sodium hydroxide are mixed.

SOLUTION: Starting with the complete ionic equation:

$$H^+ + Cl^- + Na^+ + OH^- \rightarrow Na^+ + Cl^- + H_2O(l)$$

Omit spectator ions to get the net ionic equation:

$$H^+ + OH^- \rightarrow H_2O(l)$$

Note: For most strong acid–strong base reactions, this will be the net ionic equation, but make sure that the salt formed is soluble.

WEAK ACID–STRONG BASE REACTIONS (OR STRONG ACID–WEAK BASE)

(*Chemistry* 8th ed. page 155/9th ed. page 164)

Weak acids and bases ionize only slightly. Write the formula for the weak acid or weak base in molecular form (do not separate into ions!).

EXAMPLE: Write the net ionic equation for the reaction when equimolar solutions of acetic acid and sodium hydroxide are mixed.

SOLUTION: $HC_2H_3O_2(aq) + Na^+ + OH^- \rightleftharpoons Na^+ + C_2H_3O_2^- + H_2O(l)$

Omit spectator ions to get: $HC_2H_3O_2(aq) + OH^- \rightleftharpoons C_2H_3O_2^- + H_2O(l)$

All states are aqueous, unless otherwise indicated.

EXAMPLE: Equimolar solutions of barium hydroxide and sulfuric acid are mixed and a precipitate is formed.

$$Ba(OH)_2 + H_2SO_4 \rightarrow BaSO_4(s) + H_2O(l)$$

Barium hydroxide is only slightly soluble, so it should not be written as separate ions. The first hydrogen ion separates easily from the conjugate base HSO_4^-, but the second does not. Therefore, the net ionic equation for the reaction above is

$$Ba(OH)_2 + H^+ + HSO_4^- \rightarrow BaSO_4(s) + H_2O(l)$$

OXIDATION–REDUCTION REACTIONS

(*Chemistry* 8th ed. pages 161–168/9th ed. pages 170–177)

Oxidation–reduction reactions involve the transfer of electrons from the atom(s) being oxidized to the atom(s) being reduced. Skills required for this section include the assignment of oxidation numbers and the identification of oxidation–reduction reactions. This category includes combustion and some synthesis and decomposition reactions, so check for electron transfer when classifying these kinds of reactions.

In an oxidation–reduction reaction, you need to identify the atoms that are oxidized and the atoms that are reduced. One way to keep track is "OIL RIG": Oxidation Is Loss of electrons and Reduction Is Gain of electrons.

Rules for Assigning Oxidation States (*Chemistry* 8th ed. page 163/9th ed. page 171)

The oxidation state of . . .	Examples
An atom in element is zero.	$Na(s)$, $O_2(g)$
A monatomic ion is the same as its charge.	Na^+
Oxygen is usually –2 in its compounds. Exception: peroxides (containing $O_2{}^{2-}$, ex. Na_2O_2) in which oxygen is –1.	H_2O, CO_2
Hydrogen is +1 in its covalent compounds. (Hydrogen is –1 in binary hydrides, ex. NaH).	H_2O, NH_3
For an electrically neutral compound, the sum of the oxidation states must be zero.	$KMnO_4$ Solution: K = +1, O = –2 $+1 + Mn + 4(-2) = 0$ $-7 + Mn = 0$; $Mn = +7$
For an ionic species, the sum of the oxidation states must equal the overall charge.	Ex: $Cr_2O_7{}^{2-}$ Solution: O = –2, $2\,Cr + 7(-2) = -2$; $2\,Cr = +12$; $Cr = +6$

EXAMPLE: Is the following reaction an oxidation–reduction reaction? If it is an oxidation–reduction reaction, identify which atoms are oxidized and which atoms are reduced (*Chemistry* 8th ed. pages 163–165/9th ed. pages 172–174).

$$Zn + Cu(NO_3)_2 \rightarrow Cu + Zn(NO_3)_2$$

SOLUTION: The nitrate ion appears unchanged on both sides of the reaction, so neither element in the ion is oxidized or reduced. *Copper* goes from Cu^{+2} to Cu. (It is reduced, its oxidation number goes down, and it gains 2 electrons.) *Zinc* goes from Zn to Zn^{2+}. (It is oxidized, its oxidation number goes up, and it loses 2 electrons.)

NOTE: If there is no change in oxidation numbers in the reaction, then the reaction is not an oxidation–reduction reaction.

EXAMPLE: Is the following reaction an oxidation–reduction reaction? If it is an oxidation–reduction reaction, identify which atoms are oxidized and which atoms are reduced (*Chemistry* 8th ed. pages 163–165/9th ed. pages 172–174).

$$CaCO_3 \rightarrow CaO + CO_2$$

SOLUTION: Decomposition is usually oxidation-reduction, but this one is not. *Calcium* is Ca^{2+} on both sides (paired with $CO_3{}^{2-}$ on the left and O^{2-} on the right). *Oxygen's* oxidation number does not change. The oxidation number of *carbon* is +4 in $CO_3{}^{2-}$ and in CO_2.

STEPS FOR BALANCING OXIDATION–REDUCTION REACTIONS

BALANCE OXIDATION–REDUCTION REACTIONS IN ACIDIC SOLUTION USING THE HALF-REACTION METHOD

(*Chemistry* 8th ed. pages 166–168/9th ed. pages 175–177)

EXAMPLE: $Cr_2O_7^{2-} + Cl^- \rightarrow Cr^{3+} + Cl_2$

STEP 1: *Write separate half-reactions:*

$Cr_2O_7^{2-} \rightarrow 2\ Cr^{3+}$ $\qquad\qquad$ $2\ Cl^- \rightarrow Cl_2$

STEP 2: *Balance all atoms except H and O:*

$Cr_2O_7^{2-} \rightarrow 2\ Cr^{3+}$ $\qquad\qquad$ $2\ Cl^- \rightarrow Cl_2$

STEP 3: *Balance oxygen using water:*

$Cr_2O_7^{2-} \rightarrow 2\ Cr^{3+} + 7\ H_2O$ $\qquad$ $2\ Cl^- \rightarrow Cl_2$

STEP 4: *Balance hydrogen with H^+:*

$14\ H^+ + Cr_2O_7^{2-} \rightarrow 2\ Cr^{3+} + 7\ H_2O$ $\qquad$ $2\ Cl^- \rightarrow Cl_2$

STEP 5: *Balance charge using electrons:*

$6\ e^- + 14\ H^+ + Cr_2O_7^{2-} \rightarrow 2\ Cr^{3+} + 7\ H_2O$ $\quad$ $2\ Cl^- \rightarrow Cl_2 + 2\ e^-$

STEP 6: *Equalize electron transfer.* Multiply each reaction by numbers that will allow both reactions to have the same number of electrons exchanged:

$6\ e^- + 14\ H^+ + Cr_2O_7^{2-} \rightarrow 2\ Cr^{3+} + 7\ H_2O$ $\quad$ $6\ Cl^- \rightarrow 3\ Cl_2 + 6\ e^-$

Note: 2nd reaction is multiplied by 3.

Add the two half-reactions canceling out all the electrons and the formulas which appear on both sides of the equation.

$14\ H^+ + Cr_2O_7^{2-} + 6\ Cl^- \rightarrow 2\ Cr^{3+} + 7\ H_2O + 3\ Cl_2$

Sum of Charges: $+14 - 2 - 6 = +6 \rightarrow +6 + 0 + 0 = +6$

STEP 7: *Double check that* there is the same number of each kind of atom on both sides and that the sums of all charges are the same on both sides.

BALANCE OXIDATION–REDUCTION REACTIONS IN BASIC SOLUTION USING THE HALF-REACTION METHOD

(*Chemistry* 8th ed. page 168/9th ed. page 177)

Repeat steps 1–5 above. After Step 5: Add OH^- to both sides of the equation (equal to H^+). Form H_2O on the side containing H^+ and OH^- ions. Eliminate number of H_2O appearing on both sides. Continue with steps 6 and 7.

EXAMPLE: $NO_2^- + Al \rightarrow NH_3 + AlO_2^-$

STEP 1: Write separate half-reactions.

$$Al \rightarrow AlO_2^- \qquad\qquad NO_2^- \rightarrow NH_3$$

STEP 2: All atoms except H and O are already balanced.

STEPS 3 AND 4: Balance O with H_2O and H with H^+.

$$2\ H_2O + Al \rightarrow AlO_2^- + 4\ H^+ \qquad 7\ H^+ + NO_2^- \rightarrow NH_3 + 2\ H_2O$$

STEP 5: Balance charge using electrons.

$$6\ e^- + 7\ H^+ + NO_2^- \rightarrow NH_3 + 2\ H_2O$$

$$\underline{(2\ H_2O + Al \rightarrow AlO_2^- + 4\ H^+ + 3\ e^-) \times 2}$$

$$7\ H^+ + NO_2^- + 4\ H_2O + 2\ Al \rightarrow 2\ AlO_2^- + 8\ H^+ + NH_3 + 2\ H_2O$$

CANCEL: $NO_2^- + 2\ H_2O + 2\ Al \rightarrow 2\ AlO_2^- + H^+ + NH_3$

New step for basic solution: Add OH^- to both sides equal to the number of H^+ ions:

$$OH^- + NO_2^- + 2\ H_2O + 2\ Al \rightarrow 2\ AlO_2^- + H^+ + NH_3 + OH^-$$

COMBINE THE PROTON AND HYDROXIDE TO FORM WATER:

$$OH^- + NO_2^- + 2\ H_2O + 2\ Al \rightarrow 2\ AlO_2^- + NH_3 + H_2O$$

CANCEL: $OH^- + NO_2^- + H_2O + 2\ Al \rightarrow 2\ AlO_2^- + NH_3$

ELECTRON TRANSFER TO OXYGEN (INCLUDING COMBUSTION)

(*Chemistry* 8th ed. pages 101–102/9th ed. pages 107–108)

Combustion is the name given to the complete oxidation of any organic compound containing C, H, and/or O to yield CO_2 and H_2O and heat. Other elements and compounds undergo similar reactions with oxygen, and all are oxidation–reduction reactions.

$$C_2H_4(g) + 3\ O_2(g) \rightarrow 2\ CO_2(g) + 2\ H_2O(g)$$

$$SiH_4(g) + 2\ O_2(g) \rightarrow SiO_2(s) + 2\ H_2O(g)$$

$$2\ Mg(s) + O_2(g) \rightarrow 2\ MgO(s)$$

SYNTHESIS/DECOMPOSITION

SYNTHESIS (ALSO KNOWN AS "COMBINATION")

In synthesis, two atoms and/or molecules combine to form a new molecule. These may also be redox reactions if electron transfer occurs.

EXAMPLES:
Two or more elements → 1 compound
$3\ Mg(s) + N_2(g) \rightarrow Mg_3N_2(s)$

Two or more compounds → 1 compound
$Li_2O(s) + H_2O(l) \rightarrow 2\ Li^+(aq) + 2\ OH^-(aq)$

$SO_3(g) + H_2O(l) \rightarrow H^+(aq) + HSO_4^-(aq)$

$6\ CaO(s) + P_4O_{10}(s) \rightarrow 2\ Ca_3(PO_4)_2(s)$

DECOMPOSITION

Decomposition is the opposite of synthesis, with one reactant forming two or more products. One of the examples below is oxidation-reduction.

1 compound → 2 or more elements or compounds (reverse of combination)

Magnesium carbonate is heated strongly in a crucible.
$MgCO_3(s) \rightarrow MgO(s) + CO_2(g)$

Nitrogen triiodide decomposes into two gases.
$2 NI_3(s) \rightarrow 3 I_2(g) + N_2(g)$

MULTIPLE-CHOICE QUESTIONS

No calculators are to be used in this section.

1. Consider the equation: $Cl_2(g) + 2 KI(aq) \rightarrow I_2(s) + 2 KCl(aq)$. Which species is oxidized?
   (A) Cl_2
   (B) K^+
   (C) I^-
   (D) I_2

2. Solutions of $CaCl_2$ and Na_2CO_3 are mixed and a precipitate is formed. What is the net ionic equation for the reaction?
   (A) $CO_3^{2-}(aq) + Ca^{2+}(aq) \rightarrow CaCO_3(s)$
   (B) $2 Cl^-(aq) + 2 Na^+(aq) \rightarrow 2 NaCl(s)$
   (C) $CO_3^-(aq) + Ca^{2+}(aq) + 2 Cl^-(aq) + 2 Na^+(aq) \rightarrow CaCO_3(s) + 2 NaCl(aq)$
   (D) $CO_3^-(aq) + Ca^{2+}(aq) \rightarrow Ca(CO_3)_2(s)$

3. Which of the following solutions contains the largest number of ions?
   (A) 500. mL of 0.100 M $FeCl_3$
   (B) 700. mL of 0.200 M NaOH
   (C) 400. mL of 0.100 M $Al(NO_3)_3$
   (D) 600. mL of 0.200 M $AlCl_3$

4. There are six strong acids. Which of the following is <u>not</u> a strong acid?
   (A) HCl
   (B) HF
   (C) HBr
   (D) HI

5. Spectator ions are those which are in solution but do not react. Identify any spectator ions for the reaction of sodium phosphate with calcium nitrate.
   (A) only $PO_4^{3-}(aq)$
   (B) $Na^+(aq)$ and $PO_4^{3-}(aq)$
   (C) $Na^+(aq)$ and $NO_3^-(aq)$
   (D) $Ca^{2+}(aq)$ and $PO_4^{3-}(aq)$

6. Consider the following three equations for chemical reactions:

    $2 Na(s) + Cl_2(g) \rightarrow 2 NaCl(s)$
    $2 NaCl(aq) + Pb(NO_3)_2(aq) \rightarrow PbCl_2(s) + 2 NaNO_3(aq)$
    $NaOH(aq) + HBr(aq) \rightarrow H_2O(l) + NaBr(aq)$

    These are examples of:
    (A) three acid–base reactions
    (B) a redox reaction, a precipitation reaction, then an acid–base reaction
    (C) three redox reactions
    (D) a neutralization reaction, then two precipitation reactions

7. Which of the following pairs of ions would <u>not</u> form a solid in aqueous solution?
    (A) Ba^{2+} and SO_4^{2-}
    (B) Pb^{2+} and Br^-
    (C) Na^+ and SO_4^{2-}
    (D) Pb^{2+} and S^{2-}

8. Which of the following ions are likely to form a soluble sulfate in aqueous solution?
    (A) Ba^{2+}
    (B) Pb^{2+}
    (C) Ca^{2+}
    (D) NH_4^+

9. If a solution of sodium bicarbonate is mixed with a solution containing an equal number of moles of nitric acid, then sodium nitrate, water, and carbon dioxide are produced. What is the net ionic equation representing the reaction?
    (A) $NaHCO_3(aq) + HNO_3(aq) \rightarrow NaNO_3(aq) + H_2O(l) + CO_2(g)$
    (B) $HCO_3^-(aq) + HNO_3(aq) \rightarrow NO_3^-(aq) + H_2O(l) + CO_2(g)$
    (C) $Na^+(aq) + HCO_3^-(aq) + HNO_3(aq) \rightarrow Na^+(aq) + NO_3^-(aq) + H_2O(l) + CO_2(g)$
    (D) $HCO_3^-(aq) + H^+(aq) \rightarrow H_2O(l) + CO_2(g)$

10. Classify each reaction below as one of the following: precipitation, acid-base, or oxidation-reduction (redox).

    Reaction 1 $Ca(OH)_2(aq) + 2 HNO_3(aq) \rightarrow Ca(NO_3)_2(aq) + 2 H_2O(l)$
    Reaction 2 $Fe_2O_3(s) + 3 CO(g) \rightarrow 2 Fe(s) + 3 CO_2(g)$
    Reaction 3 $CuBr_2(aq) + 2 NaOH(aq) \rightarrow Cu(OH)_2(s) + 2 NaBr(aq)$
    Reaction 4 $Cl_2(g) + 2 NaI(aq) \rightarrow I_2(aq) + 2 NaCl(aq)$

	Reaction 1	Reaction 2	Reaction 3	Reaction 4
(A)	acid-base	redox	precipitation	redox
(B)	precipitation	redox	acid-base	redox
(C)	redox	precipitation	acid-base	acid-base
(D)	precipitation	precipitation	redox	acid-base

11. The oxidation number of N in $Ca(NO_3)_2$ is
    (A) +2
    (B) +3
    (C) +4
    (D) +5

12. What is the difference between a strong acid and a weak acid?
    (A) A strong acid is more concentrated than a weak acid.
    (B) A weak acid is more soluble in water than a strong acid.
    (C) Strong acids have more hydrogen per molecule than weak acids.
    (D) Strong acids are completely dissociated in solution while weak acids are not.

13. How many moles of electrons are transferred between the substance being oxidized and the substance being reduced in the reaction given below?

$$4\ NH_3(g) + 5\ O_2(g) \rightarrow 4\ NO(g) + 6\ H_2O(l)$$

    (A) 5
    (B) 10
    (C) 16
    (D) 20

14. Which of the following is a chemical reaction?
    (A) solid carbon dioxide vaporizing
    (B) a seashell dissolving in acid
    (C) ethanol combining with water
    (D) water freezing

15. The half-reaction written correctly is
    (A) $Cl_2 + 2\ e^- \rightarrow Cl_2^-$
    (B) $Na - e^- \rightarrow Na^+$
    (C) $Cl_2 + 2\ e^- \rightarrow 2\ Cl^-$
    (D) $Ca \rightarrow Ca^+ + 2\ e^-$

FREE-RESPONSE QUESTIONS

1. Blood alcohol (C_2H_5OH) level can be determined by titrating a sample of blood plasma with an acidic potassium dichromate solution. The *unbalanced* equation for the reaction is:

$$Cr_2O_7{}^{2-}(aq) + C_2H_5OH(aq) \rightarrow Cr^{3+}(aq) + CO_2(g)$$

    (a) Identify which species is oxidized and which is reduced.
    (b) Balance the equation, using smallest whole number coefficients.
    (c) How many electrons are transferred in the balanced equation?
    (d) What visible evidence is there that a reaction has occurred?

2. Two solutions are prepared, one of $Cu(NO_3)_2$ and one of KOH.
    (a) Draw molecular representations of the two solutions, assuming that one beaker contains four formula units of $Cu(NO_3)_2$ and the other beaker contains six formula units of KOH.
    (b) Draw a molecular representation of the solution that results when the contents of the beakers are mixed. Include the correct number of formula units or ions, and the correct amounts and kinds of ions remaining.
    (c) Write the balanced net ionic equation for the reaction.

Answers

Multiple-Choice Questions

1. **C** We need only look at reactants when asked to identify the species oxidized or reduced. KI is an ionic compound and we can observe that the oxidation number of K^+ is the same in both KI and KCl. Whenever an element is found in a compound on one side of the equation and as a free element on the other side of the equation, there has to be a change in oxidation number for that species.

   By definition, oxidation is the loss of electrons. Writing the two half-reactions [$Cl_2 + 2\ e^- \rightarrow 2\ Cl^-$ and $2\ I^- - 2\ e^- \rightarrow I_2$] shows that it is the two iodide ions that lose two electrons to become diatomic iodine (*Chemistry* 8th ed. pages 161–166/9th ed. pages 170–175). LO 3.8

2. **A** In a precipitation reaction, the cations exchange anions. All compounds of Na^+ are soluble, so the solid must be formed from Ca^{2+} and CO_3^{2-} (*Chemistry* 8th ed. pages 145–150/9th ed. pages 145–147). LO 3.2

3. **D** There are three factors which must be considered in this problem, the number of ions per formula unit, the concentration of the solution, and the volume of the solution used. For example, in the first solution there are 0.200 moles of ions present: 0.500 L × 0.100 mol of formula units of $FeCl_3$ / L × 4 ions/ $FeCl_3$ = 0.200 moles of ions. In response D: 0.600 L × 0.200 mol of formula units of $AlCl_3$ × 4 ions/ $AlCl_3$ = 0.480 mol. of ions (*Chemistry* 8th ed. pages 136–140/9th ed. pages 145–149). LO 3.4

4. **B** Even though hydrofluoric acid will dissolve glass (!), it does not ionize significantly. It is important for you to know the six strong acids (then you know that all others are weak!). The six strong acids are $HClO_4$, HCl, HBr, HI, H_2SO_4, and HNO_3. These are the acids that are 100% ionized in water. You can assume that all other acids are weak (*Chemistry* 8th ed. pages 132–134, 642–644, Appendix 5.1/9th ed. pages 141–143, 656–658, Appendix 5.1). LO 3.7

5. **C** The unbalanced complete ionic equation for this reaction is: $Na^+ + PO_4^{3-} + Ca^{2+} + NO_3^- \rightarrow Ca_3(PO_4)_2 + Na^+ + NO_3^-$. Because you have memorized that all compounds containing sodium cations and nitrate anions are soluble (i.e., $NaNO_3$ is soluble in water), the only possible product is calcium phosphate (*Chemistry* 8th ed. pages 149–151, 154/9th ed. pages 157–160, 162). LO 3.2

6. **B** Being able to classify reactions will help in predicting products. In the first reaction, Na is oxidized and Cl_2 is reduced (a metal–nonmetal reaction can always be assumed to be a redox reaction); in the second reaction, insoluble lead(II) chloride forms; in the third reaction, a base and an acid form water and a salt (*Chemistry*

8th ed. pages 152–156, 164–166/9th ed. pages 161–165, 173–175). LO 3.2, LO 3.8

7. **C** The answer is reached by process of elimination. All salts containing sodium cation are soluble (*Chemistry* 8th ed. pages 147–148/9th ed. pages 155–156). LO 3.2

8. **D** Salts containing the ammonium ion are soluble (*Chemistry* 8th ed. pages 147–148/9th ed. pages 155–156). LO 3.2

9. **D** Sodium bicarbonate and sodium nitrate are both strong electrolytes (salts) and therefore are written as ions in aqueous solution. Nitric acid is a strong acid and is completely ionized in aqueous solution. Water and carbon dioxide are molecular species and have very little ionization occurring, so they stay written in the molecular form. The two spectator ions, Na^+ and NO_3^- are canceled from both sides of the equation (*Chemistry* 8th ed. pages 148–151/9th ed. pages 157–160). LO 3.2

10. **A** Reaction 1 is acid(HNO_3)-base($Ca(OH)_2$). Reaction 2 is oxidation-reduction; Fe^{3+} in Fe_2O_3 is reduced to Fe. Reaction 3 is precipitation because two aqueous solutions are producing a solid product. In Reaction 4, Cl_2 is reduced to Cl^- and I^- is oxidized to I_2 (*Chemistry* 8th ed. pages 144–150, 154–155, 161–166/9th ed. pages 153–158, 163–164, 170–175). LO 3.2, LO 3.7, LO 3.8

11. **D** Ca ion is always +2 and oxygen is –2. If you remember that the nitrate ion is –1, then 3(–2) + N = –1, and when solving for N, N = +5 (*Chemistry* 8th ed. pages 162–164/9th ed. pages 171–173). LO 3.8

12. **D** This is the definition of a strong electrolyte, which is why strong acids are labeled as "strong" (*Chemistry* 8th ed. pages 132–136/9th ed. pages 141–145). LO 3.7

13. **D** The change in oxidation number of the nitrogen is from –3 in the NH_3 to +2 in the nitrogen monoxide molecule. This requires 5 electrons/nitrogen atom, or 5 moles electrons/mol of nitrogen. Since there are 4 moles of nitrogen atoms, the total moles of electrons needed is 4 × 5 or 20 mol electrons (*Chemistry* 8th ed. pages 166–168/9th ed. pages 175–177). LO 3.8

14. **B** All other examples are phase changes or solution formation (*Chemistry* 8th ed. pages 482–483/9th ed. pages 495–496). LO 3.10

15. **C** The first option is not correct because when Cl_2 gains electrons, it forms two Cl^- anions. The second is not because by convention, when electrons are lost they are included among the products, and when they are gained, are included among the reactants. The last option does not represent the typical charge of a calcium cation (*Chemistry* 8th ed. pages 817–823/9th ed. pages 833–839). LO 3.8

FREE-RESPONSE QUESTIONS

1. Start by assigning oxidation numbers to determine which species are oxidized and which are reduced.

| +6 –2 | +2 +1 –2 | +3 | +4 –2 | individual O.N. |

$$Cr_2O_7{}^{2-}(aq) \quad + \quad C_2H_6O(aq) \longrightarrow Cr^{3+}(aq) \quad + \quad CO_2(g)$$

| +12 –14 | –4 +6 –2 | +3 | +4 –4 | group O.N. |

(a) Chromium's oxidation number has gone from +6 to +3, so chromium in dichromate has been reduced. Carbon's oxidation number has gone from +2 to +4, so the carbon in ethanol has been oxidized.

(b) Use the half-reaction method.

STEP 1: *Write separate half-reactions:*

$$Cr_2O_7{}^{2-} \rightarrow Cr^{3+} \qquad\qquad C_2H_6O \rightarrow CO_2$$

STEP 2: *Balance all atoms except H and O:*

$$Cr_2O_7{}^{2-} \rightarrow 2\,Cr^{3+} \qquad\qquad C_2H_6O \rightarrow 2\,CO_2$$

STEP 3: *Balance oxygen using water:*

$$Cr_2O_7{}^{2-} \rightarrow 2\,Cr^{3+} + 7\,H_2O \qquad\qquad 3\,H_2O + C_2H_6O \rightarrow 2\,CO_2$$

STEP 4: *Balance hydrogen with H^+:*

$$14\,H^+ + Cr_2O_7{}^{2-} \rightarrow 2\,Cr^{3+} + 7\,H_2O \qquad 3\,H_2O + C_2H_6O \rightarrow 2\,CO_2 + 12\,H^+$$

STEP 5: *Balance charge using electrons:*

$$6\,e^- + 14\,H^+ + Cr_2O_7{}^{2-} \rightarrow 2\,Cr^{3+} + 7\,H_2O \qquad 3\,H_2O + C_2H_6O \rightarrow 2\,CO_2 + 12\,H^+ + 12\,e^-$$

STEP 6: *Equalize electron transfer.* Multiply each reaction by numbers that will allow both reactions to have the same number of electrons exchanged:

$$12\,e^- + 28\,H^+ + 2\,Cr_2O_7{}^{2-} \rightarrow 4\,Cr^{3+} + 14\,H_2O$$

$$3\,H_2O + C_2H_6O \rightarrow 2\,CO_2 + 12\,H^+ + 12\,e^-$$

Note: 1st reaction is multiplied by 2.

Add the two half-reactions canceling out all the electrons and the formulas which appear on both sides of the equation.

$$16\,H^+ + 2\,Cr_2O_7{}^{2-} + C_2H_6O \rightarrow 4\,Cr^{3+} + 11\,H_2O + 2\,CO_2$$

Sum of Charges: $+16 - 4 + 0 = +12 \rightarrow +12 + 0 + 0 = +12$

STEP 7: *Double check that* there is the same number of each kind of atom on both sides and that the sums of all charges are the same on both sides.

(c) Twelve electrons are transferred

(*Chemistry* 8th ed. pages 166–168/9th ed. pages 175–177). LO 3.8

(d) There are two ways to monitor the reaction. First, a gas (CO_2) is formed. Second, the dichromate ion is orange, and the Cr(III) ion is blue-violet, so as long as there is ethanol available for reaction, the solution will be blue-violet. Once all the ethanol is consumed, the solution will stay orange, the color of unreduced dichromate (*Chemistry* 8th ed. pages 820–821/9th ed. pages 836–837). LO 3.10

2. (a)

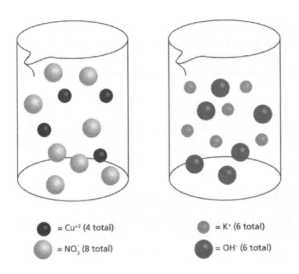

= Cu^{+2} (4 total)   = K$^+$ (6 total)

= NO$_3^-$ (8 total)   = OH$^-$ (6 total)

Both substances are soluble and will ionize completely.

(b)

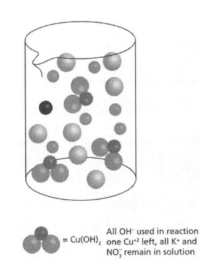

= Cu(OH)$_2$ All OH$^-$ used in reaction one Cu^{+2} left, all K$^+$ and NO$_3^-$ remain in solution

There are not enough OH$^-$ ions to react with all the Cu^{2+} ions, so there will be one Cu^{2+} ion left in solution, along with the spectators K^+ and NO_3^-.

(c) $Cu^{2+} + 2 \, OH^- \rightarrow Cu(OH)_2(s)$ (Chemistry 8th ed. pages 132–136, 145–154/9th ed. pages 141–145, 153–162). LO 3.1

8

BIG IDEA 3: STOICHIOMETRY

Big Idea 3

Changes in matter involve the rearrangement and/or reorganization of atoms and/or the transfer of electrons.

In this chapter you learn about standard analytical chemistry methods that allow determination of percent composition, molarity, empirical formula, and the quantities of materials consumed and produced in chemical reactions (stoichiometry). You may need to review the mole conversions and molar mass calculations in Chapter 2.

You should be able to

- Describe how to prepare solutions and to use titration data to determine the molarity (concentration) of solutions.
- Write balanced chemical equations and predict the amount of product formed from a given mass of reactant or the amount of reactant required to produce a desired amount of product.
- Identify limiting reactants, and calculate the amount of product formed when given the amounts of all of the reactants present.
- Calculate the percent yield of a reaction.
- For reactions in solution, given the molarity and the volume of the reactants, calculate the amount of product produced or the amount of reactant required to react.
- Use data from a titration, or describe an experiment using titration, to find the concentration of a solution.

MOLARITY

(Chemistry 8th ed. pages 136–144/9th ed. pages 145–153)

The number of moles of solute in 1 liter of solution is a measure of its molarity or solution concentration.

EXAMPLE: Prepare 2.00 L of 0.250 *M* NaOH from solid NaOH.

SOLUTION:

$$2.00 \text{ L} \times \frac{0.250 \text{ mol NaOH}}{\text{L}} \times \frac{40.00 \text{ g NaOH}}{1 \text{ mol}} = \textbf{20.0 g NaOH}$$

Place 20.0 g NaOH in a 2-L volumetric flask; add water to dissolve the NaOH, and fill to the mark with water, mixing several times along the way.

Another way to prepare a solution of a specific molarity is to dilute a more concentrated solution, using the relationship:

$$M_1 V_1 = M_2 V_2$$

EXAMPLE: Prepare 2.00 L of 0.250 *M* NaOH from 1.00 *M* NaOH.

SOLUTION:

$$1.00 \text{ } M \text{ } V_1 = 0.250 \text{ } M \times 2.00 \text{ L} \quad V_1 = \textbf{0.500 L}$$

Add 500. mL of 1.00 *M* NaOH stock solution to a 2-L volumetric flask; add deionized water in several increments with mixing until the flask is filled to the mark on the neck of the flask.

DETERMINATION OF EMPIRICAL FORMULA BY COMBUSTION ANALYSIS

(Chemistry 8th ed. pages 90–94/9th ed. pages 96–100)

You learned about the empirical formula in Chapter 2. A standard way of determining this is by combustion analysis. In this procedure, a small sample of the substance is burned in oxygen and the amount of resulting products, which may be solid or gaseous oxides, measured.

(The following problem involves two steps. First, the percent composition of the compound is determined from combustion data. Second, the empirical formula of the compound is determined from the percent composition.)

EXAMPLE: A compound contains only carbon, hydrogen, and oxygen. Combustion of 10.68 mg of the compound yields 16.01 mg CO_2 and 4.37 mg of H_2O. What is the percent composition of the compound?

SOLUTION: Assume that all the carbon in the compound is converted to CO_2 and determine the mass of carbon present in the 10.68-mg sample. The % C in CO_2 is calculated as described in percent composition, above. It can then be multiplied times the mass of CO_2 to find the mass of C.

$$16.01 \text{ mg } CO_2 \times \frac{12.01 \text{ g C}}{44.01 \text{ g } CO_2} = 4.369 \text{ mg C}$$

The mass of C can be divided by the mass of the original compound to find the mass percent of C in this compound:

$$\frac{4.369 \text{ mg C}}{10.68 \text{ mg}} \times 100\% = 40.91\% \text{ C}$$

The same procedure can be used to find the mass percent of hydrogen in the unknown compound. We assume that all the hydrogen present in 10.68 mg of compound was converted to H_2O.

$$0.0437 \text{ g } H_2O \times \frac{2.016 \text{ g H}}{18.02 \text{ g } H_2O} = 0.489 \text{ mg H}$$

The mass percent of H in the compound is

$$\frac{0.489 \text{ mg}}{10.68 \text{ mg}} \times 100\% = 4.58\% \text{ H}$$

The unknown compound contains only carbon, hydrogen, and oxygen. The remainder must be oxygen.

$$100.00\% - (40.91\% \text{ C} + 4.58\% \text{ H}) = 54.51\% \text{ O}$$

CONVERSIONS INVOLVED IN STOICHIOMETRIC CALCULATIONS

Type of Conversion	Example	Reference
g → mol (using molar mass)	$\dfrac{18 \text{ g}}{1 \text{ mol } H_2O}$	*Chemistry* 8th ed. page 85/9th ed. page 91
mol → mol (using mole ratio – coefficients from balanced chemical equation)	$\dfrac{1 \text{ mol } O_2}{2 \text{ mol } H_2O}$	*Chemistry* 8th ed. pages 102–104/9th ed. pages 108–110
mol → L (using molarity which is a solution's concentration equal to the number of mols of solute in 1 liter of solution)	$\dfrac{6 \text{ mol HCl}}{1 \text{ L}}$	*Chemistry* 8th ed. pages 136–144/9th ed. pages 145–153

SOLUTION STOICHIOMETRY

(*Chemistry* 8th ed. pages 156–160/9th ed. pages 165–170)

Solution stoichiometry involves calculations for reactions that occur in aqueous solution. The moles of product or reactant are determined by multiplying concentration by volume, being careful to keep units consistent.

EXAMPLE: Mercury(II) ion can be removed from water by precipitation with sodium sulfide. What volume of 0.100 M Na_2S must be added to 100.0 mL of a 0.150 M $HgCl_2$ solution to remove all the Hg^{2+} as HgS?

SOLUTION: First, write a balanced molecular equation.

$$HgCl_2 + Na_2S \rightarrow HgS + 2\,NaCl$$

Find the moles of Na_2S required from the volume and molarity of $HgCl_2$.

$$0.1000 \text{ L HgCl}_2 \times \frac{0.150 \text{ mol HgCl}_2}{1 \text{ L}} \times \frac{1 \text{ mol Na}_2S}{1 \text{ mol HgCl}_2} = 0.0150 \text{ mol Na}_2S$$

The volume of Na_2S solution required is:

$$0.0150 \text{ mol Na}_2S \times \frac{1 \text{ L}}{0.100 \text{ mol Na}_2S} = 0.150 \text{ L}$$

TITRATION

(*Chemistry* 8th ed. pages 713–728/9th ed. pages 727–742)

A titration can be used to determine the concentration of an unknown solution. The calculations involve stoichiometric principles. The example here is a redox titration. Acid–base titrations are discussed in Big Idea 6.

Changing the oxidation state of a substance often results in a color change that can be used to identify the endpoint of a titration. For example, the following reaction can be used to find the concentration of Fe^{2+} in solution:

$$8\,H^+(aq) + 5\,Fe^{2+}(aq) + MnO_4^-(aq) \longrightarrow 5\,Fe^{3+}(aq) + Mn^{2+}(aq) + 4H_2O(l)$$
$$\text{purple} \qquad\qquad\qquad\qquad\qquad \text{colorless}$$

Permanganate solution of known concentration is added dropwise, with a buret, to the Fe^{2+} solution. The solution will initially be colorless because the ions are reacting. When the solution stays purple, there is no Fe^{2+} remaining to react with MnO_4^-. This is the equivalence point of the reaction, when enough moles of titrant have been added to react exactly with the moles of the substance being titrated. For this reaction, at equivalence point:

$$\text{mol MnO}_4^- = 5 \times \text{mol Fe}^{2+}.$$

EXAMPLE: A 50.0-mL solution of Fe^{2+} is titrated with 0.0020 M $KMnO_4$. Find the concentration of Fe^{2+} if 20.0 mL of $KMnO_4$ is required.

SOLUTION: First, write the balanced equation for the reaction, which in this example is given above. Then use the volume and molarity of the $KMnO_4$ and the mole ratio from the balanced equation to calculate the moles of Fe^{2+} in solution.

$$0.0200 \text{ L KMnO}_4 \times \frac{0.0020 \text{ mol KMnO}_4}{1 \text{ L}} \times \frac{5 \text{ mol Fe}^{2+}}{1 \text{ mol KMnO}_4}$$
$$= 2.0 \times 10^{-4} \text{ mol Fe}^{2+}$$

The concentration of Fe^{2+} is:

$$\frac{2.0 \times 10^{-4} \text{ mol Fe}^{2+}}{0.050 \text{ L}} = 4.0 \times 10^{-3} \ M \text{ Fe}^{2+}.$$

Remember to use the initial volume of solution when determining the molarity!

LIMITING REACTANT

(*Chemistry* 8th ed. pages 107–113/9th ed. pages 114–121)

In a limiting reactant problem, the amounts of all reactants are given and the amount of product is to be determined. The limiting reactant is completely consumed when the reaction goes to completion. It determines how much product is formed.

EXAMPLE: What mass of precipitate can be produced when 50.0 mL of 0.200 M $Al(NO_3)_3$ is added to 200.0 mL of 0.100 M KOH?

SOLUTION:
Always begin with a balanced molecular equation.

$$Al(NO_3)_3(aq) + 3 \ KOH(aq) \rightarrow Al(OH)_3(s) + 3 \ KNO_3(aq)$$

For each reactant, determine the amount of a designated product produced (in mol or g).

$$0.0500 \text{ L} \times \frac{0.200 \text{ mol Al(NO}_3)_3}{\text{L}} \times \frac{1 \text{ mol Al(OH)}_3}{1 \text{ mol Al(NO}_3)_3}$$

$$= 0.0100 \text{ mol Al(OH)}_3$$

$$0.2000 \text{ L} \times \frac{0.100 \text{ mol KOH}}{\text{L}} \times \frac{1 \text{ mol Al(OH)}_3}{3 \text{ mol KOH}}$$

$$= 0.00667 \text{ mol Al(OH)}_3$$

The limiting reactant produces the least amount of product. The limiting reactant in this case is KOH. It produces only 0.00667 mol of product which is less than 0.0100 mol.

The mass of precipitate produced is:

$$0.00667 \text{ mol Al(OH)}_3 \times \frac{78.00 \text{ g Al(OH)}_3}{1 \text{ mol Al(OH)}_3} = 0.520 \text{ g Al(OH)}_3$$

PERCENT YIELD

(*Chemistry* 8th ed. pages 113–115/9th ed. pages 121–123)

The *percent yield* of a reaction is the actual yield of a product as a percentage of the theoretical yield. The *actual yield* is the amount of product obtained in an experiment. The *theoretical yield* is the amount of product calculated from the amounts of reactants used. The percent yield is generally less than 100% because the reaction doesn't go to completion, because of side reactions that occur without generating desired product, and because of difficulties in collecting the entire product. Yields greater than 100% are evidence of some contamination or error in calculation or measurement.

> EXAMPLE: If the reaction above has an 85.3% yield of precipitate, how much aluminum hydroxide is produced?
>
> SOLUTION:
>
> $$\text{Percent Yield} = \frac{\text{Actual Yield}}{\text{Theoretical Yield}} \times 100\%$$
>
> $$\text{Actual Yield} = \frac{85.3\% \times 0.520 \text{ g}}{100\%} = 0.444 \text{ g Al(OH)}_3$$

MULTIPLE-CHOICE QUESTIONS

No calculators are to be used in this section.

1. What volume of 10.0 M NaOH must be used to prepare 500. mL of a 2.50 M solution?
   (A) 125. mL
   (B) 200. mL
   (C) 250. mL
   (D) 12.5 mL

2. Analysis of a sample of an oxide of chromium is reported as 26 g of chromium and 12 g of oxygen. From these data determine the empirical formula of this compound.
   (A) CrO
   (B) Cr_2O_3
   (C) CrO_3
   (D) Cr_4O_6

3. Aluminum reacts with sulfuric acid, H_2SO_4, to form aluminum sulfate, $Al_2(SO_4)_3$, and hydrogen gas. Give the sum of all coefficients (all reactants and all products) for this balanced chemical expression.
   (A) 5
   (B) 6
   (C) 9
   (D) 12

4. Methane reacts with oxygen to form carbon dioxide and water as shown in the following chemical equation: $CH_4 + 2\,O_2 \rightarrow CO_2 + 2\,H_2O$. If 72 g of water form, how much methane must have reacted?
   (A) 16 g
   (B) 32 g
   (C) 36 g
   (D) 84 g

5. Hydrogen reacts with oxygen to form only water. If 16 grams of hydrogen is mixed with 16 grams of oxygen, how much water can form?
   (A) 0.50 grams
   (B) 8.0 grams
   (C) 18 grams
   (D) 72 grams

6. How many moles of barium sulfide, BaS, will form when 60.0 mL of 1.0 M $Ba(NO_3)_2$ are mixed with 25.0 mL of 0.80 M K_2S solution to form barium sulfide solid?
   (A) 0.020 mol
   (B) 0.040 mol
   (C) 0.060 mol
   (D) 0.10 mol

7. Consider the neutralization reaction $Be(OH)_2 + 2\ HCl \rightarrow BeCl_2 + 2\ H_2O$.
   What volume of 5.00 M HCl is required to react completely with 4.30 g of $Be(OH)_2$? (Molar mass of $Be(OH)_2$ = 43.0 g/mol.)
   (A) 10.0 mL
   (B) 30.0 mL
   (C) 40.0 mL
   (D) 50.0 mL

8. Sucrose, $C_{12}H_{22}O_{11}$, has a molar mass of 342 g/mol. How many atoms of carbon are there in 684 g of sucrose?
   (A) 6.02×10^{23} atoms
   (B) 1.45×10^{25} atoms
   (C) 1.20×10^{24} atoms
   (D) 3.01×10^{23} atoms

9. Nitric acid reacts with silver metal: $4\ HNO_3 + 3\ Ag \rightarrow NO + 2\ H_2O + 3\ AgNO_3$. Calculate the number of grams of NO formed when 10.8 g of Ag reacts with 12.6 g of HNO_3.
   (A) 0.999 g
   (B) 9.00 g
   (C) 12.0 g
   (D) 18.0 g

10. How many grams of chromium are in 58.5 g of $K_2Cr_2O_7$? (Molar mass = 294 g/mol.)
    (A) 10.4 g of Cr
    (B) 15.6 g of Cr
    (C) 20.8 g of Cr
    (D) 208 g of Cr

11. If 7.0 moles of sulfur atoms and 10 moles of oxygen molecules are combined to form the maximum amount of sulfur trioxide, how many moles of which reactant remain unused at the end?

$$2\ S + 3\ O_2 \rightarrow 2\ SO_3$$

(A) 0.25 mol O_2
(B) 0.33 mol O_2
(C) 0.33 mol S
(D) 0.67 mol S

12. What is the percent mass nitrogen in sodium cyanide, NaCN?
(A) 14.00%
(B) 24.41%
(C) 28.57%
(D) 49.10%

13. A compound of nitrogen and oxygen is 63.64% by mass nitrogen. What is the empirical formula of this compound?
(A) NO
(B) NO_2
(C) NO_3
(D) N_2O

14. When 16 g of methane (CH_4) and 32 g of oxygen (O_2) reacted to produce carbon dioxide and water, 11 g of carbon dioxide was produced. Calculate the percent yield of carbon dioxide in this reaction.
(A) 5.0%
(B) 10%
(C) 25%
(D) 50%

15. Zinc sulfide reacts with oxygen to yield zinc oxide and sulfur dioxide as follows:

$$2\ ZnS(s) + 3\ O_2(g) \rightarrow 2\ ZnO(s) + 2\ SO_2(g)$$

How many moles of ZnO are produced when 32 g of oxygen is allowed to react with an excess of ZnS?
(A) 0.67
(B) 1.0
(C) 1.3
(D) 2.0

FREE-RESPONSE QUESTIONS

Calculators may be used for this section.

1. A 10.0-g sample of an oxide of copper is heated in a stream of pure hydrogen, forming 1.26 g of water.
(a) Determine the percentage of copper in the compound.
(b) Determine the empirical formula of the copper oxide. Name it.

2. Nonprescription antacids may contain MgO, $Mg(OH)_2$, or $Al(OH)_3$.
   (a) Write a balanced equation for the neutralization of hydrochloric acid by each of these substances.
   (b) Which of these substances will neutralize the greatest amount of 0.1 M HCl per gram?

Answers

MULTIPLE-CHOICE QUESTIONS

1. **A** Rearrange the relationship $M_1V_1 = M_2V_2$ to solve for V_1. Then V_1 = (2.5 M/10.0 M) × 500. mL (*Chemistry* 8th ed. pages 145–153/9th ed. pages 153–162). LO 3.4

2. **B** You have 0.5 mol of Cr (26 g × 1 mol/52 g) and 0.75 mol of O (12 g × 1 mol/16 g). The ratio of mol Cr: mol O is 1/2:3/4 = (1/2 × 4/3) = 2/3 or 2 mol Cr: 3 mol O. While answer D gives the same ratio, it is not the smallest whole number ratio (*Chemistry* 8th ed. pages 93–97/9th ed. pages 99–103). LO 1.3

3. **C** The equation is 2 Al + 3 H_2SO_4 → $Al_2(SO_4)_3$ + 3 H_2. Note that hydrogen is diatomic. Be sure to count the coefficients for the whole equation; it is understood that the coefficient in front of the aluminum sulfate is one (*Chemistry* 8th ed. pages 97–103/9th ed. pages 103–109). LO 3.2

4. **B** The equation indicates a mole ratio of water to methane of 2:1. The 72 grams of water is 4.0 moles of water (72 g/18 g/mol = 4.0 mol), so 2.0 moles of methane are required. Two moles of methane have a mass of 32 grams (16 g/mol × 2) (*Chemistry* 8th ed. pages 102–107/9th ed. pages 108–114). LO 3.2

5. **C** Write an equation for the reaction: 2 H_2 + O_2 → 2 H_2O. The mole ratio can then be seen as 2 mol H_2 for 1 mol O_2. Determine the number of moles of each reactant: 16 g H_2 × 1 mol H_2/2.0 g = 8.0 mol H_2 and 16 g O_2 × 1 mol O_2/32 g = 0.50 mol O_2.

   Since O_2 is the limiting reagent, it determines the amount of water formed. From the mole ratio in the equation, it follows that 0.50 mol O_2 forms two times that amount of water or 1 mol of water. The molar mass of water is 18 g/mol (*Chemistry* 8th ed. pages 107–115/9th ed. pages 114–123). LO 3.4

6. **A** The equation, $Ba(NO_3)_2$ + K_2S → BaS + 2 KNO_3, indicates that with 0.060 mole $Ba(NO_3)_2$ and 0.020 mole K_2S, the potassium sulfide is the limiting reactant (they react in a one-to-one ratio). The equation also shows that for one mole of potassium sulfide, one mole of barium sulfide forms, hence 0.020 mol of potassium sulfide will allow for the formation of 0.020 mol of the solid BaS (*Chemistry* 8th ed. pages 144–149, 151–152/9th ed. pages 153–157, 160–161). LO 3.4

7. **C** The mass of 4.30 g of $Be(OH)_2$ represents 0.100 mol of this base; the equation indicates that twice that amount (0.200 mol) of acid is needed for neutralization to be complete. Since both the concentration and number of moles needed are known for the acid, the volume of the acid can be calculated (0.200 mol/5.00 mol/L = 0.0400 L = 40.0 mL) (*Chemistry* 8th ed. pages 158–160/9th ed. pages 167–170). LO 3.4

8. **B** It takes 342 g to make one mole of the compound and you have twice that amount. Therefore you have 2.00 mole of this substance (684 g/342 g/mol). Each mole of the substance contains 12 moles of carbon, for a total of 24 moles of carbon. Multiply 24 times Avogadro's number to obtain the atoms of carbon (*Chemistry* 8th ed. pages 81–87/9th ed. pages 85–92). LO 1.4

9. **A** Find the number of moles of each reactant to determine which is in excess and which is the limiting reactant: 10.8 g Ag/108 g/mol = 0.100 mol of Ag; 12.6 g HNO_3/63.0 g/mol = 0.400 mol of HNO_3. Since the Ag/HNO_3 ratio (from the equation) is 3/4, Ag is the limiting reactant. 0.100 mol of Ag will form one-third as much NO (0.100 × 1 NO/3 Ag) or 0.0333 mol of NO. Finally, 0.0333 mol NO × 30.0 g NO/mol = 0.999 g NO (*Chemistry* 8th ed. pages 107–115/9th ed. pages 114–123). LO 3.4

10. **C** First, determine the number of moles of the salt: 58.5 g/294 g/mol = 0.200 mol $K_2Cr_2O_7$. Since Cr has a molar mass of 52.0 g/mol and there are two Cr per each unit of $K_2Cr_2O_7$, 0.200 mol × 2 Cr/$K_2Cr_2O_7$ × 52.0 g/mol = 20.8 g of Cr (*Chemistry* 8th ed. pages 82–84/9th ed. pages 86–90). LO 1.4

11. **C** According to the balanced equation, for complete reaction the required ratio of moles of oxygen to sulfur is 3/2 or 1.5. In the problem we have a ratio of 10/7 or 1.43. Since this ratio is less than the required ratio, this means the oxygen is limiting; 10 moles of oxygen require 10 × (2/3) mol S = 6.67 mol S used. Therefore, 7.0 − 6.67 = 0.33 mol S remains unused (*Chemistry* 8th ed. pages 107–113/9th ed. pages 114–121). LO 3.4

12. **C** For NaCN the molar mass is 22.99 + 12.01 + 14.01 = 49.01 g/mol. % mass of N = (14.01/49.01) × 100 = 28.57%. Since you won't have a calculator, a quick estimate would be 15/50 = 30%, which is closest to 28.57% (*Chemistry* 8th ed. pages 88–90/9th ed. pages 94–96). LO 1.2

13. **D** The % oxygen is 100 − 63.64 = 36.36%.

    The steps to solving this problem are detailed below:

	N	O
Ratio by mass	63.64	36.36
Divide by molar masses	63.64/14.01	36.36/16.00
Mole ratio	4.54	2.27
Divide by smaller number	2	1

    (*Chemistry* 8th ed. pages 90–97/9th ed. pages 96–103). LO 1.2

14. **D** Start with the balanced equation: $CH_4 + 2\,O_2 \rightarrow CO_2 + 2\,H_2O$

    16 grams of methane = 1.0 mole

    32 grams of oxygen = 1.0 mole. This is the limiting reactant, since by the equation 1 mole of methane requires 2 moles of oxygen, and since there is only 1 mole of oxygen, it will be used up first leaving 0.5 mole of methane unreacted.

    Thus, if one mole of oxygen is used up, according to the equation, 0.5 mol CO_2 would be produced. The molar mass of CO_2 is 44.0 g/mol, so the expected yield would be 22 g. The actual yield was 11 g so (11 g/22 g) × 100 = 50.% (*Chemistry* 8th ed. pages 107–113/9th ed. pages 114–121). LO 3.4

15. **A** According to the equation, 1.0 mol O_2 produces 1.0 × (2/3) mol ZnO. Thus 32 grams of oxygen = 1.0 mol, 2/3 or 0.67 mol ZnO would be produced (*Chemistry* 8th ed. pages 102–107/9th ed. pages 108–114). LO 3.4

FREE-RESPONSE QUESTIONS

1. (a) 88% copper

    $$1.26 \text{ g } H_2O \times \frac{1 \text{ mol}}{18.0 \text{ g } H_2O} = 0.0700 \text{ mol } H_2O \times \frac{1 \text{ mol O}}{1 \text{ mol } H_2O}$$

    $$= 0.0700 \text{ mol O atoms}$$

    0.0700 mol × 16.0 g/mol = 1.12 g of oxygen in the oxide

    10.0 g – 1.12 g = 8.8 g of copper; 8.8 g/10.0 g × 100% = 88% copper

    (b) Cu_2O copper(I) oxide

    Consider the mole ratio of Cu to O:

    [8.8 g/63.55 g/mol = 0.14 mol Cu]

    $$\frac{0.14 \text{ mol Cu}}{0.070 \text{ mol O}} = \frac{2 \text{ mol Cu}}{1 \text{ mol O}} \quad Cu_2O \text{ is the empirical formula.}$$

    This is called copper(I) oxide since the Cu has a charge or oxidation state of +1 in this compound (*Chemistry* 8th ed. pages 87–91, 93–97, 102–107/9th ed. pages 93–97, 99–103, 108–114). LO 1.4

2. (a) $MgO(s) + 2\,HCl(aq) \rightarrow MgCl_2(aq) + H_2O(l)$

    $Mg(OH)_2(s) + 2\,HCl(aq) \rightarrow MgCl_2(aq) + 2\,H_2O(l)$

    $Al(OH)_3(s) + 3\,HCl(aq) \rightarrow AlCl_3(aq) + 3\,H_2O(l)$

    (*Chemistry* 8th ed. pages 154–155/9th ed. pages 163–164). LO 3.7

(b)

	molar mass	mol HCl/mol	mol HCl/g
MgO	40.31 g	2/1	4.96×10^{-2}
$Mg(OH)_2$	58.33 g	2/1	3.43×10^{-2}
$Al(OH)_3$	78.00 g	3/1	3.84×10^{-2}

Of the three, MgO neutralizes the most acid per gram.

(*Chemistry* 8th ed. pages 85–87/9th ed. pages 90–92). LO 3.4

9

Big Idea 3: Electrochemistry

Electrochemistry is the study of the interchange of electrical and chemical energy through transfer of electrons. There are two types of electrochemical cells, galvanic and electrolytic. In galvanic cells, spontaneous oxidation–reduction (redox) reactions generate electric current. In electrolytic cells, a nonspontaneous chemical reaction occurs with the application of an electric current.

You should be able to
- Identify and compare the two types of electrochemical cells: galvanic and electrolytic.
- Draw and label a galvanic cell, including labeling the electrodes, the flow of electrons, and the flow of ions.
- Write half-reactions and determine which reaction occurs at the anode and which reaction occurs at the cathode.
- Give the line notation for a galvanic cell or write a balanced redox reaction from the given line notation.
- Calculate the cell potential for a galvanic cell and an electrolytic cell.
- Determine if a reaction is spontaneous from its cell potential.
- Use the table of reduction potentials to determine which substances are more likely to be reduced or oxidized.

- Draw and label an electrolytic cell.
- Determine the reactions occurring at the anode and the cathode during electrolysis.
- Perform stoichiometric calculations involving electrolysis.

Galvanic Cells

Components of the Galvanic Cell

(*Chemistry* 8th ed. pages 823–825/9th ed. pages 839–842)

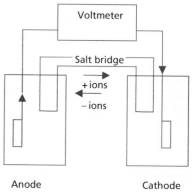

In a galvanic cell, a spontaneous chemical reaction is used to produce electrical energy. The current produced by the cell is measured in volts by a voltmeter. One compartment of the galvanic cell contains the anode, where oxidation, a loss of electrons, occurs. The other compartment contains the cathode where reduction, a gain of electrons, occurs. The electrodes (the anode and the cathode) are immersed in solutions containing metal cations. The two compartments of a galvanic cell are connected by a salt bridge or a porous disk that allows ion flow between the compartments to maintain a net zero charge in each. This is shown in the figure to the right. The anode may be a strip of zinc metal immersed in a $ZnSO_4$ solution, and the cathode may be a strip of copper metal immersed in a $CuSO_4$ solution. Zn is oxidized to Zn^{2+}, and the electrons travel to the Cu cathode, where Cu^{2+} in solution is reduced. Zn^{+2} ions travel across the salt bridge to the cathode to replace the reduced Cu^{2+}. SO_4^{2-} ions travel to the anode to balance the additional positive charge as Zn^{2+} is formed.

The oxidizing agent is the substance being reduced at the cathode. The reducing agent is the substance being oxidized at the anode.

Line Notation

(*Chemistry* 8th ed. pages 831–832/9th ed. pages 847–848)

A galvanic cell can be abbreviated with line notation.

$$\text{reactant} \mid \text{product} \parallel \text{reactant} \mid \text{product}$$
$$\text{anode reaction} \qquad \text{cathode reaction}$$

The salt bridge is indicated by the symbol ‖.
For the cell described above, the line notation would be:

$$Zn(s)|Zn^{2+}(aq) \parallel Cu^{2+}(aq)|Cu(s)$$

Sometimes an inert (nonreactive) electrode is used. The example below has a platinum cathode which transports electrons to the cations, in this case H^+.

> **Example:** Give the correct line notation for the galvanic cell pictured on the following page.

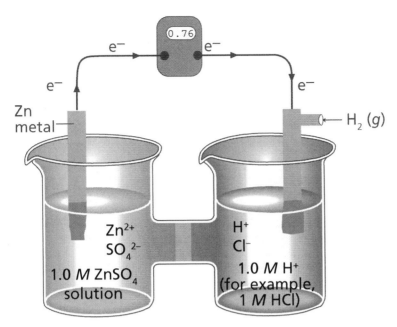

SOLUTION: $Zn(s)|Zn^{2+}(aq) \parallel H^+(aq)|H_2(g)|Pt(s)$

AP Tips

Here are some mnemonic devices to help you remember some facts about electrochemistry and redox reactions.

- "LEO" goes "GER" means <u>L</u>oss of <u>E</u>lectrons is <u>O</u>xidation and <u>G</u>ain of <u>E</u>lectrons is <u>R</u>eduction.

- To recall what happens at the anode and the cathode: RedCat and AnOx means reduction occurs at the cathode and oxidation occurs at the anode.

- To know the migration of ions toward the electrodes for both types of cells, "CAT" ions move to the "CAT" hode and "AN" ions move to the "AN" ode.

You will be provided any standard reduction potentials necessary to solve a problem on the AP test.

You should be able to sketch a galvanic cell and label the electrodes, the flow of electrons, and the flow of ions.

STANDARD REDUCTION POTENTIALS

(*Chemistry* 8th ed. pages 826–830/9th ed. pages 842–846)

The cell potential, E_{cell}, is the potential of the cell to do work on its surroundings by driving an electric current through a wire. By definition, a potential of 1 volt is produced when 1 joule of energy moves 1 coulomb of electric charge across a potential. The magnitude of the cell potential is a measure of the driving force behind an electrochemical reaction. Sometimes it is referred to as the electromotive force or emf. Tables of reduction potentials give $E°_{cell}$, standard voltages for reduction half-reactions measured at standard conditions of 1 atmosphere, 1 molar solution, and 25°C. Note that the oxidation potential is equal and opposite to the reduction potential.

CALCULATING THE CELL POTENTIAL OF A GALVANIC CELL

(*Chemistry* 8th ed. pages 830–831/9th ed. pages 846–847)

The reaction occurring in a galvanic cell can be broken down into an oxidation half-reaction and a reduction half-reaction. Calculate the cell potential of the overall reaction.

EXAMPLE: Consider a galvanic cell based on the reaction:

$$Al + Ni^{2+} \rightarrow Al^{3+} + Ni$$

Give the balanced cell reaction and calculate the cell potential, $E°_{cell}$, for the reaction.

Step 1: Write the oxidation and reduction half-reactions.

Oxidation: $Al \rightarrow Al^{3+} + 3 e^-$ **Reduction:** $Ni^{2+} + 2 e^- \rightarrow Ni$

Step 2: For the reduction half-reaction, look up the potential in the table.

$Ni^{2+} + 2 e^- \rightarrow Ni$ $\qquad\qquad\qquad$ $E°_{red} = -0.23$ V

Step 3: For the oxidation half-reaction, $E°_{ox} = -E°_{red}$.

Oxidation: $Al \rightarrow Al^{3+} + 3 e^-$

$E°_{ox} = -E°_{red} = -(-1.66$ V$) = +1.66$ V.

Step 4: The cell potential for the overall reaction is equal to the sum of the reduction potential, $E°_{red}$, and the oxidation potential, $E°_{ox}$.

$$E°_{cell} = E°_{ox} + E°_{red}$$

$$E°_{cell} = -0.23 \text{ V} + 1.66 \text{ V} = 1.43 \text{ V}$$

To obtain the balanced cell reaction, you must make sure that the electrons lost equal the electrons gained. When multiplying the half-reactions through by a coefficient, do not change the value of $E°$, because potential is an intensive property: it does not depend on how many times a reaction occurs.

3 ($Ni^{2+} + 2 e^- \rightarrow Ni$)	$E°_{red} = -0.23$ V
2 ($Al \rightarrow Al^{3+} + 3 e^-$)	$E°_{ox} = +1.66$ V
3 Ni^{2+} + 2 Al → 3 Ni + 2 Al^{3+}	$E°_{cell} = 1.43$ V

SPONTANEOUS REACTIONS

(*Chemistry* 8th ed. pages 833–836/9th ed. pages 849–852)

Gibbs free energy, $\Delta G°$, is discussed in Chapter 11. It can be calculated from the cell potential, $E°_{cell}$.

$$\Delta G° = -nFE°_{cell}$$

Faraday's constant, F, has a value of 96,500 C/mol e⁻.

The number of moles of electrons transferred in a redox reaction is represented by n.

A spontaneous reaction is one that has a negative value for $\Delta G°$ or a positive value for $E°_{cell}$.

EXAMPLE: Will 1 M HCl dissolve silver metal and form Ag^+ solution?

SOLUTION: Write the half-reactions and calculate $E°_{cell}$.

$2 H^+ + 2 e^- \rightarrow 2 H_2$	$E°_{red} = 0.00$ V
$2 Ag \rightarrow 2 Ag^+ + 2 e^-$	$E°_{ox} = -0.80$ V
$2 H^+ + 2 Ag \rightarrow H_2 + 2 Ag^+$	$E°_{cell} = -0.80$ V

The negative value for $E°_{cell}$ indicates that the reaction will not occur.

DETERMINING WHICH SUBSTANCES ARE MORE LIKELY TO BE OXIDIZED OR REDUCED

(*Chemistry* 8th ed. pages 851–852/9th ed. pages 867–868)

You may be asked if an element or ionic species is capable of reducing another element or ion. To determine if the reaction will occur, write the half-reactions and calculate the cell potential as in the previous example.

EXAMPLE: Bromine, Br_2, can oxidize iodide, I^-, to iodine, I_2. However, Br_2 cannot oxidize chloride, Cl^-, to chlorine, Cl_2. Explain why the first reaction occurs yet, the second one does not.

SOLUTION: Begin by writing the appropriate half-reactions. Then calculate the cell potential for the overall reaction.

First the reaction in which Br_2 oxidizes I^-:

$Br_2 + 2 e^- \rightarrow 2 Br^-$	$E°_{red} = 1.09$ V
$2 I^- \rightarrow I_2 + 2 e^-$	$E°_{ox} = -0.54$ V
$Br_2 + 2 I^- \rightarrow 2 Br^- + I_2$	$E°_{cell} = 0.55$ V

This reaction occurs; $E°_{cell}$ is positive.

$Br_2 + 2 e^- \rightarrow 2 Br^-$	$E°_{red} = 1.09$ V
$2 Cl^- \rightarrow Cl_2 + 2 e^-$	$E°_{ox} = -1.36$ V
$Br_2 + 2 Cl^- \rightarrow 2 Br^- + Cl_2$	$E°_{cell} = -0.27$ V

This reaction does not occur; $E°_{cell}$ is negative

For a substance to be oxidized, it must lose electrons and another substance must gain electrons because oxidation and reduction always occur together.

In any pair, the substance with the larger (more positive) $E°_{red}$ is more likely to gain electrons. It will be the reactant in the reduction half-reaction. The substance with the smaller (more negative) $E°_{red}$ is more likely to lose electrons. It will be the reactant in the oxidation half-reaction.

EXAMPLE: Classify each of the following as more likely to be oxidized, more likely to be reduced, or both. Within each list, arrange in order of increasing likelihood of being oxidized or reduced.

Br_2, Mg, Fe^{2+}, I_2, Cl^-, Cu^{2+}

SOLUTION:

Reduced: $Fe^{2+} < Cu^{2+} < I_2 < Br_2$

Oxidized: $Cl^- < Fe^{2+} < Mg$

The reduction potentials for these substances are:

$Br_2 + 2 e^- \rightarrow 2 Br^-$	$E°_{red} = 1.09$ V
$Mg^{2+} + 2 e^- \rightarrow Mg$	$E°_{red} = -2.37$ V
$Fe^{2+} + 2 e^- \rightarrow Fe$	$E°_{red} = -0.44$ V
$I_2 + 2 e^- \rightarrow 2 I^-$	$E°_{red} = 0.54$ V
$Cl_2 + 2 e^- \rightarrow 2 Cl^-$	$E°_{red} = 1.36$ V
$Cu^{2+} + 2 e^- \rightarrow Cu$	$E°_{red} = 0.34$ V

To be reduced, a substance must be capable of gaining electrons. Of the species listed, Mg and Cl^- cannot gain any more electrons. The others are listed in order of reduction potentials, with the largest positive number first.

To be oxidized, a substance must be able to lose electrons. Br_2 and I_2 are unlikely to lose electrons, and Cu^{2+} is already in its highest oxidation state. On the other hand, Cl^- and Mg can go to Cl and Mg^{2+}. Fe^{2+} can exist as Fe^{3+} or Fe so it can be oxidized or reduced. These are listed in *reverse* order of reduction potentials, with the most negative number (smallest) first.

ELECTROLYTIC CELLS

(*Chemistry* 8th ed. pages 847–850/9th ed. pages 864–867)

In an electrolytic cell, a nonspontaneous reaction is made to occur by forcing an electric current through the cell. In an earlier example, it was shown that the following reaction is spontaneous:

$$3 Ni^{2+} + 2 Al \rightarrow 3 Ni + 2 Al^{3+}$$

The reverse of this reaction: $3 Ni + 2 Al^{3+} \rightarrow 3 Ni^{2+} + 2 Al$ is nonspontaneous and can be made to occur by the addition of an external power source. This electrolytic cell can be set up with two compartments just like the galvanic cell, with the replacement of a power supply for the voltmeter.

In the process of electroplating, the electrolytic cell can also be set up using only one compartment, as shown in the figure below.

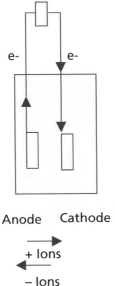

For example, an object to be plated with copper is the cathode and is immersed in a copper(II) sulfate solution. The reduction reaction $Cu^{2+} + 2\ e^- \rightarrow Cu$ will deposit copper onto the object. The anode can also be made of copper, and the oxidation of the copper anode will replace the Cu^{2+} ions.

REACTIONS THAT OCCUR IN AN ELECTROLYTIC CELL

To determine which reactions occur at the anode and the cathode during electrolysis, you must consider all possible reactions and their reduction and oxidation potentials. If the reaction takes place in an aqueous solution, the oxidation and reduction of water must be considered.

EXAMPLE: A solution of copper(II) sulfate is electrolyzed. Calculate the cell potential of the reaction, $E°_{cell}$.

SOLUTION:

	Possible reactions[1]	Cell potential, $E°$(V)
Cathode	$Cu^{2+} + 2\ e^- \rightarrow Cu$	0.34
	$SO_4^{2-} + 4\ H^+ + 2\ e^- \rightarrow H_2SO_3 + H_2O$	0.20
	$2\ H_2O + 2\ e^- \rightarrow H_2 + 2\ OH^-$	−0.83
Anode	$Cu \rightarrow Cu^{2+} + 2\ e^-$	−0.34
	$2\ H_2O \rightarrow O_2 + 4\ H^+ + 4\ e^-$	−1.23

[1]Note: There is no half-reaction for the oxidation of SO_4^{2-}. S in SO_4^{2-} is in its highest oxidation state, +6, and cannot be oxidized further.

For each electrode, the reaction with the more positive potential will occur. At the cathode, Cu^{2+} will be reduced. At the anode, Cu will be oxidized.

$Cu^{2+} + 2 e^- \rightarrow Cu$

$Cu \rightarrow Cu^{2+} + 2 e^-$

AP Tip

Frequently, the electrodes are inert for electrolysis. For example, during the electrolysis of KI(aq) K^+, I^-, and H_2O are the only species present. Only I^- and H_2O are present to be oxidized at anode. Note: In aqueous KI, there is no K(s) to be oxidized.

STOICHIOMETRY OF ELECTROLYTIC PROCESSES

(*Chemistry* 8th ed. pages 849–850/9th ed. pages 866–867)

In this section, you will review how much chemical change occurs with the flow of a given current for a specified time. You might be asked how much metal was plated (formed) or how long an electroplating process will take or how much current is required to produce a specified amount of metal over a period of time.

Some units to know how to use include A, amperes; 1 A = 1 C/s; coulombs, C; Faraday's constant is 96,500 C = 1 mol e^-.

EXAMPLE: A current of 10.0 A is passed through a solution containing M^{2+} for 30.0 min. It produces 5.94 g of metal, M. Determine the identity of metal, M.

SOLUTION: Since the metal forms a cation with a 2+ charge, 2 moles of electrons are required to reduce 1 mole of the metal.

$$10.0 \ A = \frac{10.0 \ C}{sec} \times \frac{60 \ s}{min} \times 30.0 \ min = 1.80 \times 10^4 \ C$$

$$1.80 \times 10^4 \ C \times \frac{1 \ mole \ e^-}{96500 \ C} \times \frac{1 \ mol \ M}{2 \ mol \ e^-} = 9.33 \times 10^{-2} \ mol \ M$$

$$5.94 \ g \ M \times \frac{1}{9.33 \times 10^{-2} \ mol \ M} = 63.7 \ g/mol$$

The metal is copper.

This can also be shown in one step:

$$5.94 \ g \ M \times \frac{2 \ mole \ e^-}{1 \ mol \ M} \times \frac{96500 \ C}{mole \ e^-} \times \frac{1 \ s}{10.0 \ C} \times \frac{1 \ min}{60 \ s} \times \frac{1}{30.0 \ min} = 63.7 \ g/mol$$

COMPARISON OF GALVANIC AND ELECTROLYTIC CELLS

Galvanic and electrolytic cells have a few features in common. For both types of cells, reduction always occurs at the cathode and oxidation at the anode. In an electrolytic cell, electrons travel from the battery to the cathode. In both cases, electrons travel in the wire, but you wouldn't say the electrons travel from the anode to the cathode in an electrolytic cell. Positive ions are always attracted to the cathode whether the cell is electrolytic or galvanic. The table below compares the galvanic cell to the electrolytic cell.

	Galvanic	Electrolytic
Ions attracted to the cathode	Cations (+)	Cations (+)
Ions attracted to the anode	Anions (–)	Anions (–)
Sign of $E°_{cell}$	+	–
Spontaneity	Spontaneous	Nonspontaneous

In both types of cells, the + ions or cations move toward the cathode because there is an excess of negative ions at the cathode caused by the reduction of + ions in solution. Likewise, oxidation at the anode produces + ions, so negative ions or anions in the salt bridge must move to the anode to maintain electrical neutrality.

MULTIPLE-CHOICE QUESTIONS

No calculators are to be used on this part of the exam.

1. In the reaction, $MnO_4^- + 5 Fe^{2+} + 8 H^+ \rightarrow Mn^{2+} + 5 Fe^{3+} + 4 H_2O$,
   (A) Fe^{3+} is oxidized and Mn^{2+} is reduced
   (B) H^+ is oxidized and MnO_4^- is reduced
   (C) Fe^{2+} is oxidized and MnO_4^- is reduced
   (D) electrons are transferred from Mn^{2+} to Fe^{2+}

AP Tip

Remember that you may be asked to write a balanced equation such as the one used in Question 1, and then answer a related question about the chemical species being oxidized or reduced or about the change in oxidation of one of the elements.

2. The $E°$ for $Mg \rightarrow Mg^{2+} + 2 e^-$ is +2.37 volts.
   The $E°$ for $2 Mg^{2+} + 4 e^- \rightarrow 2 Mg$ is
   (A) 2.37 volts
   (B) –2.37 volts
   (C) 4.74 volts
   (D) –4.74 volts

3. The function of a salt bridge (or porous barrier) in an electrochemical cell (galvanic cell) is to allow ions to flow
   (A) through the wire from reducing agent to oxidizing agent
   (B) to encourage charge building up on both sides of the cell
   (C) to keep the net charge on each side at zero
   (D) from the oxidizing side of the cell to the reducing side

4. What is the value of $\Delta G°$ for the reaction written below?

   $2\ MnO_4^-(aq) + 16\ H_3O^+(aq) + 5\ Zn(s) \rightarrow 2\ Mn^{2+}(aq) + 24\ H_2O(l) + 5\ Zn^{2+}(aq)$

   You are given the following standard reduction potentials for the two half-reactions:

   $E°\ (MnO_4^- \mid Mn^{2+}) = +1.49\ V$

   $E°\ (Zn^{2+} \mid Zn) = -0.76\ V$

   (A) -7.04×10^6 J
   (B) -1.34×10^6 J
   (C) -1.92×10^6 J
   (D) -2.17×10^6 J

5. Given: $Mg^{2+} + 2\ e^- \rightarrow Mg$ -2.37 V

            $Fe^{3+} + 1\ e^- \rightarrow Fe^{2+}$ $+0.77$ V

   When the reaction $2\ Mg + Fe^{3+} \rightarrow 2\ Mg^{2+} + Fe^{2+}$ comes to equilibrium, the $E°_{cell}$ value (cell potential) becomes
   (A) 3.14 V
   (B) 1.60 V
   (C) 0.83 V
   (D) 0.00 V

6. For the reaction $Cu^{2+}(aq) + Zn(s) \rightarrow Zn^{2+}(aq) + Cu(s)$, $E° = +1.10$ V. When 1.00 mole of zinc is consumed, how many faradays are transferred?
   (A) $96{,}500 \times 2.00 \times 6.023 \times 10^{23}$
   (B) 96,500
   (C) $96{,}500 \times 2$
   (D) 2.00

7. The galvanic cell based on the reactions $Ag^+ + 1\ e^- \rightarrow Ag$ ($E° = +0.80$ V) and $Fe^{3+} + 1\ e^- \rightarrow Fe^{2+}$ ($E° = +0.77$ V)
   (A) has electrons lost by Ag^+ and gained by Fe^{2+}
   (B) has the mass of the silver electrode decreasing as this reaction proceeds
   (C) has an overall cell potential difference (voltage) of +1.57 V
   (D) has electrons flowing from Fe^{2+} to Ag^+

8. Iron can be protected from oxidation by putting it into electrical contact with a substance that is more likely to be oxidized than iron. Given the reduction potentials below, which metals could be used to protect iron?

$Fe^{2+}(aq) + 2\ e^- \rightarrow Fe(s)$ $E° = -0.44$ V

$Zn^{2+}(aq) + 2\ e^- \rightarrow Zn(s)$ $E° = -0.76$ V

$Cu^{2+}(aq) + 2\ e^- \rightarrow Cu(s)$ $E° = 0.34$ V

$Sn^{2+}(aq) + 2\ e^- \rightarrow Sn(s)$ $E° = -0.14$ V

$Mg^{2+}(aq) + 2\ e^- \rightarrow Mg(s)$ $E° = -2.37$ V

(A) Zn or Mg
(B) Sn or Cu
(C) Zn or Ag
(D) Cu or Mg

9. Copper may be used for electroplating, with a half-reaction of $Cu^{2+} + 2\ e^- \rightarrow Cu$. If a current of 10.0 A is applied to a Cu^{2+} solution for 60.0 minutes, the mass of copper plated out can be calculated as
(A) $10.0 \times 3600. \times (1/96{,}500) \times (2.00/1) \times 63.5$
(B) $10.00 \times 3600. \times (6.02 \times 10^{23}) \times (1/2.00) \times 63.5$
(C) $96{,}500 \times (1/10.0) \times (1/2.00) \times (1/3600.) \times 63.5$
(D) $96{,}500 \times (1/10.0) \times (1/2.00) \times (1/3600.) \times (1/63.5)$

10. Given the following data:

$Ca^{2+}(aq) + 2\ e^- \rightarrow Ca(s)$ $E° = -2.87$ V

$Zn^{2+}(aq) + 2\ e^- \rightarrow Zn(s)$ $E° = -0.76$ V

$Co^{2+}(aq) + 2\ e^- \rightarrow Co(s)$ $E° = -0.28$ V

$Sn^{2+}(aq) + 2\ e^- \rightarrow Sn(s)$ $E° = -0.14$ V

$Pb^{2+}(aq) + 2\ e^- \rightarrow Pb(s)$ $E° = -0.13$ V

Which of the following correctly describes the ease of oxidation of the substances listed under standard state conditions?
(A) $Ca^{2+} > Zn^{2+} > Co^{2+} > Sn^{2+} > Pb^{2+}$
(B) $Pb^{2+} > Sn^{2+} > Co^{2+} > Zn^{2+} > Ca^{2+}$
(C) $Ca > Zn > Co > Sn > Pb$
(D) $Pb > Sn > Co > Zn > Ca$

Use the following data to answer questions 11, 12, and 13.

$$Ag^+ + e^- \rightarrow Ag \quad E° = 0.80 \text{ V}$$

$$Al^{3+} + 3e^- \rightarrow Al \quad E° = -1.66\text{V}$$

11. What is the balanced equation for the spontaneous reaction?
    (A) $3 Ag^+ + Al \rightarrow Al^{3+} + 3 Ag$
    (B) $3 Ag + Al^{3+} \rightarrow Al + 3 Ag^+$
    (C) $Ag + Al^{3+} \rightarrow Al + 3 Ag^+$
    (D) $Ag^+ + Al^{3+} \rightarrow Al + Ag^+$

12. What is $E°_{cell}$ for a voltaic cell using the two half-reactions at 25°C?
    (A) –2.46 V
    (B) –0.74 V
    (C) +0.74 V
    (D) +2.46 V

13. What would happen to the cell emf if NH_3 were added to the silver cell and $Ag(NH_3)_2^+$ forms?
    (A) no change
    (B) increased
    (C) reduced
    (D) cannot be determined without additional information

14. Which of the following statements concerning galvanic cells is/are true?
    (A) The two half-cells are connected by a salt bridge.
    (B) Electrons flow from the anode to the cathode.
    (C) Reduction occurs at the cathode.
    (D) All of the above are true.

15. Metal A is more easily oxidized than metal B. What is true of A^+ and B^+?
    (A) A^+ is more easily reduced than B^+.
    (B) B^+ is more easily reduced than A^+.
    (C) If a strip of metal B is plated with metal A, the metal A plating will corrode first.
    (D) Both (B) and (C) are true.

FREE-RESPONSE QUESTIONS

Calculators, Tables, and Equations may be used on this part of the exam.

1. (a) Which occurs more often in nature, oxidation or reduction? Discuss your answer.
   (b) The half-reaction for the hydrogen electrode, $2 H^+ + 2 e^- \rightarrow H_2$, has been given the $E°$ value of zero. Explain why such a standard is necessary.
   (c) The system $Mg(s) + Cu^{2+}(aq) \rightarrow Mg^{2+}(aq) + Cu(s)$ has a value of $E°_{cell}$ of +2.71 V. What is the value of $\Delta G°$ for this system?

2. Consider the following galvanic cell: $Mg(s)|Mg^{2+}(aq) \parallel Al^{3+}(aq)|Al(s)$

   Standard Reduction Potentials: $\quad Mg^{2+} + 2\ e^- \rightarrow Mg \quad -2.37\ V$

   $$Al^{3+} + 3\ e^- \rightarrow Al \quad -1.66\ V$$

   (a) Give the equation for the spontaneous cell reaction which produces charge flow.
   (b) Indicate which substance is oxidized and which is reduced in this reaction. Label the anode and the cathode electrodes for this cell.
   (c) Calculate the $E°_{cell}$.
   (d) How will the potential difference (voltage) of the galvanic cell $Cu(s) + 2\ Ag^+(aq) \rightarrow Cu^{2+}(aq) + 2\ Ag(s)$ be affected by the addition of NaCl(aq)? Explain.
   (e) How does increasing the mass of the anode affect the voltage? Justify your response.
   (f) The electrolysis of aqueous NaCl does not produce metallic sodium. Explain.

Answers

MULTIPLE-CHOICE QUESTIONS

1. **C** In changing from Fe^{2+} to Fe^{3+}, each iron(II) ion loses an electron, which is oxidation; MnO_4^- changing to Mn^{2+} is a gain of electrons, which is reduction (*Chemistry* 8th ed. page 823/9th ed. page 839). LO 3.8

2. **B** When the half-reaction is reversed, the sign of the potential is also reversed. However, the $E°$ does not change. The potential is an intensive property, which means that it is not dependent upon how many times the reaction takes place (*Chemistry* 8th ed. pages 829–830/9th ed. pages 845–846). LO 3.12

3. **C** While electrons flow through the wire from reducing agent to oxidizing agent, ions flow from one side of the cell through the salt bridge to the other side to keep the net charge at zero. If this were not done, a large amount of energy would be required to 'force' electrons to move from a positive environment into a negative environment; with such charge differences due to the charge buildup on the two sides the cell would not function; the current would be zero (*Chemistry* 8th ed. pages 823–825/9th ed. pages 839–842). LO 3.13

4. **D** In examination of the balanced oxidation–reduction reaction equation written above, you can quickly determine that the number of electrons transferred is 10 (5 Zn → 5 Zn^{2+}) and that the cell potential is determined by $E°_{cell} = E°(ox) + E°(red) = +0.76 + 1.49 = 2.25\ V$. Using $\Delta G° = -nFE°$ where $n = 10$ and F is 96,500 coulombs, $= -(10)(96500)(2.52) = -2.17 \times 10^6 J$ (*Chemistry* 8th ed. pages 835–836/9th ed. pages 851–852). LO 5.13

5. **D** When the cell reaction reaches equilibrium, no electrons flow and $E°_{cell} = 0$ (*Chemistry* 8th ed. pages 831–835, 838–839/9th ed. pages 847–851, 854–855). LO 6.25

6. **D** The charge on one mole of electrons is called the faraday (*F*, named for the Englishman Michael Faraday). In this case, two moles of electrons are transferred, hence 2.00 faradays of charge are transferred. (One faraday is 96,500 coulombs of charge, the charge on one mole of electrons.) (*Chemistry* 8th ed. pages 833–835/9th ed. pages 849–852). LO 3.13

7. **D** The overall equation for this cell reaction is $Fe^{2+}(aq) + Ag^+(aq) \rightarrow Fe^{3+}(aq) + Ag(s)$ in which Fe^{2+} is oxidized (loses electrons) and is therefore the anode. Because Fe^{2+} loses electrons, they flow from Fe^{2+} to Ag^+, which is reduced to $Ag(s)$, and the mass of the silver electrode increases (*Chemistry* 8th ed. pages 831–833/9th ed. pages 847–849). LO 3.13

8. **A** Metals with an $E°$ more negative than iron are more likely to be oxidized (*Chemistry* 8th ed. pages 846–847/9th ed. pages 861–864). LO 3.12

9. **A** Adding units to the style of responses where a setup is given is often very helpful. In this case it might better look like: (10.0 C/s)(3600/s)(1 mole e^-/96,500 C)(2.00 mole e^-/1 mole Cu)(63.5g/mol Cu) (*Chemistry* 8th ed. pages 847–850/9th ed. pages 864–868). LO 3.12

10. **C** Oxidation is the loss of electrons, and oxidation half-reactions would be the reverse of each of the above equations. This means the potential for each of the oxidation half-reactions would have a positive value; thus calcium would be most easily oxidized and lead is the least easily oxidized (*Chemistry* 8th ed. pages 828–830/9th ed. pages 844–846). LO 3.12

11. **A** Ag^+ has the more positive reduction potential, so it will be reduced and Al will be oxidized (*Chemistry* 8th ed. pages 828–830/9th ed. pages 844–846). LO 3.12

12. **D** Reverse the $Al^{3+} \rightarrow Al$ to give +1.66 V, and add to the potential for $Ag^+ \rightarrow Ag$ of +0.80 V to give +2.46 V (*Chemistry* 8th ed. pages 830–831/9th ed. pages 846–847). LO 3.13

13. **C** If you reduce the [Ag^+] by formation of $Ag(NH_3)_2^+$ then the reaction $3 Ag^+ + Al \rightarrow 3 Ag + Al^{3+}$ will be driven to the left and the cell emf will be reduced (*Chemistry* 8th ed. page 836/9th ed. page 852). LO 6.8

14. **D** In a galvanic cell, the half-cells are connected with a salt bridge. Electrons flow from the anode, where oxidation takes place, to the cathode, where reduction takes place. All are correct (*Chemistry* 8th ed. pages 831–833/9th ed. pages 847–849). LO 3.13

15. **D** If metal A is more easily oxidized, its cation is less easily reduced, and a plating of metal A will act as a sacrificial anode,

oxidizing instead of the metal B. Both (B) and (C) are true (*Chemistry* 8th ed. pages 826–831/9th ed. pages 842–847). LO 3.12

FREE-RESPONSE QUESTIONS

1 (a) They occur equally; for every electron lost by one substance an electron must be gained by another substance (*Chemistry* 8th ed. page 829/9th ed. page 845). LO 3.12

(b) Because the potential of any half-reaction cannot be measured directly, some standard is required to rank the potentials of all half-reactions. Using the hydrogen half-reaction as an arbitrary standard allows such calculations. When we say, for example, that $Zn^{2+} + 2\ e^- \rightarrow Zn$ has a potential of -0.76 V, we really mean with respect to the potential for the hydrogen half-reaction. A good comparison might be assigning sea level as the zero measure for altitude and then comparing mountain heights and ocean depths to this standard marker (*Chemistry* 8th ed. page 826/9th ed. page 842). LO 3.13

(c) Find $\Delta G°$ using the relationship $\Delta G° = -nFE°_{cell}$:
$-(2)(96,500\ C)(2.71\ V) = -5.23 \times 10^5$ V-C (1 J = 1 V-C). (*Chemistry* 8th ed. pages 833–836/9th ed. pages 849–852). LO 5.13

2. (a) $3\ Mg(s) + 2\ Al^{3+}(aq) \rightarrow 3\ Mg^{2+}(aq) + 2\ Al(s)$ (*Chemistry* 8th ed. pages 829–838/9th ed. pages 845–854). LO 3.2

(b) Mg loses e^-, therefore is oxidized and is the site of oxidation called the anode. In like manner, Al^{3+}, which is gaining these same electrons, is reduced, and the Al electrode is the site of reduction, called the cathode (*Chemistry* 8th ed. pages 829–838/9th ed. pages 845–854). LO 3.13

(c) +2.37 V

$\underline{-1.66\ V}$
+0.71 V

(*Chemistry* 8th ed. pages 829–838/9th ed. pages 845–854). LO 3.13

(d) The added $Cl^-(aq)$ will react with the $Ag^+(aq)$, precipitating as $AgCl(s)$. This lowers the silver ion concentration, which shifts the equilibrium to the left, making the silver ions less available to react with the solid copper, and <u>lowers</u> the voltage (*Chemistry* 8th ed. page 836/9th ed. page 852). LO 6.8

(e) If the mass of the anode (site of oxidation) is changed there will be no effect on the voltage. The oxidation and reduction potentials are determined by the nature of the metal and not the amount of the metal. You might be able to "run" the cell longer by changing the size of certain electrodes, but would not produce more voltage (*Chemistry* 8th ed. pages 829–838/9th ed. pages 845–854). LO 3.12

(f) When the standard reduction potentials for the two possible reactions are compared,

$$Na^+ + 1\ e^- \rightarrow Na\ E° = -2.71\ V$$

$$2\ H_2O + 2\ e^- \rightarrow H_2 + 2\ OH^- \qquad\qquad E° = -0.83\ V$$

It is evident that water is the better competitor for electrons of these two ($E°$ for water is the more positive value) (*Chemistry* 8th ed. pages 829–838/9th ed. pages 845–854). LO 3.12

10

BIG IDEA 4:
KINETICS

Big Idea 4

Rates of chemical reactions are determined by details of the molecular collisions.

Chemical reactions occur at different rates. A reaction may happen in the blink of an eye or it may take millennia to reach equilibrium. There are many different factors that affect the rate of reactions and the rate can provide evidence for the mechanism of a reaction. Reaction rates can by increased by suitable catalysts, as well.

You should be able to
- Identify factors which affect reaction rates.
- Calculate the rate of production of a product or consumption of a reactant using mole ratios and the given rate.
- Determine the rate law for a reaction from given data, overall order, and value of the rate constant, inclusive of units.
- Determine the instantaneous rate of a reaction.
- Use integrated rate laws to determine concentrations at a certain time, t, and create graphs to determine the order of a reaction. Also, determine the half-life of a reaction.
- Explain how collision theory supports observations of reactions and reaction rates.
- Write the rate law from a given mechanism given the speeds of each elementary step.

■ Write the overall reaction for a mechanism and identify catalysts and intermediates present.

■ Explain how different kinds of catalysts change reaction rates.

AP Tip

Questions on kinetics may appear in the both the multiple-choice section and free-response section. You may be asked to analyze data, plan and implement an experiment, and construct an explanation based on evidence collected in an experiment.

REACTION RATES

(*Chemistry* 8th ed. pages 540–545/9th ed. pages 553–557)

The reaction rate is the change in the concentration of a reactant or product per unit time.

Consider the reaction, A → B.

$$Rate = -\frac{\Delta[A]}{\Delta t}$$

The concentration of A in moles per liter is represented by [A]. The change in time is represented by Δt. The quantity, $-\Delta[A]/\Delta t$, is negative because the reactant concentrations are decreasing as products are formed.

EXAMPLE: Consider the reaction $4\ PH_3(g) \rightarrow P_4(g) + 6\ H_2(g)$.

If 0.0048 mol of PH_3 is consumed in a 2.0-L container during each second of the reaction, what are the rates of production for P_4 and H_2?

SOLUTION: The rate at which PH_3 is being consumed is $-\dfrac{\Delta[PH_3]}{\Delta t}$.

0.0048 mol PH_3/(2.0 L × s) = 0.0024 mol L^{-1} s^{-1} PH_3

The rate at which P_4 and H_2 are being produced can be determined by using mole ratios:

$$\frac{0.0024\ \text{mol}\ PH_3}{L \times s} \times \frac{1\ \text{mol}\ P_4}{4\ \text{mol}\ PH_3} = 0.0060\ \text{mol}\ L^{-1}\ s^{-1}\ P_4$$

$$\frac{0.0024\ \text{mol}\ PH_3}{L \times s} \times \frac{6\ \text{mol}\ H_2}{4\ \text{mol}\ PH_3} = 0.0036\ \text{mol}\ L^{-1}\ s^{-1}\ H_2$$

COLLISION THEORY

(*Chemistry* 8th ed. pages 565–566/9th ed. pages 577–578)

The collision theory model accounts for the observed characteristics of reaction rates. Molecules must collide in the correct orientation with sufficient energy, called the *activation energy*, for a reaction to occur. In most reactions only a small fraction of collisions meet these criteria.

The theory assumes that most reactions occur in a series of steps where one or more reactant particles collide. This sequence of collisions is called the reaction mechanism. In a unimolecular reaction, the reactant molecule may collide with a solvent particle or with other nonreactive particles that may be present. In a bimolecular reaction, two reactant particles collide. A termolecular reaction, where three particles collide simultaneously, is rare.

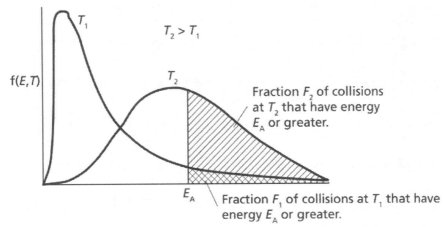

The Maxwell-Boltzmann energy diagram above shows how temperature affects the number of particles that have sufficient energy to react. At a lower temperature (T_1), the fraction of particles is very low. When temperature is higher (T_2), a higher fraction of particles has sufficient energy. Remember that in addition to having sufficient energy, the particles must collide with correct orientation. The diagram below illustrates how correct orientation is necessary for a reaction to occur.

$$HCl + C_2H_4 \rightarrow CH_3CH_2Cl$$

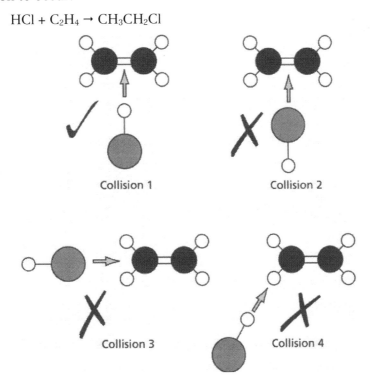

The potential energy diagram, also known as the reaction progress diagram, for the reaction

$$CO + NO_2 \rightarrow CO_2 + NO$$

is shown in the graph below. Energy must be added to break bonds of reactants in order to create a transition state at the top of the "hill," or barrier. The transition state is the highest energy state of the reactants in the reaction. Once the energy in the transition state, the activation energy, is overcome, the reactants can become products.

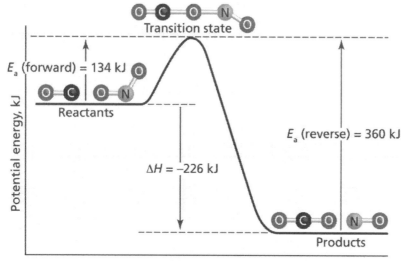

Because the products have a lower potential energy than the reactants, the reaction represented in the above diagram is exothermic. Recall that $\Delta H_{rxn} = \Delta H_{products} - \Delta H_{reactants}$. The difference between the potential energies of the products and the reactants is the enthalpy of the reaction.

If you are asked to draw the reaction progress for an endothermic reaction, the potential energy of the products will be higher than that of the reactants.

RATE LAWS

(*Chemistry* 8th ed. pages 545–559/9th ed. pages 557–571)

Rate laws show the relationship between the rate of a reaction and reactant concentrations. Except for an elementary reaction (one in which the balanced equation represents the mechanism), the rate law cannot be determined from the balanced equation.

The rate law for the reaction

$$2\,NO_2(g) \rightarrow 2\,NO(g) + O_2(g)$$

can be written as

$$\text{Rate} = k[NO_2]^n.$$

The proportionality constant, k, is called the rate constant and is determined by experiment. For a given reaction at a given temperature, this value is constant. Its units depend on the order of the reactants. The rate constant is a calculated quantity that characterizes a chemical reaction. Rate constants vary over many orders of magnitude because reaction rates vary widely.

The order, *n*, of the reactant must also be determined by experiment. It is the power to which the reactant concentration must be raised in the rate law. For example, if the reaction A → B is first order, then the rate law is Rate = $k[A]$; doubling the concentration of the reactant doubles the rate of the reaction. The units of a first-order reaction are s^{-1}. If the reaction is second order, then Rate = $k[A]^2$; doubling the concentration of the reactant will result in the rate quadrupling. The units for a second-order reaction are $L\ mol^{-1}\ s^{-1}$. If the reactant concentration is changed and the rate is not affected, the order of the reactant is zero. The rate law would be Rate = $k[A]^0$ and the units are $mol\ L^{-1}\ s^{-1}$. Note that it is possible to have fractional or negative reactant orders.

INSTANTANEOUS RATES

(*Chemistry* 8th ed. pages 542–543/9th ed. pages 555–556)

One way to determine the rate of a reaction at a particular time, the *instantaneous rate,* is to plot the reactant concentration versus time and take the slope of the tangent to the curve at time *t*.

If the slopes of tangents to the curve at two different concentrations are calculated, the rate law of a reaction can be determined by comparing the changes in rate to the changes in concentration.

In the graph to the right, when the concentration of the reactant, N_2O_5, is halved, the rate is also halved. The reaction is first order. The rate law for the reaction is Rate = $k[N_2O_5]$.

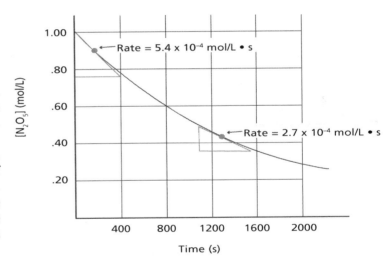

METHOD OF INITIAL RATES

(*Chemistry* 8th ed. pages 548–551/9th ed. pages 560–563)

The initial rate of a reaction is the instantaneous rate just after the reaction begins (just after *t* = 0 and before the initial concentrations of the reactants have changed.)

The rate law of a reaction can be determined by performing a few trials with different reaction concentrations and measuring the initial rate for each trial. To find the order of one reactant, change its concentration while holding the concentration of the other reactants constant.

EXAMPLE: Determine the rate law and the value of the rate constant for the reaction at $-10°C$:

$$2 \, NO(g) \; + \; Cl_2(g) \; \rightarrow \; 2 \, NOCl(g)$$

Trial	$[NO]_0$ (mol/L)	$[Cl_2]_0$ (mol/L)	Initial rate (mol L^{-1} s^{-1})
1	0.10	0.10	0.18
2	0.10	0.20	0.36
3	0.20	0.20	1.45

SOLUTION: Write the general form of the rate law:

$$Rate = k[NO]^x[Cl_2]^y$$

Your goal is to determine x and y.

To find x, the order with respect to NO, pick two trials in which NO changes and Cl_2 remains the same.

Compare Trial 3 to Trial 2.

Write a ratio of the rate law of Trial 3 to the rate of the rate law for Trial 2. Substitute the values for the rates and known concentrations and solve for the order, x.

$$\frac{Rate \, (Trial \, 3)}{Rate \, (Trial \, 2)} = \frac{k[NO]^x \cancel{[Cl_2]^y}}{k[NO]^x \cancel{[Cl_2]^y}}; \quad \frac{1.45}{0.36} = \frac{(0.20)^x}{(0.10)^x}; \quad 4.0 = 2^x; \; x = 2.0$$

The order, x, with respect to NO is 2. This means that when the concentration of NO is doubled, the rate quadruples. Note that the rate constant and the concentration of Cl_2 cancel out because they are the same in Trials 2 and 3.

To find y, the order with respect to Cl_2, pick two trials in which Cl_2 changes and NO remains the same.

Compare Trial 2 to Trial 1.

$$\frac{Rate \, (Trial \, 2)}{Rate \, (Trial \, 1)} = \frac{\cancel{k[NO]^x}[Cl_2]^y}{\cancel{k[NO]^x}[Cl_2]^y}; \quad \frac{0.36}{0.18} = \frac{(0.20)^x}{(0.10)^x}; \quad 2.0 = 2^y; \; y = 1$$

The order, y, with respect to Cl_2, is 1. This means that when the concentration of Cl_2 is doubled, the rate also doubles. Note that the rate constant and the concentration of NO cancel out because they are the same in Trials 1 and 2.

The rate law for the reaction is Rate = $k[NO]^2[Cl_2]$.

The overall order of a reaction is the sum of the reaction orders. For this example, the overall order is $2 + 1 = 3$.

Note: The order with respect to each reactant will not always be the same as the coefficients in the balanced equation and the order may be a fraction such as 1/2. Fractional rate constants are rare but have appeared on recent exams.

To determine the value of the rate constant, including its units, use the rate law and experimental data from any given trial.

$k = \text{Rate}/[\text{NO}]^2[\text{Cl}_2]$

Using values from Trial 1:

$= (0.18 \text{ M s}^{-1})/(0.10 \text{ } M)^2(0.10 \text{ } M) = 180 \text{ L}^2 \text{ mol}^{-2} \text{ s}^{-1}$.

It helps to work out the units separately.

$$\left(\frac{\text{mol}}{\text{L} \bullet \text{s}}\right)\left(\frac{\text{L}^2}{\text{mol}^2}\right)\left(\frac{\text{L}}{\text{mol}}\right) = \frac{\text{L}^2}{\text{mol}^2 \bullet \text{s}}$$

If the rate constant is known and the order with respect to one of the reactants has been determined, the order with respect to the other can be calculated even if its concentration is not held constant between any of two trials.

EXAMPLE: Determine the rate law for the reaction of ammonium and nitrite ions in aqueous solution at 25°C:

$\text{NH}_4^+(aq) + \text{NO}_2^-(aq) \rightarrow \text{N}_2(g) + 2 \text{ H}_2\text{O}(l)$

Trial	$[\text{NH}_4^+]_0$ (mol/L)	$[\text{NO}_2^-]_0$ (mol/L)	Initial rate (mol L^{-1} s^{-1})
1	0.0100	0.200	5.37×10^{-7}
2	0.0400	0.200	2.15×10^{-6}

SOLUTION: Write the general form of the rate equation.

$$\text{Rate} = k[\text{NH}_4^+]^m[\text{NO}_2^-]^n$$

Using Trials 1 and 2, determine the order, m, of NH_4^+ using the technique described above. You should find that $m = 1$. Since only 2 trials were run, you must use your newly found order with respect to NH_4^+ and the concentrations given to solve for n.

Rate (Trial 2) = $k[\text{NH}_4^+][\text{NO}_2^-]^n$

Rate (Trial 1) $k[\text{NH}_4^+][\text{NO}_2^-]^n$

$\dfrac{2.15 \times 10^{-6}}{5.37 \times 10^{-7}} = \dfrac{k(0.200)(0.0400)^n}{k(0.0100)(0.200)^n}$

$4.00 = 20(0.200)^n$

$0.200 = (0.200)^n$

$n = 1$

The reaction is first order in each reactant and the rate law is

$$\text{Rate} = k[\text{NH}_4^+][\text{NO}_2^-]$$

INTEGRATED RATE LAWS

(*Chemistry* 8th ed. pages 551–560/9th ed. pages 563–572)

An integrated rate law, derived from the differential rate law, expresses the reactant concentration as a function of time. The table below summarizes the integrated rate laws for the reaction
A → Products.

	Order		
	Zero	*First*	*Second*
Rate Law:	Rate = k	Rate = $k[A]$	Rate = $k[A]^2$
Integrated Rate Law:	$[A] = -kt + [A]_0$	$\ln[A] = -kt + \ln[A]_0$	$\dfrac{1}{[A]} = kt + \dfrac{1}{[A]_0}$
Plot Needed to Give a Straight Line:	$[A]$ versus t	$\ln[A]$ versus t	$\dfrac{1}{[A]}$ versus t
Relationship of Rate Constant to the Slope of Straight Line:	Slope = $-k$	Slope = $-k$	Slope = k
Half-Life:		$t_{1/2} = \dfrac{0.693}{k}$	

You can determine the order of the reactant graphically if you know the concentration of A at various times, t, during the reaction. For example, if you plot $\ln[A]$ vs. t and obtain a straight line, the reaction is first order in A. If the graph is not linear, then the reaction is not first order. The table above summarizes what is graphed to test for the order of the reactant.

Zero Order

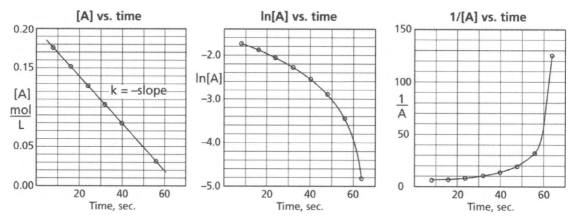

First Order

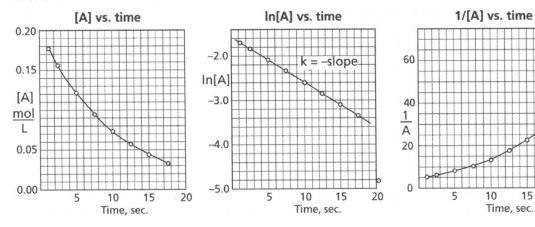

Second Order

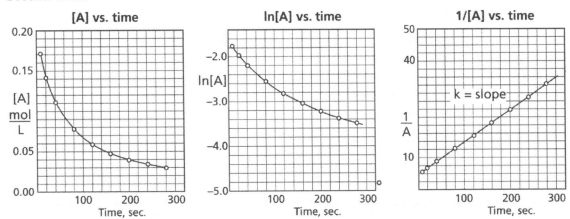

EXAMPLE: The rate of the reaction

$$NO_2(g) + CO(g) \rightarrow NO(g) + CO_2(g)$$

depends only on the concentration of nitrogen dioxide below 225°C. At a temperature below 225°C, the following data were collected.

Time (s)	$[NO_2]$ (M)	$\ln[NO_2]$	$1/[NO_2]$ (M^{-1})
0	0.500	−0.693	2.00
1.20×10^3	0.444	−0.812	2.25
3.00×10^3	0.381	−0.965	2.62
4.50×10^3	0.340	−1.079	2.94
9.00×10^3	0.250	−1.386	4.00
1.80×10^4	0.174	−1.749	5.75

SOLUTION: Assume that the data are first order and see if the plot of $\ln[NO_2]$ vs. time is linear. If this isn't linear, try the second-order plot of $1/[NO_2]$ vs. time. The data and plots follow.

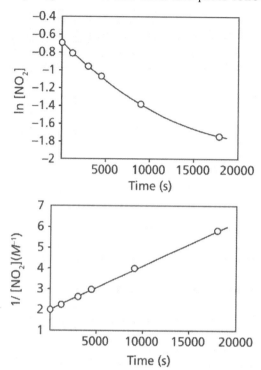

The plot of $1/[NO_2]$ vs. time is linear, which means the reaction is second order so the slope of this line gives the value of k.

$$\text{Slope} = k = \frac{\Delta y}{\Delta x} = \frac{(5.75 - 2.00)\ M^{-1}}{(1.8 \times 10^4 - 0)\ s} = 2.08 \times 10^{-4}\ \text{L mol}^{-1}\ \text{s}^{-1}$$

To determine $[NO_2]$ at 2.70×10^4 s, use the integrated rate law where $1/[NO_2]_0 = 1/0.500\ M = 2.00\ M^{-1}$.

$$1/[NO_2] = kt + 1/[NO_2]_0$$

$$\frac{1}{[NO_2]} = \frac{2.08 \times 10^{-4}\ \text{L}}{\text{mol s}} \times 2.70 \times 10^4\ s + 2.00\ \text{L mol}^{-1}$$

$$\frac{1}{[NO_2]} = 7.62\ \text{L mol}^{-1}$$

$$[NO_2] = 0.131\ M$$

The half-life of a reactant, $t_{1/2}$, is the time required for a reactant to reach half of its original concentration. The general equation for the half-life for the first order appears in the table on page 218.

THE KINETICS OF RADIOACTIVE DECAY

(*Chemistry* 8th ed. pages 878–888/9th ed. pages 896–907)

Radioactive decay is a common example of first-order kinetics in a real-life context. The decay of nuclides is represented by $\ln\left(\dfrac{N}{N_0}\right) = -kt$

where N_o = the original mass of nuclides
N = the mass remaining at time t
k = the first-order rate constant
t = time.

HALF-LIFE

(*Chemistry* 8th ed. page 879/9th ed. page 897)

The half-life, $t_{1/2}$, is the time required for the number of nuclides to reach half of their original value. It can be determined by the equation:

$$t_{1/2} = 0.693/k$$

EXAMPLE: Iodine-131, used in the diagnosis and treatment of thyroid disease, has a half-life of 8.1 days. If a patient with thyroid disease consumes a sample containing 10 µg of iodine-131, how long will it take for the amount of iodine-131 to decrease to 1/100 of the original amount?

SOLUTION: Use the equation: $\ln(N/N_o) = -kt$

Since $N = 0.010\, N_o$, substitute $0.010\, N_o$ for N.

Since $t_{1/2} = 0.693/k$, substitute 0.693/8.1 days for k.

Solving for t, you get

$\ln(0.010) = -0.693t/8.1$ days

t = 54 days.

FACTORS AFFECTING REACTION RATES

Increasing the reactant concentrations increases the chances for more molecular collisions which make products. Except for zero-order reactions, increasing reactant concentrations will usually increase the reaction rate.

Increasing the reactant's surface area increases the frequency of particle collisions. For example, granular zinc reacts more quickly with hydrochloric acid than a strip of zinc.

Increasing the reaction temperature speeds it up since the average kinetic energy of the particles is higher. More particles will have sufficient activation energy to react. Higher temperatures increase the rates of both forward and reverse reactions, increasing the number of collisions that have sufficient energy in a given period of time. The general rule-of-thumb states for each 10°C increase in temperature the reaction rate doubles and works well for reactions performed close to room temperature with activation energies of around 50 kJ mol⁻¹.

MEASURING REACTION RATES

The rate of a reaction is experimentally determined by measuring the amount of reactants converted to products in a given time. A common method of measuring the reaction rate is to use a spectrophotometer or colorimeter to monitor the absorption of light of a specific wavelength. The absorbance of the chemical is directly related to its concentration via Beer's Law.

For instance, the rate of disappearance of color from the reaction of blue food dye and bleach (NaOCl) can be analyzed. According to Beer's Law, absorbance is directly related to [dye].

$$\text{Rate} = k[\text{dye}]^x[\text{OCl}^-]^y$$

If blue food dye is the limiting reagent and the bleach concentration is so large that it remains constant throughout the reaction, then the rate expression simplifies to

$$\text{Rate} = k_{pseudo}\,[\text{dye}]^x$$

where k_{pseudo} is the pseudo rate constant for the reaction. The actual rate constant, k, can be determined by

$$k = k_{pseudo}/[\text{OCl}^-]$$

1.00 mL 0.0264 M sodium hypochlorite added to 25.00 mL of blue food dye.

Absorbance of blue food dye at 630 nm

time (min)	Abs	ln Abs
0	0.591	−0.526
1	0.369	−0.997
2	0.262	−1.339
3	0.157	−1.852
4	0.113	−2.180
5	0.071	−2.645
6	0.045	−3.101
7	0.025	−3.689

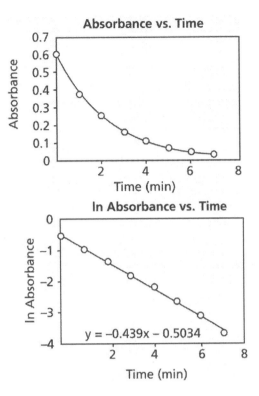

Since the graph of ln abs vs. time is linear, the reaction is first order in dye with k_{pseudo} = 0.439. The experiment was carried out under the same conditions with 0.0132 M NaOCl and the slope was half meaning the reaction is also first order in OCl⁻. The actual rate constant is

$$k = k_{pseudo}/[OCl^-]$$

$$k = 0.439/0.0264 = 16.6 \text{ L mol}^{-1}$$

and the rate law is

$$Rate = k[dye][OCl^-]$$

CATALYSIS

(*Chemistry* 8th ed. pages 570–577/9th ed. pages 583–589)

The diagram below shows the pathway for both catalyzed and uncatalyzed reactions. A catalyst speeds up a reaction by lowering the activation energy of both the forward and reverse reactions without being consumed itself. The activation energy is lowered because the mechanism of the reaction has changed and the transition state is stabilized; the pathway from reactants to products is different which is depicted by the lower squiggly line.

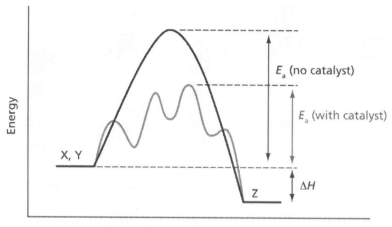

Reaction Progress

Three classes of catalysis reactions are important in AP Chemistry: acid-base, surface, and enzyme.

Acid–base catalysis involves a reactant gaining or losing a proton which causes the reaction rate to increase. In acid catalysis, the catalyst donates a proton to the reactant and the reaction rate increases with decreasing pH. A common example is the acid-catalyzed esterification reaction between a carboxylic acid and an alcohol. The acid typically used is concentrated sulfuric acid since this acid contains almost no water which can hydrolyse esters. In base catalysis, the reactant donates a proton to the basic catalyst causing an increase in reaction rate with increasing pH. An industrial application of base catalysis is the production of polyurethane foams.

Surface catalysis involves the formation of new intermediates or an increase in the probability of successful collisions by improving the orientation of the reactants. The diagram below shows the decomposition of N_2O on rhodium clusters which mimics the chemistry in catalytic converters in automobiles.

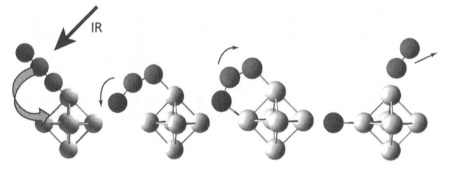

Another example of surface catalysis includes finely divided iron in the synthesis of ammonia from nitrogen and hydrogen gas. The gases adsorb onto the surface of the iron and their bonds are weakened. Since the fragments of nitrogen and hydrogen are in close proximity, formation of new nitrogen-hydrogen bonds is favored.

Enzyme catalysis plays an important role in living organisms. Enzymes are homogenous catalysts that make products necessary for the organism. After a substrate binds to the enzyme, the shape of the enzyme changes slightly. The substrate is converted into products which then leave the enzyme to be used elsewhere in the body. The enzyme is again available to bind with more substrate. Enzymes lower the activation energy by providing alternative pathways for biochemical reactions to occur.

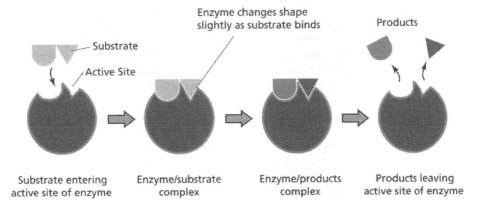

MECHANISMS

(*Chemistry* 8th ed. pages 562–565/9th ed. pages 574–577)

A mechanism is a series of steps by which a reaction occurs according to collision theory. The elementary steps, each step in the mechanism, must add up to give the overall balanced equation for the mechanism. The slowest step in the mechanism must agree with the experimentally determined rate law.

Once the rate law has been determined experimentally, chemists propose several mechanisms consistent with that rate law and design experiments to determine which mechanism fits the data. You will have to know how to identify catalysts and intermediates in a mechanism and write the overall equation for a mechanism. You will also need to be able to write a rate law from a given mechanism.

A catalyst is present in the reactants and also appears in the products. Recall that the catalyst is not consumed in the reaction. The catalyst does not appear in the overall reaction.

EXAMPLE: Identify the catalyst in the decomposition of ozone by atoms of chlorine.

$$Cl(g) + O_3(g) \longrightarrow ClO(g) + O_2(g)$$
$$O(g) + ClO(g) \longrightarrow Cl(g) + O_2(g)$$
$$\overline{O(g) + O_3(g) \longrightarrow 2\,O_2(g)}$$

SOLUTION: $Cl(g)$ is the catalyst because it is a reactant in the first reaction and a product in the second reaction. $Cl(g)$ does not appear in the overall reaction.

An intermediate is produced in one elementary step and then consumed in the next. It also does not appear in the overall equation for the reaction because it cancels out. The detection and identification of intermediates provides evidence that scientists use to justify one mechanism over another.

EXAMPLE: The synthesis of *t*-butyl alcohol, an octane booster in gasoline, is shown below. Identify the intermediate in the reaction.

$(CH_3)_3CBr \rightleftharpoons (CH_3)_3C^+ + Br^-$

$(CH_3)_3C^+ + OH^- \rightarrow (CH_3)_3COH$

SOLUTION: Since $(CH_3)_3C^+$ appears as a product in the first reaction and as a reactant in the second reaction, it is an intermediate in the overall reaction.

EXAMPLE: Consider the balanced equation for the hypothetical reaction

$2 A + 2 B \rightarrow 2 C + D_2$

The experimentally determined rate law is Rate = $k[A]^2[B]$. Which of the following two mechanisms is consistent with the rate law?

I. A + B → E + C   (slow)

   E + A → E_2 (fast)

   E_2 + B → D_2 + C   (fast)

II. A + B ⇌ E   (fast, equilibrium)

   E + A → E_2 + C   (slow)

   E_2 + B → D_2 + C   (fast)

SOLUTION: For the proposed mechanism to be correct, the overall reaction and the rate law for the mechanism must agree with the given reaction and the experimentally determined rate law.

Write the overall reaction for each mechanism. Add up the elementary steps. Cancel out the catalysts and intermediates that appear. E and E_2 are intermediates because they are produced in one step and consumed in the subsequent step of the mechanism.

I. A + B → ~~E~~ + C   (slow)

   ~~E~~ + A → ~~E_2~~   (fast)

   ~~E_2~~ + B → D_2 + C   (fast)

   $2 A + 2 B \rightarrow 2 C + D_2$ is the overall reaction.

II. A + B ⇌ ~~E~~   (fast, equilibrium)

   ~~E~~ + A → ~~E_2~~ + C   (slow)

   ~~E_2~~ + B → D_2 + C   (fast)

   $2 A + 2 B \rightarrow 2 C + D_2$ is the overall reaction.

The overall reaction for each mechanism matches the given reaction so either mechanism could be correct.

The next step is to determine which mechanism has a rate law that matches the experimental data. Write the rate law for the slowest step in each mechanism.

Mechanism I

Rate = k[A][B]

This rate law is not consistent with the rate law determined by experiment; mechanism I is not possible for this reaction.

Mechanism II

Rate = k[E][A]

[E] is an intermediate and may not be included in the rate law. Because the first step in the mechanism is reversible and fast, the rate of the forward reaction equals the rate of the reverse reaction.

Rate (forward) = k_f[A][B]

Rate (reverse) = k_r[E]

Rate (forward) = Rate (reverse), therefore k_f[A][B] = k_r[E]. Rearranging the terms gives:

[E] = (k_f/k_r)[A][B] = k'[A][B]

Substitute for [E] in the rate law for the slow step in mechanism II.

Rate = k[E][A]

Rate = $k(k'$[A][B])[A]

Combining the rate constants gives k'' and [A][A] is [A]^2 to get

Rate = k''[A]^2[B]

Mechanism II is possible because its rate law agrees with the experimentally determined rate law and the stoichiometry also agrees with the rate determining step.

DETERMINATION OF ACTIVATION ENERGY

(*Chemistry* 8th ed. pages 567–570/9th ed. pages 579–583)

Activation energy can be experimentally determined using the Arrhenius equation

$$\ln(k) = -\frac{E_a}{R}\left(\frac{1}{T}\right) + \ln(A).$$

The rate constant is represented by k.

E_a is the activation energy.

R is the gas constant, 8.3145 J mol^{-1} K^{-1}.

T is the Kelvin temperature.

A is the frequency factor that is related to the collisions and is temperature dependent.

One way to determine the activation energy, E_a, is to measure the rate constant, k, at several different temperatures, and then graph $\ln(k)$ vs. $1/T$ which gives a straight line with the slope equal to $-E_a/R$.

EXAMPLE: The activation energy for the following reaction was experimentally determined by varying the temperature at which the reaction was performed.

$6\ I^-(aq) + BrO_3^-(aq) + 6\ H^+(aq) \rightarrow 3\ I_2(aq) + Br^-(aq) + 3\ H_2O(l)$

Temperature (K)	Rate constant, k ($L^3\ mol^{-3}\ s^{-1}$)	1/Temperature (K^{-1})	ln k
275	15	0.00364	2.71
285	21	0.00351	3.04
290	26	0.00345	3.26
300	40.	0.00333	3.69
310	60.	0.00323	4.09

What is the activation energy of this reaction?

SOLUTION: The data must be graphed to determine the slope of the line.

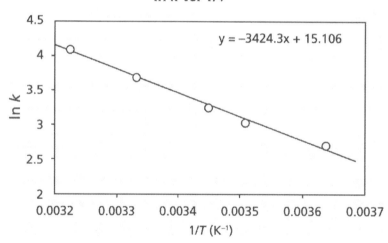

ln k vs. 1/T

$$y = -3424.3x + 15.106$$

The slope of the line is equal to $-E_a/R$ and the precision is limited by 2 significant figures in the rate constant.

$-3400\ K = -E_a/8.3145\ J\ mol^{-1}\ K^{-1}$

$E_a = 28\ kJ\ mol^{-1}$

As you can see from the data, as the temperature increases, the rate constant also increases.

MULTIPLE-CHOICE QUESTIONS

No calculators are to be used in this section.

Each of the following questions or incomplete statements has four suggested responses. Select the one which best answers the question or incomplete statement.

1. The mechanism below shows how ethanol (CH_3CH_2OH) is converted into ethene (CH_2CH_2).

    Which explanation describes the process?
    (A) HA reacts with CH_3CH_2OH to produce $CH_2CH_2 + H_2O + HA$
    (B) HA reacts with CH_3CH_2OH to produce $CH_2CH_2 + H_3OA$
    (C) HA reacts with CH_3CH_2OH to produce $CH_2CH_2 + HA$
    (D) HA reacts with CH_3CH_2OH to produce $CH_2CH_2 + H_2O$

2. A student is trying to find the activation energy of a reaction. What technique could be used?

    (A) Vary the concentrations of all reactants in several different experiments at a constant temperature.
    (B) Choose one set of reactant concentrations and run the same reaction at different temperatures.
    (C) Use a spectrophotometer to monitor the time required for a reaction to go to completion.
    (D) Add a catalyst to the reaction to see how much quicker the reaction goes.

3. The rate law of a reaction is determined to be

   rate = $k[A][B]^2$

   Which statement would most likely describe this reaction?
   (A) The reaction is catalyzed by an enzyme.
   (B) The reaction involves a one-step, termolecular mechanism.
   (C) The stoichiometry of the overall reaction must be A + 2 B → products.
   (D) The reaction involves the formation of intermediates.

4. In the reaction,

   $$NO_3(g) + CO(g) \rightleftharpoons NO_2(g) + CO_2(g)$$

   the carbon in CO must collide with an oxygen in NO_3 with sufficient energy to react. Which of the diagrams below would most likely result in the formation of products?

   (A) −40°C

   (B) 60°C

   (C) 100°C

   (D) 80°C

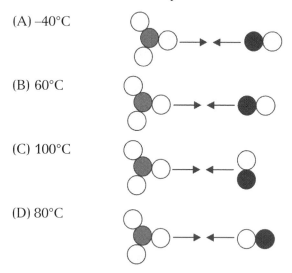

5. The graph at the right shows the number of molecules that have sufficient energy to overcome E_a for a given reaction. How would adding an enzyme change the appearance of the graph?

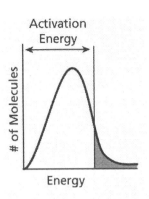

(A)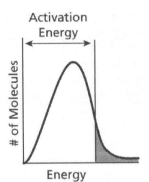

(C)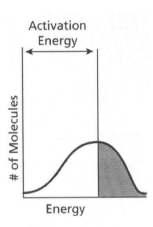

(B)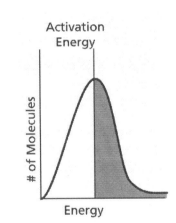

(D)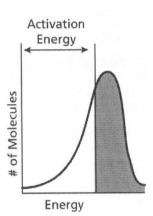

6. The values for the change in enthalpy, ΔH, and the activation energy, E_a, for a given reaction are known. The value of E_a for the reverse reaction equals
   (A) E_a for the forward reaction
   (B) $-(E_a)$ for the forward reaction
   (C) the sum of $-\Delta H$ and E_a
   (D) the sum of ΔH and E_a

7. For two first-order reactions of different substances A and X

   A → B $t_{1/2}$ = 30.0 min

   X → Y $t_{1/2}$ = 60.0 min

   This means that
   (A) a certain number of grams of A will react twice as fast as the same number of grams of X
   (B) a certain number of grams of X will react twice as fast as the same number of grams of A
   (C) the rate constant for A → B is lower than the rate constant of X → Y
   (D) 3 moles of A will react more rapidly than 3 moles of X

8. A reaction is first order with respect to [X] and second order with respect to [Y]. When [X] is 0.20 M and [Y] = 0.20 M the rate is 8.00 × 10^{-3} M min^{-1}. The value of the rate constant, including correct units, is
   (A) 1.00 M min^{-1}
   (B) 1.00 M^{-2} min^{-1}
   (C) 2.00 M^{-1} min^{-1}
   (D) 2.0 M^{-2} min^{-1}

9. The activation energy for this reaction, X + 2 Y → 3 Z, shown in the potential energy diagram, could be
   (A) increased by increasing [X] and [Y]
   (B) increased by increasing the temperature
   (C) decreased by removing Z from the system as it forms
   (D) decreased by adding a suitable catalyst

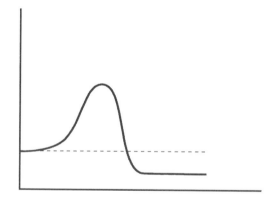

10. For all zero-order reactions
    (A) a plot of time vs. concentration squared is linear
    (B) E_a is very low
    (C) the concentration of reactants is constant
    (D) the rate is independent of time

Use the following information to answer questions 11 through 13.

Carbon monoxide reacts with oxygen according to the equation

$$CO(g) + \tfrac{1}{2} O_2(g) \rightarrow CO_2(g)$$

The rate law for the reaction is: Rate = $k[CO]^m[O_2]^n$

Experimental information for the reaction is given in the following table:

	[CO] mol L^{-1}	[O$_2$] mol L^{-1}	Initial rate, mol L^{-1} min^{-1}
Experiment 1	0.020	0.020	3.68×10^{-5}
Experiment 2	0.040	0.020	1.47×10^{-4}
Experiment 3	0.020	0.040	7.36×10^{-5}

11. Which values correspond to the reaction orders m and n for CO and O$_2$?
    (A) $m = 4$, $n = 2$
    (B) $m = 1$, $n = \tfrac{1}{2}$
    (C) $m = 1$, $n = 1$
    (D) $m = 2$, $n = 1$

12. What is the overall reaction order?
    (A) 0
    (B) 1
    (C) 2
    (D) 3

13. What is the numerical value for the rate constant, k, for this reaction?
    (A) 3.68×10^{-5} mol L^{-1}·min^{-1}
    (B) 4.60 L^2 mol^{-2} min^{-1}
    (C) 2.93×10^{-25} mol min^{-1}
    (D) 1.54×10^4 min^{-1}

14. Which of the following statements would be correct regarding the following reaction?

    $$2 H_2(g) + O_2(g) \rightarrow 2 H_2O(g)$$

    (A) The rate of O$_2$ disappearance is twice the rate of H$_2$ disappearance.
    (B) The rate of H$_2$ disappearance is twice the rate of O$_2$ disappearance.
    (C) The rate of H$_2$O disappearance is twice the rate of O$_2$ disappearance.
    (D) The rate of H$_2$O appearance is equal to the rate of O$_2$ disappearance.

15. According to the collision theory of kinetics, which statement best describes the rate of a chemical reaction?
(A) All collisions result in a chemical reaction.
(B) All collisions between molecules with at least a minimum kinetic energy result in reaction.
(C) All collisions between molecules with at least a minimum kinetic energy and the proper orientation result in reaction.
(D) The greater the difference in energy between the reactants and the products, the faster is the reaction.

FREE-RESPONSE QUESTIONS

Calculators may be used for this section.

1. The kinetics of the reaction below were studied to determine a reaction rate and to propose a mechanism.

$$2\,A + 2\,B \rightarrow C + D + E$$

Data are presented below.

Trial	$[A]_0$ (mol L^{-1})	$[B]_0$ (mol L^{-1})	Initial Rate Formation (mol L^{-1} min^{-1}), C
1	0.040	0.060	0.332
2	0.040	0.12	0.662
3	0.080	0.060	1.32

(a) (i) Determine the order of reaction with respect to each reactant.
(ii) Write the rate law expression.
(b) Calculate the value of the rate constant and include the units.
(c) Calculate the initial rate of disappearance of B in experiment 3.
(d) A proposed mechanism is shown below.

Step 1. $A + A \rightleftharpoons X$
Step 2. $X + B \rightarrow C + Y$
Step 3. $Y + B \rightarrow D + E$

(i) Identify all catalysts and intermediates.

(ii) Determine the rate determining step.

(iii) Show that the mechanism is consistent with the rate law and with the overall stoichiometry of the reaction.

2. The Haber process is used to make ammonia, an important chemical feedstock for industry. Without the use of a catalyst, the reaction proceeds too slowly to be commercially viable.

The basic reaction is $N_2 + 3\,H_2 \rightleftharpoons 2\,NH_3$.

(a) Propose a kinetic reason that the reaction does not occur in a single elementary step.

(b) If the reaction happened in a series of bimolecular steps, this is one possibility:

$N_2 + H_2 \rightleftharpoons N_2H_2$

$N_2H_2 + H_2 \rightarrow N_2H_4$

$N_2H_4 + H_2 \rightarrow 2\ NH_3$

(i) Draw the electron dot structure of N_2 and propose a reason why the reaction would be thermodynamically unfavorable.

(ii) The decomposition of hydrazine, N_2H_4 is very exothermic. Draw the energy profile for the formation of hydrazine from N_2H_2 and H_2. Propose a reason why this reaction would be thermodynamically unfavorable.

(c) The actual Haber process uses an iron catalyst.

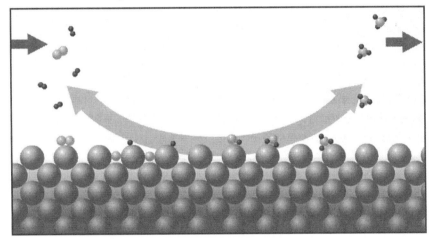

N_2 and H_2 adhere (*ad*) to the metal surface and both molecules dissociate.

Step 1. $N_2(g) \rightleftharpoons N_2(ad)$ fast

Step 2. $N_2(ad) \rightleftharpoons 2\ N(ad)$ slow

Step 3. $H_2(ad) \rightleftharpoons 2\ H(ad)$ fast

(i) Based on the diagram, propose a reason that Step 2 is the rate determining step.

Hydrogen atoms migrate across the surface in the following series of reactions.

$N(ad) + H(ad) \rightleftharpoons NH(ad)$

$NH(ad) + H(ad) \rightleftharpoons NH_2(ad)$

$NH_2(ad) + H(ad) \rightleftharpoons NH_3(ad)$

The final step is for the NH_3 to desorb from the catalyst.

$NH_3(ad) \rightleftharpoons NH_3(g)$

(ii) How does the diagram show a method to shift equilibrium to $NH_3(g)$?

(d) Describe one physical characteristic of the catalyst that would ensure its usefulness.

Answers

Multiple-Choice Questions

1. **A** This is an example of an acid-catalyzed reaction. A catalyst is a reactant in the first step of the mechanism and a product in the last step of the mechanism. LO 4.9

2. **B** Activation energy is calculated by performing a reaction using the same concentrations of reactants at different temperatures. By graphing ln$k$ vs 1/T, E_a can be calculated from the slope (*Chemistry* 8th ed. pages 565–570/9th ed. pages 577–583). LO 4.6

3. **D** Chances that three particles will collide with correct energy and orientation is very rare so this reaction most likely involves at least one intermediate (*Chemistry* 8th ed. pages 562–565/9th ed. pages 574–577). LO 4.7

4. **B** The temperature and orientation are both favorable for a reaction to occur (*Chemistry* 8th ed. pages 565–567/9th ed. pages 577–579). LO 4.4

5. **B** At a given temperature, the free energy of particles remains constant. The enzyme lowers E_a so more of the particles have sufficient energy to overcome the energy barrier (*Chemistry* 8th ed. pages 570–576/9th ed. pages 583–588). LO 4.9

6. **C** Examine the diagram on p. 216. The E_a of the reverse reaction must equal the E_a of the forward reaction plus ΔH of the reaction (*Chemistry* 8th ed. pages 565–568/9th ed. pages 577–581). LO 4.6

7. **D** It takes half as much time for A to form B as for X to form Y, as seen by the smaller half-life. Note that option "B" would be incorrect as the grams of A and the grams of X are not the same number of moles (*Chemistry* 8th ed. pages 555–556/9th ed. pages 567–568). LO 4.3

8. **B** From these data, it follows that the rate law is Rate = k[X][Y]^2. Solving for the rate constant and substituting data for this reaction:
   k = Rate / [X][Y]^2
      = 8.00×10^{-3} M/min/(0.200 M)(0.200 M)^2
      = 0.008 M/min/0.008 M^3
      = 1.00 M^{-2} min^{-1}
   (*Chemistry* 8th ed. pages 548–554, 562/9th ed. pages 560–566, 574) LO 4.2

9. **D** Adding a catalyst suitable for this reaction will lower the energy barrier (activation energy) by forming a different activated complex which has a lower potential energy (*Chemistry* 8th ed. pages 565–572/9th ed. pages 577–585). LO 4.8

10. **D** For zero-order reactions, Rate = $k[X]^0$. Because anything raised to the zero power is equal to one, Rate = k. This is another way of saying that the rates of zero-order reactions do not change; they do not speed up and they do not slow down, they either take place or they do not (*Chemistry* 8th ed. page 559/9th ed. page 571). LO 4.2

11. **D** Compare experiments 1 and 2, doubling the concentration of CO has caused the initial rate to increase by a factor of 4 or 2^2. Therefore $m = 2$. And comparing experiments 1 and 3, doubling the concentration of O_2, keeping the [CO] the same, resulted in the initial rate also being doubled, or 2^1. Therefore $n = 1$ (*Chemistry* 8th ed. pages 549–551/9th ed. pages 561–563). LO 4.2

12. **D** The overall order is simply the sum of $m + n$ or $2 + 1 = 3$ (*Chemistry* 8th ed. pages 549–551/9th ed. pages 561–563). LO 4.2

13. **B** Using experiment 1, rate = $k[CO]^2[O_2]$; $3.68 \times 10^{-5} = k(0.020)^2(0.020)$

    Solving for k, $k = 4.60$ L^2 mol^{-2} min^{-1}.

    (*Chemistry* 8th ed. pages 549–551/9th ed. pages 561–563) LO 4.2

14. **B** According to the balanced equation 2 moles of H_2 are used up for every mole of O_2, so during the same time period, the rate of disappearance of the H_2 would be twice as great (*Chemistry* 8th ed. pages 540–545/9th ed. pages 553–557). LO 4.1

15. **C** Collision theory states that the molecules colliding must not only have the minimum combined activation energy required for reaction, they must also have the proper spatial orientation when they collide (*Chemistry* 8th ed. pages 565–568/9th ed. pages 577–581). LO 4.5

FREE-RESPONSE QUESTIONS

1. (a) To determine how each of the concentrations of the reactants is related to the reaction rate, only the one reactant concentration may change.
   (i) Compare $[A]_0$ in Trial 1 and 3. Doubling the concentration increases the rate by a factor of about 4 which indicates the reaction is second order in A. Compare $[B]_0$ in Trials 1 and 2. Doubling the concentration doubles the rate which means that the reaction is first order in B.

   Rate = $k[A]^x[B]^y$

   Trial 1 $0.332 = k[0.040]^x[0.060]^y$
   Trial 3 $1.32 = k[0.080]^x[0.060]^y$

   $0.252 = 0.5^x$
   $x = 2$

Trial 1 $0.332 = k[0.040]^x[0.060]^y$
Trial 2 $0.662 = k[0.040]^x[0.12]^y$

$0.502 = 0.50^y$
$y = 1$

(ii) The rate law is rate = $k[A]^2[B]$.

(b) Solving the rate law for k yields:

$k = $ Rate/$([A]^2[B])$

$= 0.332$ mol L^{-1} min^{-1}/$(0.040$ mol L$^{-1})^2(0.060$ mol L$^{-1})$

$= 3.5 \times 10^3$ L^2 mol^{-2} min^{-1}

(c) $-1/2\Delta[B]/\Delta t = \Delta[C]/\Delta t$

$\Delta[B]/\Delta t = -2\Delta[C]/\Delta t$

$= (-2)(1.32$ mol L^{-1} min$^{-1})$

$= -2.64$ mol L^{-1} min^{-1}

(d) (i) Intermediates are X and Y because they are made in one step and used in the next. There are no catalysts.
(ii) The rate law must match the rate determining step. Step 1 cannot be the RDS because that rate law would be rate = $k[A]^2$ which does not match the experimentally determined rate law.

The rate law for Step 2 would be rate = $k[X][B]$. At first glance this does not appear to agree with the experimental rate law, either. However, intermediates are not included in the rate law. Since the first reaction is an equilibrium rate forward = rate reverse.

Rate $= k_f[A]^2 = k_r[X]$

$[X] = k_f[A]^2/ k_r$

$k_f/ k_r = k'$

$[X] = k'[A]^2$

Substituting into the rate law for the RDS,

Rate $= k_2 k'[A]^2[B]$ or Rate $= k[A]^2[B]$

(iii) The experimental rate law and the rate law of the slowest step are the same. The overall stoichiometry of the mechanism is the same as reaction which indicates the mechanism is plausible,

Step 1.   A + A ⇌ X
Step 2.   X + B → C + Y
Step 3.   Y + B → D + E
Overall. 2 A + 2 B → C + D + E

(*Chemistry* 8th ed. pages 547–565/9th ed. pages 559–577)
LO 4.2, LO 4.7

2. (a) The reaction does not occur in a single elementary step because aligning 4 particles with the correct orientation and energy would not be feasible.

   (b) (i) :N≡N: The reaction is thermodynamically unfeasible because a lot of energy would need to be added to break the very stable triple bond.

   (ii) The reaction is thermodynamically unfavorable due to the high E_a.

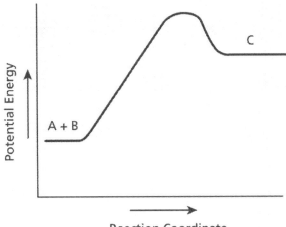

Reaction Coordinate

   (c) (i) $N_2(ad) \rightleftharpoons 2\ N(ad)$ may be the RDS because the nitrogen atoms fit very compactly between the iron atoms according to the diagram.

   (ii) As the $NH_3(g)$ desorbs, it is removed from the reaction vessel so it cannot dissociate back to reactants and so the equilibrium is shifted towards products.

   (d) One physical characteristic of the catalyst that will enhance its usefulness is high surface area so the reactants have lots of places to adsorb and react.

   (*Chemistry* 8th ed. pages 361–364, 562–572, 620–624/9th ed. pages 373–376, 574–585, 633–639) LO 4.1, LO 4.4, LO 4.5, LO 4.6, LO 4.9

11

Big Idea 5:
Thermochemistry and
Thermodynamics

> ### Big Idea 5
>
> The laws of thermodynamics describe the essential role of energy and explain and predict the direction of changes in matter.

Thermochemistry describes the heat flow of a chemical reaction or physical change. Changes in enthalpy are calculated through calorimetry, Hess's law, and standard heats of formation. Determining the value of Gibbs free energy for a process allows one to predict whether or not a process is thermodynamically favored (spontaneous). The dependence of Gibbs free energy on temperature, entropy, and enthalpy will be identified. The laws of thermodynamics will be explored.

The free-response portion of the exam may include calculations and predictions involving entropy, enthalpy, and free energy. You may be asked to interpret energy diagrams, or answer lab questions regarding the use of a calorimeter to determine the heat of a reaction.

You should be able to
  - Perform stoichiometric calculations with the enthalpy of the reaction.
  - Perform calculations with specific heat.

■ Discuss how a calorimeter is used and perform related calculations.

■ Draw, label, and perform associated calculations for heating curves involving specific heat and changes in enthalpy for phase changes.

■ Draw and label potential energy diagrams for chemical reactions.

■ Use Hess's Law, standard heats of formation, ΔH°_f, and the bond energy method to determine the heat of a reaction, and identify a process as exothermic or endothermic.

■ Write reactions representing standard heats of formation, ΔH°_f.

■ Compare the absolute entropies, S°, of elements and compounds.

■ Perform calculations with entropy S° and ΔS°.

■ Perform calculations with free energy, ΔG°_f.

AP Tips

Mathematical equations will be provided for the exam, but it would be good to be familiar with them or even better to memorize them.

TEMPERATURE VS. HEAT

(*Chemistry* 8th ed. pages 210, 236–237/9th ed. pages 220, 246–247)

Temperature is a measure of the average kinetic energy of atoms or molecules. *Heat* is the amount of energy transferred from one system to another and always flows from a hot body to a cold one.

FIRST LAW OF THERMODYNAMICS

(*Chemistry* 8th ed. pages 238–239/9th ed. pages 248–249)

The first law of thermodynamics states that energy can be converted from one form to another, but can neither be created nor destroyed: The energy of the universe is constant.

ENTHALPY

(*Chemistry* 8th ed. pages 243–244/9th ed. pages 252–253)

At constant pressure, the change in enthalpy (ΔH°) of a system is equal to the energy flow as heat. Enthalpy is a state function, so the change in H is independent of the pathway.

EXOTHERMIC

A reaction that is exothermic gives off heat and the change in enthalpy is negative ($\Delta H° < 0$). The temperature of the surroundings increases during an exothermic process.

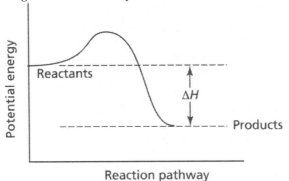

Exothermic: Products are lower energy than reactants.

ENDOTHERMIC

A reaction that is endothermic absorbs heat and the change in enthalpy is positive ($\Delta H° > 0$). The temperature of the surroundings decreases in an endothermic process.

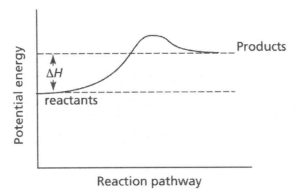

Endothermic: Products are higher energy than reactants.

EXAMPLE: How much heat is released when 4.04 g of hydrogen is reacted with excess oxygen?

SOLUTION:

$$2 \text{ H}_2(g) + \text{O}_2(g) \rightarrow 2 \text{ H}_2\text{O}(l) \qquad\qquad \Delta H° = -572 \text{ kJ}$$

$$4.04 \text{ g H}_2 \times \frac{1 \text{ mol H}_2}{2.02 \text{ g}} \times \frac{-572 \text{ kJ}}{2 \text{ mol H}_2} = -572 \text{ kJ}$$

Note that conversion factors can be written using the relationship between the enthalpy, $\Delta H°$, and the moles of reactants and products. 572 kJ of heat is produced when 1 mole of O_2 reacts with 2 moles of H_2 to produce 2 mol of H_2O.

Specific Heat

(*Chemistry* 8th ed. pages 245–246/9th ed. pages 254–255)

The specific heat capacity, s, is the amount of energy required to change the temperature of 1.0 g of a substance by 1°C and typically has units of J/(g °C). Molar heat capacity is the amount of energy required to change the temperature of 1 mole of a substance by 1°C [J/ (mol °C)].

EXAMPLE: The specific heats of solid aluminum, solid iron, mercury liquid, and carbon graphite are:

	J/(g °C)
Al(s)	0.89
Fe(s)	0.45
Hg(l)	0.14
C(s)	0.71

When the same amount of heat energy is applied to 1.0 g of each of these substances, which one will reach the highest temperature?

The answer is Hg(l). Mercury has the lowest specific heat of the four mentioned substances, which means it takes the least amount of heat to raise 1 gram of mercury 1°C.

Calorimetry

(*Chemistry* 8th ed. pages 244–249/9th ed. pages 253–258)

A calorimeter is a device used to determine experimentally the heat energy change of a chemical reaction (the "system") by observing temperature changes in the surroundings, which is usually water or another high-boiling liquid. Most calorimetry is carried out under constant pressure. In a well-insulated calorimeter, the heat change in the surroundings, q, is equal and opposite to the heat released or absorbed by the reaction, ΔH:

$$\Delta H = -q = m \times s \times \Delta T$$

Where:
- m = mass of surroundings
- s = the specific heat capacity of the surroundings
- ΔT = the temperature change in the surroundings during the reaction.

EXAMPLE: A 1.00-g sample of magnesium metal is added to a calorimeter containing 100. g of hydrochloric acid (specific heat capacity 4.184 J/(g°C) initially at 25.0°C. The solution temperature increases to 29.5°C. What is the heat of reaction, in kJ/mol?

SOLUTION: The heat gained by the solution is equal to:

$$100. \text{ g HCl} \times \frac{4.184 \text{ J}}{\text{g} \, ^\circ\text{C}} \times (29.5 ^\circ\text{C} - 25.0 ^\circ\text{C}) = 1882 \text{ J} = 1.9 \text{ kJ}$$

Since the solution's temperature increased, the reaction must be exothermic. The amount of heat released by the reaction is equal and opposite to the heat gained by the solution:

–(heat gained by solution) = (heat of reaction) = –1.9 kJ

This is the heat of reaction per gram of Mg reacted. The heat of reaction per mole of Mg reacted is:

$$\frac{-1.9 \text{ kJ}}{1 \text{ g}} \times \frac{24.31 \text{ g}}{1 \text{ mol}} = -46 \text{ kJ/mol}$$

AP Tip

Students sometimes have trouble deciding what numbers to use when calculating ΔH from calorimetry data. Remember that the thermometer is in the surroundings, so the "mass" should be the mass of water or other heat-transfer fluid. The masses of reactants and products are part of the system and should not be included in this mass. By convention, the change in temperature, ΔT, is calculated $T_{final} - T_{initial}$. According to the first law of thermodynamics, the heat lost by one substance equals the heat gained by the other substance, so ΔH will be equal in magnitude but opposite in sign to q.

HESS'S LAW

(*Chemistry* 8th ed. pages 249–255/9th ed. pages 258–264)

Hess's law states that enthalpy change, in going from a particular set of reactants to a particular set of products, is the same whether the reaction takes place in one step or in a series of elementary steps. Enthalpy is a state function. The idea is to manipulate the equations given in the problem statement so that they add up to the overall reaction. There are two ways that the equations can be manipulated.

1. Reverse the reaction. The sign of ΔH is also reversed.

2. Multiply the coefficients in a balanced reaction by an integer. The value of ΔH is multiplied by the same integer.

EXAMPLE: Given the following reactions and ΔH° values,

ΔH°

(1)	$Si(s) + 2 H_2(g) \rightarrow SiH_4(g)$	+34 kJ/mol
(2)	$Si(s) + O_2(g) \rightarrow SiO_2(s)$	–911 kJ/mol
(3)	$H_2(g) + \frac{1}{2} O_2(g) \rightarrow H_2O(g)$	–242 kJ/mol

Calculate ΔH for

$SiH_4(g) + 2 O_2(g) \rightarrow SiO_2(s) + 2 H_2O(g)$ $\Delta H^\circ = ?$

SOLUTION: Start by finding a substance that appears only once in all of the reactions, SiH_4 or H_2O. Look to see where that substance is in the final reaction and in what amount. Modify the reaction so that the substance appears where it should be and in the correct amount. SiH_4 needs to be in the reactants, so Reaction 1 is reversed. Reaction 2 is not changed. H_2O is in the products, but there are two of them in the final reaction, so Reaction 3 needs to be multiplied by two.

(1) $SiH_4(g) \rightarrow \text{S̶i̶}(s) + 2\,H_2(g)$ $-(34\ \text{kJ/mol})$

(2) $\text{S̶i̶}(s) + O_2(g) \rightarrow SiO_2(s)$ $-911\ \text{kJ/mol}$

(3) $\underline{2\,H_2(g) + O_2(g) \rightarrow 2\,H_2O(g)}$ $\underline{2(-242\text{kJ/mol})}$

$SiH_4(g) + 2\,O_2(g) \rightarrow SiO_2(s) + 2\,H_2O(g)$ $-1429\ \text{kJ} = \Delta H°$

STANDARD ENTHALPIES OF FORMATION, $\Delta H°_f$

(*Chemistry* 8th ed. pages 255–261/9th ed. pages 264–271)

The standard enthalpy of formation of a compound is the change in enthalpy that accompanies the formation of one mole of a compound from its elements with all substances in their standard states.

The degree symbol on $\Delta H°$ indicates that the process occurred under standard conditions of 25°C, 1 atm, and 1 M solutions.

By definition, the standard heat of formation for elements in their standard states equals zero.

EXAMPLE: Which of the following will have standard heats of formation equal to zero?

$H_2(g)$, $Hg(s)$, $CO_2(g)$, $H_2O(l)$, $Br_2(l)$

SOLUTION: The only elements present in their standard states are $H_2(g)$ and $Br_2(l)$. Mercury is a liquid under standard conditions. Carbon dioxide and water are compounds.

EXAMPLE: Write the balanced molecular equation representing the $\Delta H_f°$, standard heat of formation reaction of ethanol, $C_2H_5OH(l)$.

SOLUTION:

$2\,C(s) + 3\,H_2(g) + 1/2\,O_2(g) \rightarrow C_2H_5OH(l)$

Note that 1 mole of product is produced according to the definition of the standard heat of formation. All of the reactants are elements in their standard states.

Standard heats of formation can be used to calculate the enthalpy change of a reaction by subtracting the enthalpies of formation of the reactants from the enthalpies of formation of the products.

$$\Delta H°_{reaction} = \Sigma\, \Delta H°_{f\,(products)} - \Sigma\, \Delta H°_{f\,(reactants)}$$

EXAMPLE: Using the standard heats of formation, $\Delta H°_f$, calculate the change in enthalpy, $\Delta H°$, for the following reaction. The standard heats of formation for hydrogen peroxide and water are –187 kJ/mol and –285 kJ/mol, respectively.

$2 H_2O_2(l) \rightarrow 2 H_2O(l) + O_2(g)$

SOLUTION:

$\Delta H°_{reaction} = [2(-285 \text{ kJ}) + 0] - 2(-187 \text{ kJ}) = -196 \text{ kJ}$

EXAMPLE: Given the information below, calculate the heat of formation of gaseous carbon monoxide.

$2 CO(g) + C(s) \rightarrow C_3O_2(g) \quad \Delta H° = 127.3 \text{ kJ}$

$\Delta H°_f$ for $C_3O_2(g)$ is –93.7 kJ/mol.

SOLUTION:

$\Delta H°_{reaction} = \Sigma \Delta H°_{f(products)} - \Sigma \Delta H°_{f(reactants)}$

$\Delta H°_{reaction} = \Delta H°_f$ for $C_3O_2(g) - [2 \Delta H°_f$ for $CO(g) - \Delta H°_f$ for $C(s)]$

Rearrange the equation and solve for missing variable; note $\Delta H°_f$ for $C(s)$ is zero.

$\Delta H°_f$ for $CO(g) = [\Delta H°_f$ for $C_3O_2(g) - \Delta H°_{reaction}]/2$

$= (-93.7 \text{ kJ} - 127.3 \text{ kJ})/2 = -110.5 \text{ kJ/mol}$

BOND ENERGIES AND ENTHALPY

THE ENERGETICS OF BOND FORMATION

(*Chemistry* 8th ed. pages 341–342/9th ed. pages 352–353)

A chemical bond forms when a system of bonded atoms is lower in potential energy than that of independent atoms. The optimum distance between atoms is the bond length, which represents this lowest energy state. The bond length is a balance between the attractive electrostatic forces between the nucleus of one atom and the electrons of another, and the repulsive forces between the positively charged nuclei of the two atoms and negatively charged electrons of the two atoms. You should be able to explain the main features of the potential energy diagram, Figure 8.1, on page 342 of the 8th edition and page 354 of the 9th edition of *Chemistry*.

Breaking bonds requires an input of energy to overcome the attractive forces. When new bonds are formed, energy is released. The difference between input and output determines whether a process is endothermic or exothermic.

CALCULATING ENTHALPY FROM BOND ENERGIES

(*Chemistry* 8th ed. pages 361–364/9th ed. pages 373–376)

To use this method, draw Lewis structures of the reactants and products.

Example: Estimate the change in enthalpy, ΔH, for the following reaction using the table of bond energies on page 362 of the 8th edition and page 374 of the 9th edition of *Chemistry*.

$$N_2 + 3\,H_2 \rightarrow 2\,NH_3$$

Solution: First, draw the Lewis structures for the reactants and products.

$$N_2 \quad + \quad 3\,H_2 \quad \longrightarrow \quad 2\,NH_3$$

$$:N\!\equiv\!N: \qquad 3(H\!-\!H) \qquad 2\!\left(\!\overset{\cdot\cdot}{\underset{\underset{H}{|}}{H\!-\!N\!-\!H}}\!\right)$$

In the reactants, one triple bond between the atoms of nitrogen and one single bond between atoms of hydrogen are broken. Bond breaking is an endothermic process that has a positive value for enthalpy. Energy must be added to break the bonds.

Three single bonds between hydrogen and nitrogen are formed in the products. Bond formation is exothermic having a negative value for enthalpy.

$\Delta H = \Sigma$ energy to break bonds $- \Sigma$ energy released when new bonds are formed.

Reactant Bonds Broken:

N_2: 1 mol N≡N	1 mol × 941 kJ/mol = 941 kJ
H_2: 3 mol H–H	3 mol × 432 kJ/mol = 1296 kJ
	Total energy required = 2237 kJ

Product Bonds Formed:

NH_3: 2 × (3 mol N–H)	6 mol × 391 kJ/mol = 2346 kJ

$\Delta H = 2237$ kJ $- 2346$ kJ $= -109$ kJ

Intermolecular Forces

(*Chemistry* 8th ed. pages 440–443/9th ed. pages 455–458)

Intermolecular forces are attractions between molecules that arise when molecules are near each other. Breaking these forces requires the input of energy, as illustrated with the heating curve below. One way to determine the relative strengths of intermolecular forces is to measure how much energy is required to cause a phase change. However, the bonds between the atoms within a molecule (*intra*molecular forces) are not broken, so the molecules themselves remain intact. Intermolecular forces are discussed in more detail in Chapter 3, Big Idea 2.

HEATING CURVES

(Chemistry 8th ed. pages 475–476/9th ed. pages 487–488)

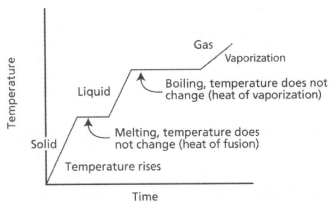

When a system is heated, energy is transferred into it. In response to the energy it receives, the system changes, for example, by increasing its temperature. A plot of the temperature versus time is called **the heating curve.** One such heating curve is shown above. The physical states of the substance and the phase transitions are identified along the curve.

The temperature of the system usually increases when energy is applied. However, when the energy absorbed is used for phase transition, a change in the physical state, the temperature (average kinetic energy) remains constant because the potential energy of the system is being increased as the molecules are rearranged in the phase change. Phase changes only affect the intermolecular forces of attraction; no intramolecular bonds are broken.

HEAT OF FUSION

(Chemistry 8th ed. page 476/9th ed. page 488)

The heat of fusion, ΔH_{fus} is the enthalpy change that occurs in melting a solid at its melting point.

> EXAMPLE: What quantity of heat is required to melt 1.00 kg of ice at its melting point? For ice, $\Delta H_{fus} = 6.02$ kJ/mol

> SOLUTION:

$$1.00 \text{ kg} \times \frac{1000 \text{ g}}{1 \text{ kg}} \times \frac{1 \text{ mol}}{18.0 \text{ g}} \times \frac{6.0 \text{ kJ}}{1 \text{ mol}} = 333 \text{ kJ}$$

HEAT OF VAPORIZATION

(Chemistry 8th ed. pages 470–471/9th ed. pages 482–483)

The heat of vaporization, ΔH_{vap}, is the energy required to vaporize one mole of a liquid at a pressure of one atmosphere.

> EXAMPLE: What quantity of heat is required to vaporize 130. g of water? For liquid, water, $\Delta H_{vap} = 43.9$ kJ/mol.

SOLUTION:

$$130. \text{ g} \times \frac{1 \text{ mol}}{18.0 \text{ g}} \times \frac{43.9 \text{ kJ}}{1 \text{ mol}} = 317 \text{ kJ}$$

EXAMPLE: The substance, X, has the following properties:

	Specific Heat
ΔH_{vap} = 20.0 kJ/mol	Solid = 3.0 J/(g °C)
ΔH_{fus} = 5.0 kJ/mol	Liquid 2.5 J/(g °C)
Boiling point 75°C	Gas 1.0 J/(g °C)
Melting point –15°C	

Calculate the energy required to convert 250.0 g of substance X from a solid at –50.0°C to a gas at 100°C. Assume that X has a molar mass of 75.00 g/mol.

SOLUTION:

There are 5 steps involved.

1. Heating the solid from –50.0°C to –15°C.

2. Melting the solid at –15°C.

3. Heating the liquid to its boiling point from –15°C to 75°C.

4. Boiling the liquid at 75°C.

5. Heating the gas to 100°C.

The energy used = sum of energies from individual steps.

There are 3.333 mol of X in 250.0 g of X.

Step 1: $q = m \times s \times \Delta T$; 250.0 g × [3.0 J/(g °C)] × 35°C = 26 kJ

Step 2: mol × ΔH_{fus} = 3.333 mol × 5.0 kJ/mol = 17 kJ

Step 3: $q = m \times s \times \Delta T$; 250.0 g × [2.5 J/(g °C)] × 90°C = 56 kJ

Step 4: mol × ΔH_{vap} = 3.333 mol × 20. kJ/mol = 67 kJ

Step 5: $q = m \times s \times \Delta T$; 250.0 g × [1.0 J/(g °C)] × 25°C = 6.2 kJ

The total energy required is the sum of the energies of the individual steps: (26 + 17 + 56 + 67 + 6.2) kJ = 172 kJ

ENTROPY

(*Chemistry* 8th ed. pages 776–779/9th ed. pages 791–794)

Entropy, S, is the driving force for a thermodynamically favored process: a spontaneous process readily occurring without intervention. Entropy measures the number of arrangements or positions available to a system in a given state. This positional entropy increases in going from a solid to liquid to gas. In the solid state, molecules are much closer together than in the gaseous state, with very few positions available for them.

Entropy during a process is said to be increasing when the value of $\Delta S > 0$; The value of ΔS is positive.

Entropy during a process is said to be decreasing when the value of $\Delta S < 0$; The value of ΔS is negative.

EXAMPLE: Which of the following pairs is likely to have the higher positional entropy per mole at a given temperature?

1) Solid CO_2 or gaseous CO_2?

2) N_2 gas at 1.0 atm and N_2 gas at 0.001 atm?

SOLUTION:

1) Gaseous CO_2 has more positional entropy than solid CO_2 since there are more positions for the molecules in the gaseous state to move to than in the solid state.

2) N_2 gas at 0.001 atm has more positional entropy than N_2 gas at 1.0 atm, because at a lower pressure, there is more volume for the molecules to move than at a higher pressure.

EXAMPLE: Describe the change in entropy when solid salt is added to water.

SOLUTION: The entropy increases when salt in its solid state is dissolved in water. The ions fixed in a crystal lattice in the solid are free to move about in the water due to solute–solvent interactions.

SECOND LAW OF THERMODYNAMICS

(*Chemistry* 8th ed. page 779/9th ed. page 794)

The second law of thermodynamics states that in any spontaneous process there is always an increase in the entropy of the universe. The change in entropy of the universe is equal to the change in the entropy of the system and the change in entropy of the surroundings.

$$\Delta S_{univ} = \Delta S_{sys} + \Delta S_{surr}$$

$$\Delta S_{surr} = -\Delta H/T$$

The sign of ΔS_{surr} depends on the direction of the heat flow. ΔS_{surr} is positive at constant temperature when the reaction is exothermic, since heat flows to the surroundings increasing the random motions and the entropy of the surroundings. The opposite is true for an endothermic reaction at constant pressure.

The magnitude of ΔS_{surr} depends on temperature. At a low temperature, the production of heat effects a much greater percent change in the randomness of the surroundings than it does at high temperature.

ENTROPY CHANGES IN A CHEMICAL REACTION

(*Chemistry* 8th ed. pages 786–790/9th ed. pages 801–805)

The change in entropy, ΔS, for a chemical reaction can be predicted without calculation.

For a chemical reaction involving only gaseous reactants and products, entropy is related to the total number of moles of gas on either side of the equation. If the moles of gas increase from reactants to products in a chemical reaction, the entropy is increasing. If the moles of gas decrease in a chemical reaction, the entropy is decreasing.

For a chemical reaction involving solid, liquids, and gases, the production of a gas will, in general, increase the entropy of the reaction much more than an increase in the number of moles of liquids or solids.

Example: Predict the sign of $\Delta S°$ for the following reaction:

$$N_2(g) + 3\,H_2(g) \rightarrow 2\,NH_3(g)$$

Solution: The entropy decreases as the reaction proceeds from reactants to products because the number of moles of gas decreases from four total moles to two moles. The sign of $\Delta S°$ is negative.

The change in entropy for a reaction, $\Delta S°$, can also be calculated using tabulated thermodynamic values in the appendix of the textbook or other reference book. These values would be provided to you in the exam.

$$\Delta S°_{reaction} = \Sigma\, S°_{(products)} - \Sigma\, S°_{(reactants)}$$

Example: Calculate $\Delta S°$ for the following reaction:

$$N_2(g) + 3\,H_2(g) \rightarrow 2\,NH_3(g)$$

Solution: $\Delta S° = 2(193) - [1(192) + 3(131)] = -199$ J/K

The sign of $\Delta S°$ is negative, confirming the prediction in the previous example.

Free Energy

(*Chemistry* 8th ed. pages 790–797/9th ed. pages 805–812)

Free energy, G, is a thermodynamic function whose value describes whether or not a process is spontaneous in the forward direction (reactions are usually written such that the forward direction is spontaneous). Gibbs free energy is dependent on the change in enthalpy, change in entropy, and temperature of the system. ΔG is negative for all spontaneous processes. Note, however, that ΔG provides no information about the rate of reaction. Spontaneous reactions can be very slow; rusting of iron is one example of a slow spontaneous reaction.

$$\Delta G = \Delta H - T\,\Delta S;\ T \text{ is the Kelvin temperature}$$

Using the chart below, you can predict if a reaction will occur without the exact value for ΔH and ΔS.

The Dependence of Spontaneity on Temperature		
ΔS	ΔH	ΔG
+	–	Spontaneous at all temperatures
+	+	Spontaneous at high temperatures
–	–	Spontaneous at low temperatures
–	+	Process not spontaneous at any temperature

FREE ENERGY AND CHEMICAL REACTIONS

(*Chemistry* 8th ed. pages 790–794/9th ed. pages 805–810)

The standard free energy change, $\Delta G°$, is the change in free energy that will occur if the reactants in their standard states are converted to the products in their standard states. This value cannot be measured directly, but it can be calculated from other measured quantities such as the equilibrium constant and the standard cell potential.

The standard free energy change, ΔG, can be calculated from the changes in enthalpy and entropy.

$$\Delta G° = \Delta H° - T\,\Delta S°$$

Note that the units of $\Delta G°$ and $\Delta H°$ are typically provided in kJ/mol, while $\Delta S°$ is provided in J/(K mol). Make sure your units are consistent before proceeding with calculations!

EXAMPLE: Consider the reaction $2\ POCl_3(g) \rightarrow 2\ PCl_3(g) + O_2(g)$.

The value of $\Delta S°$ is 179 J/K. The value of $\Delta H°$ is 542 kJ. At what temperature is this reaction spontaneous? Assume that $\Delta H°$ and $\Delta S°$ do not depend on temperature.

SOLUTION: The temperature at which $\Delta G° = 0$ is where the process shifts from spontaneous to nonspontaneous. Set $\Delta G° = 0$ and rearrange $\Delta G° = \Delta H° - T\,\Delta S°$ to solve for T.

$$T = \Delta H°/\Delta S°$$

$$3030\ K = 542\ kJ/\ (0.179\ kJ/K)$$

The standard free energy change, ΔG, is a state function and can be calculated by

$$\Delta G°_{reaction} = \Sigma\ \Delta G°_{f\,(products)} - \Sigma\ \Delta G°_{f\,(reactants)}$$

FREE ENERGY AND EQUILIBRIUM

(*Chemistry* 8th ed. pages 798–802/9th ed. pages 813–817)

$$\Delta G° = -RT\ \ln K;\ K = \text{equilibrium constant}$$

This is discussed in Chapter 12 (Big Idea 6) of this book.

FREE ENERGY AND CELL POTENTIAL

(*Chemistry* 8th ed. pages 800–803/9th ed. pages 815–818)

$$\Delta G° = -nFE°; E° \text{ is the standard cell potential}$$

This is discussed in Chapter 9 (Big Idea 3) of this book.

MULTIPLE-CHOICE QUESTIONS

No calculators may be used in this part of the exam.

1. The standard enthalpy of formation for nitrogen dioxide is the enthalpy change of the reaction
    (A) $1/2\ N_2(g) + O_2(g) \rightarrow NO_2(g)$
    (B) $N_2(g) + 2\ O_2(g) \rightarrow N_2O_4(g)$
    (C) $N_2(g) + 2\ O_2(g) \rightarrow 2\ NO_2(g)$
    (D) $NO(g) + 1/2\ O_2(g) \rightarrow NO_2(g)$

2. Which of the following has a non-zero standard enthalpy of formation?
    (A) $Na(s)$
    (B) $Hg(l)$
    (C) $H_2O(l)$
    (D) $N_2(g)$

3. For endothermic reactions at constant pressure
    (A) $\Delta H < 0$
    (B) $\Delta H > 0$
    (C) $\Delta S > 0$
    (D) $S < 0$

4. At a certain temperature $C(s) + O_2(g) \rightarrow CO_2(g)$ has a ΔG of -339.4 kJ/mol. This means that at this temperature
    (A) the system is at equilibrium
    (B) gaseous carbon dioxide spontaneously forms
    (C) this system has a high reaction rate
    (D) the system will not react

For questions 5, 6, and 7, consider the ΔG of four different combinations of ΔH and ΔS. Assume that both ΔH and ΔS are temperature independent.

5. Which processes are spontaneous at all temperatures?
    (A) $\Delta H = +$ and $\Delta S = +$
    (B) $\Delta H = +$ and $\Delta S = -$
    (C) $\Delta H = -$ and $\Delta S = -$
    (D) $\Delta H = -$ and $\Delta S = +$

6. The process which is nonspontaneous at all values of temperature is
   (A) ΔH = + and ΔS = +
   (B) ΔH = + and ΔS = –
   (C) ΔH = – and ΔS = –
   (D) ΔH = – and ΔS = +

7. Which of these four processes is improbable at a low temperature but becomes more probable as the temperature rises?
   (A) ΔH = + and ΔS = +
   (B) ΔH = + and ΔS = –
   (C) ΔH = – and ΔS = –
   (D) ΔH = – and ΔS = +

8. In which of the following four processes is there an increase in entropy?
   (A) $2 SO_2(g) + O_2(g) \rightarrow SO_3(g)$
   (B) $H_2O(g) \rightarrow H_2O(s)$
   (C) $Hg(g) \rightarrow Hg(l)$
   (D) $H_2O_2(l) \rightarrow H_2O(l) + 1/2 O_2(g)$

9. What is the enthalpy change for the following reaction under standard conditions?

   $CS_2(l) + 3 O_2(g) \rightarrow CO_2(g) + 2 SO_2(g)$

   $\Delta H°_f CS_2(l) = +88$ kJ/mol

   $\Delta H°_f CO_2(g) = -394$ kJ/mol

   $\Delta H°_f SO_2(g) = -297$ kJ/mol

   (A) –900 kJ
   (B) –779 kJ
   (C) –603 kJ
   (D) –1076 kJ

10. A 57-gram block of metal at 92°C is dropped into an insulated flask containing approximately 45.0 grams of ice and 30.0 grams of water at 0°C. After the system reaches equilibrium it is determined that 9.5 grams of the ice has melted. What is the specific heat of the metal? (Heat of fusion of water = 333 J/g)
    (A) 0.22 J/g °C
    (B) 0.32 J/g °C
    (C) 0.60 J/g °C
    (D) 0.92 J/g °C

11. A reaction takes place within a system. As a result, the entropy of the system decreases. Which of the following statements *must* be true?
    (A) The reaction is endothermic.
    (B) The entropy of the universe decreases.
    (C) The Gibbs free energy of the system increases.
    (D) The entropy of the surroundings increases.

12. When propane burns in air, heat is released:

$$C_3H_8(g) + 5\ O_2(g) \rightarrow 3\ CO_2(g) + 4\ H_2O(g)$$

What are the signs of H, S, and G for this process as illustrated by the above equation?

	ΔH	ΔS	ΔG
(A)	–	+	+
(B)	–	+	–
(C)	–	–	+
(D)	+	+	–

13. Electrolysis of water is a chemical change because
    (A) hydrogen bonds are broken
    (B) a great deal of energy is required
    (C) bonds between H atoms and O atoms in individual molecules are broken
    (D) the phase changes from liquid water to gaseous hydrogen and oxygen

14. Gas A_2 reacts with gas B_2 to form gas AB at constant temperature. The bond energy of AB is much greater than that of either reactant. For this process, what are the signs of H and S_{surr}?

	ΔH	ΔS_{surr}
(A)	–	+
(B)	–	–
(C)	+	–
(D)	+	+

15. An audio amplifier generates a great deal of heat that can be dissipated with heat-radiating metal fins. Which metal would be the best for this application?

	Metal	Specific heat capacity, J/(g °C)
(A)	Al	0.89
(B)	Fe	0.45
(C)	Cu	0.39
(D)	Cr	0.46

FREE-RESPONSE QUESTIONS

1. (a) Show the complete equation for the combustion of the flammable gas butene, C_4H_8.
   (b) Given the following table of bond energies, estimate the enthalpy change, ΔH, for the reaction noted in 1(a).

   Average Bond Energies (kJ/mol)

C–H	413	C=O	799
C–C	347 (single)	H–O	467
C=C	614 (double)	H–H	432
C≡C	839 (triple)	O=O	495
C–O	358		

(c) Often the heat of reaction (enthalpy) calculated from bond energies differs by 10–20% or more from the laboratory determined values. Suggest why this is so.

(d) Is this process thermodynamically favored at all temperatures? Justify your answer.

2. The molar heats of fusion and vaporization of benzene are 10.9 kJ/mol and 31.0 kJ/mol, respectively. The melting temperature of benzene is 5.5°C and it boils at 80.1°C.

   (a) Calculate the entropy changes for solid → liquid, and for liquid → vapor for benzene.

   (b) Would you expect the ΔS for these two changes to be about the same? Comment on the physical significance of the difference in these two values.

   (c) Why are the values for heat of vaporization usually so much greater than the heats of fusion?

Answers

MULTIPLE-CHOICE QUESTIONS

1. **A** This question should determine if you understand how to apply the definition of the term "standard enthalpy of formation." Like many terms in chemistry, this has a very specific meaning: It is the energy involved in forming one mole of a compound from elements in standard state at 25°C and 1 atm pressure. As applied here, you must write the equation showing the formation of $NO_2(g)$ as the product from the elements nitrogen and oxygen (both are diatomic elements under these conditions), and balance it so that only one mole of the product compound is formed (*Chemistry* 8th ed. pages 255–256/9th ed. pages 264–265). LO 5.8

2. **C** By definition, standard enthalpy of formation is the energy involved when one mole of a compound is formed from its elements in their standard states at 25°C and 1 atm. In this question, only water is a compound (*Chemistry* 8th ed. pages 255–256/9th ed. pages 264–265). LO 5.8

3. **B** In an endothermic reaction, heat is gained by the system. By convention, this is considered to be positive (*Chemistry* 8th ed. pages 249–253/9th ed. pages 258–262). LO 5.6

4. **B** A negative Gibbs free energy value indicates a spontaneous reaction; CO_2 forms. Note that it says nothing about the rate of reaction. Kinetics is the topic of another chapter (*Chemistry* 8th ed. pages 783–786, 797–800/9th ed. pages 798–801, 812–815). LO 5.13

5. **D** From $\Delta G = \Delta H - T\Delta S$, if ΔH is negative and ΔS is positive the reaction must be spontaneous because ΔG is negative in all such cases (*Chemistry* 8th ed. pages 783–792/9th ed. pages 798–808). LO 5.13

6. **B** From $\Delta G = \Delta H - T\Delta S$, if ΔH is positive and $T\Delta S$ is negative, then ΔG is positive in all cases, so the reaction is always nonspontaneous (*Chemistry* 8th ed. pages 783–792/9th ed. pages 798–808). LO 5.13

7. **A** From $\Delta G = \Delta H - T\Delta S$, if the temperature is high, the $T\Delta S$ factor is large and "overcomes" the influence of ΔH (+) to make ΔG negative; hence it becomes spontaneous at the higher temperatures (*Chemistry* 8th ed. pages 783–792/9th ed. pages 798–808). LO 5.13

8. **D** If there is an increase in entropy, then the products must be more disordered than the reactants. In choice (A), the system goes from 3 moles of gas to one mole of gas; in choice (B) the system goes from high entropy gas to low entropy solid; in choice (C) the system goes from high entropy gas to lower entropy liquid. The last choice goes from one mole of liquid to one mole of liquid and one-half mole of gas, an increase in entropy (*Chemistry* 8th ed. pages 786–790/9th ed. pages 801–805). LO 5.12

9. **D** Enthalpy change = [(–394 + (2 × –297)) – (+88)] = –1076 kJ. This is a basic Hess's law problem. Remind yourself that the heat of formation of any element in its standard state is defined as zero, which is why there is no value listed for oxygen gas (*Chemistry* 8th ed. pages 251–261/9th ed. pages 260–270). LO 5.8

10. **C** Heat required to melt the ice = 9.5 g × 333 J/g = 3164 J

    Heat lost by the metal block = mass of block × (specific heat capacity) × ΔT

    = 57 g × (specific heat capacity) × 92°C

    = specific heat capacity × 5244°C·g

    Since heat lost by metal block – heat gained by ice,

    3164J = specific heat capacity × 5244°C·g; and solving for specific heat capacity,

    specific heat capacity = 0.603 J/(g °C)

    (*Chemistry* 8th ed. pages 244–251/9th ed. pages 253–260). LO 5.6

11. **D** The entropy of the universe must increase and the free energy of the system must decrease, as these are expressions of the second law. If the entropy of the system decreases, the entropy of the surroundings must increase. If the entropy of the surroundings is to increase, the reaction must be exothermic. Therefore only the last statement is true (*Chemistry* 8th ed. pages 773–776, 783–790/9th ed. pages 788–791, 798–805). LO 5.13

12. **B** Since the reaction occurs we know it is spontaneous, which means ΔG must be negative. The reaction is exothermic, meaning that ΔH is negative and since there is an increase in the number of

molecules of gas, there is an increase in the randomness, meaning that ΔS is positive (*Chemistry* 8th ed. pages 783–787/9th ed. pages 798–801). LO 5.13

13. **C** Electrolysis is splitting water into hydrogen and oxygen gas. Bonds within the molecules are broken, so it is a chemical change. Hydrogen bonds are intermolecular forces and breaking those is a phase change (*Chemistry* 8th ed. pages 28, 475–478/9th ed. pages 260–270). LO 5.10

14. **A** The process must be exothermic $(\Delta H < 0)$ since the energy released when the new bond is formed is less than the energy required to break the bonds of the reactant molecules. The energy is released to the surroundings, so the entropy of the surroundings increases ($S_{surr} > 0$) (*Chemistry* 8th ed. pages 251–261/9th ed. pages 260–270). LO 5.13

15. **C** Copper has the lowest heat capacity, so it would transfer heat most efficiently (*Chemistry* 8th ed. pages 244–245/9th ed. pages 260–270). LO 5.6

FREE-RESPONSE QUESTIONS

1. (a) $C_4H_8(g) + 6\ O_2(g) \rightarrow 4\ CO_2(g) + 4\ H_2O(l)$
   (*Chemistry* 8th ed. pages 165–166/9th ed. pages 174–175) LO 3.8
   (b) $CH_2CHCHCH_3 + 6\ O=O \rightarrow 4\ O=C=O + 4\ H–O–H$

   Bonds broken (reactants):

1 C=C 1 mol × 614 kJ/mol	= 614 kJ
2 C–C 2 × 347	= 694
8 C–H 8 × 413	= 3304
6 O=O 6 × 495	= 2970

   Total energy required to break bonds = 7582 kJ.

   Bonds formed (products):

8 C=O 8 mol × 799 kJ/mol	= 6392 kJ
8 H–O 8 × 467	= 3736

   Total energy released as bonds form = 10128 kJ.

   The difference between the two is a negative value, denoting an exothermic reaction.

   $\Delta H = -2546$ kJ/mol C_4H_8 reacting.

   (*Chemistry* 8th ed. pages 362–364/9th ed. pages 373–376) LO 5.8
   (c) The surrounding bonds often affect the strength of a given bond. For example, the average C=O bond energy is 745 kJ/mol, but the C=O bond energy in CO_2 is 799 kJ/mol (the value given for your use in the table). Examining the structure

of butane, you might guess that the C–H bond energies of bonds near a C=C double bond would be somewhat different from those with a C–C single bond attached to the same carbon. The environment of the bond does make a difference (*Chemistry* 8th ed. pages 361–362/9th ed. pages 373–374). LO 5.9

(d) $\Delta G = \Delta H - T\,\Delta S$. When $\Delta G < 0$, the process is spontaneous. This process is exothermic, and but the entropy is decreasing (going from 7 moles of gas to 4 moles of gas and 4 moles of liquid), so ΔG will only be negative and the process spontaneous at lower temperatures. Note that if the equation was written with gaseous water as the product, the process would be spontaneous at all temperatures (*Chemistry* 8th ed. pages 783–787/9th ed. pages 798–801). LO 5.13

2. (a) When a liquid boils at its boiling temperature or freezes at its freezing temperature, no useful work can be done by the process, i.e., ΔG is zero. Therefore, under these conditions,

$$\Delta S = \Delta H/T$$

In melting, $\Delta S = 10.9 \times 10^3$ J/mol/(5.5 + 273 K) = +39.1 J/K•mol.

In boiling, $\Delta S = +87.8$ J/K•mol.

(*Chemistry* 8th ed. pages 781–783/9th ed. pages 796–798) LO 5.6

(b) Vaporization involves a much greater change in disorder than melting (gases are very disordered compared to liquids, whereas liquids and solids vary less in disorder, distance between molecules, and number of possible positions for molecules); hence $\Delta S_{vap} > \Delta S_{fus}$ (*Chemistry* 8th ed. pages 773–779/9th ed. pages 788–794). LO 5.12

(c) When a substance is melted, the molecules are still relatively close together and experience attractive forces. When a liquid is vaporized, however, the molecules become very widely separated and most attractive forces are overcome. This requires more energy than is needed for melting, hence $\Delta H_{vap} > \Delta H_{fus}$ (*Chemistry* 8th ed. page 439/9th ed. page 454). LO 5.6

12

Big Idea 6:
Equilibrium

Big Idea 6

Any bond or intermolecular attraction that can be formed can be broken. These two processes are in a dynamic competition, sensitive to initial conditions and external perturbations.

In this chapter, you will review the characteristics of equilibrium and calculations involving the concentrations of reactants and products for a given system at equilibrium. Your knowledge of the basic equilibrium problems in this chapter will enable you to qualitatively and quantitatively explain pH of acids, bases, salts, and buffers as well as the solubility of ionic compounds.

AP Tip

Equilibrium is one of the big ideas in AP Chemistry that underpins much of what you study. Make sure you are comfortable with particle and graphical representations as well as with the calculations.

You should be able to
- Write equilibrium expressions for a given reaction.
- Calculate Q and compare it to K to determine if a reaction is at equilibrium.
- Manipulate K if a reaction is reversed or multiplied by a coefficient.
- Calculate K from given equilibrium concentrations, or if given K and all except one equilibrium concentration, solve for the missing value.

■ Calculate equilibrium concentrations (or one of the missing variables) if given any two of the following values: K, the initial concentrations, one equilibrium concentration.

■ Do calculations involving gaseous equilibria, partial pressures, and K_p.

■ Use Le Châtelier's principle to determine in what direction the position of equilibrium will shift when a change is imposed.

■ Calculate the value of K from thermodynamic values such as $\Delta G°$.

EQUILIBRIUM CONDITION

Many chemical and physical changes are reversible. When equilibrium is reached, the rate of the forward reaction equals the rate of the reverse reaction. The ratio of the product concentrations to the reactant concentrations is constant at equilibrium. At a given set of conditions, macroscopic variables such as concentrations, partial pressures, and temperature do not change over time.

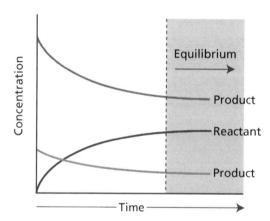

Some examples of reversible processes include biological processes such as oxygen binding to hemoglobin in red blood cells and the sense of smell due to molecules binding to receptor sites in the nose. Environmental examples include nitrogen and carbon biogeochemical cycles. Chemistry examples include dissolution of solids as well as proton transfer in acid–base reactions and electron transfer in redox reactions.

THE EQUILIBRIUM EXPRESSION

(*Chemistry* 8th ed. pages 597–598/9th ed. pages 610–611)

The equilibrium constant, K, measures the ratio of product concentrations to reactant concentrations.

For a hypothetical reaction $a\mathrm{A} + b\mathrm{B} \rightleftharpoons c\mathrm{C} + d\mathrm{D}$

$$K = \frac{[\mathrm{C}]^c[\mathrm{D}]^d}{[\mathrm{A}]^a[\mathrm{B}]^b}.$$

K is the equilibrium constant, usually given without units. Brackets, [ ], represent the concentration of the reactants and products at equilibrium in moles/liter. The concentrations of products and reactants are raised to the powers of their respective coefficients in the balanced chemical equation. Note that this is different from kinetics where the orders of each reactant must be determined by empirical evidence.

You will be expected to write the equilibrium expression for a given reaction. Remember, the concentrations of solids and liquids are not included because the concentration (amount per volume) is constant. Individual particles in a pure substance have fixed volume. Since the concentration is expressed in mol L^{-1}, changing the number of particles (mol) of a pure substance must also change the volume (L) of the pure substance.

EXAMPLE: Write the equilibrium expression for the reaction

$P_4(s) + 5\ O_2(g) \rightleftharpoons P_4O_{10}(s)$

SOLUTION: The equilibrium expression for the reaction is

$$K = \frac{1}{[O_2]^5}$$

The concentrations of the solids are not included in the expression because the concentration of a solid or liquid is a constant, so it is included in the value of *K*.

The value of the equilibrium constant measures the extent to which a reaction occurs.

K >> 1: The concentrations of the products are much greater than the concentrations of the reactants so the reaction is product-favored.

K << 1: The concentrations of the reactants are much greater than the concentrations of the products. In this case, the reaction does not proceed in the direction written to any great extent and is called a reactant-favored reaction.

K ≈ 1: Reactants and products are present in significant concentrations at equilibrium.

REACTION QUOTIENT

(*Chemistry* 8th ed. pages 608–609/9th ed. pages 620–621)

When reactants and products are mixed together, they may not be at equilibrium. The reaction quotient, *Q*, compared to the equilibrium constant, *K*, will determine which way a system will shift to reach equilibrium. If a system is not at equilibrium, it will move in a direction to reach equilibrium.

If a reactant or product in a reaction is not present and is at zero concentration, the reaction will move in the direction that produces the missing component.

If all reactants and products are present and have an initial concentration, you must determine the value of Q, the reaction quotient.

To determine if the reaction is at equilibrium or the direction it will shift to attain equilibrium, plug all of the initial concentrations into the reaction quotient, which is the same as the equilibrium expression (also called the law of mass action), and compare the value of Q to K.

Comparison of Q to K

If $Q = K$, the reaction is at equilibrium and the rate of the forward and reverse reactions are the same.

If $Q > K$, the reaction will shift to the left. A shift toward the reactants will consume products because the rate of the reverse reaction is greater than the rate of the forward reaction until equilibrium is established.

If $Q < K$, the reaction will shift to the right. A shift to produce more products will consume reactants because the rate of the forward reaction is greater than the rate of the reverse reaction until equilibrium is established.

EXAMPLE: For the reaction $2 NO(g) \rightleftharpoons N_2(g) + O_2(g)$, $K = 2.4 \times 10^3$ at a particular temperature.

(a) If the initial concentrations are 0.024 M NO, 2.0 M N$_2$, and 2.6 mol O$_2$, is the system at equilibrium?

(b) If it is not at equilibrium, in which direction will the reaction shift?

SOLUTION: The reaction is not at equilibrium, $Q > K$, so it will shift to the left.

$$Q = \frac{[N_2][O_2]}{[NO]^2} = \frac{(2.0)(2.6)}{(0.024)^2} = 9.0 \times 10^3$$

TYPES OF EQUILIBRIUM PROBLEMS

(*Chemistry* 8th ed. pages 598, 612–620/9th ed. pages 611, 625–633)

The types of equilibrium problems you can expect to solve on the AP Chemistry exam include:
1. Manipulation of the equilibrium constant, K.
   a. If the reaction is reversed, the equilibrium expression is the reciprocal of the expression for the forward reaction.

   EXAMPLE:

   $$A \rightleftharpoons B: K = \frac{[B]}{[A]}$$

   $$B \rightleftharpoons A: K' = \frac{1}{K} = \frac{[A]}{[B]}$$

b. If the coefficients in a balanced equation are multiplied by a number, n, the equilibrium constant is raised to the power n.

EXAMPLE:

$$A \rightleftharpoons B: K = \frac{[B]}{[A]}$$

$$2A \rightleftharpoons 2B: K'' = K^2 = \frac{[B]^2}{[A]^2}$$

c. If two reactions are added together through the presence of a common intermediate, the equilibrium constant of the resulting reaction is a product of the values of K for the original reactions.

EXAMPLE:

eqn 1. $A \rightleftharpoons B : K_1 = [B]/[A]$

eqn 2. $3 B \rightleftharpoons C : K_2 = [C]/[B]^3$

overall eqn. $A + 2 B \rightleftharpoons C : K = K_1 \cdot K_2 = [C]/[A][B]^2$

2. Given all equilibrium concentrations, calculate the value of the constant, K.
3. Given the value of the equilibrium constant, K, and all but one of the equilibrium concentrations, solve for the missing concentration.
4. Given the value of the initial concentrations of the reactants and one of the equilibrium concentrations of either the reactants or products, solve for all equilibrium concentrations and the value of K.
5. Given the initial concentrations and the value of K, solve by approximation for the equilibrium concentrations.

The first four types of problems listed above can be solved using basic algebra. An example of a Type 1 problem follows.

EXAMPLE: (Type 1) For the reaction

$N_2(g) + 3 H_2(g) \rightleftharpoons 2 NH_3(g)$, $K = 1.3 \times 10^{-2}$ at a certain temperature.

Calculate the value of K, called K', for the reaction

$NH_3(g) \rightleftharpoons \frac{1}{2} N_2(g) + \frac{3}{2} H_2(g)$

SOLUTION: The reaction is the reverse and one-half of the one which is given.

$$K' = [N_2]^{1/2}[H_2]^{3/2} / [NH_3] = (1/K)^{1/2}; \left(\frac{1}{1.3 \times 10^{-2}}\right)^{\frac{1}{2}} = 8.8$$

The fifth type of problem can be solved by approximation, using an ICE chart. ICE is an acronym for Initial, Change, Equilibrium and is a convenient method for organizing your work. The use of an ICE chart is illustrated below.

EXAMPLE: (Type 5) At a particular temperature, $K = 1.00 \times 10^2$ for the reaction

$$H_2(g) + I_2(g) \rightleftharpoons 2\,HI(g)$$

In an experiment, 1.00 mol H_2, 1.00 mol I_2, and 1.00 mol HI are introduced into a 1.00-L container. Calculate the equilibrium concentrations of all reactions and products.

SOLUTION: To begin, write the balanced equation for the reaction and the equilibrium expression, omitting pure solids and liquids.

	$H_2(g) +$	$I_2(g)$	$\rightleftharpoons$	$2\,HI(g)$	$K = \dfrac{[HI]^2}{[H_2][I_2]}$
I	1.00	1.00		1.00	
C	$-x$	$-x$		$+2x$	
E	$1.00 - x$	$1.00 - x$		$1.00 + 2x$	

Make an ICE chart under the balanced chemical equation.

I = initial concentration in mol/L (note units are omitted from chart)

C = the change to reach equilibrium represented by + or $-x$. A minus sign indicates a decrease in concentration; a plus sign indicates an increase. The coefficient in front of the reactant in the balanced equation is placed in front of the x in the change line.

E = Equilibrium concentrations which are obtained by adding the I and C lines together.

Plug the equilibrium values into the expression and solve for x:

$$K = 100. = \frac{(1.00 + 2x)^2}{(1.00 - x)^2}$$

Taking the square root of both sides:

$$10.0 = \frac{1.00 + 2x}{1.00 - x}$$
$$10.0 - 10.0x = 1.00 + 2x$$
$$12x = 9.0$$
$$x = 0.75\,M$$

Use this value of x to solve for the equilibrium concentrations of all reactants and products.

$[H_2] = [I_2] = 1.00 - 0.75 = 0.25\,M$; $[HI] = 1.00 + 2(0.75) = 2.50\,M$

Last, check your equilibrium concentrations by making sure that they equal the correct value of K.

EXAMPLE: (Type 4) For the reaction

$N_2O_4(g) \rightleftharpoons 2\,NO_2(g)$, $K = 4.0 \times 10^{-7}$ at a specific temperature.

In an experiment, 1.0 mol of N_2O_4 is placed in a 10.0-L vessel.

Calculate the equilibrium concentrations of NO_2 and N_2O_4.

SOLUTION: At equilibrium, $[N_2O_4] = 0.10\ M$ and

$[NO_2] = 2.0 \times 10^{-4}\ M$. To solve this problem, proceed as in the previous example.

	$N_2O_4(g)$	$\rightleftharpoons$	$2\ NO_2(g)$
I	0.10		0
C	$-x$		$+2x$
E	$0.10 - x$		$2x$

$$K = \frac{[NO_2]^2}{[N_2O_4]} = \frac{(2x)^2}{(0.10 - x)} = 4.0 \times 10^{-7}$$

Since the value of K is much smaller than 1, you can assume that the change from the initial concentration, x in $0.10 - x$, is so small that it is negligible, that is, $0.10 - x$ is about equal to 0.10.

This greatly simplifies the math to

$$K = \frac{(2x)^2}{(0.10)} = 4.0 \times 10^{-7}$$

$4x^2 = 4.0 \times 10^{-8}$, $x = 1.0 \times 10^{-4}\ M$

It is okay to make this assumption if the change from the initial concentration, in this case, x is less than 5% of the initial concentration.

$$\frac{x}{0.10} \times 100 = \frac{1.0 \times 10^{-4}}{0.10} \times 100\% = 0.10\%$$

This is less than 5%, so it is okay to make the assumption.

The equilibrium concentrations are as follows:

$[N_2O_4] = 0.10 - x = 0.10 - 1.0 \times 10^{-4} = 0.10\ M$

$[NO_2] = 2x = 2(1.0 \times 10^{-4}) = 2.0 \times 10^{-4}\ M$

GASEOUS EQUILIBRIUM

(*Chemistry* 8th ed. pages 601–604, 610–612/9th ed. pages 614–616, 622–624)

For equilibrium in the gas phase, the equilibrium expression can be written in terms of the partial pressures of the gases.

For the reaction $AsH_3(g) \rightleftharpoons 2\ As(s) + 3\ H_2(g)$

$$K_p = \frac{\left(P_{H_2}\right)^3}{P_{AsH_3}}$$

K_p is the equilibrium constant in terms of the partial pressures of the gases.

P represents the partial pressure of the gases raised to their coefficients in the balanced chemical equation. Notice that parentheses, ( ), are used for the partial pressure. The use of brackets, [ ], in this instance would result in deduction of points on the exam since brackets represent concentration in mol/L.

EXAMPLE: Given the following reaction:

$2\ NO(g) + Br_2(g) \rightleftharpoons 2\ NOBr(g)$, $K_p = 109$ at 25°C

The equilibrium partial pressure of $Br_2 = 0.0159$ atm and NOBr = 0.0768 atm. Calculate the equilibrium partial pressure of NO.

SOLUTION:

$$K_p = \frac{(P_{NOBr})^2}{(P_{NO})^2(P_{Br_2})}$$

$$109\ \text{atm}^{-1} = \frac{(.0768\ \text{atm})^2}{(P_{NO})^2(0.0159\ \text{atm})}$$

$$P_{NO} = 0.0583\ \text{atm}$$

The relationship between K_p and K is given by $K_p = K(RT)^{\Delta n}$.

K_p is the equilibrium constant in terms of partial pressures.

K is the equilibrium constant in terms of concentration.

R is the ideal gas constant (0.08206 atm L mol^{-1} K^{-1}).

T is the absolute (Kelvin) temperature.

Δn is the sum of the coefficients of the gaseous products minus the sum of the coefficients of the gaseous reactants.

EXAMPLE: $2\ NO(g) + Cl_2(g) \rightleftharpoons 2\ NOCl(g)$ $K_p = 1.9 \times 10^3$ at 25°C. Calculate the value for K_c at 25°C.

$\Delta n = 2 - (2 + 1) = -1$

$K_p = K(RT)^{-1} = K/RT$

$K = K_pRT = (1.9 \times 10^3)(0.08206)(298) = 4.6 \times 10^4$

LE CHÂTELIER'S PRINCIPLE

(*Chemistry* 8th ed. pages 620–625/9th ed. pages 633–639)

The value of K is a constant at a particular temperature. The only factor that changes the value of K is temperature. Pressure, a catalyst, and changes in concentration will not affect the value of K.

Le Châtelier's principle states that if a change is imposed in a system at equilibrium, the position of the equilibrium will shift in a direction that will counteract the change.

EXAMPLE 1: Consider the following changes on the system below at equilibrium.

$2\ SO_3(g) \rightleftharpoons 2\ SO_2(g) + O_2(g)$, $\Delta H = 197$ kJ

(a) Addition of O_2

SOLUTION: The equilibrium will shift to the left to form more reactants. The addition of oxygen increases the rate of the reverse reaction so more reactants will form, until the rate of the forward reaction again equals the rate of the reverse reaction. On the particulate level, more O_2 is available to collide with the SO_2 so more reactant will be made. Another way to explain the shift is that with the added O_2, Q is now greater than K. The reverse reaction is favored so the product concentrations decrease and reactant concentrations increase until $Q = K$ again.

(b) Removal of SO_2

SOLUTION: Removal of an equilibrium component such as SO_2 at constant pressure and temperature will cause the equilibrium to shift toward the removed component to increase its concentration. The reaction in this example will shift to products. When SO_2 is removed, Q is less than K. The forward reaction is favored until enough product has been made for $Q = K$.

(c) Increase in temperature

SOLUTION: The direction of the shift can be predicted in the same way as the addition or removal of a reactant or product.

The decomposition of SO_3 is endothermic. Treating heat as a reactant, an increase in temperature will cause the reaction to shift right, producing more products, increasing the value of K. More SO_3 molecules will have sufficient energy to break the bonds and make products. A decrease in temperature will cause a shift to the left, increasing the reactant concentrations, and lowering the value of K.

(d) An increase in pressure

SOLUTION: If the pressure is increased in an equilibrium system, the reaction will shift toward the side with fewer moles of gas. Decreasing the volume has the same effect because the only way the pressure can be increased without changing the temperature or number of moles is to decrease the volume. In this example, the reaction will shift to the left, toward SO_3, when the pressure is increased or the volume is decreased. If the moles of gas are the same on both sides of the reaction, no shift will occur.

(e) Addition of a solid or inert gas, such as Ne

SOLUTION: If a solid or an inert gas (with no change in volume) is added to the reaction, there will be no shift in equilibrium. Neither the solid nor the inert gas is part of the equilibrium expression. The concentrations of all the components of the equilibrium expression remain unchanged.

(f) An inert gas, such as Ne, is added at constant pressure.

SOLUTION: There will be a shift in the equilibrium to the side of the equation with more moles of gas. To add Ne at constant pressure, the volume of the container must increase so the concentrations or partial pressures of all gases have decreased.

If the moles of gas are greater in the reactants, then $Q < K$, so equilibrium can be reestablished only by increasing the products.

EXAMPLE 2: Dilution of a reaction system with a solvent may have an effect on the equilibrium concentrations. Consider how the following will affect equilibrium.

Water is added to a dilute $Fe(SCN)^{2+}$ solution.

$$Fe^{3+} + SCN^- \rightleftharpoons Fe(SCN)^{2+}$$

SOLUTION: This is the opposite of the acetic acid example. When water is added to this equilibrium, the reaction will shift to the reactants because the more dilute the solution, the fewer chances the individual ions have of colliding to make the complex ion.

EXAMPLE 3: Create a particulate model to illustrate the system described below.

6 molecules of NO_2 and 2 molecules of N_2O_4 are at equilibrium. 10 molecules of NO_2 are added and equilibrium is reestablished. Temperature and pressure remain constant.

SOLUTION:

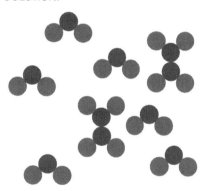

Initial Equilibrium
    6 NO_2 molecules
    2 N_2O_4 molecules
    3 : 1 ratio

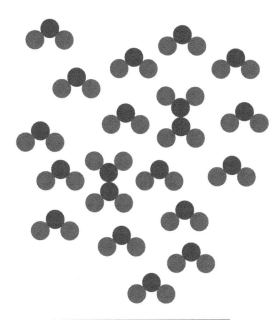

Disturb Equilibrium
    add 10 NO_2 molecules

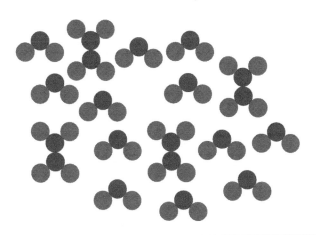

Restore Equilibrium
    12 NO_2 molecules
    4 N_2O_4 molecules
    3 : 1 ratio

RELATIONSHIP OF *K* TO FREE ENERGY, $\Delta G°$

(*Chemistry* 8th ed. pages 798–802/9th ed. pages 813–817)

The magnitude of the equilibrium constant, *K*, is directly related to the change in Gibbs free energy associated with the reaction, $\Delta G°$. The species that have lower free energy will have larger relative concentrations at equilibrium. When both reactants and products have significant concentrations at equilibrium, the magnitude of $\Delta G°$ is similar to the thermal energy (RT).

The equilibrium constant at standard temperature can be determined from the thermodynamic values of a reaction using the equation:

$\Delta G° = -RT \ln K$
$R = 8.314$ J/(K•mol)

Alternatively, the equation can be expressed in terms of the equilibrium constant:

$K = e^{-\Delta G°/RT}$

The equilibrium constant can be determined quantitatively through calculation or qualitatively through estimation. The thermal energy (RT) at room temperature is 2.4 kJ/mol. If $\Delta G°$ is large compared to RT, then K will be significantly larger than 1.

> **EXAMPLE:** Calculate the value of K at 25.0°C for the reaction 2 $NO_2(g) \rightleftharpoons N_2O_4(g)$
>
> The values of $\Delta H°$ and $\Delta S°$ are –58.03 kJ/mol and –176.6 J/K•mol, respectively.
>
> **SOLUTION:**
>
> Notice that the units for energy must both be in J.
>
> At 25°C, $\Delta G° = \Delta H° - T\Delta S°$
>
> $\qquad = -58.03 \times 10^3$ J/mol $- (298$ K$)(-176.6$ J K^{-1} mol^{-1})
>
> $\qquad = -5.40 \times 10^3$ J mol^{-1}
>
> $\Delta G° = -RT \ln K$
>
> $\ln K = -\Delta G°/RT = (-5.40 \times 10^3$ J mol$^{-1})/[(8.3145$ J K^{-1} mol$^{-1})(298$ K$)]$
>
> $\qquad = 2.18$
>
> $\quad K = 8.846$
>
> This reaction is product-favored since $K > 1$.

Comparison of $\Delta G°$ to K

If $\Delta G° < 0$, then $K > 1$ and the reaction is product-favored.
If $\Delta G° > 0$, then $K < 1$ and the reaction is reactant-favored.

Exergonic reactions ($\Delta G° < 0$) and endergonic reactions ($\Delta G° > 0$) are important in many biological applications where the magnitude of the equilibrium constant is important.

MULTIPLE-CHOICE QUESTIONS

No calculators are to be used in this section.

1. In the reaction $3 W + X \rightleftharpoons 2 Y + Z$, all substances are gases. The reaction is initiated by adding an equal number of moles of W and of X. When equilibrium is reached,
   (A) [Y] = [Z]
   (B) [X] = [Y]
   (C) [W] = [X]
   (D) [X] > [W]

2. An esterification reaction occurs when an alcohol reacts with a carboxylic acid as shown below.

   | Ethanol | Acetic Acid | Ethyl Acetate |

   The equilibrium constant is approximately 5 at room temperature, but the rate of reaction without a catalyst is very slow. How do the rates of the forward and reverse reactions compare at equilibrium?
   (A) The forward rate is 5 times faster than the reverse rate.
   (B) The reverse rate is the same as the forward rate.
   (C) The reverse rate is 5 times faster than the forward rate.
   (D) The rate can only be determined experimentally.

3. The reaction $3 H_2(g) + N_2(g) \rightleftharpoons 2 NH_3(g)$ has an enthalpy of change of –92 kJ. Increasing the temperature of this equilibrium system causes
   (A) an increase in $[NH_3]$
   (B) an increase in $[N_2]$
   (C) a decrease in $[H_2]$
   (D) an increase in K

4. Consider $N_2(g) + O_2(g) \rightleftharpoons 2 NO(g)$. The reaction was initiated by adding 15.0 moles of NO to a 1.0-L flask. At equilibrium, 3.0 moles of oxygen are present in the 1.0-L flask. The value of K must be
   (A) 0.33
   (B) 3.0
   (C) 5.0
   (D) 9.0

5. At a certain temperature, the synthesis of ammonia gas from nitrogen and hydrogen gases, shown as $N_2 + 3 H_2 \rightleftharpoons 2 NH_3$, has a value for K of 3.0×10^{-2}. If $[H_2] = [N_2] = 0.10\ M$ and $[NH_3] = 0.20\ M$,
   (A) the reaction would shift toward the ammonia
   (B) the reaction would shift toward the N_2 and the H_2
   (C) the system is at equilibrium, therefore no shifting will occur
   (D) the reaction will shift toward a new equilibrium position, but the direction cannot be determined from these data

6. One way to produce nitric acid is through the Ostwald process. In the first reaction ammonia is oxidized to nitrogen monoxide.

$$4\,NH_3(g) + 5\,O_2(g) \rightleftharpoons 4\,NO(g) + 6\,H_2O(g) \qquad \Delta H = -905.2 \text{ kJ}$$

Which of the following would shift equilibrium to products?
(A) Raise the temperature of the reaction and remove nitrogen monoxide as it is made.
(B) Lower the temperature of the reaction and remove nitrogen monoxide as it is made.
(C) Raise the temperature of the reaction to keep water in its gaseous form.
(D) Lower the temperature of the reaction to condense ammonia into a liquid.

7. Which of the following is an example of carbon dioxide/carbonate equilibrium?
(A) acid rain deforestation
(B) stalagtite formation in caves
(C) salting icy roads in winter
(D) ozone depletion

8. Which of the following systems at equilibrium are not affected by a change in pressure caused by changing the volume at constant temperature?
(A) $H_2(g) + Cl_2(g) \rightleftharpoons 2\,HCl(g)$
(B) $H_2(g) + I_2(s) \rightleftharpoons 2\,HI(g)$
(C) $N_2(g) + 3\,H_2(g) \rightleftharpoons 2\,NH_3(g)$
(D) $2\,NH_3(g) \rightleftharpoons N_2(g) + 3\,H_2(g)$

9. The equilibrium $P_4(g) + 6\,Cl_2(g) \rightleftharpoons 4\,PCl_3(l)$ is established at –10°C. The equilibrium constant expression is

(A) $K = \dfrac{[PCl_3]}{[P_4][Cl_2]}$

(B) $K = \dfrac{[PCl_3]^4}{[P_4][Cl_2]^6}$

(C) $K = \dfrac{[P_4][Cl_2]^6}{[PCl_3]^4}$

(D) $K = \dfrac{1}{[P_4][Cl_2]^6}$

10. Ammonium hydrogen sulfide will decompose into ammonia gas and hydrogen sulfide gas when heated. Consider the equilibrium system

$$NH_4HS(s) \rightleftharpoons NH_3(g) + H_2S(g)$$

which is developed from 1.000 mole of NH_4HS in a 100-L cylinder. At equilibrium the total pressure is found to be 0.400 atm. K_p will be equal to
(A) 2.00×10^{-1}
(B) 1.00×10^{-2}
(C) 4.00×10^{-2}
(D) 4.00

11. The equilibrium constant for the ionization of hypochlorous acid is 3.0×10^{-8}. If a 1.0 M solution is at pH 2, what is the equilibrium condition of the system?

$$HClO + H_2O \rightleftharpoons H_3O^+ + ClO^-$$

(A) The system is at equilibrium.
(B) The system will shift to the right to make products.
(C) The system will shift to the left to make reactants.
(D) The equilibrium cannot be determined without more information.

12. According to the graph below, what chemical was added to the equilibrium mixture and how did the system respond?

$$N_2(g) + 3 H_2(g) \rightleftharpoons NH_3(g)$$

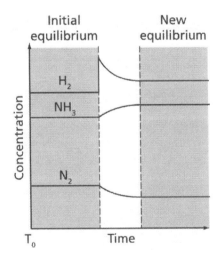

(A) Hydrogen was added and the concentration of nitrogen decreased.
(B) Ammonia was added and the concentration of ammonia increased.
(C) Hydrogen was added and the concentration of ammonia decreased.
(D) Ammonia was added and the concentration of hydrogen increased.

13. For which of the following values of K will the equilibrium mixture consist almost entirely of reactants:
    (A) 0.030
    (B) 1.00
    (C) 1×10^{10}
    (D) 30

14. $K = 0.25$ for $2\, NOBr(g) \rightleftharpoons 2\, NO(g) + Br_2(g)$. At the same T and P, what is the K for $NO + \frac{1}{2}\, Br_2 \rightleftharpoons NOBr$?
    (A) 2.0
    (B) 4.0
    (C) 0.50
    (D) 0.63

15. Ammonia and oxygen react to establish the following equilibrium:

    $$4\, NH_3(g) + 3\, O_2(g) \rightleftharpoons 2\, N_2(g) + 6\, H_2O(g)$$

    If a 1-L flask is filled with 4.0 mol of oxygen and 3.0 mol of ammonia and the system is allowed to come to equilibrium, the flask is found to contain 1.0 mol of nitrogen. How much oxygen is present at equilibrium?
    (A) 0.50 mol
    (B) 1.0 mol
    (C) 1.5 mol
    (D) 2.5 mol

FREE-RESPONSE QUESTIONS

1. The Haber process for the synthesis of ammonia is kinetically and thermodynamically controlled.

    $N_2(g) + 3\, H_2(g) \rightleftharpoons 2\, NH_3(g)$

    for the reaction above: $\Delta H° = -92$ kJ, $\Delta S° = -199$ J K^{-1}
    (a) Calculate $\Delta G°$ from the thermodynamic data and comment on the spontaneity of the reaction at room temperature.
    (b) Calculate the equilibrium constant at room temperature.
    (c) At what temperature does $\Delta G°$ become zero? What does this mean in regards to the temperature at which this reaction can be carried out at?
    (d) The rate of reaction at room temperature is very low. Give an explanation for this fact.
    (e) Propose a way to shift the rate of the reaction and also shift equilibrium towards products.

2. Refer to the system $PCl_3(g) + Cl_2(g) \rightleftharpoons PCl_5(g)$. To an empty 15.0-L cylinder, 0.500 mol of gaseous PCl_5 are added and allowed to reach equilibrium. The concentration of PCl_3 is found to be 0.0220 M. Assume a temperature of 375 K.
    (a) How many mol of PCl_5 remain at equilibrium?
    (b) Write the equilibrium constant expression for the above reaction.
    (c) Determine the value of K.

(d) Determine the value of K_p for this same system at the same temperature.
(e) How would the value of K_p be effected by increasing the temperature of the system at equilibrium for this exothermic reaction?

Answers

MULTIPLE-CHOICE QUESTIONS

1. **D** Since every time a mole of X reacts, 3 moles of W must react, so the amount of W remaining must be less than the amount of X remaining (recall that you started with an equal number of moles of W and of X) (*Chemistry* 8th ed. pages 594–597/9th ed. pages 607–610). LO 6.6

2. **B** Equilibrium is established when the forward rate is equal to the reverse rate (*Chemistry* 8th ed. pages 594–597/9th ed. pages 607–610). LO 6.3

3. **B** Increasing the temperature causes the equilibrium to shift to the left. For an exothermic reaction, increasing the temperature increases the rate of both the forward and reverse reactions, but proportionally makes a greater increase in the reverse reaction since it has the higher activation energy, favoring the formation of more hydrogen gas and more nitrogen gas, and lowering the concentration of the ammonia. This forms more gaseous particles; therefore, the pressure increases at constant volume (*Chemistry* 8th ed. pages 624–626/9th ed. pages 637–639). LO 6.8

4. **D** If 3.0 moles of oxygen are formed, 6.0 moles of NO must have reacted, leaving 9.0 moles of NO at equilibrium (15.0 − 6.0 = 9.0 mol/L for [NO]). Each time 3.0 moles of oxygen form, the same number of moles of nitrogen are produced. Since the reaction (take care here) is written showing NO as a product, the equilibrium constant expression is $K = \dfrac{[NO]^2}{[N_2][O_2]} = \dfrac{(9.0)^2}{(3.0)(3.0)} = \dfrac{81}{9.0} = 9.0$

   (*Chemistry* 8th ed. pages 612–617/9th ed. pages 624–630). LO 6.5

5. **B**

   $$Q = \frac{[NH_3]^2}{[H_2]^3[N_2]} = \frac{(0.20)^2}{(0.10)^3(0.10)} = 400$$

   Since Q is greater than K, the reaction will shift toward N_2 and H_2

   (*Chemistry* 8th ed. pages 608–610/9th ed. pages 620–622). LO 6.10

6. **B** The reaction is exothermic so lowering the temperature and removing the nitrogen monoxide will both shift the reaction to

products according to Le Châtelier's principle (*Chemistry* 8th ed. pages 620–626/9th ed. pages 633–639). LO 6.9

7. **B** Chemistry concepts should not be learned in a vacuum. You need to be able to connect chemistry concepts with other science concepts. Cave formations occur when carbon dioxide in the air forms carbonic acid. The very weak acid reacts with calcium carbonate in limestone forming calcium bicarbonate. This compound is also in equilibrium with carbon dioxide, water, and calcium carbonate.

$$H_2CO_3 + CaCO_3 \rightleftharpoons Ca(HCO_3)_2 \rightleftharpoons H_2O + CO_2 + CaCO_3$$

(*Chemistry* 8th ed. pages 620–622, 624–626/9th ed. pages 633–635, 637–639). LO 6.1

8. **A** Because you are seeking an equilibrium system which has not changed with a change in pressure due to a volume change, look for a system with an equal number of moles of both gaseous reactants and products (*Chemistry* 8th ed. pages 621–624/9th ed. pages 634–637). LO 6.8

9. **D** The equilibrium constant is a ratio of the concentration of products divided by the concentration of reactants, each taken to a power represented by their coefficients. Pure liquids and solids are not shown in the equilibrium constant expression (*Chemistry* 8th ed. pages 597–599, 603–606/9th ed. pages 610–612, 615–618). LO 6.2

10. **C** The two gases are formed in equal molar amounts (1:1); therefore half of the pressure is due to each gas $\left(\dfrac{0.400 \text{ atm}}{2} = 0.200 \text{ atm}\right)$. $K_p = \left(P_{NH_3}\right)\left(P_{H_2S}\right) = (0.200) \times (0.200) = 0.0400 = 4.00 \times 10^{-2}$ (*Chemistry* 8th ed. pages 602–606/9th ed. pages 615–618). LO 6.6

11. **C** Hypochlorous acid is a weak acid, but the pH can be used to calculate $[H_3O^+]$ and by stoichiometry, $[ClO^-]$.

At pH 2, $[H_3O^+] = 0.01 \, M = [ClO^-]$

$Q = [H_3O^+]_0[ClO^-]_0/[HClO]_0$
$Q = (0.01)(0.01/1) = 1 \times 10^{-4}$

Recall that $K = 3.0 \times 10^{-8}$ so $Q > K$. Equilibrium with shift to reactants (*Chemistry* 8th ed. pages 608–611/9th ed. pages 620–623). LO 6.4

12. **A** The graph shows a spike where H_2 was added. This extra H_2 reacted with some N_2 and decreased $[N_2]$ in the system (*Chemistry* 8th ed. pages 620–622/9th ed. pages 633–635). LO 6.10

13. **C** A small value for K indicates that in the ratio of products to reactants, there are considerably more reactants than products, resulting in a very small number significantly less than one (*Chemistry* 8th ed. page 608/9th ed. page 620). LO 6.7

14. **A** First, recognize that the reaction requested is the reverse of the one for which the K is given. The value of K for the reversed equilibrium reaction is the reciprocal of K or $1/K$, which is $1/0.25 = 4$. The new reaction as written is then multiplied by a factor of ½, therefore the equilibrium expression for the new reaction is the original K raised to the ½ power or in this case, the square root of 4, which is 2.0 (*Chemistry* 8th ed. pages 598–600/9th ed. pages 611–613). LO 6.2

15. **D** Solve the problem using an ICE table. A useful technique is to underline the information given to you in the problem (3.0 mole NH_3 and 4.0 mole O_2 as well as 1.0 mole N_2 at equilibrium).

	$4\,NH_3(g)\,+$	$3\,O_2(g)\,\rightleftharpoons$	$2\,N_2(g)\,+$	$6\,H_2O(g)$
initial	<u>3.0</u>	<u>4.0</u>	0	0
change	$-4x = -2.0$	$-3x = -1.5$	$+2x = 1.0$	$+6x = 3.0$
equilibrium	1.0	2.5	<u>1.0</u>	3.0

Since the coefficient for N_2 is 2, the concentration must increase by $2x$. The reactant concentrations decrease by their coefficients times x and the water concentration increases by its concentration times x (see chart). Since $2x = 1$, $x = 0.5$. Plug that value into the other "change" boxes to calculate the values of all of the species at equilibrium (*Chemistry* 8th ed. pages 606–615/9th ed. pages 618–628). LO 6.6

FREE-RESPONSE QUESTIONS

1. (a) $\Delta G° = \Delta H° - T\Delta S°$

   $\Delta G° = -92\ \text{kJ} - (298\ \text{K})(0.199\ \text{kJ/K})$

   $\Delta G° = -33\ \text{kJ}$; spontaneous at room temperature

   (b) $K = e^{-\Delta G°/RT}$

   $K = e^{-33000J/(8.814J/K\ mol)(298K)}$

   $K = 5.4 \times 10^5$

   LO 6.25

   (c) $\Delta G° = \Delta H° - T\Delta S°$

   $0\ \text{kJ mol}^{-1} = 92\ \text{kJ mol}^{-1} - T(0.199\ \text{kJ K}^{-1}\text{mol}^{-1})$

   $T = 462\ \text{K}$; at temperatures higher than 462 K, the reaction becomes nonspontaneous.

   (d) The rate of reaction is probably very low due to a high E_a that must be overcome. The very stable triple bond of nitrogen requires a lot of energy to break; that is the activation energy for the reaction.

(e) To maximize the yield of this reaction, raise the temperature up to around 426 K to maximize the thermodynamics. Increase the pressure to force the reaction to products to relieve the stress on the system. Find a suitable catalyst to lower the activation energy by taking a different path from reactants to products (*Chemistry* 8th ed. pages 565–570, 790–794, 798–802/9th ed. pages 577–583, 805–810, 813–817). LO 6.3, LO 6.9

2. (a) 0.0220 mol/L PCl_3 × 15.0 L = 0.330 mole PCl_3 = 0.330 mole PCl_5 that reacted.

   0.500 – 0.330 = 0.170 mole PCl_5 remains.

   (b) $K_c = \dfrac{[PCl_5]}{[PCl_3][Cl_2]}$

   (c) $\dfrac{\left(\dfrac{0.170}{15.0\ \text{L}}\right)}{(0.0220)(0.0220)} = 23.4$

   (d) $K_p = K_c\,(RT)^{\Delta n}$

   In this case, 1 + 1 mol of gas → 1 mol of gas, so $\Delta n = -1$ mol

   $K_p = 23.4\,(0.08206 \times 375)^{-1} = 0.760$

   (e) Raising the temperature of an exothermic reaction opposes the forward reaction. Further, from $K_p = K_c(RT)^{\Delta n}$, if T increases, the value of K_p decreases (*Chemistry* 8th ed. pages 602–603, 609–612/9th ed. pages 615–616, 621–625). LO 6.8

13

BIG IDEA 6: APPLICATIONS OF EQUILIBRIA: PROTON TRANSFER AND SOLUBILITY

Big Idea 6

Any bond or intermolecular attraction that can be formed can be broken. These two processes are in a dynamic competition, sensitive to initial conditions and external perturbations.

Concepts from the last chapter will be applied in this section covering the equilibria of weak acids, weak bases, and salts. In addition, acid–base theories and properties of acids will be reviewed. Calculations involved in acid–base titrations, preparation of buffers, and salt hydrolysis will be demonstrated. In addition, you will apply basic equilibrium concepts involving solids dissolving to form aqueous solutions.

You should be able to
- Understand the Brønsted–Lowry acid–base theory.
- Identify strong acids and bases and calculate their pH's.
- Calculate the pH of a weak acid or base.
- Calculate the concentration of a strong or weak acid or base from its pH.

- Calculate the pH and ion concentrations in a polyprotic acid.
- Predict the pH of a salt from its formula and then calculate the pH of the salt.
- Identify the components of a buffer and perform calculations involving the preparation of a buffer and the addition of strong acid or strong base to a buffer.
- Perform calculations involving strong acid–strong base titrations as well as weak acid–strong base and weak base–strong acid calculations.
- Be familiar with titration curves and selection of an acid–base indicator.
- Write balanced equations for the dissolution of a salt and its corresponding solubility product expression.
- Predict the relative solubilities of salts which dissolve to give the same number of ions from their K_{sp} values.
- Calculate the K_{sp} value from the solubility of a salt and also calculate the solubility of the salt in units of mol/L or g/L from the given K_{sp} value.
- Predict the effect of a common ion on the solubility of a salt and perform calculations.
- Perform calculations to predict if a precipitate will form when two solutions are mixed.

AP Tip

Be systematic. All solution equilibrium problems have the same basic features—a ratio of product concentrations and reactant concentrations raised to their stoichiometric coefficients. Remember that pure substances are not involved in equilibrium calculations.

ACID–BASE THEORY

BRØNSTED–LOWRY

(*Chemistry* 8th ed. pages 639–642/9th ed. pages 653–656)

The Brønsted–Lowry theory says that an acid is a proton (H^+) donor and a base is a proton acceptor.

In the reaction below, HNO_3 transfers a proton to H_2O forming H_3O^+, the hydronium ion. H_3O^+ is the conjugate acid of H_2O and NO_3^- is the conjugate base of HNO_3. The formulas in a conjugate acid–base pair differ by one H^+.

$$HNO_3 + H_2O \rightarrow H_3O^+ + NO_3^-$$
Acid　　　Base　　Conjugate acid　Conjugate base

EXAMPLE: Give the formulas for the conjugate base of H_2SO_4 and the conjugate acid of CH_3NH_2.

SOLUTION: HSO_4^- is the conjugate base of H_2SO_4.

$CH_3NH_3^+$ is the conjugate acid of CH_3NH_2.

Note that each conjugate acid–base pair differs by 1 H^+:

$HSO_4^- + 1H^+ = H_2SO_4$

$CH_3NH_3^+ = 1H^+ + CH_3NH_2$

ACID AND BASE STRENGTH

(*Chemistry* 8th ed. pages 642–645, 661–662/9th ed. pages 656–659, 675–676)

The names and formulas of the six strong acids must be memorized. The six strong acids are HCl, HBr, HI, HNO_3, H_2SO_4, and $HClO_4$.

If an acid is not one of the six in the list, then for purposes of the AP exam, you can assume it is a weak acid. Common weak acids include carboxylic acids and most oxyacids. Several factors affect the magnitude of K_a of weak acids: bond strength, solvation, and electronegativity of the atom bonded to the proton that will ionize.

A particulate model is especially useful for understanding the differences between strong and weak acids.

Dissociation of a Strong Acid
$HA + H_2O \rightarrow H_3O^+ + A^-$

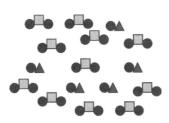

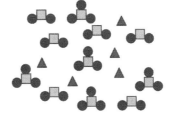

before dissociation   after dissociation

Ionization of a Weak Acid
$HA + H_2O \rightleftharpoons H_3O^+ + A^-$

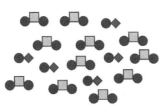

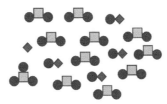

before ionization   after ionization

Weak acids exist in equilibrium with their ions in aqueous solution. The equilibrium constant, K_a, measures the extent to which the acid dissociates in water:

$$HA(aq) + H_2O(l) \rightleftharpoons H_3O^+(aq) + A^-(aq)$$

The equilibrium expression for the reaction is

$$K_a = \frac{\left[H_3O^+\right]\left[A^-\right]}{[HA]}$$

A table of K_a values for monoprotic acids, containing one acidic hydrogen, appears in the appendix of *Chemistry* (8th ed. page A22/9th ed. page A22) and many other textbooks and is worth studying. The larger the K_a value, the stronger the acid.

Comparison of Strong and Weak Acids				
Type of acid, HA	Reversibility of reaction	K_a value	pK_a Value	Ions existing when acid, HA, dissociates in H_2O
Strong	not reversible	very large	negative	H_3O^+ and A^-, only. No HA present.
Weak	reversible	small	positive Smaller values indicate equilibrium lies more toward products.	H_3O^+, A^-, and HA

EXAMPLE: List the acids in order of increasing strength: HCN, HCl, $HClO_2$, HNO_2.

SOLUTION: HCN < HNO_2 < $HClO_2$ < HCl. The first three weak acids are listed in order of increasing K_a values. HCl is stronger than all of the weak acids given. HCl is a strong acid.

EXAMPLE: Arrange the following species in order of increasing base strength: NO_2^-, ClO_2^-, CN^-, Cl^-.

SOLUTION: Cl^- < ClO_2^- < NO_2^- < CN^-. The bases are listed in reverse order of their conjugate acids in the previous example because the stronger the acid, the weaker its conjugate base.

Strong bases include group 1A and 2A hydroxides such as NaOH. Weak bases include ammonia, amines, and pyridines, and other nitrogenous bases. The equilibrium constant, K_b, measures the extent to which a base reacts with water. The reaction of a weak base, B, with water and its corresponding equilibrium expression is

$$B(aq) + HOH(l) \rightleftharpoons BH^+(aq) + OH^-(aq) \rightarrow K_b = \frac{[BH^+][OH^-]}{[B]}.$$

The acid and base equilibrium constants, K_a and K_b are related to each other through the equilibrium constant of water, K_w.

$$K_w = K_a K_b$$

AP Tip

Writing the reaction for base ionization can be tricky. Always remember to react the base with water. For example, the base reacts with water to produce hydroxide ions and accepts a hydrogen ion to become protonated. Remember to check the charges of the reactants and products and be sure that the sums of the charges on both sides of the reaction are equal.

THE EFFECT OF STRUCTURE ON ACID–BASE PROPERTIES

(*Chemistry* 8th ed. pages 667–678/9th ed. pages 681–693)

For binary acids, HX, the strength of the H–X bond and the polarity of the bond will determine the behavior of the acid. The polarity of the bonds in hydrogen halides become less polar going down a group. The very strong H–F bond is what makes it a weak acid: F^- has a very high attraction for H^+ so a great deal of energy is needed to break the bond. The rest of the hydrogen halides are strong acids: HI > HBr > HCl.

For a given series of oxyacids such as $HClO_4$, $HClO_3$, $HClO_2$, and $HClO$, the acid strength increases with increasing number of oxygen atoms attached to the central atom. $HClO_4$ is a strong acid. The remaining oxyacids are listed in order of decreasing strength (decreasing number of oxygen atoms). The O–H bond becomes more polarized and weakened due to the electron density drawn toward the highly electronegative oxygen atoms.

CALCULATING THE pH OF STRONG ACIDS AND BASES

(*Chemistry* 8th ed. pages 650–651, 662–663/9th ed. pages 665–666, 676–677)

The pH of a strong acid can be calculated directly from the hydronium (or hydrogen) ion concentration,

$$pH = -\log [H_3O^+]$$

$[H_3O^+]$, the molar concentration of the hydronium ion, is obtained from the molarity of the acid.

EXAMPLE: Calculate the pH of 0.025 *M* HCl.

SOLUTION: The pH equals 1.60; $-\log (0.025) = 1.60$. Recall that in strong acids the concentration of the acid equals $[H_3O^+]$.

The pH of a strong base can be calculated from its hydroxide ion concentration.

$$pOH = -\log [OH^-]$$

$$pH + pOH = 14.00$$

The concentration of a strong acid or strong base can be determined from the solution's pH.

EXAMPLE: The pH of a $Sr(OH)_2$ solution is 13.50. Calculate the concentration of $Sr(OH)_2$.

SOLUTION: $pOH = 14 - pH = 14 - 13.50 = 0.50$

$[OH^-] = 10^{(-pOH)}$; $10^{(-0.50)} = 0.32\ M\ OH^-$

$$\frac{0.32\ mol\ OH}{1\ L} \times \frac{1\ mol\ Sr(OH)_2}{2\ mol\ OH^-} = 0.16\ M\ Sr(OH)_2$$

AP Tip

The number of significant figures in a pH measurement is equal to the number of decimal places in the pH. For example, a pH of 1.70 has 2 significant figures.

CALCULATING THE pH OF WEAK ACIDS

(*Chemistry* 8th ed. pages 651–656/9th ed. pages 666–671)

The pH of a weak acid cannot be calculated directly from the concentration of the acid since all of the acid does not dissociate to form H_3O^+. The equilibrium reaction of the acid must be considered.

AP Tip

Always follow these steps when performing calculations involving the disassociation of weak acids or weak bases.
1. Write the reaction of the acid or base with water. (Use Brønsted–Lowry acid–base theory and check charges.)
2. Set up an ICE chart.
3. Write the equilibrium expression in terms of reactant and product concentrations (without numbers).
4. Solve for x, using the method of approximation. Test approximation. Solve a quadratic equation if necessary.
5. Solve for pH. (Be careful with base equilibria: $x = OH^-$. You need to find pOH and then pH.)
6. Always remember that for weak acids and bases, at equilibrium, $pH = -\log [H_3O^+]$.

EXAMPLE: Calculate the pH of 0.025 M HCN.

SOLUTION: First, write the reaction of the acid with water. Use the Brønsted–Lowry theory to help you write the products. Check that you have the correct charges on the products.

$HCN + H_2O \rightleftharpoons H_3O^+ + CN^-$

Second, set up an ICE chart as you did in the previous chapter for equilibrium problems.

	HCN +	$H_2O \rightleftharpoons$	H_3O^+ +	CN^-
I	0.025		0	0
C	$-x$		$+x$	$+x$
E	$0.025 - x$		x	x

Third, write the equilibrium expression for K_a in the same manner as you did in the last chapter. Plug in the values from the equilibrium line of the ICE chart.

$$K_a = 6.2 \times 10^{-10} = \frac{[H_3O^+][CN^-]}{[HCN]}; \quad \frac{x^2}{(0.025 - x)} \cong \frac{x^2}{0.025}$$

If x is very small compared to the concentration of the acid you are subtracting it from, then you can assume $[HA - x]$ is approximately equal to $[HA]$. One way to determine if this approximation is valid is to compare the magnitude of K to $[HA]$; if $[HA]$ is greater than K by a factor of 10^3 or more then x can be safely ignored. You can always assume that x is small and then check the value of x you calculate to see if $[HA - x]$ is within 5% of $[HA]$.

Fourth, solve for x which equals H_3O^+.

$x^2 = (6.2 \times 10^{-10})(0.025)$

$x = [H_3O^+] = 3.9 \times 10^{-6} M$

Finally calculate the pH from the value of x, the H_3O^+ concentration.

$pH = -\log (3.9 \times 10^{-6}) = 5.40$

As you can see, acid strength and concentration both play a role in the pH of a solution. At the same concentration, the strong acid was pH 1.60 while the weak acid was pH 5.40. The difference is due to the higher $[H_3O^+]$ in the strong acid.

CALCULATING THE PERCENT IONIZATION

(*Chemistry* 8th ed. pages 657–660/9th ed. pages 672–675)

The percent ionization of an acid (or a base) is the amount of the acid, HA, which has ionized, x, divided by the acid's initial concentration, $[HA]_0$, multiplied by 100.

$$\% \text{ ionization} = \frac{x}{[HA]_0} \times 100$$

When making assumptions in an equilibrium calculation, it is best to test the assumption by making sure that the percent dissociation is less than or equal to 5%. The test for the assumption is the same as the calculation for the percent dissociation.

EXAMPLE: The percent ionization of an acid, HA, which is 0.100 M is 2.5%. Calculate the K_a of the acid.

Solution: $x/0.100\ M \times 100 = 2.5\%$; $x = 2.5 \times 10^{-3}\ M$

$$K_a = \frac{[H_3O^+][A^-]}{[HA]}$$

$$K_a = \frac{(2.5 \times 10^{-3})^2}{0.100 - 2.5 \times 10^{-3}} = 6.4 \times 10^{-5}$$

Calculating the pH of Weak Bases

(*Chemistry* 8th ed. pages 662–666/9th ed. pages 675–680)

The calculations involving weak base equilibria are similar to the weak acid equilibria problems except that the equation is written for a base reacting with water and the calculation initially involves finding $[OH^-]$. You will need to find the pOH and then the pH. pK_b values can be used to determine the position of equilibrium: smaller values indicate equilibrium favors products.

EXAMPLE: The pH of a 0.20 M solution of H_2NNH_2 is 11.38. Calculate K_b for H_2NNH_2.

Write the reaction with water. Bases accept H^+. Watch charges! One hint to help in writing the reaction is that the pH is 11.38. The basic pH indicates that OH^- must be one of the products.

Fill out the ICE chart under the reaction.

	H_2NNH_2 +	HOH $\rightleftharpoons$	OH^- +	$H_2NNH_3^+$
I	0.20		0	0
C	$-x$		$+x$	$+x$
E	$0.20 - x$		x	x

You are given the pH, but x equals $[OH^-]$.

Find pOH; pH + pOH = 14.00; pOH = 14.00 − 11.38 = 2.62

pOH = −log $[OH^-]$; Find $[OH^-] = 10^{(-pOH)}$;

$10^{(-2.62)} = 2.4 \times 10^{-3}\ M$

Plug this value of x into the K_b expression:

$$K_b = \frac{\left[OH^-\right]\left[H_2NNH_3^+\right]}{\left[H_2NNH_2\right]} = \frac{x^2}{(0.20 - x)}$$

$$K_b = \frac{\left(2.4 \times 10^{-3}\right)^2}{0.20} = 2.9 \times 10^{-5}$$

Conjugate Acid–Base Pairs

(*Chemistry* 8th ed. page 645/9th ed. page 659)

Water is an amphoteric substance; it can act as an acid or a base according to the reaction

$$H_2O + H_2O \rightleftharpoons H_3O^+ + OH^-$$

The equilibrium expression for this reaction is

$$K_w = [H_3O^+][OH^-]$$

where K_w is the equilibrium constant for the ionization of water. Water is neutral whenever $[H_3O^+] = [OH^-]$. At 25°C $[H_3O^+] = [OH^-] = 1.0 \times 10^{-7}$ M, but since this is an endothermic equilibrium reaction, the concentrations are temperature dependent.

This relationship can be expressed as

$$pK_w = pH + pOH$$

Since pK_w is 14.00 at 25°C, the equation is often written as

$$14.00 = pH + pOH$$

The equation can be generalized for any acid–base pair in aqueous solution at 25°C as

$$14.00 = pK_a + pK_b$$

POLYPROTIC ACIDS

(*Chemistry* 8th ed. pages 666–671/9th ed. pages 681–686)

Polyprotic acids can donate more than one proton, H^+, and dissociate by losing 1 H^+ at a time. Sulfuric acid, H_2SO_4 is the only strong acid that is polyprotic.

EXAMPLE: Calculate the pH of a 0.10 M solution of H_2SO_4. K_{a1} = very large; $K_{a2} = 1.2 \times 10^{-2}$.

SOLUTION: The dissociation of H_2SO_4 occurs in a stepwise fashion where the first step goes to completion and the second step is an equilibrium.

Step 1. $H_2SO_4 + H_2O \rightarrow H_3O^+ + HSO_4^-$

$$[H_2SO_4] = [H_3O^+] = [HSO_4^-] = 0.50\ M$$

Step 2. $HSO_4^- + H_2O \rightleftharpoons H_3O^+ + SO_4^{2-}$

	HSO_4^- +	$H_2O \rightleftharpoons$	H_3O^+ +	SO_4^{2-}
I	0.10		0.10	0
C	$-x$		$+x$	$+x$
E	$0.10 - x$		$0.10 + x$	x

Because K_a and the acid concentration are close to each other, x cannot be ignored and a quadratic equation must be solved to determine $[H_3O^+]$.

$$K_a = \frac{[H_3O^+][SO_4^{2-}]}{[HSO_4^-]} \qquad K_a = [H_3O^+][SO_4^{2-}]/[HSO_4^-]$$

$$1.2 \times 10^{-2} = \frac{(0.10 + x)(x)}{(0.10 - x)}$$

$$0 = x^2 + 0.112x - 1.2 \times 10^{-3}$$

$$X = \frac{-b \pm \sqrt{b^2 - 4ac}}{2a}$$

$$X = \frac{-0.112 \pm \sqrt{0.112^2 - 4(1)(-1.2 \times 10^{-3})}}{2(1)}$$

x = 9.8 × 10⁻³

[H₃O⁺] = 0.10 + 0.0098 M = 0.11 M

pH = –log[H₃O⁺] = –log(0.11) = 0.96

EXAMPLE: Calculate the [H₃O⁺] of a 0.20 M solution of H₃AsO₄.

Also determine the concentrations of H₃AsO₄, H₂AsO₄⁻, HAsO₄²⁻, and AsO₄³⁻.

For H₃AsO₄, K_{a_1} = 5 × 10⁻³, K_{a_2} = 8 × 10⁻⁸, K_{a_3} = 6 × 10⁻¹⁰.

	H₃AsO₄ +	H₂O ⇌	H₃O⁺ +	H₂AsO₄⁻
I	0.20		0	0
C	–x		+x	+x
E	0.20 – x		x	x

H₃AsO₄ + H₃O⁺ ⇌ H₃O⁺ + H₂AsO₄⁻

$$K_{a_1} = \frac{[H_3O^+][H_2AsO_4^-]}{[H_3AsO_4]}$$

$$5 \times 10^{-3} = \frac{x^2}{0.20 - x}$$

Note: You cannot assume x is small since the K and 0.20 only differ by a factor of 10². You will need to solve the quadratic equation to solve for x.

x = 3 × 10⁻² M

[H₃O⁺] = [H₂AsO₄⁻] = 3 × 10⁻² M

[H₃AsO₄] = 0.20 – 0.03 = 0.17 M

Since K_{a_3} <<< K_{a_2} <<< K_{a_1}, very little of H₂AsO₄⁻ and HAsO₄²⁻ dissociates compared to H₃AsO₄, so [H₃O⁺] and [H₂AsO₄⁻] will not change very much by the K_{a_2} dissociation, and we can use their concentrations to find the concentration of HAsO₄²⁻.

	H₂AsO₄⁻ +	H₂O ⇌	H₃O⁺ +	HAsO₄²⁻
I	3 × 10⁻²		3 × 10⁻²	0
C	–x		+x	+x
E	3 × 10⁻² – x		3 × 10⁻² + x	x

$$K_{a_2} = 8 \times 10^{-8} = \frac{(3 \times 10^{-2})[HAsO_4^{2-}]}{(3 \times 10^{-2})}$$

$[HAsO_4^{2-}] = 8 \times 10^{-8}$ M; the assumption that K_{a_2} does not contribute significantly to $[H_3O^+]$ and $[H_2AsO_4^-]$ is good.

Repeat the process to find $[AsO_4^{3-}]$.

	$HAsO_4^{2-} +$	$H_2O \rightleftharpoons$	$H_3O^+ +$	AsO_4^{3-}
I	8×10^{-8}		3×10^{-2}	0
C	$-x$		$+x$	$+x$
E	$8 \times 10^{-8} - x$		$3 \times 10^{-2} + x$	x

$$K_{a_3} = 6 \times 10^{-10} = \frac{(3 \times 10^{-2})\,[AsO_4^{3-}]}{(8 \times 10^{-8})}$$

$[AsO_4^{3-}] = 2 \times 10^{-15}$ M. Assumption that x is small is valid.

ACID–BASE PROPERTIES OF SALTS

(*Chemistry* 8th ed. pages 671–677/9th ed. pages 686–691)

PREDICTING THE pH OF SALTS

You may be asked to determine if a salt is acidic, basic, or neutral by looking at its chemical formula. This process involves two steps, as outlined in the flowcharts which follow. In the first flowchart, you determine the acidity or basicity of the individual ions. Then, using the second chart and the results from the first flowchart, you can determine if the salt is acidic, basic, or neutral.

Determining the Approximate pH of Ions in a Salt

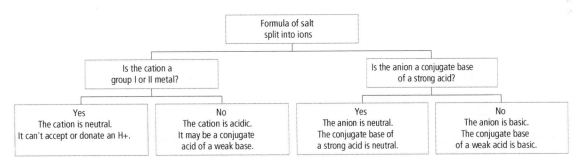

Determining the Approximate pH of a Salt

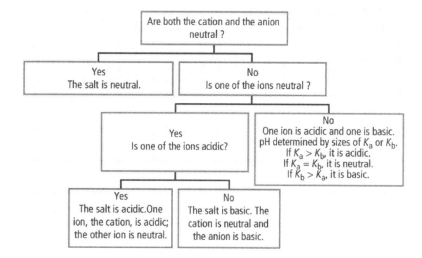

EXAMPLE: Determine whether an aqueous solution of $KC_2H_3O_2$ is acidic, basic, or neutral.

SOLUTION: KCH_3O_2 is basic. Use the method of asking questions outlined above.

Split the salt into its cation, K^+, and its anion, $C_2H_3O_2^-$.

Is the cation a Group I metal? Yes; the cation does not affect the pH.

Is the anion a conjugate base of a strong acid? No; $C_2H_3O_2^-$ is the conjugate base of a weak acid, $HC_2H_3O_2$, which makes the solution basic.

Because we have a salt with a cation which doesn't affect the pH and a basic anion, an aqueous solution of the salt is basic.

CALCULATING THE pH OF SALTS

To calculate the pH of a salt, first you must decide whether the salt is acidic, basic, or neutral. If the salt is basic, then its anion is the conjugate base of a weak acid. The anion will undergo hydrolysis. Write an equation for the reaction of that ion with water to form the acid and OH^- ions: $A^- + H_2O \rightleftharpoons HA + OH^-$. Then write the equilibrium expression:

$$K_b = \frac{K_w}{K_a} = \frac{[HA][OH^-]}{[A^-]}$$

If the salt is basic, then the hydrolysis reaction will produce an acid.

EXAMPLE: Determine the pH of a 0.100 M aqueous solution of NaCN. The K_a for HCN is 5.8×10^{-10}.

SOLUTION: In aqueous solutions, NaCN ionizes completely into Na^+ and CN^-. However, the cyanide ions ionize in water according to the following equation:

$CN^-(aq) + H_2O(l) \rightleftharpoons HCN(aq) + OH^-(aq)$.

Na^+ ions do not affect the pH. Ions from Group IA and IIA never undergo hydrolysis because they are cations of strong bases. The equilibrium expression for the solution is

$$K_b = \frac{[OH^-][HCN]}{[CN^-]}$$

We need a value for K_b. Since we have K_a for HCN, we can calculate the value of K_b for CN^-.

$$K_b = \frac{1.0 \times 10^{-14}}{K_a} = \frac{1.0 \times 10^{-14}}{5.8 \times 10^{-10}}$$

$K_b = 1.7 \times 10^{-5}$

Constructing a table for filling in the available information, we get

	CN⁻ +	H₂O ⇌	HCN +	OH⁻
I	0.100		0	0
C	−x		+x	+x
E	0.100 − x		x	x

Since K is much smaller than 0.100, assume that $0.100 - x \approx 0.100$.

$$K_b = \frac{[OH^-][HCN]}{[CN^-]}; \quad 1.7 \times 10^{-5} = \frac{x^2}{0.100}$$

Solving for x, we have

$x = [OH^-] = 1.3 \times 10^{-3}$

pOH = 2.89;   pH = 14.00 − pOH

pH = 11.11

BUFFERS

(*Chemistry* 8th ed. pages 701–713/9th ed. pages 715–727)

Buffers resist changes in pH when acids or bases are added. The components of a buffer are summarized in the next table.

Buffer	
Components	**Examples**
Similar concentrations of weak acid + salt containing the conjugate base	HCN and NaCN
Similar concentrations of weak base + salt containing the conjugate acid	CH_3NH_2 and CH_3NH_3Cl
Excess weak acid + strong base	2 mol of HCN + 1 mol NaOH react to yield 1 mol HCN and 1 mol NaCN
Excess weak base + strong acid	2 mol NH_3 + 1 mol HCl react to yield 1 mol NH_3 and 1 mol NH_4Cl

Buffers cannot be made with strong acids or strong bases because their conjugate forms are extremely weak and the system is not in equilibrium; it has gone to completion.

Buffer pH is related to the pK_a and the relative amounts of the acid and base forms. Buffer capacity is proportional to the actual concentrations of the acid and base forms. A buffer will maintain pH as long as both the acid and base forms are present.

CALCULATING THE PH OF A BUFFER

The calculation to find the pH of a buffer is similar to all equilibrium calculations *except* there are now two initial concentrations, one for each part of the buffer pair.

EXAMPLE: Calculate the pH of a solution that is 0.60 M HF and 1.00 M KF. K_a for HF is 7.2×10^{-4}.

SOLUTION: First, write the reaction of the acid with water. (You are given K_a, and the buffer is a made of a weak acid and its conjugate base.)

$$HF + H_2O \rightleftharpoons H_3O^+ + F^-$$

Second, set up an ICE chart. Since KF is a soluble salt, $[F^-] = [KF] = 1.00\ M$.

	HF +	$H_2O \rightleftharpoons$	H_3O^+ +	F^-
I	0.60		0	1.00
C	$-x$		$+x$	$+x$
E	$0.60 - x$		x	$1.00 + x$

Third, write the equilibrium expression for K_a.

Plug in the values from the equilibrium line of the ICE chart. Check to see if x is small.

$$K_a = 7.2 \times 10^{-4} = \frac{[H_3O^+][F^-]}{[HF]} = \frac{x(1.00 - x)}{(0.60 - x)} = \frac{x(1.00)}{0.60}$$

Fourth, solve for x which equals H_3O^+.

$$K_a = 7.2 \times 10^{-4} = \frac{x(1.00)}{0.60}$$

$$x = [H_3O^+] = 4.3 \times 10^{-4}\ M$$

$$pH = -\log[H_3O^+]$$

$$pH = -\log(4.3 \times 10^{-4}) = 3.36$$

An alternative method of solving a buffer problem is to use the Henderson–Hasselbalch equation

Henderson–Hasselbalch Equation
$pH = pK_a + \log\left(\dfrac{[\text{conjugate base}]}{[\text{weak acid}]}\right)$

where $pK_a = -\log K_a$.

EXAMPLE: Repeat the example above with the Henderson–Hasselbalch equation.

SOLUTION: $pH = pK_a + \log\left(\dfrac{F^-}{HF}\right)$

$$pH = -\log\left(7.2 \times 10^{-4}\right) + \log\left(\dfrac{1.00}{0.60}\right)$$

pH = 3.14 + 0.22 = 3.36

Comparing the pH and pK_a of a buffer can give a qualitative indication of the predominant species present. When pH = pK_a, [A$^-$] = [HA]. When pH > pK_a, [A$^-$] > [HA] and when pH < pK_a, [HA] > [A$^-$]. Applications of this relationship include acid–base indicators and protonation of amino acids in polypeptides and proteins.

EXAMPLE: Identify the forms of phenylalanine in highest concentration at pH 2 and 10. pK_a = 2.58 (acid), 9.24 (amine)

SOLUTION: pH 2 is less than the pK_a, so the amino group in phenylalanine will be fully protonated. It will attract the hydrogen from H_3O^+ and will leave H_2O behind.

pH 10 is greater than the pK_a of the amine, so the molecule will be fully deprotonated—the hydrogen on the carboxylic acid group will be attracted to OH$^-$ in the solution forming water.

PREPARATION OF A BUFFER

A buffer can be made from a weak acid and a salt containing its conjugate base or from a weak base and a salt containing its conjugate acid.

EXAMPLE: Calculate the mass of $NaC_2H_3O_2$ required to prepare a buffer of pH 4.55 when added to 0.500 L of 0.67 M acetic acid. (Assume no change in volume.) $K_a = 1.8 \times 10^{-5}$ for $HC_2H_3O_2$.

SOLUTION: This problem can be solved using an ICE chart or by using the Henderson–Hasselbalch equation. Once $[C_2H_3O_2^-]$ is calculated, stoichiometry is used to relate concentration to mass.

$$pH = pK_a + \log\left(\frac{[C_2H_3O_2^-]}{[HC_2H_3O_2]}\right)$$

$$4.55 = 4.74 + \log\left(\frac{[C_2H_3O_2^-]}{0.67\ M}\right)$$

$$-0.19 = \log\left(\frac{[C_2H_3O_2^-]}{0.67\ M}\right)$$

$$0.65 = \frac{[C_2H_3O_2^-]}{0.67\ M}$$

$$\text{mass } NaC_2H_3O_3 = \frac{0.44\ \text{mol } [C_2H_3O_2^-]}{L} \times \frac{1\ \text{mol } NaC_2H_3O_2}{1\ \text{mol } [C_2H_3O_2^-]} \times \frac{0.500\ L \times 82.0\ g}{1\ \text{mol } NaC_2H_3O_2}$$

mass $NaC_2H_3O_2$ = 1.8 g

ADDITION OF STRONG ACID AND STRONG BASE TO A BUFFER

When the [A⁻]/[HA] ratio is 1, the pH of the buffer equals the pK_a of the weak acid. Addition of small amounts of strong acid or base will not significantly change this ratio because the large amount of weak acid is available to react with the strong base and the large amount of conjugate base is available to react with the strong acid. It is not until the [A⁻]/[HA] ratio changes by a factor of 10 that the pH changes by 1 unit.

TITRATION

(*Chemistry* 8th ed. pages 713–728/9th ed. pages 727–742)

A titration can be used to determine the concentration of an unknown solution. The neutralization reaction generally has $K > 1$ so these reactions can be considered to go to completion. At the equivalence point, the moles of titrant and moles of analyte are present in stoichiometric ratios; neither one is in excess. Near the equivalence point the pH changes rapidly as fewer moles of analyte are present.

The table below summarizes the other types of problems involving acid–base titrations. Examples of each type of titration problem follow the table.

Characteristics of Titrations

Titrations	Before equivalence point	At equivalence point	After equivalence point
Strong acid titrated with a strong base	Use excess $[H_3O^+]$ to calculate the pH pH < 7	pH = 7	Use excess $[OH^-]$ to calculate the pH pH > 7
Species in solution which affect the pH (in addition to H_2O)	H_3O^+	H_2O	OH^-
Weak acid titrated with a strong base	Weak acid + conjugate base (buffer calculation) pH < 7	Salt hydrolysis calculation pH > 7	Use excess $[OH^-]$ to calculate pH pH > 7
Species in solution which affect the pH (in addition to H_2O)	HA, A^-	A^-	OH^-
Weak base titrated with a strong acid	Weak base + conjugate acid (buffer calculation) pH > 7	Salt hydrolysis calculation pH < 7	Use excess $[H_3O^+]$ to calculate pH pH < 7
Species in solution which affect the pH (in addition to H_2O)	B, HB^+	HB^+	H_3O^+

TITRATION OF A STRONG ACID WITH A STRONG BASE

(*Chemistry* 8th ed. pages 713–717/9th ed. pages 727–731)

At any point during the titration of a strong acid with a strong base (or a strong base with a strong acid), the pH can be calculated from the molarity of the ion present in excess after the complete reaction. Halfway to the equivalence point the main species present are H_3O^+, the anion from the acid, and the cation from the base. The total positive charge is equal to the total negative charge; the mixture is electrically neutral.

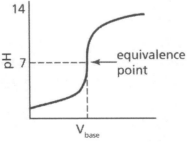

At the equivalence point of any type of titration,

$$\text{moles } H_3O^+ = \text{moles } OH^-.$$

For a strong acid–strong base titration, the pH equals 7.

> EXAMPLE: Consider the titration of 40.0 mL of 0.200 M HBr by 0.100 M KOH. Calculate the pH of the resulting solution when the following volumes of KOH have been added.
>
> a. 10.0 mL   b. 80.0 mL   c. 100.0 mL
>
> SOLUTION: First, using the volume and molarity of the HBr, calculate the moles of H_3O^+ to be titrated. The resulting moles of H_3O^+ appear in the first column in the table at the end of the problem.
>
> $M = n/V$
>
> $n = (0.200$ mol/L$)(0.0400$ L$) = 8.00 \times 10^{-3}$ mol HBr
>
> Next, for the titration in question, calculate the moles of OH^- added from the volume and concentration of KOH. The resulting moles of OH^- used in each titration appear in the second column of the table.
>
> $M = n/V$
>
> $n = (0.100$ mol/L$)(0.0100$ L$) = 1.00 \times 10^{-3}$ mol KOH
>
> Calculate the moles of ion in excess, H_3O^+ or OH^-.

	HBr +	KOH →	KBr +	HOH
Init mol	8.00×10^{-3}	1.00×10^{-3}	0	
Change mol	-1.00×10^{-3}	-1.00×10^{-3}	$+1.00 \times 10^{-3}$	
Final mol	7.00×10^{-3}	0	1.00×10^{-3}	

> The results for each titration appear in column four in the table below.
>
> Using the total volume, in column five of the table, and the moles of ion in excess in column four, determine the molarity of the ion in excess. The molarity of the ion in excess for each of the three titrations is in column six.
>
> 40.0 mL acid + 10.0 mL base = 50.0 mL solution
>
> $M = n/V$
>
> $M = 7.00 \times 10^{-3}$ mol/0.0500 L $= 0.0140$ M
>
> It is the molarity of the ion in excess which determines the pH.
>
> $pH = -\log[H_3O^+]$
>
> $pH = -\log(0.0140) = 0.854$
>
> In part b of the example, neither ion is in excess. The pH equals 7 because the titration is at the equivalence point.
>
> Be careful, in part c of the example, the excess ion is the OH^- ion. To calculate the pH, you must determine pOH and then the pH.

Problem Part	Mol H_3O^+	Mol OH^-	Mol Ion in Excess	Total Volume (When acid and base react)	Molarity Ion in Excess	pH
A	8.00×10^{-3}	1.00×10^{-3}	7.00×10^{-3} (H_3O^+)	0.0500 L	0.140 (H_3O^+)	0.854
B	8.00×10^{-3}	8.00×10^{-3}	None Equivalence point	Not needed	None	7.00
C	8.00×10^{-3}	10.0×10^{-3}	2.0×10^{-3} (OH^-)	0.140 L	0.014 (OH^-)	12.15

AP Tip

When you are calculating the pH during a titration, be careful to take the negative log of the concentration of H_3O^+, not just the moles of H_3O^+ which is a common mistake. And if the excess ion or the value of x is OH^-, be sure that you calculate the pOH and then the pH.

TITRATION OF A WEAK ACID WITH A STRONG BASE

There are four characteristic types of calculations for the titration of a weak acid with a strong base: before the equivalence point (1), halfway to equivalence point (2), at the equivalence point (3), and after the equivalence point (4). For this type of titration, always do stoichiometric calculations followed by equilibrium calculations.

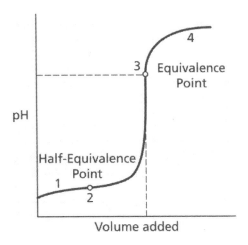

EXAMPLE: A 25.0-mL sample of 0.100 M $HC_3H_5O_2$ is titrated with 0.100 M NaOH. Calculate the pH when the following volumes of 0.100 M NaOH are added: $K_a = 1.3 \times 10^{-5}$ for $HC_3H_5O_2$.

a) 8.0 mL   b) 12.5 mL   c) 25.0 mL   d) 30.0 mL

SOLUTION: <u>Titration Point 1</u> – Calculation of the pH before the Equivalence Point

Part a of the example above involves the titration before the equivalence point. Perform the stoichiometry and record the results in a table under the reaction.

Stoichiometry:

Calculate the initial moles of the weak acid present in the sample.

0.0250 L × 0.100 mol /L = 2.50 × 10^{-3} mol $HC_3H_5O_2$

Calculate the moles of strong base, OH$^-$, added.

0.0080 L × 0.100 mo/L = 8.0 × 10^{-4} mol

The total volume of the solution is now 33.0 mL. Calculate the concentration of each species that remains.

[$HC_3H_5O_2$] = 1.70 × 10^{-3} mol/0.0330 L = 0.0515 M

	$HC_3H_5O_2$ +	OH$^-$ →	$C_3H_5O_2^-$ +	H_2O
Init mol	2.50 × 10^{-3}	8.0 × 10^{-4}	0	
Change mol	–8.0 × 10^{-4}	–8.0 × 10^{-4}	+8.0 × 10^{-4}	
Final mol	1.70 × 10^{-3}	0	8.0 × 10^{-4}	
Final [ ]	0.0515		0.0242	

Equilibrium:

Calculate the new initial moles of weak acid and its conjugate base present after the OH$^-$ has reacted.
    This problem is now identical to a "buffer" problem.
    Make an ICE table to do an equilibrium calculation. Note the minus sign to show the amount of acid decreasing upon added OH$^-$ and the plus sign to show the amount of conjugate base increasing.
    Calculate the new initial moles of weak acid and its conjugate base, after the weak acid has reacted with the strong base, by subtracting or adding the number of moles OH$^-$ added.

	$HC_3H_5O_2$ +	H_2O ⇌	H_3O^+ +	$C_3H_5O_2^-$
I	0.0515			0.0242
C	–X		+X	+X
E	0.0515 – X		X	0.0242 + X

You can now perform the equilibrium calculation.

$$K_a = \frac{[H_3O^+] [C_3H_5O_2^-]}{[HC_3H_5O_2]}$$

$$1.3 \times 10^{-5} = \frac{[H_3O^+] (0.0242 + x)}{0.0515 + x} \approx \frac{[H_3O^+]0.0242}{0.0515}$$

$2.77 \times 10^{-5} \, M = [H_3O^+]$

$pH = -\log [H_3O^+] = 4.56$

Alternatively, you can use the Henderson–Hasselbalch equation.

$pH = pK_a + \log[C_3H_5O_2^-]/[HC_3H_5O_2]$

$pH = -\log(1.3 \times 10^{-5}) + [\log(0.0242 + x)/(0.0515 - x)] = 4.56$

Titration Point 2 – Halfway to the Equivalence Point

In part b of the example on the previous page, a 25.00-mL sample of 0.100 M HC$_3$H$_5$O$_2$ is titrated with 12.5 of 0.100 M NaOH. K_a is 1.3×10^{-5} for HC$_3$H$_5$O$_2$.

Half of the acid being titrated is neutralized. This point is halfway to the equivalence point.

Since half the acid is neutralized and half remains, [HA] = [A$^-$]. The major species present at this point in the titration are H$_3$O$^+$, the anion from the acid, the cation from the base, and the weak acid. The total positive charge is equal to the total negative charge; the mixture remains electrically neutral.

$K_a = \dfrac{[H^+] \, [\cancel{A^-}]}{[\cancel{HA}]}$

$pK_a = pH$

$pK_a = -\log K_a = -\log (1.3 \times 10^{-5}) = 4.89$

Titration Point 3 – At the Equivalence Point

In part c of the example on the previous page, a 25.00-mL sample of 0.100 M HC$_3$H$_5$O$_2$ is titrated with 25.0 mL of 0.100 M NaOH.

K_a is 1.3×10^{-5} for HC$_3$H$_5$O$_2$.

Stoichiometry:

Calculate the initial moles of the weak acid in the sample.

Calculate the moles of strong base, OH$^-$, added.

0.0250 L $\times$ 0.100 mol/ L = 2.50×10^{-3} mol OH$^-$ = mol C$_3$H$_5$O$_2^-$

The total volume of the solution is now 50.0 mL. Calculate the concentration of each species that remains.

$[C_3H_5O_2^-] = 2.50 \times 10^{-3}$ mol/0.0500 L = 0.0500 M

	$HC_3H_5O_2$ +	OH^- →	$C_3H_5O_2^-$ +	H_2O
Init mol	2.50×10^{-3}	2.50×10^{-3}	0	
Change mol	-2.50×10^{-3}	-2.50×10^{-3}	$+2.50 \times 10^{-3}$	
Final mol	0	0	2.50×10^{-3}	
Final [ ]			0.0500	

There is no weak acid present once the strong base added completely reacts. All that is present is A^- ($C_3H_5O_2^-$), the conjugate base of weak acid, HA ($HC_3H_5O_2$). An aqueous solution of A^- will be basic due to its reaction with water.

~~HA + NaOH~~ → NaA + HOH

The problem from this point on is a salt hydrolysis problem.

	$C_3H_5O_2^-$ +	HOH ⇌	$HC_3H_5O_2$ +	OH^-
I	0.0500		0	0
C	$-x$		$+x$	$+x$
E	$0.500 - x$		x	x

$$K_b = \frac{K_w}{K_a} = \frac{1.0 \times 10^{-14}}{1.3 \times 10^{-5}} = 7.7 \times 10^{-10}$$

$$K_b = \frac{[OH^-][HC_3H_5O_2]}{[C_3H_5O_2^-]} = \frac{x^2}{0.0500 - x} \approx \frac{x^2}{0.0500}$$

$x = [(7.7 \times 10^{-10})(0.0500)]^{1/2} = 6.2 \times 10^{-6}$ M OH^-

pOH = 5.21; pH = 14.00 − 5.21 = 8.79

<u>Titration Point 4</u> – After the Equivalence Point

The calculations involved here are identical to those in a strong acid–strong base titration.

In part d of the example on the previous page, a 25.0-mL sample of 0.100 M $HC_3H_5O_2$ is titrated with 30.0 mL of 0.100 M NaOH. K_a is 1.3×10^{-5} for $HC_3H_5O_2$.

0.0300 L × 0.100 mol/L = 3.00×10^{-3} mol NaOH

0.02500 L × 0.100 mol/L = 2.50×10^{-3} mol $HC_3H_5O_2$

$[OH^-] = 5.0 \times 10^{-4}$ mol/0.0550 L = 9.1×10^{-3} M

Stoichiometry:

	$HC_3H_5O_2$ +	OH^- →	$C_3H_5O_2^-$ +	H_2O
Init mol	2.50×10^{-3}	3.00×10^{-3}	0	
Change mol	-2.50×10^{-3}	-2.50×10^{-3}	$+2.50 \times 10^{-3}$	
Final mol	0	5.0×10^{-4}	2.50×10^{-3}	
Final [ ]		9.1×10^{-3}	0.0500	

The hydrolysis of $C_3H_5O_2^-$ will not significantly change the $[OH^-]$, so the pH is only dependent on the excess $[OH^-]$.

pOH = 2.0; pH = 12.0

Titration of a Weak Base with a Strong Acid

The calculations for a weak base–strong acid titration are very similar to the weak acid–strong base titration.

The differences are these:

- The pH before the equivalence point is greater than 7.
- At the equivalence point, the pH is less than 7 since the salt formed is acidic.
- After the equivalence point, the pH is determined by the molarity of the excess H^+.

Characteristics of Titration Curves

It is important for you to be able to sketch and identify the key points on titration curves for the AP exam. The next example will help you to review titration curves for the different types of titrations discussed in this section. Calculations involving titrations of polyprotic acids are beyond the scope of the AP exam, but qualitative questions may be asked.

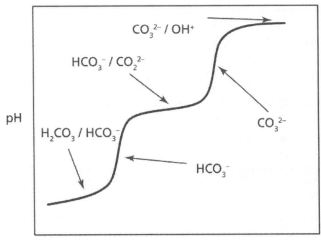

mL Base

$$H_2CO_3 + OH^- \rightleftharpoons HCO_3^- + H_2O$$

$$HCO_3^- + OH^- \rightleftharpoons CO_3^{2-} + H_2O$$

The graph above shows a titration of carbonic acid (a diprotic acid) with a strong base. Two fairly vertical regions (labeled HCO_3^- and

CO_3^{2-}) indicate rapid pH changes resulting from a small change in volume. This indicates 2 *labile protons*. Labile protons are protons prone to separate or be removed from the rest of the molecule; they are the "acidic" protons. The labile protons in H_2CO_3 are circled in the structure below.

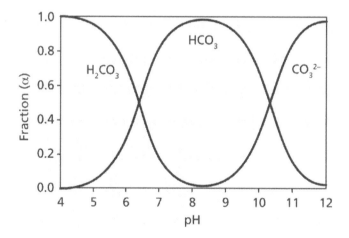

The species present at different points in the titration depend on the pH of the solution. Protonation is an equilibrium situation: a competition between the H_2CO_3, HCO_3^-, CO_3^{2-}, and H_2O. In aqueous solution at 25°C, $pK_{a_1} = 6.3$ and $pK_{a_2} = 10.3$.

$$H_2CO_3 + OH^- \rightleftharpoons HCO_3^- + H_2O \qquad pK_{a_1} = 6.3$$

$$HCO_3^- + OH^- \rightleftharpoons CO_3^{2-} + H_2O \qquad pK_{a_2} = 10.3.$$

H_2CO_3 is the predominant species present at pH < 6.3 because the carbonic acid has a greater affinity for protons than water does. Bicarbonate ion (HCO_3^-) is predominant at 6.3 < pH < 10.3 and carbonate ion (CO_3^{2-}) predominates at pH > 10.3. The speciation graph below shows how the fraction of H_2CO_3, HCO_3^-, and CO_3^{2-} depend on the pH of the solution.

EXAMPLE: The questions that follow refer to the following three titration curves. All solutions are equimolar.

Figure 1:

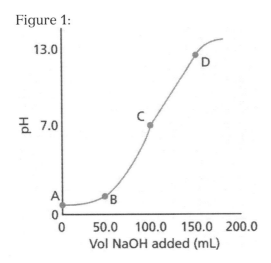

Figure 2:

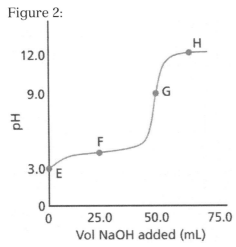

Figure 3:

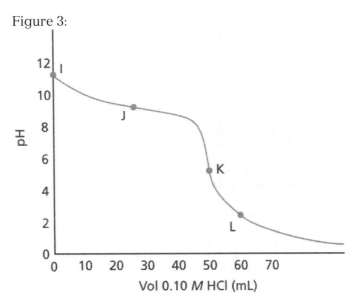

(a) Which titration curve represents a strong acid titrated by a strong base? Explain your answer.

(b) Which titration curve represents a weak acid titrated by a strong base? Explain your answer.

(c) Which titration curve represents a weak base titrated by a strong acid? Explain your answer.

(d) For each lettered part of each curve, A through L, identify the major species which affects the pH.

SOLUTION: (a) Figure 1 represents a strong acid titrated by a strong base. The pH is very low when no base has been added. The pH at the equivalence point is 7.00.

SOLUTION: (b) Figure 2 represents a weak acid titrated by a strong base. The pH is acidic, but slightly higher than the titration curve in Figure 1. The equivalence point occurs at pH 9, signifying the presence of the conjugate base of the weak acid being titrated.

SOLUTION: (c) Figure 3 represents a weak base titrated by a strong acid. When no acid has been added, the pH is basic. Notice that at the equivalence point the pH is acidic in this titration.

SOLUTION: (d) The points are labeled as follows:

Figure 1:

A strong acid, H⁺

B strong acid, H⁺

C water

D strong base, OH⁻

Figure 2:

E weak acid, HA

F weak acid, HA and its conjugate base, A⁻

G conjugate base, A⁻

H strong base, OH⁻

Figure 3:

I weak base, B

J weak base, B, and its conjugate acid, HB⁺

K conjugate acid, HB⁺

L strong acid, H⁺

THERMODYNAMICS OF SOLUTION FORMATION

(*Chemistry* 8th ed. pages 501–504/9th ed. pages 514–517)

The common axiom, "like dissolves like" is an inadequate explanation for any AP Chemistry exam question that asks you to explain why 2 substances may be soluble or insoluble. In order to understand why that axiom is used, you need to understand solution formation in terms of thermodynamics: enthalpy, entropy, and free energy.

The attractive forces that hold the solute and solvent together must first be overcome before a solution can form. Since both of these processes involve overcoming intermolecular attractions, expanding the solute (ΔH_1) and expanding the solvent (ΔH_2) are always endothermic. Attraction between the solute and solvent (ΔH_3) is usually (but not always) an exothermic process. The enthalpy of solution (ΔH_{soln}) is the sum of the ΔH for the entire process.

$$\Delta H_{soln} = \Delta H_1 + \Delta H_2 + \Delta H_3$$

If ΔH_{soln} is positive (as is for the case of dissolving NaCl: $\Delta H_{soln} = 3$ kJ/mol), then entropy must be the driving force that makes $\Delta G°$ negative and explains why salt spontaneously dissolves in water.

SOLUBILITY PRODUCT

(*Chemistry* 8th ed. pages 744–745, 748/9th ed. pages 759–760, 763)

You must memorize the fact that all sodium, potassium, ammonium, and nitrate salts are soluble in water. For all other salts, you will either be given solubility information or will need to calculate solubility based on equilibrium data and/or constants provided to you.

For slightly soluble or insoluble salts, equilibrium exists between the solid and its aqueous ions. For example, lead(II) chloride dissolves in water as follows:

$$PbCl_2(s) \rightleftharpoons Pb^{2+}(aq) + 2\ Cl^-(aq)$$

At first, when the salt is added to the water, there are no ions present. As the solid dissolves, the concentration of the ions increases. A simultaneous competing process is the reverse of the dissolution, that is, the reforming of the solid called crystallization. At some point, the maximum amount of dissolution is achieved, which is called the saturation point. However, remember that on a molecular level, a dynamic equilibrium exists between dissolved solute and undissolved solid. (The rate of dissolution equals the rate of crystallization.) The solution is saturated when no more solid dissolves and equilibrium is reached.

The equilibrium expression for the dissolution of lead(II) chloride is

$$K_{sp} = [Pb^{2+}][Cl^-]^2$$

The constant, K_{sp}, is the solubility product constant. For salts producing the same number of ions, the K_{sp} value can be used to measure the extent to which the solid dissolves. The larger the K_{sp} value, the more soluble the salt.

EXAMPLE: Given the following salts and their K_{sp} values, which salt is the most soluble? Which salt is the least soluble?

Formula	K_{sp}
$NiCO_3$	1.4×10^{-7}
MnS	2.3×10^{-13}
$CaSO_4$	6.1×10^{-5}

SOLUTION: The most soluble salt is the salt with the largest K_{sp} value, $CaSO_4$.

The least soluble salt is the salt with the lowest value of K_{sp}, MnS. You are able to compare the K_{sp} values to determine the relative solubilities of the salts because they all produce the same number of ions.

CALCULATIONS INVOLVING SOLUBILITY

(*Chemistry* 8th ed. pages 743–749/9th ed. pages 758–765)

The solubility of a salt is the amount of salt that will dissolve in 1 liter of water. The solubility of a salt can be given in units of mol/L or g/L. The solubility of a salt can be used to determine the K_{sp} value for the salt.

CALCULATING K_{SP} FROM SOLUBILITY

EXAMPLE: The solubility of $Pb_3(PO_4)_2$ is 6.2×10^{-12} M. Calculate the K_{sp} value for the solid.

K_{sp} equals 9.9×10^{-55}.

Step 1: Write the reaction for the dissolution of the solid.

$Pb_3(PO_4)_2(s) \rightleftharpoons 3\ Pb^{2+}(aq) + 2\ PO_4^{3-}(aq)$

Step 2: Underneath the reaction, make an ICE chart.

	$Pb_3(PO_4)_2(s) \rightleftharpoons$	$3\ Pb^{2+}(aq) +$	$2\ PO_4^{3-}(aq)$
I		0	0
C		$+3x$	$+2x$
E		$3x$	$2x$

In the ICE chart above, x represents x mol/L of $Pb_3(PO_4)_2(s)$ dissolving to reach equilibrium which equals 6.2×10^{-12} M. Remember that pure solids are not included in equilibrium expressions.

For every 1 mol per liter of $Pb_3(PO_4)_2$ which dissolves, 3 moles per liter of Pb^{2+} and 2 moles per liter of PO_4^{3-} form.

$3x$ is the mol/L of $Pb^{2+}(aq)$ produced when the solid, $Pb_3(PO_4)_2$, dissolves.

$2x$ is the mol/L of $PO_4^{3-}(aq)$ produced when the solid, $Pb_3(PO_4)_2$, dissolves.

Step 3: Write the equilibrium expression for the reaction and plug in the values from the equilibrium line of the ICE chart.

$$K_{sp} = [Pb^{2+}]^3[PO_4^{3-}]^2 = (3x)^3(2x)^2 = 108x^5$$

The value of x is the solubility of $Pb_3(PO_4)_2$, which equals 6.2×10^{-12} M.

$$K_{sp} = 108(6.2 \times 10^{-12})^5 = 9.9 \times 10^{-55}$$

Alternate solution:

$$6.2 \times 10^{-12} \; \frac{mol\; Pb_3(PO_4)_2}{1\; L} \times \frac{3\; mol\; Pb^{2+}}{1\; mol\; Pb_3(PO_4)_2} = 1.9 \times 10^{-11} M \; Pb^{2+}$$

$$6.2 \times 10^{-12} \; \frac{mol\; Pb_3(PO_4)_2}{1\; L} \times \frac{2\; mol\; Pb_4^{3-}}{1\; mol\; Pb_3(PO_4)_2} = 1.2 \times 10^{-11} M \; PO_4^{3-}$$

Plug these values into the K_{sp} expression and solve for K_{sp}.

$$K_{sp} = [Pb^{2+}]^3[PO_4^{3-}]^2 = (1.9 \times 10^{-11})^3(1.2 \times 10^{-11})^2 = 9.9 \times 10^{-55}$$

CALCULATING SOLUBILITY FROM K_{SP}

If you are given a group of salts which do not all have the same cation to anion ratio and asked which is more soluble, you must perform a calculation to determine the solubility of each salt.

EXAMPLE: Given the two salts in the table below, which is more soluble? Show calculations to support your answer.

	K_{sp}
FeC_2O_4	2.1×10^{-7}
$Cu(IO_4)_2$	1.4×10^{-7}

SOLUTION: You cannot directly compare the K_{sp} values to predict which is more soluble because the salts dissolve to produce a different number of ions. FeC_2O_4 dissolves to produce two ions and $Cu(IO_4)_2$ produces three ions. You must calculate the solubility for each salt from its K_{sp} value.

Step 1: Write the reaction for the dissolution of the solid.

$$FeC_2O_4(s) \rightleftharpoons Fe^{2+}(aq) + C_2O_4^{2-}(aq)$$

Step 2: Underneath the reaction, make an ICE chart.

$$FeC_2O_4(s) \rightleftharpoons Fe^{2+}(aq) + C_2O_4^{2-}(aq)$$

I		0	0
C		$+X$	$+X$
E		X	X

Step 3: Write the equilibrium expression for K_{sp}, plug in the equilibrium line, and solve for x.

$K_{sp} = [Fe^{2+}][C_2O_4^{2-}]$

$2.1 \times 10^{-7} = x^2$

$x = 4.6 \times 10^{-4}$ mol Fe^{2+}/L

$$4.6 \times 10^{-4} \text{mol } Fe^{2+} \times \frac{1 \text{ mol } FeC_2O_4}{1 \text{ L}} = 4.6 \times 10^{-4} \text{mol } FeC_2O_4/\text{L}$$

Repeat the same calculations for the next salt.

Step 1: Write the reaction for the dissolution of the solid.

$Cu(IO_4)_2(s) \rightleftharpoons Cu^{2+}(aq) + 2 IO_4^-(aq)$

Step 2: Underneath the reaction, make an ICE chart.

$$Cu(IO_4)_2(s) \rightleftharpoons Cu^{2+}(aq) + 2 IO_4^-(aq)$$

I		0	0
C		$+X$	$+2X$
E		X	$2X$

Step 3: Write the equilibrium expression for K_{sp}, plug in the equilibrium line, and solve for x.

$K_{sp} = [Cu^{2+}][IO_4^-]^2$

$1.4 \times 10^{-7} = x(2x)^2$

$1.4 \times 10^{-7} = 4x^3$

$x = 3.3 \times 10^{-3}$ mol/L

$$3.3 \times 10^{-3} \text{ mol } Cu^{2+} \times \frac{1 \text{ mol } Cu(IO_4)_2}{1 \text{ L}} = \frac{3.3 \times 10^{-3} \text{ mol } Cu(IO_4)_2}{\text{L}}$$

3.3×10^{-3} mol $Cu(IO_4)_2$/L is greater than 4.6×10^{-4} mol FeC_2O_4 /L.

Therefore $Cu(IO_4)_2$ is more soluble even though K_{sp} for FeC_2O_4 is slightly larger than K_{sp} for $Cu(IO_4)_2$.

COMMON ION EFFECT

(Chemistry 8th ed. pages 750–752/9th ed. pages 765–767)

When a salt is dissolved in water containing a common ion, its solubility is decreased.

For example, consider the solubility equilibrium of silver sulfate.

$$Ag_2SO_4(s) \rightleftharpoons 2\ Ag^+(aq) + SO_4^{2-}(aq)$$

When silver sulfate is dissolved in 0.100 M $AgNO_3$, the Ag^+ ion from silver nitrate causes the equilibrium to shift to the left, decreasing the solubility of silver sulfate.

pH AND SOLUBILITY

Chromium(III) hydroxide dissolves according to the equilibrium

$$Cr(OH)_3(s) \rightleftharpoons Cr^{3+}(aq) + 3\ OH^-(aq)$$

An increase in pH, caused by the addition of OH^- ions, will shift the equilibrium to the left, decreasing the solubility of $Cr(OH)_3$.

A decrease in pH, caused by the addition of H^+ ions, will shift the equilibrium to the right, increasing the solubility of $Cr(OH)_3$. The H^+ ions remove the OH^- ions from the solution.

A salt with the general formula, MX, will show increased solubility in acidic solution if the anion, X^-, is an effective base (if HX is a weak acid). Common anions that make effective bases include S^{2-}, OH^-, and CO_3^{2-}.

PRECIPITATE FORMATION

(Chemistry 8th ed. pages 752–755/9th ed. pages 768–771)

A precipitate may or may not form when two solutions are mixed, depending on the concentrations of the ions involved in the formation of the solid.

ION PRODUCT

The ion product, Q, is written in the same way as the K_{sp} expression. For lead(II) chloride, $Q = [Pb^{2+}][Cl^-]^2$

Calculation of the value, Q, involves the use of the initial concentrations of the solutions mixed, $[Pb^{2+}]_0$ and $[Cl^-]_0$, instead of the equilibrium concentrations.

A comparison of the value of Q to K_{sp} determines if a precipitate is formed.

$Q > K_{sp}$: precipitation occurs

$Q < K_{sp}$: no precipitation occurs

$Q = K_{sp}$: the solution is saturated

EXAMPLE: Will a precipitate form when 100.0 mL of 4.0×10^{-4} M $Mg(NO_3)_2$ is added to 100.0 mL of 2.0×10^{-4} M NaOH?

SOLUTION: Step 1: Determine the identity of the precipitate formed.

$Mg(OH)_2$ is the precipitate. $NaNO_3$ is always soluble.

Step 2: Determine the concentration of the ions after they are mixed and before any reaction occurs.

Determine the moles of concentration of each solute present. Be sure to divide by the total volume of the two solutions mixed.

$[Mg^{2+}]_0 = (0.1000 \text{ L} \times 4.0 \times 10^{-4} \text{ mol/L})/0.2000 \text{ L} = 2.0 \times 10^{-4} M$

$[OH^-]_0 = (0.1000 \text{ L} \times 2.0 \times 10^{-4} \text{ mol/L})/0.2000 \text{ L} = 1.0 \times 10^{-4} M$

Step 3: Write the ion product expression, calculate its value, and compare it to K_{sp}, which equals 8.8×10^{-12}.

$Q = [Mg^{2+}][OH^-]^2$

$Q = (2.0 \times 10^{-4})(1.0 \times 10^{-4})^2 = 2.0 \times 10^{-12}$

Since $Q < K_{sp}$, no precipitate will form.

MULTIPLE-CHOICE QUESTIONS

No calculators are to be used in this section.

1. Equal volumes of equimolar H_2S and OH^- are combined. Which diagram represents the resultant solution?

S = △   O = ●   H = ■

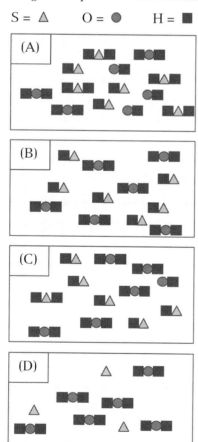

2. The autoionization of water is an endothermic process. How would pH of pure water change if the water was at 100°C?
   (A) pH would remain 7 because water is neutral.
   (B) pH would decrease because equilibrium shifts towards $[H_3O^+]$ and $[OH^-]$.
   (C) pH would increase because equilibrium shifts towards $[H_3O^+]$ and $[OH^-]$.
   (D) pH could not be measured because water boils at 100°C.

3. Consider the phosphoric acid equilibria.

   $$H_3PO_4 + H_2O \rightleftharpoons H_3O^+ + H_2PO_4^- \qquad K_{a_1} = 7.5 \times 10^{-3}$$

   $$H_2PO_4^- + H_2O \rightleftharpoons H_3O^+ + HPO_4^{2-} \qquad K_{a_2} = 6.2 \times 10^{-8}$$

   $$HPO_4^{2-} + H_2O \rightleftharpoons H_3O^+ + PO_4^{3-} \qquad K_{a_3} = 4.8 \times 10^{-13}$$

   What species is predominant at pH 12?

   (A) H_3PO_4
   (B) $H_2PO_4^-$
   (C) HPO_4^{2-}
   (D) PO_4^{3-}

4. Each of the following salts has a solubility of $1.0 \times 10^{-5}\ M$. Rank the salts in order of lowest to highest K_{sp}.
   AX, B_2X, C_2X_3, D_3X
   (A) $C_2X_3 < D_3X < B_2X < AX$
   (B) $C_2X_3 < D_3X < AX < B_2X$
   (C) $D_3X < C_2X_3 < B_2X < AX$
   (D) $D_3X < B_2X < AX < C_2X_3$

5. 0.10 mol $NaC_2H_3O_2$ and 0.050 mol HCl was added to 1.0 L of 0.075 M $HC_2H_3O_2$. List the species in order of decreasing equilibrium concentration.
   (A) $[HC_2H_3O_2] > [C_2H_3O_2^-] > [Cl^-] > [H_3O^+]$
   (B) $[H_3O^+] > [Cl^-] > [C_2H_3O_2^-] > [HC_2H_3O_2]$
   (C) $[HC_2H_3O_2] = [C_2H_3O_2^-] > [Cl^-] = [H_3O^+]$
   (D) $[Cl^-] = [H_3O^+] > [HC_2H_3O_2] = [C_2H_3O_2^-]$

6. Two unlabeled Erlenmeyer flasks each contained 25.00 mL of solution at pH 4.00. Each flask was titrated with the same standardized NaOH solution. The volumes needed to reach the endpoint are listed in the table below. What claim can be made about the acids in flasks A and B?

Flask	Titrant Volume (mL)
A	11.29
B	37.07

(A) The concentration of the acids was the same because both solutions were pH 4.00.
(B) The strength of the acids was the same because both solutions were pH 4.00.
(C) Flask A was a strong acid because less titrant was needed to reach the endpoint.
(D) Flask B was a strong acid because more titrant was needed to reach the endpoint.

7. Consider the following data for the dissolution of an alcohol, R–OH, in a solvent, X–OH. $\Delta H_1 = 65$ kJ/mol, $\Delta H_2 = 340$ kJ/mol, $\Delta H_3 = -8$ kJ/mol. Predict and explain the solubility of this compound.
(A) The compound would be soluble because the solute and solvent both have –OH in their formulas.
(B) The compound would not be soluble because ΔH_3 is negative and exothermic.
(C) The compound would not be soluble because $\Delta H_{soln} = 397$ kJ/mol which is very endothermic.
(D) The compound would not be soluble because ΔS is unknown.

8. HA is a weak acid which is 4.0% dissociated at 0.100 M. Determine the K_o for this acid.
(A) 0.0040
(B) 0.00016
(C) 0.040
(D) 1.6

9. What point on the graph represents pK_{a_2}?

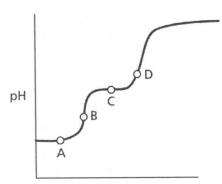

(A) A
(B) B
(C) C
(D) D

10. A buffer can maintain pH upon addition of small amounts of a strong base because
    (A) small amounts of base do not drastically alter an aqueous solution's pH
    (B) the strong base is balanced by the weak acid and conjugate base in the buffer
    (C) the weak acid reacts with the strong base to make more conjugate base
    (D) the strong base has a different pH than the buffer

11. Which acid is the strongest acid?

Acid	K_a
HF	7.2×10^{-4}
HNO_2	4.0×10^{-4}
HCO_2H	1.8×10^{-4}
$HC_3H_5O_3$	1.38×10^{-4}

(A) HF
(B) HNO_2
(C) HCO_2H
(D) $HC_3H_5O_3$

12. Which of the following describes what happens to the solubility of a slightly soluble ionic compound when a common ion is added to the solution?
    (A) The solubility of the ionic compound is reduced.
    (B) The solubility of the ionic compound is increased.
    (C) There is no effect on the solubility of the ionic compound.
    (D) The ionic compound dissolves more rapidly.

13. A researcher needs to prepare a pH 5 buffer. What solutions would be best?
    (A) 0.20 M boric acid ($K_a = 5.8 \times 10^{-10}$) + 0.10 M sodium borate
    (B) 0.20 M ammonia ($K_b = 1.8 \times 10^{-5}$) + 0.10 M ammonium chloride
    (C) 0.20 M propanoic acid ($K_a = 1.3 \times 10^{-5}$) + 0.10 M sodium hydroxide
    (D) 0.20 M lactic acid ($K_a = 1.38 \times 10^{-4}$) + 0.10 M hydrochloric acid

I.

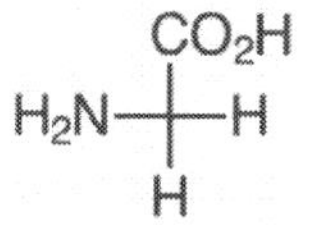

$$\begin{array}{c} CO_2H \\ H_2N{-}\!\!\!\!-\!\!\!\!-H \\ H \end{array}$$

II.

$$\begin{array}{c} \overset{-}{C}OO \\ {}^+H_3N{-}C{-}H \\ H \end{array}$$

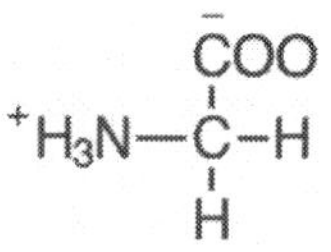

pK_a carboxylic acid = 2.34
pK_a protonated amine = 9.6

14. The structures of the amino acid, glycine, are shown above. What is the predominant form of the amino acid at physiological pH 7.3?
    (A) only structure I
    (B) fairly equal amounts of structures I and II
    (C) more structure II than structure I
    (D) only structure II

15. Two salts, AX and BX$_2$, have identical K_{sp} values at a given temperature. We can say
    (A) the salts are more soluble in 0.1 M NaX than in water
    (B) the molar solubility of AX is identical to BX$_2$
    (C) addition of NaX will not affect the solubilities of the salts
    (D) the molar solubility of AX is greater than that of BX$_2$

FREE-RESPONSE QUESTIONS

1. Methanoic (formic) acid is responsible for the pain of bee stings and stinging nettles. $K_a = 1.8 \times 10^{-4}$
    (a) Circle the labile proton in the structure.

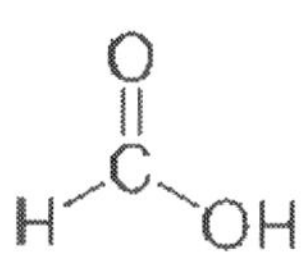

$$\begin{array}{c} O \\ \| \\ H{-}C \\ \quad \ \ OH \end{array}$$

    (b) 15.00 mL of formic acid was titrated with 29.07 mL of 0.0896 M potassium hydroxide.
        (i) Write the net ionic equation for the reaction.
        (ii) Calculate the concentration of formic acid solution.
        (iii) Is the pH at the equivalence point <7, 7, or >7? Explain your answer.
    (c) A different solution of formic acid had a pH of 1.62. Calculate the concentration of formic acid in that solution.

(d) Calculate the pH of a mixture of 1.5 M formic acid and 0.500 M sodium formate.

2. Human bodies maintain their balance (homeostasis) through a series of equilibria. One important equilibrium involves calcium ion because Ca^{2+} is important for muscle contractions in the heart as well as for strong bones. Bone is a complex tissue consisting of living cells and non-living material. Calcium phosphate is part of the non-living material and is how the body stores calcium.
   (a) Write the solubility product expression for the dissolution of calcium phosphate.
   (b) When blood calcium ion concentration decreases, a hormone is released that causes calcium ions from the bones to be released into the bloodstream. What effect does this have on the concentration of calcium phosphate in the bones?

$$H_3PO_4 + H_2O \rightleftharpoons H_3O^+ + H_2PO_4^- \qquad K_{a_1} = 7.5 \times 10^{-3}$$

$$H_2PO_4^- + H_2O \rightleftharpoons H_3O^+ + HPO_4^{2-} \qquad K_{a_2} = 6.2 \times 10^{-8}$$

$$HPO_4^{2-} + H_2O \rightleftharpoons H_3O^+ + PO_4^{3-} \qquad K_{a_3} = 4.8 \times 10^{-13}$$

   (c) Blood pH is approximately 7.4 in healthy people. What are the predominant forms of phosphate in the blood at this pH? Justify your answer.
   (d) One way skeletons can be cleaned for study is to boil the bones in a solution to remove all material and leave the bone. Based on the equilibrium equations above, would a highly acidic or highly basic solution be best to clean the bones? Explain your answer.

Answers

MULTIPLE-CHOICE QUESTIONS

1. **B** Equal volumes of equimolar solutions have the same number of moles. The products of the reaction are equal moles of HS^- and H_2O (*Chemistry* 8th ed. pages 103–107/9th ed. pages 108–114). LO 6.11

2. **B** Endothermic reactions shift to products to relieve stress. Higher $[H_3O^+]$ means lower pH (*Chemistry* 8th ed. pages 624–626/9th ed. pages 637–639). LO 6.14

3. **D** At high pH, OH^- is the predominant H^+ acceptor so PO_4^{3-} is the predominant form of phosphate (*Chemistry* 8th ed. pages 639–642/9th ed. pages 653–656). LO 6.19

4. **A** C_2X_3 forms the most ions so it will have the lowest calculated K_{sp}. AX forms the fewest ions so it will have the highest K_{sp}.

Compound	K_{sp}
AX	1.0×10^{-10}
B_2X	4.0×10^{-15}
C_2X_3	1.1×10^{-23}
D_3X	2.7×10^{-19}

(*Chemistry* 8th ed. pages 749–750/9th ed. pages 764–765). LO 6.22

5. **A** Do a stoichiometry table and then an equilibrium table.

	$NaC_2H_3O_2$ +	HCl →	$HC_2H_3O_2$ +	NaCl
init mol	0.10	0.050	0.075	0
change in mol	–0.050	–0.050	+0.050	+0.050
final mol	0.05	0	0.125	0.050

	$HC_2H_3O_2$ +	H_2O ⇌	$C_2H_3O_2^-$ +	H_3O^+
I	0.125		0.05	0
C	–x		+x	+x
E	0.125 + x		0.05 + x	x

$[HC_2H_3O_2] \approx 0.125\ M$

$[C_2H_3O_2^-] = (0.05 + x)\ M$

$[Cl^-] = 0.050\ M$

$[H_3O^+] = x\ M$

(*Chemistry* 8th ed. page 701–704/9th ed. pages 715–718). LO 6.17

6. **C** At the same pH, a strong acid has a lower concentration because all of the acid is dissociated. In order for the weak acid to ionize to have the same $[H_3O^-]$, the concentration of HA must be much higher (*Chemistry* 8th ed. pages 650–657/9th ed. pages 665–671). LO 6.12

7. **C** A very endothermic process could not be mitigated by an increase in entropy so the dissolution is not favorable at this particular temperature (*Chemistry* 8th ed. pages 501–504/9th ed. pages 514–517). LO 6.24

8. **B**

$[HA]_0 = 0.100\ M$

$[H^+] = [A^-] = 0.004\ M$

$K_a = [H^+][A^-]/[HA] = (0.004)(0.004)/0.100 =$

(seen more simply for our purposes here)

$$(4 \times 10^{-3})(4 \times 10^{-3})/(10^{-1}) = 1.6 \times 10^{-4}$$

Note that although the actual value for [HA] is 0.100 – 0.004 = 0.096 *M*, this approximation is within the 5% rule, and students do not have calculators for this part of the test (*Chemistry* 8th ed. pages 657–659/9th ed. pages 672–673). LO 6.12

9. **C** Halfway to the second equivalence point (*Chemistry* 8th ed. pages 719–720/9th ed. pages 732–734). LO 6.13

10. **C** Buffers have WA-CB equilibrium so small additions of base will just react with the WA forming CB. CB will react with water to reform WA until equilibrium is reestablished (*Chemistry* 8th ed. pages 704–706/9th ed. pages 718–720). LO 6.20

11. **A** HF has the largest K_a which means its equilibrium lies farthest to products (*Chemistry* 8th ed. pages 642–643/9th ed. pages 656–657). LO 6.11

12. **A** The solubility of a slightly soluble ionic compound is always lowered whenever the solution already contains ions common in the solid or ions common to the solid that are added after a solution is prepared. The common-ion effect is an example of Le Châtelier's principle (*Chemistry* 8th ed. pages 750–752/9th ed. pages 766–768). LO 6.23

13. **C** The NaOH (limiting reagent) will react with half of the propanoic acid leaving equal concentrations of propanoic acid and propanoate ion (*Chemistry* 8th ed. pages 701–710/9th ed. pages 715–724). LO 6.18

14. **C** Equilibrium lies closer to structure II at pH 7.3. However, since structure does not fully deprotonate until pH 9.6 there will still be some structure I. LO 6.19

15. **D** For each salt, the respective solubility equilibrium expressions are:

$$AX(s) \rightleftharpoons A^+(aq) + X^-(aq) \text{ and } BX_2(s) \rightleftharpoons B^{2+}(aq) + 2 X^-(aq)$$

Since they have the same K_{sp} values, let us call that value N.

Let "a" represent the solubility of AX. Thus, $(a)(a) = N$ or $a = \sqrt{N}$.

Let "b" represent the solubility of BX_2. Thus $(b)(2b)^2 = N$ or $b = \sqrt[3]{N/4}$.

Since a > b the molar solubility of AX is greater than that of BX_2 (*Chemistry* 8th ed. pages 748–750/9th ed. pages 763–766). LO 6.21

FREE-RESPONSE QUESTIONS

1. (a)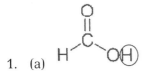

The labile proton is the one that will be ionized. Because oxygen is more electronegative, it pulls electrons away from hydrogen allowing hydrogen to become more attracted to water (*Chemistry* 8th ed. pages 677–678/9th ed. pages 691–693). LO 6.19

(b) (i) $HCOOH + OH^- \rightarrow HCOO^- + H_2O$

(ii) For a 1:1 stoichiometric titration, $M_A V_A = M_B V_B$

$M_A(15.00 \text{ mL}) = (0.0896 \text{ } M)(29.07 \text{ mL})$

$M_A = 0.174 \text{ } M$

(iii) The pH will be >7 because a WA-SB titration makes the conjugate base of a WA as a product. The CB competes for H^+ from water leaving OH^- in solution (*Chemistry* 8th ed. pages 717–722/9th ed. pages 731–736). LO 6.13

(c) $[H_3O^+] = 10^{-1.62} = 0.024 \text{ } M = [HCOO^-]$

	HCOOH +	$H_2O \rightleftharpoons$	HCOO⁻ +	H_3O^+
I	x		0	0
C	−0.024		+ 0.024	+ 0.024
E	$x - 0.024$		0.024	0.024

$K_a = [H_3O^+][HCOO^-]/[HCOOH]$

$[HCOOH] = (x - 0.024) = (0.024)^2/1.8 \times 10^{-4}$

$[HCOOH] = 3.2 \text{ } M$

(d) You can use the Henderson–Hasselbalch equation because the equilibrium concentrations of HA and A^- are more than 1000 times greater than K_a.

$H = pK_a + \log[A^-]/[HA]$

$= 3.74 + \log (0.500/1.5)$

$= 3.27$

(*Chemistry* 8th ed. pages 701–710/9th ed. pages 715–724). LO 6.15

2. (a) $Ca_3(PO_4)_2(s) \rightleftharpoons 3 \text{ } Ca^{2+}(aq) + 2 \text{ } PO_4^{2-}(aq)$

$K_{sp} = [Ca^{2+}]^3[PO_4^{3-}]^2$

(b) The concentration of calcium phosphate does not change since it is a pure solid. The moles per volume remains constant.

(c) At pH 7.4 the predominant forms of phosphate are HPO_4^{2-} and $H_2PO_4^-$. pK_{a_2} is 7.21 which is the pH at which the HPO_4^{2-} and $H_2PO_4^-$ would be in equal concentration. Since the physiological pH is slightly higher than this, HPO_4^{2-} has a slightly higher concentration because the labile proton is more attracted to water.

(d) A highly basic solution will prevent the bones from being damaged in the cleaning. At high pH, acid–base equilibrium favors PO_4^{3-}. Higher PO_4^{3-} concentrations shift the solubility equilibrium back to solid $Ca_3(PO_4)_2$ (*Chemistry* 8th ed. pages 744–752/9th ed. pages 759–768). LO 6.23

Part III

Practice Tests

Periodic Table of Elements

1																	18
1 H 1.008																	2 He 4.003
3 Li 6.941	4 Be 9.012											5 B 10.81	6 C 12.01	7 N 14.01	8 O 16.00	9 F 19.00	10 Ne 20.18
11 Na 22.99	12 Mg 24.31											13 Al 26.98	14 Si 28.09	15 P 30.97	16 S 32.07	17 Cl 35.45	18 Ar 39.95
19 K 39.10	20 Ca 40.08	21 Sc 44.96	22 Ti 47.88	23 V 50.94	24 Cr 52.00	25 Mn 54.94	26 Fe 55.85	27 Co 58.93	28 Ni 58.69	29 Cu 63.55	30 Zn 65.38	31 Ga 69.72	32 Ge 72.59	33 As 74.92	34 Se 78.96	35 Br 79.90	36 Kr 83.80
37 Rb 85.47	38 Sr 87.62	39 Y 88.91	40 Zr 91.22	41 Nb 92.91	42 Mo 95.94	43 Tc (98)	44 Ru 101.1	45 Rh 102.9	46 Pd 106.4	47 Ag 107.9	48 Cd 112.4	49 In 114.8	50 Sn 118.7	51 Sb 121.8	52 Te 127.6	53 I 126.9	54 Xe 131.3
55 Cs 132.9	56 Ba 137.3	57 La* 138.9	72 Hf 178.5	73 Ta 180.9	74 W 183.9	75 Re 186.2	76 Os 190.2	77 Ir 192.2	78 Pt 195.1	79 Au 197.0	80 Hg 200.6	81 Tl 204.4	82 Pb 207.2	83 Bi 209.0	84 Po (209)	85 At (210)	86 Rn (222)
87 Fr (223)	88 Ra 226	89 Ac† (227)	104 Rf	105 Db	106 Sg	107 Bh	108 Hs	109 Mt	110 Ds	111 Rg (272)							

*Lanthanides

58 Ce 140.1	59 Pr 140.9	60 Nd 144.2	61 Pm (145)	62 Sm 150.4	63 Eu 152.0	64 Gd 157.3	65 Tb 158.9	66 Dy 162.5	67 Ho 164.9	68 Er 167.3	69 Tm 168.9	70 Yb 173.0	71 Lu 175.0

†Actinides

90 Th 232.0	91 Pa (231)	92 U 238.0	93 Np (237)	94 Pu (244)	95 Am (243)	96 Cm (247)	97 Bk (247)	98 Cf (251)	99 Es (252)	100 Fm (257)	101 Md (258)	102 No (259)	103 Lr (260)

Practice Test 1

These questions are representative of the AP Chemistry examination, but keep in mind that it is impossible to predict exactly how well you will do on the actual exam. The first section of this test is 50% of your total test grade. Time yourself so that you finish this part in 90 minutes. Remember that on the actual examination, there is no penalty for guessing, so you should answer every question.

AP CHEMISTRY EXAMINATION
Section I: Multiple-Choice Questions
Time: 90 minutes
Number of Questions: 60

No calculators can be used in this section. A periodic table and a formula chart with constants is provided.

Directions: Each of the questions or incomplete statements below is followed by four suggested answers or completions. Select the one that is best in each case.

Questions 1–3 refer to the reaction 2 Al + 6 HCl → 3 H$_2$ + 2 AlCl$_3$. The H$_2$ produced is collected by water displacement.

1. If 0.636 L of H$_2$ is collected at 27°C (vapor pressure of H$_2$O = 21 torr) and a barometric pressure of 757 torr, the partial pressure of the H$_2$, in torr, is
   (A) 0.636 × (273 + 27)
   (B) 0.636 × 757
   (C) 757 – 27
   (D) 757 – 21

2. The gas has a volume of 0.560 L at STP. The number of moles of H$_2$ present is
   (A) 0.025 mole
   (B) 0.050 mole
   (C) equal to the Kelvin scale
   (D) an indicator of the average kinetic energy of gas particles

3. H$_2$(g) is considered to be "ideal," while H$_2$O(g) deviates from "ideal" behavior. What is the best explanation for this observation?
   (A) The volume of H$_2$(g) is less than that of an equal number of H$_2$O(g) gas molecules.
   (B) H$_2$(g) molecules are nonpolar and not attracted to each other, while highly polar H$_2$O(g) molecules do experience intermolecular attractions.
   (C) The expression PV = nRT only applies to substances that are gases as STP.
   (D) None of the above explains the observation.

4. The engines of boats that sail in salt water have an iron shaft that is protected from corrosion by using a zinc collar. The purpose of this collar is
    (A) to improve shaft movement by reducing friction
    (B) to act as a sacrificial anode, protecting the shaft from corrosion
    (C) to act as a sacrificial cathode, protecting the shaft from corrosion
    (D) to act as an insulator

5. This question refers to the water heating curve below. Why is the slope in the section for water heating different from the slope for steam heating?
    (A) It takes more energy to vaporize water than to melt ice.
    (B) When steam is cooled at 100°C, little energy is needed.
    (C) When ice is cooled at 0°C, little energy is needed.
    (D) Water and steam have different molar heat capacities.

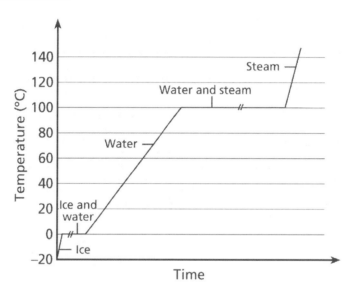

Questions 6–10 refer to a solution formed by dissolving lead(II) bromide in water.

6. The K_{sp} expression for lead(II) bromide is
    (A) $[Pb^{2+}][2Br^-]$
    (B) $[Pb^{2+}]^2[Br^-]$
    (C) $[Pb^{2+}][Br^-]^2$
    (D) $[Pb^{2+}]^2[Br^-]^2$

7. The concentration of bromide ions in a saturated lead(II) bromide solution
    (A) is equal to $[Pb^{2+}]$
    (B) is two times that of $[Pb^{2+}]$
    (C) is one-half that of $[Pb^{2+}]$
    (D) cannot be determined without knowing the value of K_{sp}

8. Grinding the salt into a fine powder accomplishes which of the following:
    (A) increases its solubility
    (B) increases the value of the K_{sp}
    (C) increases the rate of dissolving
    (D) breaks the bonds between the ions

9. An aqueous solution of lead(II) bromide is a weak electrolyte. Therefore the salt
    (A) has ions which are strongly attracted to each other
    (B) is very soluble
    (C) forms many ions when dissolving
    (D) is covalently bonded

10. If a solution of potassium bromide is added to a saturated solution of lead(II) bromide
    (A) a precipitate of lead(II) bromide forms
    (B) the concentration of Br^- increases
    (C) the concentration of lead(II) bromide increases
    (D) the common ion effect does not apply

Questions 11–14 refer to molecular geometry and its effects on the properties of molecules.

11. The VSEPR model predicts that the structure of XeF_4 is square planar. This is due to
    (A) the tendency of four electron pairs always to form a square
    (B) the tendency of four electron pairs always to form a tetrahedron
    (C) bond angles of 90°
    (D) the high degree of repulsion between the two lone pairs

12. The geometry of carbon disulfide, CS_2, can be described by the VSEPR model as
    (A) bent or angular
    (B) linear
    (C) trigonal pyramid
    (D) tetrahedral

13. The hybridization of carbon in carbon disulfide is
    (A) sp
    (B) sp^2
    (C) sp^3
    (D) the orbitals in carbon are not hybridized

14. Compared to CO_2, we would predict the vapor pressure of CS_2 to be
    (A) the same, because both are nonpolar molecules
    (B) higher, because CS_2 has a higher molar mass
    (C) lower, because S has more electrons and thus is more polarizable than O
    (D) lower, because CS_2 has double bonds and CO_2 does not

15. The vapor pressure of C_8H_{18} will be lower than that of C_4H_{10}, all other things being equal, because
    (A) of weaker intermolecular forces in C_4H_{10}
    (B) the longer molecule has more polarizable electrons
    (C) of less hydrogen bonding in C_8H_{18}
    (D) vapor pressure is a constant for a given substance

16. Naturally occurring copper is composed of two isotopes, ^{63}Cu and ^{65}Cu. If copper is 69.1% ^{63}Cu and 30.9% ^{65}Cu, the average atomic mass could be estimated as
    (A) (63 + 65)/2
    (B) (65 × 30.9) + (63 × 69.1)
    (C) (0.309 × 65) + [0.691 × 63)
    (D) [(0.309 × 65) + (0.691 × 63)]/2

17. A sample of $CuSO_4 \cdot 5H_2O$ is heated gently just above 100°C for 15 minutes and then cooled to room temperature in a dessicator. The mass will now be
    (A) lower because the compound has decomposed into CuO
    (B) higher because the compound will react with oxygen in the air
    (C) lower because waters of hydration have been removed
    (D) unchanged

GO ON TO NEXT PAGE

18. The number of calcium atoms in a sliver of calcium of mass 5.234 mg may be calculated as
   (A) $(5.234/1000) \times (1/40.08) \times (6.02 \times 10^{23})$
   (B) $(5.234 \times 40.08) \times (6.02 \times 10^{23})$
   (C) $(40.08/5.234) \times (6.02 \times 10^{23})$
   (D) $(6.02 \times 10^{23}) \times (40.08 \times 1000)$

19. Which of the following pairs illustrates the law of multiple proportions?
   (A) KCl, KBr
   (B) P_2O_5, N_2O_5
   (C) NO, NO_2
   (D) CO_2, SiO_2

20. A one liter quantity of 1.0 M HCl(aq) would usually be prepared in the laboratory from concentrated HCl, using
   (A) a buret
   (B) a balance
   (C) a volumetric flask
   (D) a graduated cylinder

21. To neutralize this solution of 1.0 M HCl and use the least volume of base, you should select
   (A) 1.0 M NaOH
   (B) 1.0 M Ba(OH)$_2$
   (C) 1.0 M NH$_3$
   (D) 1.0 M KOH

22. In the reaction:
   $H_2O(l) + HCl(g) \rightarrow H_3O^+(aq) + Cl^-(aq)$
   (A) H_2O donates an electron pair to the H^+ in HCl
   (B) H_2O donates an electron pair to the Cl^- in HCl
   (C) H_2O accepts an electron pair from the Cl^- in HCl
   (D) H_2O accepts an electron pair from the H^+ in HCl

23. The HCl is added dropwise to a saturated solution of magnesium hydroxide until the pH = 4. This results in
   (A) a precipitate forming
   (B) much bubbling and frothing occurring
   (C) the solution becoming increasingly basic
   (D) water forming

24. Two solutions are mixed: 1.0 L of 0.20 M NaOH and 1.0 L of 0.10 M H_3PO_4. After reaction, the ions in the largest concentration are Na$^+$ and
   (A) H_3O^+
   (B) PO_4^{3-}
   (C) HPO_4^{2-}
   (D) $H_2PO_4^-$

25. A small portion of acid is added to an aqueous solution, but the pH does not change. What is the best explanation for this observation?
   (A) The acid is not soluble in the solution.
   (B) The solution contains species that can react with both H^+ and OH^-.
   (C) The solution contains species that can precipitate with the acid.
   (D) The acid reacts to form H_2 gas.

26 The K_a for acetic acid, $HC_2H_3O_2$, is 1.8×10^{-5} at 25°C. In a 0.10 M solution of potassium acetate, which of the following is true?
   (A) $[HC_2H_3O_2] = [OH^-]$
   (B) $[H^+] = [OH^-]$
   (C) $[C_2H_3O_2^-] < 0.10\ M$
   (D) (A) and (C) are true.

27. Which of the following salts will form a basic solution in water?
   (A) KCl
   (B) CuCl$_2$
   (C) Na$_2$CO$_3$
   (D) NH$_4$NO$_3$

28. Solutions of Na_2S and $AgNO_3$ are mixed. A precipitate will form if
    (A) the ion product (Q) is a high value
    (B) the ion product (Q) is a low value
    (C) the ion product (Q) exceeds the K_{sp} value
    (D) the solubility product exceeds the ion product (Q)

29. Of the following salts, which is insoluble in water?
    (A) Na_2S
    (B) $Pb(NO_3)_2$
    (C) KCl
    (D) All sodium, potassium, and nitrate salts are soluble.

30. Knowing only the temperature and the K_{sp} value will not provide the relative solubility of unknown ionic salts because
    (A) different salts sometimes produce different numbers of ions when dissolving
    (B) solubility does not consider lattice energy effects
    (C) not all ionic salts are soluble
    (D) the two ions formed are of different sizes

31. When 1.0 L of 1.0 M lead(II) nitrate is added to 1.0 L of 1.0 M potassium nitrate the concentration of ions in solution is
    (A) 1.0 M Pb^{2+}, 2.0 M NO_3^-, 1.0M K^+
    (B) 0.50 M Pb^{2+}, 2.0 M NO_3^-, 0.50 M K^+
    (C) 0.50 M Pb^{2+}, 1.5 M NO_3^-, 0.50 M K^+
    (D) 0.50 M Pb^{2+}, 0.50 M NO_3^-, 0.50 M K^+

32. The 1.0 M solution which provides the fewest ions in solution is
    (A) CH_3COOH
    (B) $Ca(NO_3)_2$
    (C) $NaNO_3$
    (D) NaCl

33. For the reaction $O_2(g) \rightarrow 2\,O(g)$,
    (A) ΔH would be +, ΔS would be +
    (B) ΔH would be –, ΔS would be –
    (C) ΔH would be +, ΔS would be –
    (D) ΔH would be –, ΔS would be +

Questions 34–36 refer to systems of salts dissolved in water.

34. When NaCl is dissolved in room temperature water, the water temperature decreases. Therefore, the enthalpy of dissolving is
    (A) positive, because the temperature of the surroundings has decreased
    (B) negative, because the temperature of the surroundings has decreased
    (C) positive, because the temperature of the system has increased
    (D) cannot be determined from these data

35. When NaCl dissolves
    (A) ΔS is + because one particle changes into two ions
    (B) ΔS is – because one particle changes into two ions
    (C) ΔS is unchanged because the atoms are the same
    (D) ΔS cannot be determined from this information

36. Under what conditions will dissolving NaCl <u>not</u> be spontaneous?
    (A) high temperatures
    (B) low temperatures
    (C) spontaneous at all temperatures
    (D) spontaneous only if the water is stirred

GO ON TO NEXT PAGE

37. In all cases, a reaction is spontaneous if
    (A) $\Delta S < 0$ and $\Delta H > 0$
    (B) $\Delta S > 0$ and $\Delta H > 0$
    (C) $\Delta S > 0$ and $\Delta H < 0$
    (D) $\Delta S < 0$ and $\Delta H < 0$

38. For which of the following is the sign of the enthalpy change different from the others?
    (A) $CO_2(s) \rightarrow CO_2(g)$
    (B) $H_2O(l) \rightarrow H_2O(s)$
    (C) $Br_2(g) \rightarrow 2Br(g)$
    (D) $H_2O(l) \rightarrow H_2O(g)$

39. For which of the following equations is the sign of entropy as shown?

    $$\Delta S$$

    (A) $H_2(g) + 3N_2(g) \rightarrow 2NH_3(g)$ $+$

    (B) $Hg(l) \rightarrow Hg(g)$ $+$

    (C) $CO_2(s) \rightarrow CO_2(g)$ $-$

    (D) $C_6H_{12}O_6(aq) \rightarrow C_6H_{12}O_6(s)$ $+$

40. Find the ΔG for $S(s) + O_2(g) \rightarrow SO_2(g)$, given

    $$S(s) + 1.5\ O_2(g) \rightarrow SO_3(g)$$
    $$\Delta G = -370\ kJ$$
    $$O_2(g) + 2\ SO_2(g) \rightarrow 2\ SO_3(g)$$
    $$\Delta G = -140\ kJ$$

    (A) +510 kJ
    (B) –510 kJ
    (C) +300 kJ
    (D) –300 kJ

41. The process with the highest rate of reaction would be one in which
    (A) $\Delta G = -30$ kJ
    (B) $\Delta G = -60$ kJ
    (C) $\Delta G = +60$ kJ
    (D) impossible to predict from only ΔG values

42. The $E° = -0.60$ V for $FeS(s) \rightarrow Fe^{2+}(aq) + S^{2-}(aq)$. This indicates that
    (A) FeS has very low solubility
    (B) K_{sp} for FeS is very large
    (C) S^{2-} ions are unstable
    (D) Fe^{2+} ions are unstable

Questions 43–47 refer to the electrochemical cell:

$$Zn(s) \,|\, Zn^{2+}(aq) \,\|\, Ag^+(aq) \,|\, Ag(s)$$

43. The anode for this cell is the
    (A) Zn
    (B) Zn^{2+}
    (C) Ag^+
    (D) Ag

44. As this cell functions
    (A) electrons flow from the Zn electrode to the Ag electrode
    (B) the mass of the Ag electrode decreases
    (C) the $[Ag^+]$ increases
    (D) $E°_{cell} = 0$

45. In the half-reaction that occurs at the cathode, the number of electrons
    (A) lost is 1
    (B) lost is 2
    (C) gained is 1
    (D) gained is 2

46. The net equation for this cell is
    (A) $Ag(s) + Zn(s) \rightarrow Al^+(aq) + Zn^{2-}(aq)$
    (B) $Ag^+(aq) + Zn(s) \rightarrow Ag(s) + Zn^{2-}(aq)$
    (C) $2\ Ag^+(aq) + Zn(s) \rightarrow 2\ Ag(s) + Zn^{2+}(aq)$
    (D) $2\ Ag^+(aq) + Zn(s) \rightarrow Ag_2(s) + Zn^{2+}(aq)$

47. The purpose of a salt bridge in this electrochemical cell is
    (A) to make possible electron flow through the external circuit
    (B) to provide for ion flow through the cell
    (C) to provide for oxidation at the cathode
    (D) to provide for reduction at the anode

48. A quarter is plated with copper in an electrolytic cell. To determine how long the process will take, you must also be given
    (A) the mass of the copper to be plated and the current available
    (B) the number of moles of electrons transferred and the voltage available
    (C) the number of coulombs required to deposit one mol of copper
    (D) the mass of the copper to be plated and the voltage measured

49. To calculate the molarity of a solution, it is necessary to know
    (A) molar mass of the solute
    (B) the molar mass of the solvent
    (C) the mass of the solvent
    (D) the volume of the solvent

Questions 50–53 refer to the reaction: A + 2 B → C + 2 D, and these data:

Exp. No.	Initial [A]	Initial [B]	Initial Rate $\Delta[A]/\Delta t$ in mol L^{-1} s^{-1}
1	0.100 M	0.050 M	7.00×10^{-6}
2	0.200 M	0.050 M	14.0×10^{-6}
3	0.100 M	0.100 M	7.00×10^{-6}

50. The initial reaction rates reported above
    (A) do not change as the reaction proceeds
    (B) can be calculated from slope of a line tangent to a concentration vs. time curve
    (C) are not temperature dependent
    (D) can only be used to find the reaction order with respect to reactant A

51. Rate laws can be written
    (A) only from experimental data
    (B) directly from the coefficients of the reactants
    (C) as a ratio of the coefficients of reactants to coefficients of products
    (D) only if the rate constant is known

52. The rate law for this reaction is
    (A) Rate = k[A][B]
    (B) Rate = k[A][B]^2
    (C) Rate = k[A]
    (D) Rate = k[B]

53. For Experiment 2, the rate of appearance of product D is
    (A) 7.00×10^{-6} mol L^{-1} s^{-1}
    (B) 14.0×10^{-6} mol L^{-1} s^{-1}
    (C) 28.0×10^{-6} mol L^{-1} s^{-1}
    (D) cannot be determined from these data

54. One function of a catalyst is to
    (A) shift the equilibrium toward products
    (B) lower the activation energy
    (C) increase the value of ΔH
    (D) lower the value of the rate constant

55. Another reaction, X → Y, is second-order and its rate is 6.0×10^{-4} mol L^{-1} s^{-1} when the value of [X] = 0.22 M. When the concentration of X is 0.66 M, the rate, in mol L^{-1} s^{-1}, will be
    (A) $(6.0 \times 10^{-4})/9$
    (B) $(6.0 \times 10^{-4}) \times 9$
    (C) $(6.0 \times 10^{-4})^2$
    (D) $(6.0 \times 10^{-4}) \times 3$

GO ON TO NEXT PAGE

56. Ethanol (CH_3CH_2OH) is not soluble in carbon tetrachloride (CCl_4) because
    (A) only substances that experience London dispersion forces of attraction are soluble in CCl_4
    (B) only substances that can form hydrogen bonds are soluble in CCl_4
    (C) only ionic substances are soluble in CCl_4
    (D) only substances with dipole–dipole forces of attraction are soluble in CCl_4

57. The oxidation state assigned to nitrogen in NO_3^- is
    (A) +2
    (B) +5
    (C) +6
    (D) –1

58. Consider two solutions: Solution X with a pH of 7 and Solution Y with a pH of 9. The hydronium ion ratio, X/Y, would be
    (A) 7/9
    (B) 2/1
    (C) 1/3
    (D) 100/1

Questions 59–60 refer to a strong acid–weak base titration.

59. A weak base is neutralized with the solution of 1.0 M HCl. The pH at the equivalence point will be
    (A) equal to 7
    (B) less than 7
    (C) greater than 7
    (D) cannot be predicted

60. The volume of HCl needed to reach the equivalence point of this titration is determined by
    (A) the concentration of the acid and the amount of the base
    (B) the relative strength of the acid and the base
    (C) the concentration of the base
    (D) the K_b value for the base

Advanced Placement Chemistry Equations and Constants

Throughout the test the following symbols have the definitions specified unless otherwise noted.

L, mL	=	liter(s), milliliter(s)	mm Hg	= millimeters of mercury
g	=	gram(s)	J, kJ	= joule(s), kilojoule(s)
nm	=	nanometer(s)	V	= volt(s)
atm	=	atmosphere(s)	mol	= mole(s)

ATOMIC STRUCTURE

$$E = h\nu$$
$$c = \lambda\nu$$

E = energy
ν = frequency
λ = wavelength

Planck's constant, $h = 6.626 \times 10^{-34}$ J s

Speed of light, $c = 2.998 \times 10^8$ m s^{-1}

Avogadro's number $= 6.022 \times 10^{23}$ mol^{-1}

Electron charge, $e = -1.602 \times 10^{-19}$ coulomb

EQUILIBRIUM

$$K_c = \frac{[C]^c[D]^d}{[A]^a[B]^b}, \text{ where } a\,A + b\,B \rightleftarrows c\,C + d\,D$$

$$K_p = \frac{(P_C)^c(P_D)^d}{(P_A)^a(P_B)^b}$$

$$K_a = \frac{[H^+][A^-]}{[HA]}$$

$$K_b = \frac{[OH^-][HB^+]}{[B]}$$

$$K_w = [H^+][OH^-] = 1.0 \times 10^{-14} \text{ at } 25°C$$
$$= K_a \times K_b$$

$$\text{pH} = -\log[H^+], \quad \text{pOH} = -\log[OH^-]$$

$$14 = \text{pH} + \text{pOH}$$

$$\text{pH} = pK_a + \log\frac{[A^-]}{[HA]}$$

$$pK_a = -\log K_a, \quad pK_b = -\log K_b$$

Equilibrium Constants

K_c (molar concentrations)
K_p (gas pressures)
K_a (weak acid)
K_b (weak base)
K_w (water)

KINETICS

$$\ln[A]_t - \ln[A]_0 = -kt$$

$$\frac{1}{[A]_t} - \frac{1}{[A]_0} = kt$$

$$t_{1/2} = \frac{0.693}{k}$$

k = rate constant
t = time
$t_{1/2}$ = half-life

GO ON TO NEXT PAGE

GASES, LIQUIDS, AND SOLUTIONS

$$PV = nRT$$

$$P_A = P_{total} \times X_A, \text{ where } X_A = \frac{\text{moles A}}{\text{total moles}}$$

$$P_{total} = P_A + P_B + P_C + \ldots$$

$$n = \frac{m}{M}$$

$$K = {}^\circ C + 273$$

$$D = \frac{m}{V}$$

$$KE \text{ per molecule} = \frac{1}{2}mv^2$$

Molarity, M = moles of solute per liter of solution

$$A = abc$$

P = pressure
V = volume
T = temperature
n = number of moles
m = mass
M = molar mass
D = density
KE = kinetic energy
v = velocity
A = absorbance
a = molar absorptivity
b = path length
c = concentration

Gas constant, $R = 8.314 \text{ J mol}^{-1} \text{K}^{-1}$
$= 0.08206 \text{ L atm mol}^{-1} \text{K}^{-1}$
$= 62.36 \text{ L torr mol}^{-1} \text{K}^{-1}$
1 atm = 760 mm Hg
= 760 torr
STP = $0.00\,^\circ$C and 1.000 atm

THERMOCHEMISTRY/ ELECTROCHEMISTRY

$$q = mc\Delta T$$

$$\Delta S^\circ = \sum S^\circ \text{ products} - \sum S^\circ \text{ reactants}$$

$$\Delta H^\circ = \sum \Delta H_f^\circ \text{ products} - \sum \Delta H_f^\circ \text{ reactants}$$

$$\Delta G^\circ = \sum \Delta G_f^\circ \text{ products} - \sum \Delta G_f^\circ \text{ reactants}$$

$$\Delta G^\circ = \Delta H^\circ - T\Delta S^\circ$$

$$= -RT \ln K$$

$$= -n F E^\circ$$

$$I = \frac{q}{t}$$

q = heat
m = mass
c = specific heat capacity
T = temperature
S° = standard entropy
H° = standard enthalpy
G° = standard free energy
n = number of moles
E° = standard reduction potential
I = current (amperes)
q = charge (coulombs)
t = time (seconds)

Faraday's constant, F = 96,485 coulombs per mole of electrons

$$1 \text{ volt} = \frac{1 \text{ joule}}{1 \text{ coulomb}}$$

Introduction to Section II: Free-Response Questions

Section II of the AP Chemistry Examination counts for 50% of the total test grade and involves several parts. Answering these questions gives you an opportunity to demonstrate your ability to present your material in clear, orderly, and convincing language. Your answers will be graded on the basis of accuracy, the kinds of information you include to support your responses, and the importance of the descriptive material used. Be specific; general, all-encompassing answers will not be graded as well as detailed answers with examples and equations. CLEARLY SHOW THE METHOD USED AND THE STEPS INVOLVED IN ARRIVING AT YOUR ANSWERS. It is to your advantage to do this, since you may obtain partial credit if you do and you will receive little or no credit if you do not. Attention should be paid to significant figures. On the AP exam, be sure to write all your answers to the questions on the lined pages following each question in the test booklet. Do not write your answers in the white space between questions.

Section II: Free-Response Questions
Time: 90 minutes
Number of Questions: 7

Allow yourself no more than 90 minutes to answer these questions. You may use a calculator, the equations sheet, and the periodic table throughout this section. All questions must be answered.

1. A student is asked to determine the heat of formation of MgO and is given the following equipment:
    coffee cup calorimeter
    Celsius thermometer
    balance
    chemicals: magnesium oxide, magnesium ribbon, 1.00 M hydrochloric acid
    (density 1.00 g/mL)

The student performs experiments to determine the value of ΔH for the reactions of

(1) magnesium + hydrochloric acid → $\Delta H_1 = ?$

(2) magnesium oxide + hydrochloric acid → $\Delta H_2 = ?$

The data for these two experiments are listed below.

Magnesium + Hydrochloric Acid	
magnesium mass (g)	0.121
hydrochloric acid volume (mL)	50.0
initial temperature (°C)	20.0
final temperature (°C)	30.7

GO ON TO NEXT PAGE

Magnesium Oxide + Hydrochloric Acid	
magnesium oxide mass (g)	0.348
hydrochloric acid volume (mL)	50.0
initial temperature (°C)	14.9
final temperature (°C)	20.0

The student is also given the following:

(3) $H_2(g) + 1/2\ O_2(g)\ H_2O(l)$ $\Delta H_3° = -285.8$ kJ mol^{-1}

    (a) Write the net ionic equations for the reaction of magnesium with hydrochloric acid and of magnesium oxide with hydrochloric acid.

    (b) Calculate ΔH_1. Assume the specific heat capacity of the solution is 4.184 J/(g °C).

    (c) Calculate ΔH_2. Assume the specific heat capacity of the solution is 4.184 J/(g °C).

    (d) Show how the 3 equations above can be rearranged to calculate $\Delta H_f°$ of magnesium oxide.

    (e) Calculate $\Delta H_f°$ of magnesium oxide.

    (f) The accepted value for $\Delta H°_f = -602$ kJ/mol. Calculate the percent error.

    (g) The calorimeter constant is the amount of heat that the calorimeter must gain to change temperature by one degree. Why would the use of a calorimeter constant improve the accuracy of the results?

2. A reverse phase chromatography column (with a hydrophobic stationary phase) is set up to separate octanol, $CH_3(CH_2)_6CH_2OH$, from butanol, $CH_3(CH_2)_2CH_2OH$ using a mobile phase of 80:20 ethanol:water. Which substance will be eluted from the column first? Use molecular representations to justify your answer.

3. The reported solubility of NaCl at 20°C is 35.89 g/100 g water, whereas that of $NaCH_3COO$ is 54.6 g/100 g of water.

    (a) Explain these observations using bonding theories and/or intermolecular forces of attraction.

    (b) How would adding 1.0 M HCl affect the solubilities?

    (c) Explain how the solubilities would change if ethanol were the solvent instead of water.

    (d) When these salts are dissolved, the water temperature decreases. How would increasing the initial water temperature affect solubility?

4. A 1.00-gram sample of solid sodium metal is dropped into water.

    (a) Write the balanced net ionic equation and indicate the type of reaction.

    (b) Determine the volume of gas produced at STP.

    (c) Write the balanced equation for the reaction of the gas with oxygen, using smallest whole number coefficients.

5. The first ionization energies, in kJ/mole, of elements in row 3 of the periodic table are as follows:

Na	Mg	Al	Si	P	S	Cl	Ar
496	738	577	786	1060	999.6	1256	1520

   Explain the trend in energies, including the discontinuities at aluminum and sulfur.

6. Plants convert water and carbon dioxide to glucose via the following reaction:
   $6 H_2O(l) + 6 CO_2(g) + heat \rightarrow C_6H_{12}O_6(s) + 6 O_2(g)$
   Discuss three ways to increase the rate of reaction. Include a molecular-level explanation of how each will affect the rate.

7. (a) Calculate the pH of 0.833 M acetic acid, $HC_2H_3O_2$, $K_a = 1.8 \times 10^{-5}$.
   (b) Calculate the pH of 0.833 M sodium acetate.
   (c) Calculate the pH of the mixture of 100.0 mL of 0.833 M acetic acid to which 0.0833 mol solid sodium acetate has been added.
   (d) Explain the pH of the mixture in (c) in terms of Le Chatelier's principle. Include a particulate model in your explanation.

END OF EXAMINATION

Answers to Practice Test 1

Section I: Multiple-Choice Questions

Score your test using the table below.

Determine how many questions you answered correctly. You will find explanations of the answers on the following pages.

1. D	2. A	3. B	4. B	5. D
6. C	7. B	8. C	9. D	10. A
11. D	12. B	13. A	14. C	15. B
16. C	17. C	18. A	19. C	20. C
21. B	22. A	23. D	24. C	25. B
26. C	27. C	28. C	29. D	30. A
31. C	32. A	33. A	34. A	35. A
36. B	37. C	38. B	39. B	40. D
41. D	42. A	43. A	44. A	45. C
46. C	47. B	48. A	49. A	50. B
51. A	52. C	53. C	54. B	55. B
56. A	57. B	58. D	59. B	60. A

Calculate Your Score:

Number answered correctly: _____

What Your Score Means:

Each year, since the test is different, the scoring is a little different. But generally, if you scored 20 or more on the multiple-choice questions, you'll most likely get a 3 or better on the test. If you scored 28 or more, you'll probably score a 4 or better. And if you scored a 40 or more, you'll most likely get a 5. Keep in mind that the multiple-choice section is worth 50% of your final grade, and the free-response section is worth 50% of your final grade. To learn more about the scoring for the free-response questions, turn to the last page of this section.

Answers and Explanations

Section I: Multiple-Choice Questions

1. **Answer: D** Because $P_{H_2} + P_{H_2O} = P_{total}$, $P_{H_2} = P_{total} - P_{H_2O} = 757 - 21$ (*Chemistry* 8th ed. pages 203–205/9th ed. pages 212–214). LO 2.6

2. ANSWER: **A** The molar volume of any ideal gas at STP is 22.4 L. From 0.560 L × 1 mol/22.4 L = mol we see that response A is correct (*Chemistry* 8th ed. pages 194–195/9th ed. pages 203–204). LO 2.6

3. ANSWER: **B** Ideal gases have particles of zero volume, no forces between the particles, and are described by the relationship $PV = nRT$ (*Chemistry* 8th ed. pages 183, 188–190/9th ed. pages 192, 197–199). LO 2.12

4. ANSWER: **B** Because the reaction for the collar is $Zn \rightarrow Zn^{2+} + 2e^-$, it is undergoing oxidation. The site of oxidation is known as the anode (*Chemistry* 8th ed. pages 845–847/9th ed. pages 861–864). LO 3.12

5. ANSWER: **D** Molar heat capacity refers to the energy required to change the temperature of one mole of the substance (in this case, steam or water), by 1°C (*Chemistry* 8th ed. page 476/9th ed. page 488). LO 5.6

6. ANSWER: **C** The K_{sp} is an equilibrium constant with the usual expression, $K_{sp} = [Pb^{2+}][Br^-]^2$. The solid, of course, has a constant concentration and so is not a part of the equilibrium expression (*Chemistry* 8th ed. pages 743–744/9th ed. pages 758–759). LO 6.21

7. ANSWER: **B** Each mole of $PbBr_2$ contributes three moles of ions: one mole of Pb^{2+} and two moles of Br^- (*Chemistry* 8th ed. pages 136–137/9th ed. pages 145–146). LO 3.2

8. ANSWER: **C** Increasing the surface area does increase the amount of solid that will dissolve in a given period of time. However, since ions reform the solid on the surface of the solid, the rate of reforming the solid also increases, and at the same rate. Therefore, solubility is not increased by grinding; only the rate of dissolving is increased (*Chemistry* 8th ed. pages 743–744/9th ed. pages 758–759). LO 6.23

9. ANSWER: **A** Weak electrolytes ionize very slightly because their ions are strongly attracted to each other, so few ions are formed when they dissolve (*Chemistry* 8th ed. page 134/9th ed. page 143). LO 2.15

10. ANSWER: **A** The additional Br^- causes the equilibrium to shift to the left, forming more solid $PbBr_2$ (common ion effect). Note that the concentration of a solid is constant; therefore response C is incorrect (*Chemistry* 8th ed. pages 746–747/9th ed. pages 761–762). LO 6.8

11. **Answer: D** The two lone pairs of electrons on Xe favor a position of 180° from each other, leaving the four bonded pairs pointing toward the four corners of a square (*Chemistry* 8th ed. pages 384–385/9th ed. pages 395–396). LO 2.21

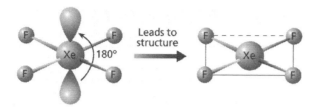

12. **Answer: B** Note that the compound must be similar to CO_2 and that for purposes of determining shape, a double bond is treated the same as a single bond (*Chemistry* 8th ed. pages 378–387/9th ed. pages 389–398). LO 2.21

13. **Answer: A** The double bonds between the carbon and the sulfurs are made of one sigma bond and one pi bond each. No orbitals are hybridized to form the pi bonds (unhybridized *p* orbitals). The sigma bonds between the carbon and sulfurs are formed by two *sp* hybrid orbitals on each carbon (*Chemistry* 8th ed. pages 404–414/9th ed. pages 416–426). LO 2.21

14. **Answer: C** Sulfur is in the third row of the periodic table, so it has more electrons and is more subject to induced dipole attractions than oxygen (*Chemistry* 8th ed. pages 471–474/9th ed. pages 483–486). LO 2.11

15. **Answer: B** Larger substances with more electrons are more subject to induced dipoles due to interaction with other molecules (*Chemistry* 8th ed. pages 471–474/9th ed. pages 483–486). LO 2.11

16. **Answer: C** Because 30.9/100 atoms are Cu mass 65, and 69.1/100 atoms are Cu mass 63, the average mass of a copper atom is $(0.309 \times 65) + (0.691 \times 63)$ (*Chemistry* 8th ed. pages 77–80/9th ed. pages 82–85). LO 1.2

17. **Answer: C** Heating the substance just above the boiling point of water will evaporate the waters of hydration, so the mass will be lower (*Chemistry* 8th ed. page 219/9th ed. page 228). LO 1.19

18. **Answer: A** Units will help explain this calculation: 5.234 mg/1000 mg/g × 1 mol / 40.18 g × (6.02×10^{23}) atoms/mol (*Chemistry* 8th ed. page 81/9th ed. page 85). LO 1.4

19. **Answer: C** This law describes the mass ratios for two elements which form two different compounds. These mass ratios can be reduced to small whole numbers (*Chemistry* 8th ed. pages 42–43/9th ed. pages 45–46). LO 1.1

20. ANSWER: **C** The use of a 1-liter flask constructed with a hairline thin volume marker (calibration mark) at just the 1-liter volume is most likely (*Chemistry* 8th ed. pages 140–141/9th ed. pages 149–150). LO 3.4

21. ANSWER: **B** 1.0 *M* NaOH, 1.0 *M* KOH, and 1.0 *M* NH_3 can deliver the same number of moles of OH^- to neutralize the acid. $Ba(OH)_2$ has twice as many OH^- groups and can neutralize twice as much HCl (*Chemistry* 8th ed. pages 149–151/9th ed. pages 157–160). LO 3.4

22. ANSWER: **A** Water acts as a Brønsted–Lowry base by donating an electron pair to H^+, forming H_3O^+ (*Chemistry* 8th ed. pages 639–642/9th ed. pages 653–656). LO 3.7

23. ANSWER: **D** $Mg(OH)_2(s) \rightarrow Mg^{2+}(aq) + 2\ OH^-(aq)$. The added H^+ (the pH is 4, therefore acidic) leads to reaction with the OH^- from the $Mg(OH)_2$ to form water. The reaction shifts toward the Mg^{2+} and OH^- ions; some of the $Mg(OH)_2$ dissolves (*Chemistry* 8th ed. page 752/9th ed. page 768). LO 6.8

24. ANSWER: **C** 0.20 mol OH^- + 0.10 mol $H_3PO_4 \rightarrow$ 0.20 mol H_2O + 0.10 mol HPO_4^{2-} (*Chemistry* 8th ed. pages 154–161/9th ed. pages 163–170). LO 3.4

25. ANSWER: **B** The solution must be a buffer, which resists pH change by reaction with either added H^+ or added OH^-. An acid buffer consists of a weak acid and the salt of its conjugate base. In this case, the relatively strong conjugate base must react with the added acid (*Chemistry* 8th ed. pages 704–705, 764–765/9th ed. pages 718–719, 779–780). LO 6.20

26. ANSWER: **C** Due to the hydrolysis of the acetate ion, the solution will be basic (therefore H^+ and OH^- cannot be equal); because some of the acetic acid formed from this hydrolysis reaction will react with water leaving less acetic acid, the acetic acid and OH^- will not be equal. Because some of the acetate ion reacts with water (the hydrolysis reaction again), the $[C_2H_3O_2^-]$ will be somewhat less than 0.10 *M* (*Chemistry* 8th ed. pages 671–673/9th ed. pages 686–688). LO 6.8

27. ANSWER: **C** The CO_3^{2-} reacts with H_2O as: $CO_3^{2-} + H_2O \rightarrow HCO_3^- + OH^-$, which gives a basic solution. You can determine that the salts are acidic, basic, or neutral by determining the parent acid and parent base. For salt Na_2CO_3, the parent base NaOH is strong and the parent acid is weak H_2CO_3, so the salt is basic. This is a memory aid and does not really explain the chemistry of why this occurs (*Chemistry* 8th ed. pages 671–677/9th ed. pages 686–691). LO 6.23

28. ANSWER: **C** If the *Q* exceeds the K_{sp} a precipitate forms. Think of the ion product, *Q*, as a limit which if exceeded causes the equilibrium to shift toward the solid (*Chemistry* 8th ed. pages 752–754/9th ed. pages 768–770). LO 6.21

29. **Answer: D** All 1A compounds and all nitrates are soluble in water (*Chemistry* 8th ed. pages 148–149/9th ed. pages 156–157). LO 6.21

30. **Answer: A** A salt like AgOH (K_{sp} = 10^{-8}) and a salt like Ca(OH)$_2$ (K_{sp} = 10^{-6}) form a different number of ions in solution. With AgOH, for example, solubility = $\sqrt{K_{sp}}$; whereas with Ca(OH)$_2$, the solubility = $\sqrt[3]{K_{sp}/4}$ (*Chemistry* 8th ed. pages 743–746/9th ed. pages 758–761). LO 6.22

31. **Answer: C** The 1.0 mol of Pb^{2+} (1.0 mol/L × 1.0 L) is now occupying 2.0 L of the solution, so
$$[Pb^{2+}] = 1.0 \text{ mol}/2.0 \text{ L} = 0.50 \ M.$$
The [K^+] can be found in like manner.
The [NO_3^-] = (1.0 mol/L × 1.0 L + 2.0 mol/L × 1.0 L) / 2.0L = 1.5 M (*Chemistry* 8th ed. pages 137–139/9th ed. pages 146–148). LO 3.4

32. **Answer: A** This weak acid, acetic acid, dissociates (ionizes) only to a slight extent in aqueous solution (*Chemistry* 8th ed. page 134/9th ed. page 143). LO 6.12

33. **Answer: A** H = (+) for bond breaking, which is always an endothermic process. S = (+) for an increase in disorder due here to the increase in the number of particles (*Chemistry* 8th ed. pages 783, 785, 790–792/9th ed. pages 798, 800, 805–807). LO 5.13

34. **Answer: A** The temperature of the surroundings decreases because heat energy transfers from the surroundings to the system. The system is the reaction, which requires heat so it must be endothermic (*Chemistry* 8th ed. pages 243–251/9th ed. pages 252–260). LO 5.7

35. **Answer: A** An increase in the number of particles increases entropy of a system (*Chemistry* 8th ed. pages 777–779/9th ed. pages 792–794). LO 5.12

36. **Answer: B** Reactions are spontaneous if $\Delta G°$ (the Gibbs free energy) is negative. When ΔH is (+) and ΔS is (+), the term "$T\Delta S$" must be greater than ΔH for ΔG to be negative. As the temperature drops, "$T\Delta S$" eventually becomes lower than ΔH (*Chemistry* 8th ed. pages 780–786/9th ed. pages 795–801). LO 5.13

37. **Answer: C** Reactions are spontaneous if $\Delta G°$ (the Gibbs free energy) is negative. This must be the case if ΔH is (–) and ΔS is (+), (from: $\Delta G = \Delta H - T\Delta S$) (*Chemistry* 8th ed. pages 780–786/9th ed. pages 795–801). LO 5.13

38. **Answer: B** Three of the choices are endothermic. Going from solid to gas phase or liquid to gas phase requires an input of energy, as does bond breaking. When water freezes (goes to a lower energy state), energy is released. (*Chemistry* 8th ed. pages 236-242/9th ed. pages 246–252). LO 5.8, LO 5.9

39. **Answer: B** Entropy or disorder is increasing when a liquid becomes a gas; this is shown with a positive value for entropy (*Chemistry* 8th ed. pages 773–779/9th ed. pages 788–794). LO 5.12

40. **Answer: D** Keep the first equation as is, but reverse the second equation, divide it by two, and add the equations:

$$S(s) + 1.5\ O_2(g) \rightarrow SO_3(g) \qquad \Delta G = -370\ \text{kJ}$$
$$\underline{SO_3(g) \rightarrow 0.5\ O_2(g) + SO_2(g) \qquad \Delta G = 140/2\ \text{kJ}}$$

$$S(s) + O_2(g) \rightarrow SO_2(g) \qquad \Delta G = -370 + 70\ \text{kJ} = -300\ \text{kJ}$$

(*Chemistry* 8th ed. pages 792–793/9th ed. pages 807–809). LO 5.14

41. **Answer: D** The value for ΔG indicates how far the process is from equilibrium (which direction is favored). The speed of reaction is independent of the final equilibrium condition (*Chemistry* 8th ed. page 773/9th ed. page 788). LO 5.18

42. **Answer: A** From log $K = nE°/0.0591 = (2)(-0.60)/0.06 = -1.20/0.06 = -20$, you can see (even if you cannot calculate the exact value of K) that a negative value means a very small value for K. Because K in this case is K_{sp}, the solubility would be very low (*Chemistry* 8th ed. pages 888–889/9th ed. pages 907–908). LO 6.25

43. **Answer: A** The anode is the site of oxidation. $Zn \rightarrow Zn^{2+} + 2\ e^-$ is oxidation (*Chemistry* 8th ed. pages 830–831/9th ed. pages 846–847). LO 3.12

44. **Answer: A** In this cell the zinc loses electrons ($Zn \rightarrow Zn^{2+} + 2\ e^-$) and the Ag^+ gains electrons ($Ag^+ + 1\ e^- \rightarrow Ag$) (*Chemistry* 8th ed. pages 830–831/9th ed. pages 846–847). LO 3.12

45. **Answer: C** The reaction is $Ag^+ + 1\ e^- \rightarrow Ag$ (*Chemistry* 8th ed. pages 823–825/9th ed. pages 839–842). LO 3.12

46. **Answer: C** The silver ion gains 1 electron and Zn loses 2 electrons. The overall reaction must reflect an equal number of electrons gained and lost (*Chemistry* 8th ed. pages 829–831/9th ed. pages 845–847). LO 3.4

47. **Answer: B** Without a salt bridge, one side of the cell would become increasingly positive (on the oxidation side, where electrons leave) and the other side would become increasingly negative. The salt bridge allows for ions to flow between the compartments, to keep the net charge zero as electrons flow through the external circuit (*Chemistry* 8th ed. pages 823–825/9th ed. pages 839–842). LO 3.12

48. **Answer: A** If you know the mass of copper, you can determine the moles of Cu^{2+}, then the moles of electrons required, and the number of coulombs of charge needed. This must be multiplied by

the current (1A = 1C/s) (*Chemistry* 8th ed. pages 849–850/9th ed. pages 866–867). LO 3.12

49. **Answer: A** Molarity = mol solute / L of solution. The solvent is added to the mark on the volumetric flask, so you do not need to know the exact mass, molar mass, or volume of the solvent (*Chemistry* 8th ed. pages 136–137/9th ed. pages 145–146). LO 2.9

50. **Answer: B** The average rate and the initial rate should not be confused. If the concentration is plotted on the *y*-axis vs. time, a curve is generated. For any given point on this curve (i.e., any given time), a tangent may be drawn. The slope of this tangent line is the change in concentration/change in time, which is rate. The rate generally decreases as reactant is used up, and rates are temperature dependent. Since concentrations of both reactants are varied, the order with respect to both reactants can be determined (*Chemistry* 8th ed. pages 540–546/9th ed. pages 553–558). LO 4.1

51. **Answer: A** You cannot determine the rate law by just looking at the chemical equation (unlike the equilibrium constant). The rate law and consequently the order are determined by observing how the rate varies with the concentration of reactants (*Chemistry* 8th ed. pages 547–548/9th ed. pages 559–560). LO 4.2

52. **Answer: C** Note that doubling [A] doubles the rate of this reaction, suggesting that this is a first-order reaction with respect to [A]. Keeping the [A] constant and changing [B] (comparing Exp. 1 to 3), has no effect on the reaction rate, so the order of reaction with respect to [B] is zero (*Chemistry* 8th ed. pages 548–550/9th ed. pages 560–562). LO 4.2

53. **Answer: C** Note from the stoichiometry of the equation, every time a mol of A disappears, two moles of D appear. . . twice the rate of the disappearance of A (*Chemistry* 8th ed. pages 550–551/9th ed. pages 562–563). LO 4.1

54. **Answer: B** The addition of a catalyst lowers the activation energy by finding a less energy demanding pathway. It does this by forming different intermediate substances (*Chemistry* 8th ed. pages 570–572/9th ed. pages 583–585). LO 4.9

55. **Answer: B** Using the fact that this is a second-order reaction, rate = $k[X]^2$. Because the concentration of X is tripled (goes from 0.22 *M* to 0.66 *M*), the rate is $(3)^2$, or 9 times greater (*Chemistry* 8th ed. pages 548–555/9th ed. pages 560–567). LO 4.2

56. **Answer: A** Be familiar with intermolecular forces and how they affect solubility (*Chemistry* 8th ed. pages 440–443/9th ed. pages 455–458). LO 2.1

57. **Answer: B** Because each oxygen has an oxidation state of –2 for a total of $3x - 2 = -6$, and the net charge on this ion is 1–, the

nitrogen must have an oxidation state of 5+ (*Chemistry* 8th ed. pages 162–163/9th ed. pages 171–172). LO 3.8

58. ANSWER: D Keep in mind that the pH scale is a log scale based on 10; pH = –log[H⁺]. X/Y = $10^{-7}/10^{-9}$ = 10^2/1 = 100/1 (*Chemistry* 8th ed. pages 647–650/9th ed. pages 661–664). LO 6.12

59. ANSWER: B When a weak base is completely neutralized, its conjugate acid remains. The conjugate acid of a weak base is relatively strong. It will release some hydronium ions into solution, and the pH will be less than 7 at the equivalence point (*Chemistry* 8th ed. pages 717–725/9th ed. pages 731–739). LO 6.13

60. ANSWER: A The equivalence point will occur when the mol of OH⁻ from the base and H+ from the acid are equal (*Chemistry* 8th ed. pages 717–725/9th ed. pages 731–739). LO 6.13

SECTION II: FREE-RESPONSE QUESTIONS

Question 1: Answers
(a) reaction (1) $Mg(s) + 2\,H^+(aq) \rightarrow Mg^{2+}(aq) + H_2(g)$
    reaction (2) $MgO(s) + 2\,H^+(aq) \rightarrow Mg^{2+}(aq) + H_2O(l)$
(b) Use $q = mC\Delta T$ to calculate the heat gained by the surroundings.
    $q = (50.0\ g)(4.184\ J\ g^{-1}\ °C^{-1})(10.7°C) = 2.240\ J$

The energy absorbed by the surroundings must be equal and opposite in sign to the energy released by the reaction. Convert Mg mass to Mg mol and divide the energy released by the moles of Mg.

Moles Mg = 0.121 g/(24.305 g Mg/1 mol Mg) = 4.98×10^{-3} mol Mg

ΔH_1 = (-2240 J/4.98 × 10⁻³ mol Mg)(1 kJ/1000 J) = 4.50×10^2 kJ mol⁻¹
(c) Use $q = mC\Delta T$ to calculate the heat gained by the surroundings.
    $q = (50.0\ g)(4.184\ J\ g^{-1}\ °C^{-1})(5.1°C) = 1.07 \times 10^3\ J$

The energy absorbed by the surroundings must be equal and opposite in sign to the energy released by the reaction. Convert MgO mass to MgO mol and divide the energy released by the moles of MgO.

Moles MgO = 0.348 g/(40.30 g MgO/1 mol MgO) = 8.64×10^{-3}

ΔH_2 = (–1.07 × 10³ J/8.64 × 10⁻³ mol MgO)(1 kJ/1000 J) = -1.24×10^2 kJ mol⁻¹
(d) Mg + ~~2 HCl~~ → ~~MgCl₂~~ + ~~H₂~~ ΔH_1 = -4.50×10^2 kJ mol⁻¹
    ~~MgCl₂~~ + ~~H₂O~~ → MgO + ~~2 HCl~~ ΔH_2 = 1.24×10^2 kJ mol⁻¹ (note this reaction is reversed so the sign on ΔH_2 is reversed)

    ~~H₂~~ + ½ O₂ → ~~H₂O~~ ΔH_3 = -2.858×10^2 kJ mol⁻¹
(e) Summing the equations and enthalpies from (d) gives
    Mg + ½ O₂ → MgO ΔH_f = -6.12×10^2 kJ mol⁻¹
(f) % error = [(lab value – theoretical value) ÷ theoretical value] × 100
    % error = [(–6.12 × 10² kJ mol⁻¹ – (-6.02 × 10² kJ/mol))/–6.02 × 10² kJ mol⁻¹] × 100
        = –1.7 % error (note 2 significant figures from the subtraction)

(g) Including the calorimeter constant in the calculations would account for any heat gained or lost by the apparatus itself (the calorimeter includes the thermometer as well as the coffee cup calorimeter) and therefore provides a more accurate value for ΔH.

(*Chemistry* 8th ed. pages 243–251/9th ed. pages 252–260) LO 5.7

Question 2: Answer

A hydrophobic stationary phase is nonpolar and will attract nonpolar molecules. The more polar of the two molecules will be eluted first. Both butanol and octanol have hydroxyl (–OH) groups so they can form hydrogen bonds with water or compounds containing –OH groups. However, octanol has a longer nonpolar hydrocarbon chain so it will be less soluble in the polar mobile phase and more attracted to the hydrophobic stationary phase. Butanol will elute first (*Chemistry* 8th ed. pages 440–443/9th ed. pages 455–458). LO 2.7

butanol

octanol

Question 3: Answers

(a) An ionic compound will be more soluble in water if the forces of attraction between the cation and anion are weaker than the forces of attraction between the individual ions and water molecules. The force of attraction between ions is governed by Coulomb's law. Smaller ions will be more strongly attracted to each other, and more highly charged ions will be more strongly attracted to each other.

Cl^- is a smaller anion than CH_3COO^-, so "r" (the distance between the ion nuclei) term is smaller for NaCl than for $NaCH_3COO$ and application of Coulomb's law predicts that the force of attraction is greater between Na^+ and Cl^- than between Na^+ and CH_3COO^-. This is reflected in the lower solubility of NaCl (*Chemistry* 8th ed. pages 440–443/9th ed. pages 455–458). LO 2.14

(b) The dissolution equations for the two salts are:

$NaCl \rightarrow Na^+ + Cl^-$

$NaCH_3COO \rightarrow Na^+ + CH_3COO^-$

HCl is a strong acid that dissociates completely in water. Therefore, adding HCl adds H^+ and Cl^- ions to the solution. In the case of a solution of NaCl, this adds product (Cl^-) and shifts the equilibrium left, reducing the salt's solubility. In the case of $NaCH_3COO$, the H^+ can react with CH_3COO^-, the conjugate base of the weak acid CH_3COOH. This removes product and shifts the equilibrium right, increasing the salt's solubility (*Chemistry* 8th ed. pages 620–622/9th ed. pages 633–635). LO 6.8

(c) Solubilities would be lower in ethanol because ethanol is not as polar as water, and so the forces of attraction between ethanol and ions are not as strong as between water and ions (*Chemistry* 8th ed. pages 440–443/9th ed. pages 455–458). LO 2.14

(d) Because the solution's temperature decreases when the salts dissolve, the processes must be endothermic and heat appears on the reactant side of the equation. Raising the water's initial temperature would shift the equilibrium right, increasing the solubility of both salts (*Chemistry* 8th ed. pages 238–240, 624–626/9th ed. pages 248–250, 637–639). LO 5.4, LO 6.8

Question 4: Answers

(a) $2\ Na(s) + 2\ H_2O(l) \rightarrow H_2(g) + 2\ Na^+(aq) + 2\ OH^-(aq)$

This is an oxidation–reduction reaction (or single-displacement reaction) (*Chemistry* 8th ed. pages 161–166/9th ed. pages 170–175). LO 3.2, LO 3.8

(b) Find the moles of Na reacted:

$$1.00\ g\ Na\ \times \left(\frac{1\ mol\ Na}{22.9\ g}\right) = 4.37 \times 10^{-2}\ mol\ Na$$

Use the mole ratio to find the moles of H_2 produced:

$$4.37 \times 10^{-2}\ mol\ Na\ \times\left(\frac{1\ mol\ H_2}{2\ mol\ Na}\right) = 2.18 \times 10^{-2}\ mol\ H_2$$

Use the STP relationship to find the volume of H_2:

$2.18 \times 10^{-2}\ mol\ H_2 \times (22.4\ L/1mol\ at\ STP) = 0.489\ L$ of H_2 gas

(*Chemistry* 8th ed. pages 194–199/9th ed. pages 203–208). LO 3.4

(c) $2\ H_2 + O_2 \rightarrow 2\ H_2O$ (*Chemistry* 8th ed. pages 161–166/9th ed. pages 170–175). LO 3.2

Question 5: Answer

Ionization energy increases from left to right across rows in the periodic table because, while the electrons are being added to the same valence shell, there are more protons to attract these electrons, increasing Z_{eff}. The discontinuities at Al and S are due to electron configuration.

Al $1s^2 2s^2 2p^1$
S $1s^2 2s^2 2p^4$

The outermost electron of Al is in a slightly higher energy p orbital. It is further from the nucleus than the electrons in the 2s orbital, so the Z_{eff} is lower for that electron and less energy is required to remove it.

The S atom has a pair of electrons in a p orbital. These electrons repel each other, and this electron–electron repulsion results in a slightly lower first ionization energy (*Chemistry* 8th ed. pages 318–322/9th ed. pages 329–333). LO 1.9

Question 6: Answers

An effective way to increase the rate of reaction is to increase collision frequency of reactants. The more frequently they collide, the more likely they are to form product. Three ways to do this are:

  i. Increase the system temperature, which makes the molecules move faster and increases the number of collisions with sufficient activation energy to react.

  ii. Increase the amount of either or both reactants, which increases the odds that one reactant will encounter another.

  iii. Add a catalyst, which facilitates getting molecules close enough and in the proper orientation to react.

Another way to increase the rate of reaction is to remove product as soon as it is formed. Most reactions are reversible to some extent, and preventing the reverse reaction increases the rate of product formation (*Chemistry* 8th ed. pages 565–573/9th ed. pages 577–586). LO 4.4, LO 4.9

Question 7: Answers

(a) Acetic acid is a weak acid so you must determine $[H_3O^+]$ in the solution. Set up an ICE table.

	$HC_2H_3O_2$ +	H_2O ⇌	H_3O^+ +	$C_2H_3O_2^-$
I	0.833		0	0
C	$-x$		$+x$	$+x$
E	$0.833 - x$		x	x

$$K_a = \frac{\left[H_3O^+\right]\left[C_2H_3O_2^-\right]}{\left[HC_2H_3O_2\right]}$$

Since $[HC_2H_3O_2] \gg K_a$ ignore x in (conc$-x$)

$1.8 \times 10^{-5} = (x)(x)/0.833$

$x = 3.87 \times 10^{-3}\ M = [H_3O^+]$

$pH = -\log[H_3O^+] = 2.41$

Note that you report 2 significant figures because K_a is given to 2 significant figures.

(b) Sodium acetate is the conjugate base of a weak acid and will hydrolyze in water. Set up an ICE table.

	$C_2H_3O_2^-$ +	H_2O ⇌	$HC_2H_3O_2$ +	OH^-
I	0.833		0	0
C	$-x$		$+x$	$+x$
E	$0.833 - x$		x	x

$K_w = K_a K_b$

$$K_b = \frac{K_w}{K_a}$$

$$= \frac{1 \times 10^{-14}}{1.8 \times 10^{-5}}$$

$$= 5.6 \times 10^{-10}$$

$$K_b = \frac{\left[HC_2H_3O_2\right]\left[OH^-\right]}{\left[C_2H_3O_2^-\right]}$$

$$5.6 \times 10^{-10} = \frac{(x)(x)}{0.833}$$

$x = 2.2 \times 10^{-5} = [OH^-]$

$pOH = -\log[OH^-] = 4.67$

$14 = pH + pOH$

$pH = 9.33$

(c) This is a buffer problem. Note that 0.0833 mol $C_2H_3O_2^-$ in 100.0 mL is 0.833 M.

	$HC_2H_3O_2$	+	H_2O	$\rightleftharpoons$	H_3O^+	+	$C_2H_3O_2^-$
I	0.833				0		0.833
C	$-x$				$+x$		$+x$
E	$0.833 - x$				x		$0.833 + x$

$$K_a = \frac{\left[H_3O^+\right]\left[C_2H_3O_2^-\right]}{\left[HC_2H_3O_2\right]}$$

$$1.8 \times 10^{-5} = \frac{(x)(0.833)}{0.833}$$

$x = 1.8 \times 10^{-5}\ M = [H_3O^+]$

$pH = -\log[H_3O^+] = 4.74$

Note that this problem is equimolar in weak acid and conjugate base. When this occurs, $pH = pK_a$ according to the Henderson–Hasselbalch equation.

(d) The pH of the buffer is higher than the acid but lower than the conjugate base because addition of the conjugate base shifts the equilibrium towards the reactant (acetic acid). The higher concentration of acetate will have a larger frequency of collisions with hydronium ion which will make more molecules of acetic acid.

The particulate model shows as more acetate ion is added, more molecular acetic acid is formed.

$H = \square$ $C_2H_3O_2^- = \bigcirc$

Initial equilibrium conditions

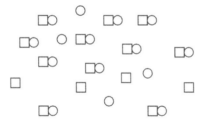

Add acetate

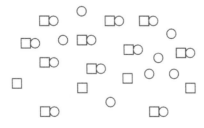

Reestablish equilibrium

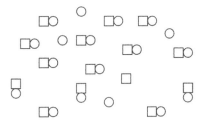

(*Chemistry* 8th ed. pages 652–656, 672–673, 701–707/9th ed. pages 666–670, 687–688, 715–721) LO 6.11, LO 6.12, LO 6.13, LO 6.18

Scoring the Free-Response Questions

It is difficult to come up with an exact score for this section of test. However, if you compare your answers to the answers in this book, remembering that each part of the test you answer correctly is worth points even if the other parts of the answer are incorrect (see the section titled "Types of Free-Response Questions" on page 12 of this book), you can get a general idea of the percentage of the questions for which you would get credit. If you believe that you got at least one-third of the possible credit, you would probably receive a 3 on this part of the test. If you believe that you would receive close to half or more of the available credit, your score would more likely be a 4 or a 5.

Practice Test 2

These questions are representative of the AP Chemistry examination, but keep in mind that it is impossible to predict exactly how well you will do on the actual exam. The first section of this test is 50% of your total test grade. Time yourself so that you finish this part in 90 minutes.

AP CHEMISTRY EXAMINATION
Section I: Multiple-Choice Questions
Time: 90 minutes
Number of Questions: 60

No calculators can be used in this section. A periodic table and a formula chart with constants is provided.

<u>Directions:</u> Each of the questions or incomplete statements below is followed by four suggested answers or completions. Select the one that is best in each case.

1. The element that has atoms with the largest atomic radius is
   (A) He
   (B) Na
   (C) Si
   (D) Mg

2. The element that has the highest first ionization energy is
   (A) Na
   (B) Si
   (C) Mg
   (D) Ar

3. The element that is the most metallic in character is
   (A) He
   (B) C
   (C) Si
   (D) Mg

4. The element that most easily forms an ion with a 2+ charge is
   (A) Na
   (B) Si
   (C) Mg
   (D) Ar

5. If two atoms have different atomic numbers but the same mass number, what must be true?
   (A) They must be atoms of the same element.
   (B) Each must contain the same total number of neutrons and protons.
   (C) The number of neutrons in both must be the same.
   (D) The number of protons in each atom must be the same.

6. An element has two naturally occurring isotopes. One isotope has an abundance of 80% and a mass of 122.0 amu. The other has a mass of 120.0 amu. What is the atomic mass of the element?
   (A) 121.6
   (B) 122.0
   (C) 120.6
   (D) 120.8

Periodic Table of Elements

1 H 1.008																	2 He 4.003
3 Li 6.941	4 Be 9.012											5 B 10.81	6 C 12.01	7 N 14.01	8 O 16.00	9 F 19.00	10 Ne 20.18
11 Na 22.99	12 Mg 24.31											13 Al 26.98	14 Si 28.09	15 P 30.97	16 S 32.07	17 Cl 35.45	18 Ar 39.95
19 K 39.10	20 Ca 40.08	21 Sc 44.96	22 Ti 47.88	23 V 50.94	24 Cr 52.00	25 Mn 54.94	26 Fe 55.85	27 Co 58.93	28 Ni 58.69	29 Cu 63.55	30 Zn 65.38	31 Ga 69.72	32 Ge 72.59	33 As 74.92	34 Se 78.96	35 Br 79.90	36 Kr 83.80
37 Rb 85.47	38 Sr 87.62	39 Y 88.91	40 Zr 91.22	41 Nb 92.91	42 Mo 95.94	43 Tc (98)	44 Ru 101.1	45 Rh 102.9	46 Pd 106.4	47 Ag 107.9	48 Cd 112.4	49 In 114.8	50 Sn 118.7	51 Sb 121.8	52 Te 127.6	53 I 126.9	54 Xe 131.3
55 Cs 132.9	56 Ba 137.3	57 La* 138.9	72 Hf 178.5	73 Ta 180.9	74 W 183.9	75 Re 186.2	76 Os 190.2	77 Ir 192.2	78 Pt 195.1	79 Au 197.0	80 Hg 200.6	81 Tl 204.4	82 Pb 207.2	83 Bi 209.0	84 Po (209)	85 At (210)	86 Rn (222)
87 Fr (223)	88 Ra 226	89 Ac+ (227)	104 Rf	105 Db	106 Sg	107 Bh	108 Hs	109 Mt	110 Ds	111 Rg (272)							

*Lanthanides

58 Ce 140.1	59 Pr 140.9	60 Nd 144.2	61 Pm (145)	62 Sm 150.4	63 Eu 152.0	64 Gd 157.3	65 Tb 158.9	66 Dy 162.5	67 Ho 164.9	68 Er 167.3	69 Tm 168.9	70 Yb 173.0	71 Lu 175.0

+Actinides

90 Th 232.0	91 Pa (231)	92 U 238.0	93 Np (237)	94 Pu (244)	95 Am (243)	96 Cm (247)	97 Bk (247)	98 Cf (251)	99 Es (252)	100 Fm (257)	101 Md (258)	102 No (259)	103 Lr (260)

7. A monoatomic ion contains 15 protons, 16 neutrons, and 18 electrons. What ion of what isotope is this?
(A) $^{31}P^{3+}$
(B) $^{34}Se^{2-}$
(C) $^{31}P^{3-}$
(D) $^{34}As^{3-}$

8. Which one of the following is an example of a physical property whose value is not dependent on the amount of substance?
(A) Aluminum burns in bromine.
(B) A balloon of hydrogen and oxygen explodes.
(C) A bottle of rubbing alcohol has a mass of 900 grams.
(D) The molar mass of sodium is 22.99 g/mol.

9. Of the colors listed below that are part of the visible portion of the electromagnetic spectrum, which one has the highest frequency?
(A) blue
(B) green
(C) yellow
(D) red

10. Atomic size increases going from top to bottom in a group of the periodic table because
(A) the number of protons increases
(B) the number of electron shells increases
(C) the atomic mass increases
(D) the atomic volume increases

Questions 11–15 refer to the structure and geometry of molecules:

11. What is the arrangement of electron pairs around the central atom in the molecule krypton difluoride, KrF_2?
(A) linear
(B) trigonal planar
(C) tetrahedral
(D) trigonal bipyramidal

12. Which of the following require(s) resonance to reconcile the Lewis electron representations with the actual or real structure?
CO_2 O_3 SO_4^{2-} NO_3^-
(A) CO_2 only
(B) O_3 only
(C) O_3 and NO_3^- only
(D) O_3 and SO_4^{2-} only

13. What is the condensed (shorthand) electron configuration for the phosphide ion, P^{3-}?
(A) $[Ne]3s^2$
(B) $[Ar]$
(C) $[Ar]4s^2$
(D) $[Ne]3s^23p^5$

14. What is the average bond order in the nitrate ion, NO_3^-?
(A) 1.0
(B) 1.33
(C) 1.5
(D) 2.0

15. In the Lewis dot structure for the molecule S_2O, how many lone pairs of electrons are there around the central atom?
(A) 4
(B) 3
(C) 2
(D) 1

Questions 16–19 refer to the system of reactions below:

$2\ NO(g) \rightarrow N_2O_2(g)$ *Fast*

$N_2O_2(g) + H_2(g) \rightarrow N_2O(g) + H_2O(g)$ *Slow*

$N_2O(g) + H_2(g) \rightarrow N_2(g) + H_2O(g)$ *Fast*

16. What is (are) reaction intermediate(s) in this reaction mechanism?
(A) NO and N_2O
(B) N_2O and N_2O_2
(C) N_2O_2
(D) N_2O and H_2

GO ON TO NEXT PAGE

17. What is the rate law for the reaction according to this mechanism?
(A) Rate = $k[N_2O_2][H_2]$
(B) Rate = $k[NO]^2$
(C) Rate = $k[N_2O_2]^2[H_2]^2$
(D) Rate = $k[NO]^2[H_2]$

18. Adding a catalyst to this reaction
(A) increases the amount of product at equilibrium
(B) changes the route the reaction takes between reactants and products
(C) increases the activation energy required for the reaction
(D) shifts the equilibrium toward the product side

19. The overall equation for the reaction is
(A) $N_2O(g) + H_2(g) \rightarrow N_2(g) + H_2O(g)$
(B) $2\ NO(g) + 2\ H_2(g) \rightarrow N_2(g) +$ $2\ H_2O(g)$
(C) $2\ NO(g) + H_2(g) \rightarrow N_2(g) + H_2O(g)$
(D) $NO(g) + H_2(g) \rightarrow N(g) + H_2O(g)$

Questions 20–22 refer to the reaction of ammonia with nitrogen monoxide, which is described by the following equation:

$$4\ NH_3(g) + 6\ NO(g) \rightarrow 5\ N_2(g) + 6\ H_2O(g)$$

20. In one particular experiment, equal molar amounts of the reactants were mixed and concentrations of the reactants and products were plotted against time. The graph below was obtained. Identify the components A, B, C, and D, and choose the line where all the components are identified properly.

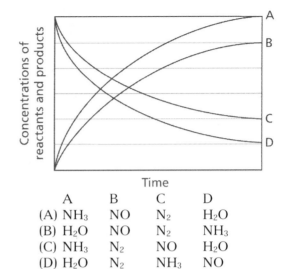

	A	B	C	D
(A)	NH_3	NO	N_2	H_2O
(B)	H_2O	NO	N_2	NH_3
(C)	NH_3	N_2	NO	H_2O
(D)	H_2O	N_2	NH_3	NO

21. At one stage in the reaction, nitrogen is produced at a rate of 30 mol $L^{-1} s^{-1}$. At what rate is nitrogen monoxide used up at this stage?
(A) 36 mol $L^{-1} s^{-1}$
(B) 30 mol $L^{-1} s^{-1}$
(C) 24 mol $L^{-1} s^{-1}$
(D) 6.0 mol $L^{-1} s^{-1}$

22. A proposed rate law for this reaction is: Rate of reaction = $k[NO]^2[NH_3]$ where k is the rate constant for the reaction. What happens to the rate of the reaction if the concentration of NO is doubled and the concentration of NH_3 is halved? (The temperature remains unchanged.)
(A) The rate halves.
(B) The rate stays the same.
(C) The rate doubles.
(D) The rate increases by four.

Questions 23–27 refer to the system of gases below:

23.

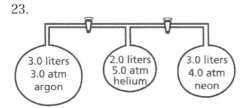

With the stopcocks closed, the three bulbs in the apparatus shown above are filled with the quantities indicated of argon, helium, and neon, respectively. Assume the gases are ideal and that the volumes include the volumes of the connecting tubes. What is the partial pressure of helium inside the apparatus when the taps are opened?
(A) 1.00 atm
(B) 1.25 atm
(C) 1.50 atm
(D) 2.00 atm

24. The graph below shows the speed distributions for the three gases, Ar, He, and Ne, at the same temperature.

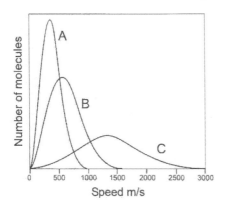

Match the gas with the distribution.

	A	B	C
(A)	Ar	Ne	He
(B)	Ar	He	Ne
(C)	Ne	He	Ar
(D)	Ar	He	Ne

25. Which of the gases exhibits the greatest deviation from ideal behavior?
(A) He, because it is the smallest atom.
(B) Ar, because it has the most electrons and is therefore the most polarizable.
(C) Ar, because it is the biggest atom.
(D) None, because inert gases are all ideal.

26. The pressure of the system is increased by decreasing the system volume and the temperature is decreased. How will the system conditions as predicted by the ideal gas law be affected?
(A) There will be no effect as long as all of the substances are in the gas phase.
(B) Intermolecular attractions between gas molecules will become more significant.
(C) The volume of the gas molecules will become significantly large relative to the volume of the container.
(D) Both (B) and (C) are true.

27. The temperature of the system is increased from 0°C to 273°C, and half the moles of gas are released. What happens to the pressure?
(A) It is unchanged.
(B) It doubles.
(C) It decreases by one half.
(D) It increases four times.

GO ON TO NEXT PAGE

28. A U-tube mercury manometer is open to the atmosphere (1 atm = 760 mm Hg) on the right arm and is connected to a glass vessel containing a gas on the left arm as shown.

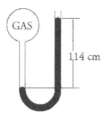

The level of the mercury in the tube is 114 cm (1140 mm) higher in the right arm. What is the pressure of the gas in the glass vessel?
(A) 0.50 atm
(B) 1.0 atm
(C) 1.5 atm
(D) 2.5 atm

29. 0.24 mole of sodium carbonate is dissolved in sufficient water to make 300.0-mL of solution. What is the molarity of the sodium carbonate solution?
(A) 0.24 M
(B) 0.72 M
(C) 0.32 M
(D) 0.80 M

30. The concentration of sodium ions in a 300.0-mL solution made from 0.24 mole of sodium carbonate dissolved in water is
(A) 3.6 M
(B) 1.6 M
(C) 1.2 M
(D) 4.8 M

31. Distilled vinegar purchased at the grocery store is a 0.833 M solution of acetic acid. What is the concentration in mole L^{-1} of acetic acid in a solution prepared by taking 100. mL of vinegar and adding it to enough water to make 2.00 L of solution?
(A) 0.0417 M
(B) 0.0833 M
(C) 0.0975 M
(D) 0.167 M

32. The correct balanced equation for the reaction of sodium carbonate solution with acetic acid is:
(A) $NaHCO_3(aq)$ + $CH_3COOH(aq)$ → $H_2O(l)$ + $CO_2(g)$ + $NaCH_3COO(aq)$
(B) 2 $Na_2CO_3(aq)$ + 2 $CH_3COOH(aq)$ → $H_2O(l)$ + $CO_2(g)$ + 4 $NaCH_3COO(aq)$
(C) $Na_2CO_3(aq)$ + 2 $CH_3COOH(aq)$ → $H_2O(l)$ + $CO_2(g)$ + 2 $NaCH_3COO(aq)$
(D) $Na_2CO_3(aq)$ + $CH_3COOH(aq)$ → $H_2O(l)$ + $CO_2(g)$ + 2 $NaCH_3COO(aq)$

33. The reaction of sodium carbonate and hydrochloric acid is an example of
(A) oxidation-reduction
(B) synthesis
(C) acid-base
(D) combustion

34. Which of the following is an oxidation–reduction reaction?
(A) $Ca(OH)_2(aq)$ + 2 $HNO_3(aq)$ → $Ca(NO_3)_2(aq)$ + 2 $H_2O(l)$
(B) 2 $H_2(g)$ + $O_2(g)$ → 2 $H_2O(g)$
(C) $CuBr_2(aq)$ + 2 $NaOH(aq)$ → $Cu(OH)_2(s)$ + 2 $NaBr(aq)$
(D) Both (A) and (B)

Questions 35–37 refer to the following reaction:

2 $MnO_4^-(aq)$ + 16 $H_3O^+(aq)$ + 5 $Zn(s)$ → 2 $Mn^{2+}(aq)$ + 24 $H_2O(l)$ + 5 $Zn^{2+}(aq)$

35. In this reaction, which species is oxidized, and which is reduced?
(A) MnO_4^- is oxidized, and Zn is reduced.
(B) Zn is oxidized, and MnO_4^- is reduced.
(C) H_3O^+ is oxidized, and Zn is reduced.
(D) Zn^{2+} is oxidized, and Mn^{2+} is reduced.

36. How many electrons are transferred in this reaction?
    (A) 5
    (B) 7
    (C) 10
    (D) 14

37. This reaction is typically performed as a titration, but no indicator is added. How is the endpoint identified?
    (A) When all the Zn has reacted, the solution will stay purple, the color of the permanganate ion.
    (B) A precipitate forms.
    (C) When all the Zn has reacted, additional permanganate reacts with water to form a gas.
    (D) The pH of the solution increases to 14.

38. What is the change in oxidation number of sulfur in the following half-reaction?
    $$S_4O_6^{2-} + 10\ H_2O \rightarrow SO_4^{2-} + 2\ OH^- + 14\ e^-$$
    (A) –2 to –8
    (B) +4 to +1
    (C) +4 to +6
    (D) +2 ½ to +6

39. Balance the following equation for the reaction of dimethylhydrazine with dinitrogen tetroxide:

    __$C_2H_8N_2$ + __N_2O_4 → __N_2 + __CO_2 + __H_2O

    The sum of all the coefficients in the balanced equation is
    (A) 9
    (B) 11
    (C) 12
    (D) 14

40. In which compound does nitrogen have the highest (most positive) oxidation number?
    (A) NO_2
    (B) NH_3
    (C) N_2
    (D) NO_3^-

Questions 41–43 refer to the following reaction:

$$2\ CH_3OH(g) + 3\ O_2(g) \rightarrow 2\ CO_2(g) + 4\ H_2O(l)$$

41. When this reaction is performed in a calorimeter, the water temperature increases. Therefore, the heat of reaction
    (A) is negative
    (B) is positive
    (C) is equal to zero
    (D) cannot be determined from the data

42. From the equation of the reaction, what is most likely happening to entropy during this process?
    (A) Entropy of the system decreases, entropy of the surroundings increases
    (B) Entropy of the system increases, entropy of the surroundings increases
    (C) Entropy of the system decreases, entropy of the surroundings decreases
    (D) Entropy of the system increases, entropy of the surroundings decreases

43. Given the following bond energies (kJ/mol), what is the ΔH_{rxn} in kJ for the reaction?

    | C–H | 413 | C–O | 358 | O=O | 495 |
    | C=O | 799 | O–H | 467 | | |

    (A) 2559 kJ
    (B) –2559 kJ
    (C) –1319 kJ
    (D) 1319 kJ

44. For which substance does the standard enthalpy of formation ΔH_f° equal zero?
    (A) $H_2O(l)$
    (B) $Cu(s)$
    (C) $O_3(g)$
    (D) $Fe(l)$

GO ON TO NEXT PAGE

45. Which process is always exothermic?
    (A) evaporation of a liquid
    (B) dissolving a typical salt in water
    (C) breaking a hydrogen molecule into atoms
    (D) freezing water

Questions 46–47 refer to the thermodynamics of dissolving ammonium nitrate in water.

46. When crystalline ammonium nitrate dissolves in water to make a solution, the solution gets very cold, dropping in temperature about 20°C. What are the signs of ΔH, ΔS, and ΔG for this process?

	ΔH	ΔS	ΔG
(A)	(–)	(+)	(+)
(B)	(–)	(+)	(–)
(C)	(+)	(–)	(+)
(D)	(+)	(+)	(–)

47. Under what conditions is the process spontaneous?
    (A) The process is spontaneous at all temperatures.
    (B) The process is not spontaneous at any temperature.
    (C) The process is spontaneous at high temperatures and not at low temperatures.
    (D) The process is spontaneous at low temperatures and not at high temperatures.

48. Arrange the following substances in order of increasing entropy.
    $H_2O(l)$ $CO_2(s)$ $N_2(l)$ $N_2(g)$
    (A) $CO_2(s) < H_2O(l) < N_2(l) < N_2(g)$
    (B) $N_2(g) < CO_2(s) < N_2(l) < H_2O(l)$
    (C) $H_2O(l) < CO_2(s) < N_2(l) < N_2(g)$
    (D) $CO_2(s) < N_2(l) < H_2O(l) < N_2(g)$

Questions 49–50 refer to the following reaction:

$$3\ F_2(g) + Cl_2(g) \rightleftharpoons 2\ ClF_3(g)$$

49. When the system is at equilibrium at 298 K, $[F_2] = 2.0\ M$; $[Cl_2] = 2.5\ M$; $[ClF_3] = 3.0\ M$. Calculate the value of K, the equilibrium constant.
    (A) 0.45
    (B) 0.90
    (C) 1.2
    (D) 0.25

50. The system volume is decreased at constant temperature. In which direction, if any, will the system shift to restore equilibrium?
    (A) There will be no change.
    (B) It will shift to the left.
    (C) It will shift to the right.
    (D) The value of K will change because the volume has decreased.

Questions 51–52 refer to a solution prepared by dissolving hydrogen sulfide in water to form hydrosulfuric acid, $H_2S(aq)$:

51. The Brønsted–Lowry conjugate base of $H_2S(aq)$ is
    (A) S^{2-}
    (B) HS^-
    (C) OH^-
    (D) H_3O^+

52. The K_a of $H_2S(aq)$ is equal to 1.0×10^{-7} at 25°C. What is the K_b for its conjugate base?
    (A) 1.0×10^{-7}
    (B) 1.0×10^{-14}
    (C) 1.8×10^{-5}
    (D) $1.0 \times 10^{+7}$

53. Which one of the following equimolar solutions will act as a buffer solution?
(A) H_2SO_4 and Na_2SO_4
(B) H_2SO_4 and H_2SO_3
(C) KOH and KCN
(D) HI and KI

54. What is the molar solubility of cadmium sulfide, CdS? (K_{sp} of CdS = 3.6×10^{-29})
(A) 3.6×10^{-16} M
(B) 6.0×10^{-15} M
(C) 1.8×10^{-16} M
(D) 6.0×10^{-14} M

55. A substance with strong intermolecular forces of attraction would be expected to have
(A) a low boiling point
(B) a low vapor pressure
(C) a low melting point
(D) a low boiling point and a low vapor pressure

56. The molecules HF, $CaCO_3$, and $BaSO_4$ are weak electrolytes in aqueous solution. This must be because
(A) the molecules dissolve without breaking up into cations and anions
(B) water is polar and the molecules are nonpolar
(C) the atoms in the molecules are covalently bonded to each other
(D) the forces of attraction between the ions are stronger than those between the ions and water

57. How can the solubility of silver carbonate be increased?
(A) Add silver nitrate, $AgNO_3$
(B) Add sodium carbonate, Na_2CO_3
(C) Add calcium nitrate, $Ca(NO_3)_2$
(D) None of these will increase its solubility.

58. A solution with a low pH
(A) has a low concentration of acid
(B) has a high concentration of hydronium ions
(C) has a low concentration of hydronium ions
(D) is a basic solution

59. Below are representations of energy levels (drawn to scale) in the Bohr model of the hydrogen atom. Which electron making a transition, denoted by the arrows, results in the emission of a photon of shortest wavelength?

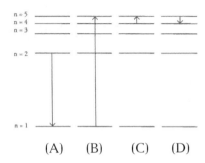

60. Calculate the standard cell potential for the cell

$Sr(s)|Sr^{2+}(aq) \parallel Sn^{2+}(aq)|Sn(s)$ given the half-cell standard potentials:

$E°\ Sr^{2+}(aq)|Sr(s) = -2.89$ V

$E°\ Sn^{2+}(aq)|Sn(s) = -0.14$ V

(A) -3.03 V
(B) $+3.03$ V
(C) -2.75 V
(D) $+2.75$ V

GO ON TO NEXT PAGE

Advanced Placement Chemistry Equations and Constants

Throughout the test the following symbols have the definitions specified unless otherwise noted.

L, mL	=	liter(s), milliliter(s)	mm Hg	= millimeters of mercury
g	=	gram(s)	J, kJ	= joule(s), kilojoule(s)
nm	=	nanometer(s)	V	= volt(s)
atm	=	atmosphere(s)	mol	= mole(s)

ATOMIC STRUCTURE

$$E = h\nu$$
$$c = \lambda\nu$$

E = energy
ν = frequency
λ = wavelength

Planck's constant, $h = 6.626 \times 10^{-34}$ J s

Speed of light, $c = 2.998 \times 10^8$ m s^{-1}

Avogadro's number = 6.022×10^{23} mol^{-1}

Electron charge, $e = -1.602 \times 10^{-19}$ coulomb

EQUILIBRIUM

$$K_c = \frac{[C]^c[D]^d}{[A]^a[B]^b}, \text{ where } a\,A + b\,B \rightleftarrows c\,C + d\,D$$

$$K_p = \frac{(P_C)^c (P_D)^d}{(P_A)^a (P_B)^b}$$

$$K_a = \frac{[H^+][A^-]}{[HA]}$$

$$K_b = \frac{[OH^-][HB^+]}{[B]}$$

$$K_w = [H^+][OH^-] = 1.0 \times 10^{-14} \text{ at } 25°C$$
$$= K_a \times K_b$$

$$pH = -\log[H^+], \ pOH = -\log[OH^-]$$

$$14 = pH + pOH$$

$$pH = pK_a + \log\frac{[A^-]}{[HA]}$$

$$pK_a = -\log K_a, \ pK_b = -\log K_b$$

Equilibrium Constants

K_c (molar concentrations)
K_p (gas pressures)
K_a (weak acid)
K_b (weak base)
K_w (water)

KINETICS

$$\ln[A]_t - \ln[A]_0 = -kt$$

$$\frac{1}{[A]_t} - \frac{1}{[A]_0} = kt$$

$$t_{1/2} = \frac{0.693}{k}$$

k = rate constant
t = time
$t_{1/2}$ = half-life

GASES, LIQUIDS, AND SOLUTIONS

$$PV = nRT$$

$$P_A = P_{total} \times X_A, \text{ where } X_A = \frac{\text{moles A}}{\text{total moles}}$$

$$P_{total} = P_A + P_B + P_C + \ldots$$

$$n = \frac{m}{M}$$

$$K = °C + 273$$

$$D = \frac{m}{V}$$

$$KE \text{ per molecule} = \frac{1}{2}mv^2$$

Molarity, M = moles of solute per liter of solution

$$A = abc$$

P = pressure
V = volume
T = temperature
n = number of moles
m = mass
M = molar mass
D = density
KE = kinetic energy
v = velocity
A = absorbance
a = molar absorptivity
b = path length
c = concentration

Gas constant, R = 8.314 J mol^{-1} K^{-1}
= 0.08206 L atm mol^{-1} K^{-1}
= 62.36 L torr mol^{-1} K^{-1}
1 atm = 760 mm Hg
= 760 torr
STP = 0.00 °C and 1.000 atm

THERMOCHEMISTRY/ ELECTROCHEMISTRY

$$q = mc\Delta T$$

$$\Delta S° = \sum S° \text{ products} - \sum S° \text{ reactants}$$

$$\Delta H° = \sum \Delta H_f° \text{ products} - \sum \Delta H_f° \text{ reactants}$$

$$\Delta G° = \sum \Delta G_f° \text{ products} - \sum \Delta G_f° \text{ reactants}$$

$$\Delta G° = \Delta H° - T\Delta S°$$

$$= -RT \ln K$$

$$= -nFE°$$

$$I = \frac{q}{t}$$

q = heat
m = mass
c = specific heat capacity
T = temperature
$S°$ = standard entropy
$H°$ = standard enthalpy
$G°$ = standard free energy
n = number of moles
$E°$ = standard reduction potential
I = current (amperes)
q = charge (coulombs)
t = time (seconds)

Faraday's constant, F = 96,485 coulombs per mole of electrons

$$1 \text{ volt} = \frac{1 \text{ joule}}{1 \text{ coulomb}}$$

GO ON TO NEXT PAGE

Introduction to Section II: Free-Response Questions

Section II of the AP Chemistry Examination counts for 50% of the total test grade and involves several parts. Answering these questions gives you an opportunity to demonstrate your ability to present your material in clear, orderly, and convincing language. Your answers will be graded on the basis of accuracy, the kinds of information you include to support your responses, and the importance of the descriptive material used. Be specific; general, all-encompassing answers will not be graded as well as detailed answers with examples and equations. CLEARLY SHOW THE METHOD USED AND THE STEPS INVOLVED IN ARRIVING AT YOUR ANSWERS. It is to your advantage to do this, since you may obtain partial credit if you do and you will receive little or no credit if you do not. Attention should be paid to significant figures. On the AP exam, be sure to write all your answers to the questions on the lined pages following each question in the test booklet. Do not write your answers in the white space between questions.

Section II: Free-Response Questions
Time: 90 minutes
Number of Questions: 7

Allow yourself no more than 90 minutes to answer these questions. You may use a calculator, the equations sheet, and the periodic table throughout this section. All questions must be answered.

1. For the reaction $PCl_3(g) + Cl_2(g) \rightarrow PCl_5(g)$, $K_p = 0.0870$ at $300\,^\circ C$. A flask is charged with 0.30 atm PCl_3, 0.60 atm Cl_2, and 0.10 atm PCl_5 at this temperature.
   (a) Determine whether the above conditions (the added gases) are at equilibrium. If not, determine to which direction the reaction must proceed to reach equilibrium.
   (b) Calculate the equilibrium partial pressures of the gases.
   (c) Predict and justify what effect increasing the volume of the system will have on the mole fraction of PCl_5 in the mixture.
   (d) The reaction as written is exothermic. Predict and justify what effect decreasing the temperature of the system will have on the mole fraction of PCl_5 in the mixture.

2. A 0.495 M solution of nitrous acid, HNO_2, has a pH of 1.83.
   (a) Find the $[H^+]$ and the percent ionization of nitrous acid in this solution.
   (b) Write the equilibrium expression and calculate the value of K_a for nitrous acid.
   (c) Sketch the pH curve that results when 20.0 mL of a 0.0125 M nitrous acid solution are titrated with 0.0125 M NaOH solution. Label the axes, the equivalence point, and the buffer region clearly.

3. Given the following data:

$$Fe^{2+} + 2\,e^- \rightarrow Fe \qquad E^\circ_{red} = -0.44\ V$$
$$Ag^+ + e^- \rightarrow Ag \qquad E^\circ_{red} = 0.80\ V$$

Answer the following questions with respect to the reaction

$$Fe^{2+}(aq) + 2\,Ag(s) \rightarrow Fe(s) + 2\,Ag^+(aq)$$

(a) What is the cell potential, E°, for the reaction?
(b) Is the reaction spontaneous at standard state conditions? Justify your answer.
(c) What is the value of E° at equilibrium?
(d) What is the value of the equilibrium constant at 25°C?
(e) For the spontaneous reaction, what is the maximum amount of work that can be performed?

4. Answer the following questions about reaction kinetics.
(a) Sketch a potential energy versus reaction progress plot for an exothermic reaction, labeling ΔH and E_a. Use collision theory to justify the shape of the curve and to explain how changing the temperature affects the rate of reaction.
(b) On the same plot, sketch a line representing the potential energy versus reaction progress for the same reaction run using a catalyst. Account for the difference in energy between the catalyzed and uncatalyzed reaction.

5. A student weighs out equal amounts of magnesium hydroxide, calcium carbonate, calcium sulfate, and sodium bicarbonate but carelessly forgets to label the containers in which each sample is placed. If the only chemicals available are a bottle of dilute hydrochloric acid and some distilled water, describe a procedure that could be used to identify each solid. Write the net ionic equations for reactions that assist in identification.

6. Nitrogen forms NF_3 but not NF_5 whereas phosphorus forms PF_3 and PF_5. The trifluorides are both trigonal pyramidal and the pentafluoride is trigonal bipyramidal. Draw Lewis diagrams of the molecules and account for these observations.

7. Calcium oxide has a much higher melting point (2580°C) than potassium fluoride (858°C). Use Coulomb's law to explain these observations.

END OF EXAMINATION

Answers to Practice Test 2

Section I: Multiple-Choice Questions

Score your test using the table below.

Determine how many questions you answered correctly. You will find explanations of the answers on the following pages.

1. B	2. D	3. D	4. C	5. B
6. A	7. C	8. D	9. A	10. B
11. D	12. C	13. B	14. B	15. D
16. B	17. D	18. B	19. B	20. D
21. A	22. C	23. B	24. A	25. B
26. D	27. A	28. D	29. D	30. B
31. A	32. C	33. C	34. B	35. B
36. C	37. A	38. D	39. C	40. D
41. A	42. A	43. C	44. B	45. D
46. D	47. C	48. D	49. A	50. C
51. B	52. A	53. A	54. B	55. B
56. D	57. C	58. B	59. A	60. D

Calculate Your Score:

Number answered correctly: _____

What Your Score Means:

Each year, since the test is different, the scoring is a little different. But generally, if you scored 20 or more on the multiple-choice questions, you'll most likely get a 3 or better on the test. If you scored 28 or more, you'll probably score a 4 or better. And if you scored a 40 or more, you'll most likely get a 5. Keep in mind that the multiple-choice section is worth 50% of your final grade, and the free-response section is worth 50% of your final grade. To learn more about the scoring for the free-response questions, turn to the last page of this section.

Answers and Explanations

Section I: Multiple-Choice Questions

1. **Answer: B** In the periodic table, radius increases going down a group because the number of electron shells increases. The radius decreases across a row because the Z_{eff} (number of positive charges in the nucleus) increases (*Chemistry* 8th ed. pages 318–323, 909–910/9th ed. pages 329–334, 928–929). LO 1.9

2. ANSWER: D First ionization energy follows the same trend as atomic radius. Less energy is required to remove electrons that are further from the nucleus. More energy is required to remove electrons from atoms with high Z_{eff} (*Chemistry* 8th ed. pages 318–323/9th ed. pages 329–334). LO 2.28

3. ANSWER: D Metallic character refers to ability to lose electrons and conductivity. The other substances are nonmetals (*Chemistry* 8th ed. pages 318–323/9th ed. pages 329–334). LO 1.9

4. ANSWER: C Group 2 elements have an ns^2 valence configuration and will form 2+ cations (*Chemistry* 8th ed. pages 318–323/9th ed. pages 329–334). LO 1.9

5. ANSWER: B Different atomic numbers, therefore different number of protons. Same mass numbers, therefore same total number of protons and neutrons (*Chemistry* 8th ed. pages 49–52/9th ed. pages 52–55). LO 1.4

6. ANSWER: A No calculator is necessary to solve this problem. More than half of the substance is the higher mass isotope, so the weighted average mass should be greater than 121. Weighted average = $(0.80 \times 122) + (0.20 \times 120) = 121.6$ (*Chemistry* 8th ed. pages 341–344/9th ed. pages 352–356). LO 1.4

7. ANSWER: C

   15 protons means the atomic number is 15, which is P.

   16 neutrons means that the mass number is 15+16 = 31.

   18 electrons compared to 15 protons means that the charge is 3– (*Chemistry* 8th ed. pages 49–52/9th ed. pages 52–55). LO 1.5

8. ANSWER: D Molar mass is a physical property; it does not involve chemical change. It is also independent of the amount present (*Chemistry* 8th ed. pages 244–246/9th ed. pages 253–255). LO 3.10

9. ANSWER: A High frequency light is high energy. The visible spectrum is bracketed by UV on the high energy side, and IR on the low energy side. Blue is the closest color to UV (*Chemistry* 8th ed. pages 285–287/9th ed. pages 296–298). LO 1.15

10. ANSWER: B Each row on the periodic table represents another electron shell. The more electron shells an atom has, the larger its radius (*Chemistry* 8th ed. pages 322–323/9th ed. pages 333–334). LO 1.9

11. Answer: D

    Kr: 8 valence electrons

    2 F: 14 valence electrons

    Total: 22 valence electrons. Around Kr there are 2 bonding pairs and 3 lone pairs = 5 pairs total

    Therefore: trigonal bipyramidal (*Chemistry* 8th ed. pages 378–388/9th ed. pages 389–399). LO 2.21

12. Answer: C O_3 has one single bond and one double bond. The double bond can be drawn in either position. The nitrate ion has two single bonds and one double bond; the double bond is drawn in one of three positions (*Chemistry* 8th ed. pages 373–378/9th ed. pages 384–389). LO 2.21

13. Answer: B Review the rules for writing electron configurations (*Chemistry* 8th ed. pages 312–318/9th ed. pages 322–329). LO 1.6

14. Answer: B There are two N–O single bonds and one double bond; the average bond order is 1.3 (*Chemistry* 8th ed. pages 373–378/9th ed. pages 384–389). LO 2.21

15. Answer: D   Total valence electrons = 2 × 6 for S + 6 for O = 18 total. Divide 18 by 8, for 2 bonding pairs, leaving 2 electrons or one lone pair (*Chemistry* 8th ed. pages 365–369/9th ed. pages 376–380). LO 2.21

16. Answer: B Reactants are NO and H_2. Products are N_2 and H_2O. Intermediates are N_2O_2 and N_2O; they are formed and used up (*Chemistry* 8th ed. pages 562–565/9th ed. pages 574–577). LO 4.7

17. Answer: D Slowest step: Rate = $k[N_2O_2][H_2]$, but N_2O_2 is a reaction intermediate. Assume first step reaches steady state: $K' = [N_2O_2]/[NO]^2$, so $[N_2O_2] = K[NO]^2$ and Rate = $kK[NO]^2[H_2]$ (*Chemistry* 8th ed. pages 562–565/9th ed. pages 574–577). LO 4.2

18. Answer: B Adding a catalyst causes the reaction to follow a different route with a lower activation energy, allowing the process to proceed at a higher rate. It does not affect equilibrium position (amount of product formed overall) (*Chemistry* 8th ed. pages 570–575/9th ed. pages 583–587). LO 4.9

19. Answer: B This is a Hess's law problem. Sum the three equations, eliminating terms that are the same on both sides.
    $$2\ NO(g) \rightarrow \cancel{N_2O_2}(g)$$
    $$\cancel{N_2O_2}(g) + H_2(g) \rightarrow \cancel{N_2O}(g) + H_2O(g)$$
    $$\cancel{N_2O}(g) + H_2(g) \rightarrow N_2(g) + H_2O(g)$$
    $$2\ NO(g) + 2\ H_2(g) \rightarrow N_2(g) + 2\ H_2O(g)$$
    (*Chemistry* 8th ed. pages 562–565/9th ed. pages 574–577) LO 4.7

20. **ANSWER: D** The reactants diminish in concentration (C and D). D [NO] goes down 6/4 faster than C [NH_3]. The products are formed (A and B). A [H_2O] is formed 6/5 times faster than B [N_2] (*Chemistry* 8th ed. pages 540–545/9th ed. pages 553–557). LO 4.2

21. **ANSWER: A** Rate at which NO is used = rate of production of N_2 × (6/5) = 36 mol/L/s (*Chemistry* 8th ed. pages 540–545/9th ed. pages 553–557). LO 4.1

22. **ANSWER: C** Rate = $k[A]^2[B]$ = $(2)^2(1/2)$ = 4 × ½ = 2 (*Chemistry* 8th ed. pages 547–551/9th ed. pages 559–563). LO 4.7

23. **ANSWER: B** The partial pressure of the helium = 5.0 atm × (2.0L/8.0L) = 1.25 atm (*Chemistry* 8th ed. pages 199–213/9th ed. pages 208–223). LO 2.6

24. **ANSWER: A** Average speeds increase as the molecular masses decrease (*Chemistry* 8th ed. pages 205–214/9th ed. pages 214–224). LO 2.4

25. **ANSWER: B** Ar is the largest atom, but the reason it deviates from ideal gas behavior is its larger number of electrons, which makes it more polarizable (*Chemistry* 8th ed. pages 214–216/9th ed. pages 224–226). LO 2.12

26. **ANSWER: D** Be familiar with the assumptions underpinning the ideal gas law, and why changing conditions cause deviation from ideal behavior (*Chemistry* 8th ed. pages 183–193/9th ed. pages 192–203). LO 2.4

27. **ANSWER: A** Be familiar with solving problems using the ideal gas law, and remember always to convert temperature from °C to K. Since the volume is not mentioned in the problem statement, it must be constant.

    $P_2 = P_1 (n_2/n_1)(T_2/T_1) = P_1(0.5 \, n_1/n_1)(546 \text{ K}/273\text{K})$ so $P_2 = P_1$

    (*Chemistry* 8th ed. pages 183–193/9th ed. pages 192–203). LO 2.4

28. **ANSWER: D** The difference in levels is 1.5 atm. The pressure outside is 1.0 atm; therefore, the total pressure of the gas is 2.5 atm (*Chemistry* 8th ed. pages 181–183/9th ed. pages 190–192). LO 2.4

29. **ANSWER: D** Molarity = number of moles/volume of solution (in liters) = 0.24 moles/0.300 L = 0.80 *M* (*Chemistry* 8th ed. pages 136–145, 498–500/9th ed. pages 145–153, 511–513). LO 2.9

30. **ANSWER: B** There are two sodium ions per formula unit, so the concentration is twice $8.0 × 10^{-1} M$ (*Chemistry* 8th ed. pages 136–145/9th ed. pages 145–153). LO 2.9

31. ANSWER: **A** Use the relationship $M_1V_1 = M_2V_2$; rearrange to solve for $M_2 = M_1(V_1/V_2) = 0.833\ M\ (0.100L/2.00L) = 0.0417\ M$ (*Chemistry* 8th ed. pages 141–144/9th ed. pages 150–153). LO 2.9

32. ANSWER: **C** Sodium carbonate can neutralize two monoprotic acids, whereas sodium hydrogen carbonate can only neutralize one. Remember that when carbonates react with acid, CO_2 is formed in addition to water and a salt (*Chemistry* 8th ed. pages 154–159/9th ed. pages 163–169). LO 3.7

33. ANSWER: **C** Carbonates act as bases when added to acids (*Chemistry* 8th ed. pages 154–159/9th ed. pages 163–169). LO 3.7

34. ANSWER: **B** The first choice is acid-base; the third choice is precipitation. In answer B, the oxidation numbers change so only this choice is oxidation-reduction (*Chemistry* 8th ed. pages 161–166/9th ed. pages 170–175). LO 3.8

35. ANSWER: **B** The Mn in MnO_4^- goes from oxidation number of 7+ to 2+ in Mn^{2+} so it is reduced. Zn is oxidized to Zn^{2+} (*Chemistry* 8th ed. pages 165–166/9th ed. pages 174–175). LO 3.8

36. ANSWER: **C** For the oxidation, $5\ Zn(s) \rightarrow 5\ Zn^{2+}(aq)$, 10 electrons are lost. Ten electrons are gained in the reduction, so the equation is balanced (*Chemistry* 8th ed. pages 166–169/9th ed. pages 175–177). LO 3.9

37. ANSWER: **A** Permanganate is purple; a solution of Mn^{+2} ions is light yellow (*Chemistry* 8th ed. page 962/9th ed. page 981). LO 3.9

38. ANSWER: **D** In $S_4O_6^{2-}$, $4x + 6(-2) = -2$, so $x = +2\ ½$ (*Chemistry* 8th ed. pages 161–166/9th ed. pages 170–175). LO 3.8

39. ANSWER: **C** $C_2H_8N_2 + 2\ N_2O_4 \rightarrow 3\ N_2 + 2\ CO_2 + 4\ H_2O$

    (*Chemistry* 8th ed. pages 99–103/9th ed. pages 105–109). LO 3.2

40. ANSWER: **D** In NO_3^-, N has an oxidation number of +5 whereas its oxidation number is +4 in NO_2. Its oxidation number is 0 in N_2, and –3 in NH_3 (*Chemistry* 8th ed. pages 161–166/9th ed. pages 170–175). LO 3.8

41. ANSWER: **A** An exothermic reaction releases heat to the surroundings, whose temperature will increase (*Chemistry* 8th ed. pages 248–249/9th ed. pages 257–258). LO 5.7

42. ANSWER: **A** Entropy of the system decreases in going from 5 moles of gas to 2 moles of gas and 4 of liquid. The exothermic reaction releases heat to the surroundings, whose entropy then increases (*Chemistry* 8th ed. pages 780–783/9th ed. pages 795–798). LO 5.12

43. ANSWER: **C** Draw the Lewis structures and identify the kind and number of bonds. ΔH_{rxn} will be equal to the difference between the energy required to break bonds and the energy released when bonds are formed.

$$2 \; H-\underset{\underset{H}{|}}{\overset{\overset{H}{|}}{C}}-O-H \quad + \; 3 \; O{=}O \quad \rightarrow \quad 2 \; O{=}C{=}O \quad + \; 4 \; H-O-H$$

Reactants		Products	
C–H	413 kJ × 3 × 2	C=O	799 kJ × 2 × 2
C–O	358 kJ × 1 × 2	O–H	467 kJ × 2 × 4
O–H	467 kJ × 1 × 2		
O=O	495 kJ × 1 × 3		
TOTALS	5613 kJ	– 6932 kJ =	–1319 kJ

(*Chemistry* 8th ed. pages 361–364/9th ed. pages 373–376). LO 5.8

44. ANSWER: **B** An element in its standard state has a defined standard heat of formation of zero (*Chemistry* 8th ed. pages 255–261/9th ed. pages 264–270). LO 5.8

45. ANSWER: **D** The freezing of water involves the release of energy since the water molecules are moving very close to one another to maximize the formation of hydrogen bonds. Bond formation is always exothermic (*Chemistry* 8th ed. pages 798–802/9th ed. pages 813–817). LO 5.6

46. ANSWER: **D** The process is endothermic, so ΔH = (+). There in an increase in disorder so ΔS = (+). The process happens, so ΔG = (–) (*Chemistry* 8th ed. pages 783–794/9th ed. pages 798–810). LO 5.13

47. ANSWER: **C** Compare the values of the terms in the expression

$$\Delta G = \Delta H - T\Delta S$$

Since ΔS is positive, the value of the term $T\Delta S$ is positive and "$-T\Delta S$" will always be negative. When T decreases, the value of "$-T\Delta S$" decreases until it is less than the positive ΔH. At this point, the process will no longer be spontaneous (*Chemistry* 8th ed. pages 783–794/9th ed. pages 798–810). LO 5.13

48. ANSWER: **D** A gas phase molecule has the most entropy, and a solid phase the least. For the liquids, the more complex molecule, H_2O, has more entropy than N_2 (*Chemistry* 8th ed. pages 773–779/9th ed. pages 788–794). LO 5.12

49. **Answer: A**

$$K = \frac{[ClF_3]^2}{[F_2]^3[Cl_2]} = \frac{(3)^2}{(2)^3(2.5)} = 0.45$$

(*Chemistry* 8th ed. pages 545–547/9th ed. pages 557–559). LO 6.5

50. **Answer: C** Decreasing volume will force the reaction to the side with fewer moles of gas, the right (*Chemistry* 8th ed. pages 620–626/9th ed. pages 633–639). LO 6.8

51. **Answer: B** The only difference in a conjugate acid–base pair is the removal of a H^+ going from the acid to the base or the addition of a H^+ going from the base to acid (*Chemistry* 8th ed. pages 642–647/9th ed. pages 656–661). LO 3.7

52. **Answer: A** $K_w/K_a = 1.0 \times 10^{-14}/1.0 \times 10^{-7} = 1.0 \times 10^{-7}$
(*Chemistry* 8th ed. pages 651–666/9th ed. pages 666–680). LO 6.12

53. **Answer: A** The pair must be a weak electrolyte and its conjugate partner (*Chemistry* 8th ed. pages 701–710/9th ed. pages 715–724). LO 6.18

54. **Answer: B**

$$K_{sp} = [Cd^{2+}][S^{2-}] = 3.6 \times 10^{-29}$$

$$[Cd^{2+}] = \sqrt{3.6 \times 10^{-29}} = \sqrt{3.6 \times 10^{-30}} = 6.0 \times 10^{-15}$$

(*Chemistry* 8th ed. pages 744–752/9th ed. pages 759–768). LO 6.21

55. **Answer: B** Strong intermolecular forces means that additional energy must be supplied in order to increase the physical distance between the molecules when they move from liquid to vapor state. This results in a greater heat of vaporization. It also means that fewer molecules at a given temperature are able to move into the vapor state; thus the vapor pressure is lower than for other liquids with weaker intermolecular forces (*Chemistry* 8th ed. pages 440–443, 504/9th ed. pages 455–458, 517). LO 2.1

56. **Answer: D** Substances that are weak electrolytes ionize to a limited extent in water, so the solutions they form are not strongly conductive. Therefore, the ions must be more attracted to each other than they are to polar water. The fact that the solutions are somewhat conductive indicates that the substances do dissociate to some extent (*Chemistry* 8th ed. pages 132–136/9th ed. pages 141–145). LO 2.14

57. **Answer: C** $Ag_2CO_3 \rightarrow 2\,Ag^+ + CO_3^{2-}$

Silver nitrate contains Ag^+, a common ion, so this will suppress solubility. Sodium carbonate contains the carbonate ion, a common ion and so this will also suppress solubility.

Calcium nitrate is soluble and will release Ca^{+2}, which reacts with the carbonate ion to form insoluble calcium carbonate. This will increase solubility because the carbonate ion will be removed from solution (*Chemistry* 8th ed. pages 606–613, 620–626/9th ed. pages 618–626, 633–639). LO 6.23

58. ANSWER: B Review definitions of acids and of pH (*Chemistry* 8th ed. pages 647–650/9th ed. pages 661–664). LO 6.12

59. ANSWER: A The arrow must point down to show emission and the largest difference corresponds to the greatest difference in energy which means highest frequency and shortest wavelength (*Chemistry* 8th ed. pages 294–300/9th ed. pages 305–310). LO 1.6

60. ANSWER: D Change the sign for the oxidation at the anode and add the two half-cell potentials

$$+2.89 - 0.14 \text{ V} = +2.75 \text{ V}$$

(*Chemistry* 8th ed. pages 876–883/9th ed. pages 894–902). LO 3.12

SECTION II: FREE-RESPONSE QUESTIONS

Question 1: Answers

(a)

$$Q = \frac{P_{PCl_5}}{P_{PCl_3} \times P_{Cl_2}} = \frac{0.10}{(0.30)(0.60)} = 0.56$$

Since 0.56 (*Q*) > 0.0870 (*K*), the reaction proceeds to the left.

(b)

	$PCl_3(g)$	+	$Cl_2(g)$	⇌	$PCl_5(g)$
Initial	0.30 atm		0.60 atm		0.10 atm
Change	$+x$		$+x$		$-x$
Equil	$(0.30 + x)$ atm		$(0.60 + x)$ atm		$(0.10 - x)$

Since the reaction proceeds to the left, PCl_5 must decrease and the reactants increase.

$$K_p = 0.0870 = \frac{(0.10 - x)}{(0.30 + x)(0.60 + x)} = \frac{(0.10 - x)}{0.18 + 0.90x + x^2}$$

Using the quadratic equation and solving for *x*, *x* = 0.078.
Therefore, at equilibrium, $P_{PCl_5} = (0.10 - 0.078) = 0.022$ atm $= 0.02$ atm

$$P_{PCl_3} = (0.30 + 0.078) = 0.378 \text{ atm} = 0.38 \text{ atm}$$

$$P_{PCl_2} = (0.60 + 0.078) = 0.678 \text{ atm} = 0.68 \text{ atm}$$

(c) Increasing the volume of the container favors the process where more moles of gas are produced, so the reverse reaction is favored; the equilibrium shifts to the left; the mole fraction of PCl_5 decreases.

(d) For an exothermic reaction decreasing the temperature increases the value of *K*, favoring the products. The partial pressure of PCl_5 increases. Decreasing the

temperature always favors the exothermic direction of a reaction, and increasing the temperature favors the endothermic direction
(*Chemistry* 8th ed. pages 601–604, 606–626/9th ed. pages 614–616, 618–639). LO 6.4, LO 6.8

Question 2: Answers

(a) pH = 1.83 [H⁺] = 1.5 × 10⁻² *M*

So percent ionized = $\dfrac{0.015 \times 100}{0.495}$ = 3.0%

(b)

$$K_a = \frac{[H^+][NO_2^-]}{[HNO_2]} = \frac{(1.5 \times 10^{-2})^2}{0.495} = 4.5 \times 10^{-4}$$

The answer will vary slightly if the ionized acid is subtracted from the initial amount of acid present.

$$K_a = \frac{(1.5 \times 10^{-2})^2}{0.480} = 4.7 \times 10^{-4}$$

(c)

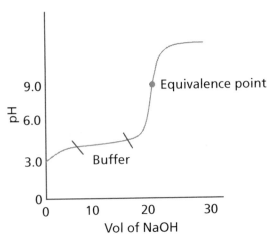

(*Chemistry* 8th ed. pages 713–733/9th ed. pages 727–747). LO 6.4, LO 6.12, LO 6.13

Question 3: Answers

(a)

$$Fe^{2+} + 2\,e^- \rightarrow Fe \qquad E^\circ_{red} = -0.44 \text{ V}$$
$$2(Ag \rightarrow Ag^+ + e^-) \qquad E^\circ_{oxid} = -0.80 \text{ V}$$
_____
$$Fe^{2+} + 2\,Ag \rightarrow 2\,Ag^+ + Fe \qquad E^\circ = -1.24 \text{ V}$$

(b) The reaction is not spontaneous because $E^\circ < 0$.

(c) $E = 0$ for any reaction at equilibrium.

(d) You can calculate log *K* by using the equation

$$\log K = \left(\frac{nE^\circ}{0.0592 \text{ V}}\right)V$$

$$= \frac{2(-1.24 \text{ V})}{(0.0592 \text{ V})} = -42.0$$

Taking the antilog of both sides yields $K = 1.0 \times 10^{-42}$

(e) The reaction that is spontaneous is the reverse of the one above, with $E = 1.24$ V.
$W_{max} = -nFE = -(2 \text{ mol e}^-)(96{,}500 \text{ C mol}^{-1})(1.24 \text{ V})(1\text{J C}^{-1}\text{V}^{-1}) = 2.39 \times 10^5$ J
(*Chemistry* 8th ed. pages 833–842/9th ed. pages 849–858). LO 3.12

Question 4: Answers

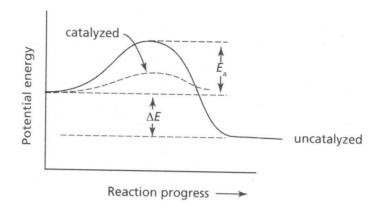

(a) Collision theory postulates that molecules must collide in order to react, and that not all collisions lead to reactions. Only when molecules with sufficient kinetic energy collide will there be enough energy to go over the activation energy barrier and create products. In addition, the reactants must approach each other in the proper orientation in order for the collision to result in product formation. Increasing the temperature increases the rate of reaction by increasing the fraction of molecules that have sufficient kinetic energy to overcome the energy barrier (*Chemistry* 8th ed. pages 565–568/9th ed. pages 577–581). LO 4.6

(b) Using a catalyst speeds the rate of reaction by lowering the activation energy barrier, thus increasing the number of collisions with sufficient energy to form products. A catalyst does this by providing a different reaction route, and it is not consumed in the course of the reaction (*Chemistry* 8th ed. pages 570–575/9th ed. pages 583–587). LO 4.9

Question 5: Answers

The net ionic equations for the identification reactions are:

$CaCO_3(s) + 2 H^+(aq) \rightarrow CO_2(g) + H_2O(l) + Ca^{2+}(aq)$

$NaHCO_3(s) + H^+(aq) \rightarrow CO_2(g) + H_2O(l) + Na^+(aq)$

$Mg(OH)_2(s) + 2 H^+(aq) \rightarrow 2 H_2O(l) + Mg^{2+}(aq)$

Add water to each solid. The calcium sulfate and the calcium carbonate will be insoluble; however, the magnesium hydroxide and sodium bicarbonate will each be soluble to some degree. Then add the acid to a sample of each insoluble solid; the one which produces bubbles of gas (carbon dioxide) is the calcium carbonate. Then take a sample of each solid that dissolved in water and add acid to each one. The sodium bicarbonate will also produce bubbles of gas (carbon dioxide). The magnesium hydroxide will react with the acid and increase in solubility, but will not produce any gaseous products (*Chemistry* 8th ed. pages 154–160, 218–219, 732/9th ed. pages 163–170, 228–229, 746). LO 2.22

Question 6: Answers

N can form three bonds (NF_3) but not five (NF_5) because it lacks d orbitals that are energetically available for the formation of hybrid orbitals (or alternatively, because it is too small to accommodate five atoms). Both NF_3 and PF_3 are trigonal pyramidal because the central atom has three bonding pairs and one lone pair of electrons. PF_5 is trigonal bipyramidal because it has five bonding pairs.

NF₃   PF₃

F–N–F   F–P–F
  F   F

4 e⁻ pairs
trigonal pyramidal

PF₅

F–P–F

(*Chemistry* 8th ed. pages 378–388, 404–407, 410–411, 932–933/9th ed. pages 389–399, 416–419, 422–423, 952). LO 2.21

Question 7: Answers

Coulomb's law states that the force of attraction between two oppositely charged particles is directly proportional to the product of the absolute value of the charges, and inversely proportional to distance between the ion centers.

$$E = (2.31 \times 10^{-19} \text{ J} \bullet \text{nm}) \left(\frac{Q_1 Q_2}{r} \right)$$

Because of their charges, Ca^{2+} and O^{2-} ions are attracted about four times more strongly than K^+ and F^- ions. Ca^{+2} is smaller than K^+ because it has more protons pulling on the same number of electrons (greater Z_{eff}). Even though O^{2-} is somewhat larger than F^-, overall the calcium-to-oxygen distance is less than the potassium-to-fluoride distance, leading to a smaller distance between ion centers in CaO. Therefore, CaO has a larger numerator and smaller denominator, and a lower solubility than KF (*Chemistry* 8th ed. pages 341–342/9th ed. pages 352–353). LO 2.14

SCORING THE FREE-RESPONSE QUESTIONS

It is difficult to come up with an exact score for this section of test. However, if you compare your answers to the answers in this book, remembering that each part of the test you answer correctly is worth points even if the other parts of the answer are incorrect (see the section titled "Types of Free-Response Questions" on page 12 of this book), you can get a general idea of the percentage of the questions for which you would get credit. If you believe that you got at least one-third of the possible credit, you would probably receive a 3 on this part of the test. If you believe that you would receive close to half or more of the available credit, your score would more likely be a 4 or a 5.

INTERPRETERS AND TRANSLATORS IN COMMUNICATION DISORDERS

A Practitioner's Handbook

Henriette W. Langdon, EdD

THINKING PUBLICATIONS®

09 08 07 06 05   8 7 6 5 4 3 2

Library of Congress Cataloging-in-Publication Data

Langdon, Henriette W., date.
        Interpreters and translators in communication disorders : a practitioner's
        handbook/Henriette W. Langdon.
           p. cm.
        Includes bibliographical references.
        ISBN 1-888222-89-1 (pbk.)
           1. Communicative disorders—Patients—Rehabilitation. 2. Translators. I. Title.

     RC423 .L328 2002
     616.85'5—dc21

                                                            2002022169

Printed in the United States of America
Cover design by Kristin Kulig Sosalla

THINKING
PUBLICATIONS®
A Division of McKinley Companies, Inc.
424 Galloway Street • Eau Claire, WI 54703
715.832.2488 • Fax 715.832.9082
Email: custserv@ThinkingPublications.com

COMMUNICATION SOLUTIONS THAT CHANGE LIVES®

To Linda Halog, Michele Sánchez-Boyce, and Vicki Siegel
who helped me initiate and disseminate information on this topic
many years ago.

ABOUT THE AUTHOR

Henriette W. Langdon, EdD, CCC-SLP, is an associate professor at San José State University in the Communicative Disorders and Sciences Department and is a fellow of the American Speech-Language-Hearing Association (ASHA). Henriette has more than 25 years of experience working with bilingual students who have a variety of speech, language, and learning disabilities. She has published several papers, book chapters, and books and has presented on this topic at state, national, and international levels. As a speaker of four different languages, one of her interests is the process of interpreting and translating and its relationship to practice in the fields of speech-language pathology and audiology.

CONTENTS

LIST OF FIGURES AND TABLES

Figures

Tables

PREFACE

This handbook was written specifically for you, the interpreter and translator, who will be collaborating with communication disorders professionals (i.e., speech-language pathologists and/or audiologists). The handbook includes strategies and helpful information that is organized into five sessions. Four of the five sessions also include case studies for practice. A glossary of 100⁺ terms is included to facilitate learning new terminology.

The strategies outlined in this handbook and the content included in the companion book by Langdon and Cheng (*Collaborating with Interpreters and Translators: A Guide for Communication Disorders Professionals,* 2002) are based on practices followed in other professions where services from interpreters and translators are needed, such as deaf interpreting, conference interpreting, and medical and court interpreting. The interpreting and translating process is very complex, and very few people appreciate the many responsibilities and roles of interpreters and translators. Interpreters and translators are the bridge, connecting communication between parties who do not share the same language. Without your help, communication between these two parties would not be possible.

My hope is that the content of his handbook will be useful in your work. I would like to hear from you about how this handbook was useful and how I might improve its content in future editions. You can write to me at *hlangdon@email.sjsu.edu* or through the publisher, Thinking Publications.

ACKNOWLEDGMENTS

This handbook could not have been completed without the support and feedback of many people whose backgrounds include interpreting (oral and sign) as well as working in special education (speech-language pathologists and psychologists). Thank you Vivian Amador, Bilingual Speech-Language Pathologist, Li-Rong Lilly Cheng, Professor of Communicative Disorders, Diane Hijos Di Bari, Bilingual Psychologist, Ellen Lamberth, Bilingual Speech-Language Pathologist, Margarita L. Murillo, Interpreter and Translator, and Neva J. Turoff, Interpreter for the Deaf, for taking the time to read earlier drafts of this handbook and for providing helpful comments to make the manual more readable. June McCullough, Professor of Audiology, offered much appreciated supplemental information and feedback.

The publication of the manual could not have become a reality without the help and resources from three people who were instrumental in accepting the project and providing invaluable editorial comments and immeasurable assistance: Nancy McKinley, Editor in Chief of Thinking Publications, and Editors Joyce Olson and Heather Johnson Schmitz. Your assistance, precision, care, and encouragement provided very needed energy in completing this project. I also appreciate the helpful editorial comments from Elisabeth Wiig, William Prather, and Mary Blake Huer. Dzieskuje, Gracias, Merci, and Thank You!

THE INTERPRETING AND TRANSLATING PROCESS

In this session, you will learn:

- Definitions and types of interpreting and translating

- The roles and responsibilities of interpreters and translators

- A code of ethics for interpreters and translators working with communication disorders professionals

- The skills needed by interpreters and translators practicing in communication disorders

- How to facilitate the interpreting and translating process

- Tips for successful interpreting and translating

- Basic knowledge about the speech-language pathology field

- Basic knowledge about the audiology field

- A code of ethics for communication disorders professionals working with interpreters and translators

- How to refine your skills through translation exercises

INTRODUCTION

Your role as an interpreter or translator is essential to the success of speech-language pathologists and audiologists working with clients who are culturally/linguistically diverse (CLD). In this first session, you will learn about your role as an interpreter or translator and the skills you will need in a variety of clinical and educational settings. You will also learn about the fields of speech-language pathology and audiology and what to expect when working with professionals in those fields. Ethical practices are important for you and for professionals in communication disorders, and guidelines are provided for both roles. You will also have the opportunity to begin translating common statements used with a variety of clients. This session provides you with skills that will be used in every interaction you have with a communication disorders professional.

SELF-ASSESSMENT ITEMS

1. Compare and contrast interpreting and translating. Which required skills are your strengths and which do you need more practice with?

2. Refer to the code of ethics for interpreters and translators (see page 5). Select one item and identify potential negative effects of not following the code.

3. Describe the way(s) you expand your knowledge of professional terminology.

4. The communication disorders professional knows how and why to avoid idiomatic expressions, but a family may not. What will you say to a family member who uses idiomatic expressions?

5. Identify at least three pieces of information you would want to learn about before beginning an interpreting session with a speech-language pathologist and your reasons for needing this information.

6. Based on your knowledge of an audiologist's responsibilities, do you believe interpreting services would be used more often during assessment or during interviews and conferences? Why?

7. Select an item from the code of ethics for communication disorders professionals working with interpreters and translators. How would you address a problem that arises if the communication disorders professional does not follow that guideline?

8. Refer to the translation exercises on pages 16–17. Which sentences were easier? Which were more difficult? Please state why.

SUGGESTED READINGS AND RESOURCES

Baker, C. (2001). *A parents' and teachers' guide to bilingualism*. Clevedon, England: Multilingual Matters.

This book discusses various issues that concern parents who are raising their children bilingually. The book is written in an easy-to-read question/answer format. A Spanish version of the book is available, translated by Alma Flor Ada.

Carr, S.E., Roberts, R., Dufour, A., and Steyn, D. (Eds.). (1997). *The critical link: Interpreters in the community*. Philadelphia: Johns Benjamins.

The daily duties and responsibilities of interpreters and translators in the community are discussed by various authors. The content focuses on various roles played by the interpreter/translator in several sectors, such as the courts and medical professions. Training issues are also discussed from perspectives of the interpreter, the professional, and the consumer.

Lustig, M.W., and Koester, J. (1999). *Intercultural competence: Interpersonal communication across cultures*. New York: Longman.

Helpful information on understanding and facilitating communication across various cultural and linguistic groups is discussed in this book.

Nicolosi, L., Harryman, E., and Kresheck, J. (Eds.). (1996). *Terminology of communication disorders*. Baltimore: Williams and Wilkins.

This dictionary includes a comprehensive list of terms used in the field of communication disorders and many diagrams. The book includes tables on various topics, such as descriptions and implications of various hearing impairments, speech-language milestones, and lists of various tests used in speech-language pathology and audiology.

INTERPRETING AND TRANSLATING TERMINOLOGY

Interpreting involves orally transmitting the same message from the first language to the second language. *Translating* involves transmitting the same written message from the first language to the second language.

Interpreting is considered to be more demanding than translating because the interpreter needs to continually shift from the first language to the second language and vice versa. Interpretation takes place during interviews, conferences, assessments, and intervention. Interpreters must have knowledge and use of specific vocabulary, good auditory memory, and the ability to respond quickly while under pressure. There are two types of interpreting:

- **Consecutive interpreting** involves transmitting segments of a speaker's message while the speaker pauses for the interpreting to be carried out. The segments that are conveyed should be neither too long nor too short to be well understood. In consecutive interpreting, there is lag time between what is said by each speaker. This is the most frequent type of interpreting used in clinical settings.

- **Simultaneous interpreting** involves interpreting the message from one language to the other without lag time. This method is used primarily in the international relations field. An interpreter may want to use this method in clinical settings to keep the meeting flowing without interruption.

Using either type of interpretation, the interpreter may whisper the interpretation to the parents or family members as the meeting is proceeding if it can be done without disrupting communication.

Translation is used to transmit information from letters and documents or from formal and informal tests. Knowledge of specific vocabulary is necessary for translation. Translation speed is important in some cases (e.g., when the translator is asked to translate a written document orally). There are two types of translation:

- **Prepared translation** involves preparing a written version of any type of document, such as a letter or a report, in advance. This is the most common type of translating in communication disorders settings.

- **Sight translation** involves providing a spoken translation while reading a written document. Fewer formal terms and structures are used in sight translation than in prepared translation.

WHAT YOU SHOULD KNOW ABOUT INTERPRETERS AND TRANSLATORS

The interpreter's or translator's responsibility is to bridge communication in various contexts between parties who do not share the same language. Consider the following list of roles and responsibilities. Table 1.1 provides a summary of dos and don'ts.

- **Maintain neutrality.** Remain neutral about the behaviors and statements conveyed by all parties involved in the interpreting process. No value judgments should be made about a person's beliefs, practices, or skills. Maintaining neutrality also means not becoming actively involved in a situation. You may be tempted to take on an advocacy role or to provide advice to a client or a family member. However, your role is to represent the other speaker's meanings, not to interject your own ideas.

- **Respect confidentiality.** All information shared during a session must remain behind when you leave. Information learned during interpretation or translation should not be used or shared with others outside the professional setting.

- **Interpret faithfully.** Serve as a bridge between two or more parties and interpret everything that is said, including offensive and negative remarks. You must interpret all that is said or expressed, including both verbal and nonverbal messages, as accurately as possible in order to convey the underlying meaning.

- **Participate in ongoing learning and remain flexible.** Respond positively to constructive criticism to increase success on the job. Continue to update your knowledge about procedures to follow in a given work setting, and follow up on suggestions made by the communication disorders professionals you work with. Identify areas where you need more training, and ask for assistance in locating sources of information or training.

Table 1.1 **Dos and Don'ts of Interpreter's and Translator's Roles**

Do	Don't
Remain neutral.	Take over the role of the professional or make judgments.
Respect confidentiality.	Discuss a case outside a given setting.
Interpret faithfully.	Add or leave out information.
Become a lifelong learner.	Accept jobs that are too difficult.

CODE OF ETHICS FOR INTERPRETERS AND TRANSLATORS WORKING IN COMMUNICATION DISORDERS

1. Be certified through formal training.

2. Accept work or assignments only where linguistically and culturally competent.

3. Be adequately prepared for a given assignment.

4. Interpret the message, the material, or the interaction accurately.

5. Keep the information conveyed confidential.

6. Ask for clarification from the speech-language pathologist or audiologist, the client, the parent, the family member, or any other participant if uncertain about the meaning of a message, document, or interaction.

7. Decline a job where there might be a conflict of interest.

8. Refrain from providing independent advice or information without consultation or guidance from the communication disorders professional.

9. Be punctual in responding to various assignments or attending meetings.

10. Show respect for all parties involved.

11. Continue professional development in the field of interpretation or translation and in aspects of speech-language pathology and audiology.

From *Collaborating with Interpreters and Translators: A Guide for Communication Disorders Professionals* (p. 110), by H.W. Langdon and L.L. Cheng, 2002, Eau Claire, WI: Thinking Publications. © 2002 by Thinking Publications. Reprinted with permission.

SKILLS NEEDED TO INTERPRET AND TRANSLATE IN COMMUNICATION DISORDERS

Six linguistic skills are needed to ensure that you can successfully bridge the communication between two parties who do not share the same language (Langdon and Cheng, 2002). Several procedural skills are also necessary. Both types of skills are listed in the following sections.

Linguistic Skills

- **Oral and written proficiency with two languages**—You must understand and speak both languages fluently and at a normal rate. You must also have accurate written language skills, including grammar and spelling, for both languages.

- **Knowledge of two cultures and nonverbal communication**—You must be sensitive to social and cultural variations, including dialectal variations, pronunciation differences, and paralinguistic messages (e.g., intonation, use of gestures, and facial expressions). You must also be sensitive to differences that are tied to a given culture and that may affect the client's understanding of procedures, interpretation of assessment results, or acceptance of medical and educational labels. Common cultural differences fall in the areas of child-rearing practices, beliefs, and understanding the roles of parents and families in carrying out communication disorders professionals' suggestions and recommendations.

- **Ability to convey the same meaning in two languages**—When interpreting or translating, you must convey messages without changing the meaning. A word-by-word translation or interpretation cannot convey the same meaning because grammar and word use are different in each language. For example, translation of a Spanish statement that means "Would you please sign this assessment plan" would become "Do me the favor of signing this plan of assessment" with a word-by-word translation.

- **Knowledge of professional terminology**—You should be familiar with specific terminology and procedures used in speech-language pathology and audiology to perform with greater speed and accuracy. When a word does not exist in a language, a definition for a given concept may be necessary.

- **Familiarity with dialectal differences**—You must be aware of potential dialectal variations of a language. Vocabulary differences may lead to confusion of word meanings. Differences in grammar or speech sounds may be misinterpreted as errors.

- **Ability to adapt to the speech and language of people with communication disorders**—You need to use careful listening skills when working with people who have communication disorders. A client may present varying degrees of challenges in comprehending and expressing information. Quite often, a client's pronunciation of words may be difficult to understand due to misarticulation or sound omission, both of which interfere with intelligibility. During assessments, pay very close attention and transcribe what the client says verbatim; do not edit what is said and do not change sounds. (Note: You will need to explain to speech-language pathologists what is said versus what should have been said.)

Procedural Skills

- **Familiarity with specific procedures followed in each job setting—** You must be familiar with procedures followed by the specialties of speech-language pathology and audiology. Procedures vary between school and clinical settings. Ask the communication disorders professional you work with for clarification of procedures as needed; never make assumptions about procedures.

- **Understanding of your function and role**—You must remain neutral and accurate in your communications. Your responsibilities may be redefined as your relationship with the communication disorders professional develops. Remember to function within the guidelines of the code of ethics (see page 5) at all times.

- **Flexibility**—You must be able to work with a variety of people with all sorts of personalities and levels of education. In all cases, you should be patient and respectful. Flexibility is also required when called on to provide services with short notice or no advance preparation time.

Notes

_____

_____

_____

_____

_____

_____

_____

_____

_____

_____

_____

FACILITATING THE INTERPRETING AND TRANSLATING PROCESS

As you engage in interpreting or translating for interviews, conferences, assessments, or intervention, you must remember your role in facilitating the communication process. Keep the following strategies in mind:

- **Maintain a continual dialogue during all phases of the process.** Request that the communication disorders professional provide ongoing supportive feedback to you and stress the importance of his or her participation in the process. (See Session 5 for specific evaluation forms.) Encourage the communication disorders professional to support your development as a well-informed member of the team. Resist the occasional desire to provide advice or advocacy for a client or family. Instead, discuss any needs you observe with the communication disorders professional so assistance can be provided through appropriate channels.

- **Keep grammatical constructions as simple as possible.** Help the communication disorders professional understand that an interpretation or translation can only be as good as what the original speaker says or writes. Ask the communication disorders professional to use language that is easy to understand and translate. Request that lengthy and complex sentences be avoided.

- **Remain as clear as possible.** Ask the communication disorders professional to keep the use of prepositions, conjunctions, and other function words to a minimum. The communication disorders professional needs to convey ideas clearly, one idea at a time, checking regularly to make sure the message has been understood. Speech rate should be neither too fast nor too slow.

- **Avoid idiomatic expressions.** Monitor for idioms and explain why they should be avoided. *Idioms* use one or more words that have a figurative meaning (e.g., *pull one's hair out* or *talk one's ear off*). The intended meaning is often lost in a literal translation, and it is difficult for nonnative speakers to memorize and quickly recall meanings of idioms.

- **Define professional terms.** Professional terms such as *auditory processing skills*, *visual motor integration*, or *percentile* may have no equivalent words in other languages. To be clear, the term should be followed by a definition and a concrete example applicable to the home or work context. The definition and example should be provided by the speech-language pathologist or the audiologist, not by you. Ask for a definition and an example if one is not forthcoming.

- **Watch for indicators of translation difficulty.** Join everyone in the interpretation or translation process in watching for indicators of difficulty. For example, you may see a puzzled expression that may signal that what was said was too long or too complex or that a response does not coincide with the original question or statement. Avoid assuming the meaning of nonverbal communication, which may vary widely due to cultural and individual differences. For example, a smile may indicate embarrassment, friendliness, or warning of tension (Lustig and Koester, 1999). When in doubt, it is the communication disorders professional's responsibility to ensure that what is said is clear and understandable to all parties involved.

- **Address the client directly.** Position yourself so the speech-language pathologist or audiologist can face the client and his or her family and address all comments directly to them. Maintaining eye contact facilitates more direct communication and helps the professional establish rapport with the client.

- **Maintain linguistic skills.** Constantly refine the six skills cited previously (see pages 6–7) that are necessary to successfully bridge the communication between two parties who do not share the same language: (1) oral and written proficiency with two languages, (2) knowledge of two cultures and nonverbal communication, (3) ability to convey the same meaning in two languages, (4) knowledge of professional terminology, (5) familiarity with dialectal differences, and (6) ability to adapt to the speech and language of people with communication disorders.

Notes

_____

_____

_____

_____

_____

_____

_____

_____

_____

_____

_____

_____

TIPS FOR SUCCESSFUL INTERPRETING AND TRANSLATING

Keep these tips in mind during all phases of the interpreting and translating process:

- Listen and read carefully to convey accurate messages.

- Take notes and review the information if necessary.

- Ask for repetition or clarification whenever necessary.

- When in doubt about meaning, consult a dictionary.

- Be aware of dialectal differences in word meaning.

- Confirm accuracy of translated documents by translating the second language version back into the first language and comparing it to the original (also called *back translation*).

- Assist in identifying culturally biased items or situations.

- Support the communication disorders professional as the person responsible.

Notes

_____

_____

_____

_____

_____

_____

_____

_____

_____

_____

_____

_____

WHAT YOU SHOULD KNOW ABOUT SPEECH-LANGUAGE PATHOLOGY

Job Responsibilities of Speech-Language Pathologists

The job responsibilities of a speech-language pathologist that most directly affect your interpretation or translation work include the following:

- Identify and assess clients of various ages who have one or more challenges in communicating adequately.

- Plan and implement intervention programs for individuals who have communication challenges (e.g., difficulties in articulating sounds; fluency challenges [stuttering]; difficulties using adequate voice pitch, stress, or loudness; and challenges in performing adequately in tasks requiring reading and writing.

- Conduct interviews and conferences with clients and their parents or families to obtain additional information to facilitate the assessment or intervention plan.

- Collaborate with other professionals to enhance the success of the intervention plan.

Interviews or Conferences

An interview or a conference follows a certain format. Specific topics are covered in each situation. Most typically, information about a client's difficulty is collected during an interview. Results of an assessment or intervention are discussed during a conference.

The use of specific vocabulary is needed when conducting an interview or a conference. For example, during an interview, the speech-language pathologist might bring up medical issues that relate to information about birth and early infancy history as well as motor and speech developmental milestones. During a conference, the speech-language pathologist reports the results of an assessment or intervention and may use many other terms related to the profession. Refer to the Glossary to begin learning specific terms.

Assessment and Intervention

Various types of tests exist (e.g., normed, criterion-referenced, and inventories). Speech-language pathologists choose tests based on their purpose and their usefulness with various age groups or suspected disabilities. Each type of test has limitations on its usefulness, so the communication disorders professional may use a variety of instruments to develop a fuller picture of the client's disabilities. The speech-language pathologist you work with will teach you what you need to know regarding various methods of assessment.

Specific assessment techniques and instrumentation are used in the various job contexts where your services are needed. Certain procedures are more common in a clinical hospital setting, such as feeding techniques, endoscopy, radiographic studies, use of oral manometer, use of stroboscopy to assess voice quality, and various devices and prostheses that may be used for larnygectomee patients. Computerized therapy materials and augmentative communication devices are used with greater frequency in educational settings. Again, the speech-language pathologist you work with will help you learn the language needed for the setting; ask for help if none is forthcoming.

Paperwork Procedures

The success of the interpreting or translating process is enhanced if you are familiar with the admission and dismissal procedures and the paperwork involved in a school, hospital, clinic, or rehabilitation center. Understanding the referral, assessment, and conference process related to the development of an individualized family service plan (IFSP) for a newborn to 3-year-old child or an individualized education program (IEP) for a 3–21 year old enhances the efficiency of your job performance. Your speech-language pathologist is responsible for teaching you the specific information you will need to be successful in each setting.

Notes

WHAT YOU SHOULD KNOW ABOUT AUDIOLOGY

Job Responsibilities of an Audiologist

The job responsibilities of an audiologist that directly affect your interpretation or translation work include the following:

- Assess and identify clients of various ages who have one or more challenges in hearing or processing linguistic information.

- Conduct a variety of sessions to interview clients and their families, to counsel them regarding the use of hearing aids and devices, and to suggest specific educational programs for hearing impaired individuals.

- Collaborate with other professionals to enhance the success of assessment and intervention plans.

Interviews or Conferences

Specific issues are addressed in each type of context. For example, during an interview, the audiologist asks questions about the extent of the hearing problem and its possible origin, asks about the situations where the client feels most uncomfortable, and collects pertinent background medical history. If hearing aids are prescribed, the audiologist has a conference with the client to discuss recommendations regarding the use of the hearing aids and the best learning and communication environment for the client.

The audiologist uses specific vocabulary related to this specialty. Your understanding of these terms is important in facilitating the interpreting or translating process. Refer to the Glossary to begin learning specific terms.

Assessment and Intervention

Many types of tests are used (e.g., pure tone, air and bone conduction, auditory brainstem response [ABR], speech discrimination, speech reception, tympanogram, and acoustic impedance). Test results may be recorded on an audiogram or other report formats. The kinds of hearing losses that are identified may involve deafness, conductive hearing loss due to otitis media, sensorineural hearing loss, tinnitus, otosclerosis, and presbycusis.

Intervention may involve a session to fit a hearing aid and to explain its use and care, followed by one or more return visits to check on its effectiveness. In schools, the audiologist may participate in an annual IEP meeting to update information on the student's needs and progress and make recommendations for the following year.

Paperwork Procedures

The success of the interpreting or translating process is enhanced if you are familiar with the admission and dismissal procedures and paperwork involved in a school, hospital, clinic, or rehabilitation center. Understanding the referral, assessment, and conference process related to the development of an IFSP for a newborn to 3-year-old child or an IEP for a 3–21 year old enhances the efficiency of your job performance.

Notes

CODE OF ETHICS
FOR COMMUNICATION DISORDERS PROFESSIONALS
WORKING WITH INTERPRETERS OR TRANSLATORS

You may find it helpful to know the contents of the code of ethics for speech-language pathologists and audiologists with regard to the use of interpreters and translators.

1. Have knowledge of bilingual language development and assessment and intervention issues.

2. Work with a trained interpreter or translator only.

3. Continue to update knowledge through continuing education in the field of bilingualism, including assessment of and intervention with bilingual speakers.

4. Adequately prepare the interpreter or translator for a given conference, assessment, or intervention.

5. Participate in improving the process of working with the interpreter or translator.

6. Document successful strategies in working with the interpreter or translator to serve bilingual clients more equitably.

A complete code of ethics for the entire scope of practice can be found on the American Speech-Language-Hearing Association (ASHA) website (*http://professional.asha.org/*).

From *Collaborating with Interpreters and Translators: A Guide for Communication Disorders Professionals* (p. 94), by H.W. Langdon and L.L. Cheng, 2002, Eau Claire, WI: Thinking Publications. © 2002 by Thinking Publications. Adapted with permission.

TRANSLATION EXERCISES

The following are common sentences used by communication disorders professionals during various types of conferences or interviews and during the assessment process. They are listed here so that you can practice relating them both orally and in writing.

Conferences or Interviews

With Children

- When did you first notice that your child had a speech/language/hearing problem?

- Do you feel your child has difficulty understanding oral directions? For example, if you ask him or her something, does he or she stare at you rather than do it?

- Students with speech and language impairments have a primary problem in either the understanding or the expression of oral language.

- An individualized education program (IEP) can be implemented only after the parent has given written consent for placement in special education.

- A student should receive special education in the least restrictive environment (LRE).

With Adults

- Tell me a little about your husband's daily activities and his hobbies.

- Tell me about your job before you had your accident.

- The type of stroke you had will limit the use of your right hand for some time.

- Who are the primary people that you need to communicate with everyday at your job?

- Do you have problems understanding the newspaper?

With Clients Who Have Hearing Impairments

- This audiogram shows that your child has a conductive hearing loss in the left ear in the low frequencies. You need to see the physician to seek medical management.

- This type of hearing aid will be best for the hearing loss that you have. You need to adjust the volume between 4 and 5 to get the best results.

- I am afraid that you have the type of hearing loss that is typical for people who are in your age bracket.

- When you communicate with your spouse, you should be sure that the TV is not on at a high volume.

- There is an excessive accumulation of wax in your ears. Make sure you visit us regularly to have it removed.

Assessment

With Clients Who Have Hearing Impairments

- Please put the headphones on your ears.

- Please repeat these phrases after me.

- When you hear a signal, raise your hand, even if it is very soft like this one.

- Put the block in the box when you hear a beep, even if it is as soft as this.

- Tell me if these two words sound the same or different.

With Clients Who Have Speech-Language Disorders

- After you look at this book with pictures, I want you to tell me a story about what is happening.

- I want you to complete the following sentences. Please remember that I can say the information only once.

- I am going to read you something. After I finish, I am going to ask you some questions to find out how much you can remember.

- I want you to name these colors and figures as fast as you can. Go.

- Point to the picture that goes with the word I say.

Notes

_____

_____

_____

_____

_____

_____

_____

_____

_____

CASE STUDIES TO PRACTICE INTERPRETING SKILLS

Meetings

1. Select Case 1.1 or 1.2 to use with your team. Scripts are excerpted from longer interactions.

2. Make sure that each team includes the members identified in the script plus one or more observers/evaluators.

3. Decide if you will use consecutive or simultaneous interpreting during the role-playing.

4. Perform the role-playing, following the script.

5. Have role players and observers/evaluators discuss the effectiveness of the interaction. Discuss how role players decided where to stop to enable the interpreter to communicate the information in the other language.

6. Role-play case 1.3 once with simultaneous whispered interpreting and then with consecutive interpreting. Discuss the advantages and disadvantages of each method.

Sight Translation

1. The information provided in Case 1.4 is from a printed notice about parent and child rights in special education (Wisconsin Department of Public Instruction, 2002). Use this information to role-play an interaction explaining these rights to a parent whose child has recently been referred for an evaluation.

2. Assign team members to be the parent, interpreter, and speech-language pathologist. One or more others may be assigned as observers/evaluators.

3. Decide the format of the conference. Should the speech-language pathologist present the information with interpreter assistance, or should the interpreter be taught how to present this information directly?

4. Role-play the conference, making sure the parent understands the rights.

5. Role players and observers/evaluators discuss the effectiveness of the interaction.

Case 1.1: Meeting to Write an Annual IEP

Team Members: parent, interpreter, and speech-language pathologist

SPEECH-LANGUAGE PATHOLOGIST: We have been working on helping John understand and remember directions. Do you remember when we talked about how he had trouble following along in class?

PARENT: Yes.

SPEECH-LANGUAGE PATHOLOGIST: We have been having John use a tape recorder at the end of each social studies class. He goes to the back of the room and talks in the recorder about what was covered in class that day. He tells the tape recorder what the assignment is too. It really helps him remember the important ideas if he talks about them right away before he starts doing the assignment. Has he told you about doing this?

PARENT: Yes, but I didn't know why he was doing it.

SPEECH-LANGUAGE PATHOLOGIST: It was to help his memory and to learn the important words and ideas in the lesson. He's getting very good at doing this without help.

PARENT: Is he going to keep doing this?

SPEECH-LANGUAGE PATHOLOGIST: Well, that's what this first goal is about. It's going to be important for him to keep reviewing what he has been listening to. This will help him remember the important points and directions. But it will be better if he can learn to do this without using the tape recorder. So our goal for this year is to help him learn to review the lesson in his head by telling it to himself and jotting down notes of important things to remember before he starts doing the assignment. We'll also want him to notice when he is not sure about what the directions were and ask the teacher for help if he is confused or forgets. It's going to be more important for him to do this when he goes to middle school. Do you have any suggestions or questions about this goal?

PARENT: No. It's fine.

Case 1.2: Consultation Regarding Care of Child's Hearing Aid

Team Members: parent, interpreter, and audiologist

AUDIOLOGIST: Set the hearing aid to the M position like this. Then connect the stethoscope here. OK? You try it.

PARENT: Like this?

AUDIOLOGIST: Yes. That's the way. Now you put on the stethoscope and put the hearing aid volume at the low setting. Start turning the volume control wheel up and listen to make sure that the sound is getting louder. Turn the volume up and down to make sure it's working. Make sure there is no crackling sound or circuit noise. You try it now.

PARENT: *[Looks confused]* What sounds?

AUDIOLOGIST: The sounds or noises are like static on your radio. It might indicate the battery is getting weak. Usually that's the cause of the problem.

PARENT: Then I should change the battery?

AUDIOLOGIST: Yes. And we'll want to teach your child about the noises.

Case 1.3: A Medical Staffing for Patient with Aphasia

Team Members: spouse, interpreter, physician, and speech-language pathologist

PHYSICIAN: The electroencephalogram shows a focal lesion in the left parietal-temporal region. She has no vision in the right visual field. She has a right hemiplegia. Physical therapy reports increased functioning of leg strength and control, but we see that her arm and hand are still very weak. What have you found regarding her speech and language?

SPEECH-LANGUAGE PATHOLOGIST: Her processing is very slow. She understands better when we use short sentences. Speech is about 60% unintelligible, partly due to transpositions of sounds within and between words.

SPOUSE: *[To interpreter]* I don't understand what they are saying.

INTERPRETER: Excuse me. Mr. Garcia has a question.

PHYSICIAN: Go ahead, Mr. Garcia.

Case 1.4: Conference with Parent to Explain Rights in Special Education

Team Members: parent, interpreter, and speech-language pathologist

The school must tell you about decisions about your child's special education. They must tell you in writing a reasonable time before they carry out the decision. When your child reaches 18 years of age, you will continue to receive any required notices. The decisions can be about something the school plans to do. The decisions can be about something the school is refusing to do. The school must tell you before starting or changing your child's identification as a child with a disability. The school must tell you before starting or changing something about your child's evaluation for a disability. They must tell you before starting or changing your child's placement. The school must tell you before starting or changing your child's FAPE. The school must tell you why they plan to do something or refuse to do something. They must tell you about other actions they considered and why they did not choose those. The school must describe each evaluation procedure, test, record, or report they used to make the decision. They must describe any other reason for the decision. They must tell you that you have protection under the procedural safeguards (rights) of special education law. The school must tell you the qualifications of the people who will evaluate your child and their names, if known.

From *Special Education Rights for Parents and Children,* by Wisconsin Department of Public Instruction, January 14, 2002, http://www.dpi.state.wi.us/een/pcrights.html

SESSION 2

COLLABORATION WHEN WORKING WITH CULTURALLY/LINGUISTICALLY DIVERSE (CLD) CLIENTS

In this session, you will learn:

- Environment, seating arrangement, and a protocol to facilitate the flow of interviews and conferences

- How to collect information during an interview

- How to share information during a conference

- The three steps that should take place when collaborating with a communication disorders professional: briefing, interaction, and debriefing (BID)

- The procedure to follow when collaborating with a communication disorders professional to assess: review, interview, observe, and test (RIOT)

- Features of standardized tests affected by language and cultural differences

INTRODUCTION

This session provides guidance for the situations most commonly needing the services of an interpreter or translator in communication disorders: interviews or conferences with clients and their families and assessments of a client's communication performance. The procedures recommended here will help make your interactions with communication disorders professionals as productive as possible. Procedures include the BID process, which will be your guide for preparing in advance for collaborating with the communication disorders professional during interaction with a client, and the RIOT procedure, which will help ensure a complete and accurate client assessment. You will also learn some cautions about using standardized tests so that you understand the need to confer closely with the communication disorders professional when these are translated or administered.

SELF-ASSESSMENT ITEMS

1. When preparing the environment, summarize what you would do differently for a meeting with 3 people versus a meeting with 10 people.

2. Is it important for the communication disorders professional to be present when an interview is conducted in a language other than English? Why?

3. How will you handle side conversations that occur during a conference despite your request that they not happen?

4. Imagine that you are called to a facility whose staff has never used interpreter services. How would you explain the need for following the BID process?

5. Identify the steps of the RIOT procedure where interpreter or translator services are most needed and least needed. Explain your reasoning.

6. Explain why standardized tests should be used with caution for speakers of languages other than English.

SUGGESTED READING AND RESOURCES

Campbell, G.L. (1995). *Compendium of the world's languages*. London: Rouledge.

Almost 100 languages are described in this resource. Descriptions include sounds of the language, its structure and use, and examples.

Cheng, L.L., Langdon, H.W., and Davies, D. (1991). *The art of interpreting: A dynamic process* [Video]. San Diego, CA: Department of Communication Disorders, San Diego State University.

This videotape includes a summary of the interpreting process and illustrations of an interview and a conference with a parent.

Haynes, W.O., Pindzola, R.H., and Emerick. L.L. (1998). Interviewing. In *Diagnosis and evaluation in speech pathology* (5th ed.) (pp. 30–57). Boston: Allyn and Bacon.

This clearly written chapter offers helpful strategies to ensure a successful interview. It includes a checklist that considers many of the points discussed in this chapter, but specific issues pertaining to CLD clients are not addressed.

Langdon, H.W. (in press). *Assessment of English learners with the collaboration of an interpreter/translator* [Video]. Rockville, MD: American Speech-Language-Hearing Association.

This video illustrates procedures that communication disorders professionals should follow step by step in working with an interpreter or a translator to assess clients. Includes examples of working with three Spanish-speaking students ages 8, 9, and 10. The strategies that are illustrated can be applied to any other age and language group.

Shipley, K.G., and McAfee, J.G. (1999). *Assessment in speech-language pathology: A resource manual* (2nd ed.). San Diego, CA: Singular.

This manual describes methods to assess a variety of speech and language disorders. It is written in a very clear manner and includes numerous protocols and charts.

WEBSITE

CultureGrams (*www.CultureGrams.com*)

Provides information on 177 countries' cultural practices.

THE INTERVIEW OR CONFERENCE ENVIRONMENT

Along with the communication disorders professional, and before gathering a group of people, prepare in the following ways:

1. Discuss the purpose of the upcoming meeting.

2. Limit the number of participants to decrease the stress on the client, the parent, and/or the family members and to make your interpreting task more manageable.

3. Find out which disciplines other than communication disorders will be represented at the meeting and if there is specialized terminology you will need to interpret.

4. Make the setting as comfortable and non-threatening as possible.

5. Seat all people so that they are able to make eye contact with each other. However, consider that in some cultures direct eye contact is avoided as a sign of respect.

6. Immediately before the meeting begins, politely ask participants to refrain from side conversations so you are able to interpret everything that is said during the meeting.

7. Avoid being a direct participant in the interaction. All those involved should address their gaze and attention directly to the client, the parent, or the family member.

Use the checklist provided in Figure 2.1 (see page 26) to ensure that these preparation steps and other issues have been considered.

Figure 2.1
Collaborating during Interviews and Conferences: A Checklist

Briefing

Format of the interview or conference is explained	Y	N
Purpose of the interview or conference is explained	Y	N
Critical pieces of information are reviewed	Y	N
Critical questions are reviewed (where applicable)	Y	N
Type of interpreting (consecutive or simultaneous) is discussed	Y	N

Comments: _____

_____

Interaction

Seating arrangement is appropriate	Y	N
Communication disorders professional introduces participants	Y	N
Communication disorders professional defines roles	Y	N
Communication disorders professional states the purpose of the conference	Y	N
Interpreter interprets using "I" instead of "Mr. X says"	Y	N
Interpreter transmits all that the parent says	Y	N
Team maintains eye contact with the parent (if culturally appropriate)	Y	N
Team's language is understandable to the parent	Y	N
Team appears ultimately responsible for the conference procedure, information sharing, and intent	Y	N
Team presents itself as a unit	Y	N
Environment is comfortable	Y	N
Attention is paid to nonverbal cues	Y	N
Interpreter interprets clearly and precisely	Y	N
Interpreter asks for clarification when necessary	Y	N

Figure 2.1—*Continued*

Comments: _____

_____

Debriefing

Was the interview or conference productive?   Y   N

Areas that went well: _____

Areas to emphasize in the future: _____

Comments: _____

_____

_____

_____

_____

From *Collaborating with Interpreters and Translators: A Guide for Communication Disorders Professionals* (pp. 116–117), by H.W. Langdon and L.L. Cheng, 2002, Eau Claire, WI: Thinking Publications. © 2002 by Thinking Publications. Reprinted with permission.

Notes

_____

_____

_____

_____

_____

_____

_____

_____

_____

_____

_____

_____

_____

INTERVIEWS: COLLECTING INFORMATION

Two different questionnaires are provided to interview clients; these questionnaires include examples of typical questions asked during initial interviews, thus allowing you some translation practice. One is for younger clients (Figure 2.2); the other is for adult clients (Figure 2.3; see pages 33–34). The questionnaires can be translated into other languages. Spanish versions are available on the Thinking Publications website (*www.ThinkingPublications.com*). Communication disorders professionals working with other languages are invited to submit to the author versions of questionnaires as well as informal test protocols in the languages they have used with clients.

Ultimately, the communication disorders professional you work with will select the questionnaire that is used; it is not your responsibility to supply one. You will find that useful questionnaires usually include the following types of information:

- Identification, date and place of birth, grade or occupation, and language use

- Educational, occupational, health, and developmental history

- Teachers' and family members' observations of the client's typical day, favorite pastimes, and the effect of the communication problem

Notes

_____

_____

_____

_____

_____

_____

_____

_____

_____

_____

_____

_____

_____

_____

Figure 2.2
Interview of a Child's Family Member

Name: _____

DOB: _____ Age: _____ Grade: _____

Number and age of siblings: _____

Parents' occupation: (M) _____ (F) _____

Parents' highest level of education: (M) _____ (F) _____

Language Use and Preferences

Language(s): _____ Country of origin: _____

Has the child resided in countries where other languages were spoken?   ❑ Yes ❑ No
   Where? _____ When? _____ How long? _____

Describe the child's experiences with other languages: _____
_____

How long has the family resided in the United States?
   Father _____ Mother _____ Child _____

Language(s) of interaction between the child and:
   Father _____ Mother _____ Child _____
   Other family members: _____

Who converses most often with the child at home?   _____

What is the main language used at home (i.e., home language)? _____

Language preference in listening to the radio or watching TV?
   ❑ Home language   ❑ English   ❑ No preference

Language preference for reading and writing (if applicable)?
   ❑ Home language   ❑ English   ❑ No preference

Education

Did the child attend school in country of origin or other countries?
   ❑ Yes   If yes, how many years? _____ ❑ No

How long has the child attended school in the United States? _____

Continued on next page

Figure 2.2—*Continued*

Has the child attended any other U.S. school before this school?   ❏ Yes   ❏ No
  If yes, where and when _____

Type of educational program:
  ❏ Only English—Which grades? _____   ❏ ESL—Which grades? _____
  ❏ Bilingual—Which grades?_____

Did the student attend preschool?   ❏ Yes   ❏ No

Formal education has been   ❏ Continuous   ❏ Interrupted

If interrupted, describe: _____

_____

_____

Any problems at school with: (*circle response*)

Listening to the teacher	Yes	No
Remembering what is taught	Yes	No
Following directions	Yes	No
Finishing homework	Yes	No
Participating in activities	Yes	No
Learning to read	Yes	No
Learning math	Yes	No
Writing	Yes	No
Behavior	Yes	No
Making friends	Yes	No
Expressing ideas clearly	Yes	No
Others understanding child	Yes	No

Health and Developmental Information

Any problems with: (*circle response*)

Pregnancy	Yes	No
Birth process	Yes	No
Hearing	Yes	No
Vision	Yes	No
Allergies	Yes	No
Health	Yes	No
Hospitalizations	Yes	No

Figure 2.2—*Continued*

Born at:　　　　　❑ Home　　　　　❑ Clinic　　　　　❑ Hospital

Birth weight: _____

Comments: _____

_____

Family's Perception of the Child's Language Performance at Home

Have you noticed any difficulties the child has with? *(circle response)*

Understanding　　　Speaking　　　Writing　　　Reading

Home language　　　English

How does the child's speech and language development compare to his or her siblings?

Describe problems: _____

_____

_____

_____

Any problems at home with: *(circle response)*

Following directions	Yes	No
Understanding what others say	Yes	No
Others understanding what child says	Yes	No
Expressing ideas	Yes	No
Behavior	Yes	No
Making friends	Yes	No
Learning new concepts	Yes	No

Describe problems: _____

_____

Do you or any family member: *(circle response)*

Tell the child stories?	Yes	No
Read stories to the child?	Yes	No

Continued on next page

Figure 2.2—*Continued*

Talk about activities ?	Yes	No
Discuss what you saw on TV?	Yes	No

What reading material is available at home for children or adults? _____

_____

Child's interests and favorite pastimes: _____

_____

Briefly describe the child's typical day: _____

_____

_____

_____

_____

Notes: _____

_____

_____

_____

_____

Name and position of person conducting the interview:

_____

Date: _____

Figure 2.3
Adult Interview

Name: _____

DOB: _____ Age: _____

Current occupation: _____ How long? _____

Language Use and Preferences

Language(s): _____ _____Country of origin: _____

How long has the adult resided in the United States? _____

Has the adult resided in countries where other languages were spoken? ❑ Yes ❑ No

Where? _____When? _____How long? _____

Describe the adult's experiences with other languages: _____

_____

What is the main language used at home (i.e., home language)? _____

Language(s) of interaction between the adult and:

Spouse_____Siblings_____Children_____Parents_____

Other family members/friends _____

Language preference in listening to the radio or in watching TV?

❑ Home language   ❑ English   ❑ No preference

Language preference for reading and writing?

❑ Home language   ❑ English   ❑ No preference

Rate the adult's proficiency in English:

❑ Very low   ❑ Low Average   ❑ Above average   ❑ Very high

Education and Occupation

Did the adult attend school in his or her country of origin, if other than the United States?

❑ Yes   If yes, how many years? _____ ❑ No

Did the adult attend school in the United States?

❑ Yes   If yes, how many years? _____ ❑ No

Highest level of education: _____

List jobs held in the past five years: _____

_____

Continued on next page

Figure 2.3—*Continued*

Health Information

Any problems with: (*circle response*)

Listening	Yes	No
Hearing	Yes	No
Remembering what others say	Yes	No
Following directions	Yes	No
Speaking clearly	Yes	No
Expressing ideas clearly	Yes	No
Finishing tasks	Yes	No
Performing home or work activities	Yes	No
Walking	Yes	No
Using hands	Yes	No
Writing	Yes	No
Reading	Yes	No
Previous significant health problems	Yes	No

Describe problems: _____

_____

_____

Describe any differences in communication skills you have noticed since the current medical problem: _____

_____

_____

Describe the adult's typical day when at home: _____

_____

_____

List the adult's favorite activities and hobbies: _____

_____

Additional comments: _____

_____

Name and position of person conducting the interview:

_____

Date: _____

CONFERENCES: SHARING INFORMATION

Information shared during conferences may relate to results obtained in a speech-language or audiological evaluation or may focus on progress made in intervention. You will typically experience the following commonalities from conference to conference:

1. Before the meeting begins, you will determine what interpreter services each person desires. Some bilingual speakers may not need interpreter services. Others may not need interpretation of what is said to them in English, but may prefer to make their comments and questions in the other language. Others may need interpreter services for all interactions.

2. You will help to arrange the seating so that no one is isolated from the interaction. All participants should be able to see each other clearly. (Again, remember that in some cultures direct eye contact is avoided as a sign of respect.)

3. The person leading the conference will state the purpose of the meeting (e.g., to share assessment results or to report progress in intervention). This may include an estimate of the amount of time the meeting will take.

4. The person leading the meeting will introduce those at the meeting and describe their roles in the assessment or intervention process.

5. The person leading the meeting will ask participants to refrain from side conversations. Alternatively, you may make this request.

6. The person leading the meeting will describe the order in which information will be shared.

7. Communication disorders professionals will present their key findings, with clear explanations of how results affect the client's communication skills and daily communication.

8. Communication disorders professionals may use concrete examples, pictures, or diagrams to make a point. These may include a normal curve diagram to help explain test scores, a picture of the vocal cords to demonstrate the location of nodules, or an illustration of the hearing mechanism to indicate where the hearing difficulty might originate.

9. Communication disorders professionals may invite the client and the family members to offer comments or ask questions. You should be alert to nonverbal communication and inform the professionals when there may be confusion or unspoken questions.

10. Communication disorders professionals may ask the client to summarize the key information to check if the information has been clearly understood. Be especially careful to interpret these responses precisely because vague or inaccurate responses will let the communication disorders professional know that he or she needs to explain some information again.

11. Communication disorders professionals may provide the client or family with one or two ideas for follow-up activities. Make sure the client or family members clearly understand the directions, and ask the communication disorders professional for further explanation or clarification when needed.

12. At any point during the meeting, you may need to ask for clarification from a participant to ensure clear and precise interpretation.

13. When the meeting ends, the person leading the meeting will summarize the main points and recommendations.

Notes

_____

_____

_____

_____

_____

_____

_____

_____

_____

_____

_____

_____

_____

WHAT YOU SHOULD KNOW ABOUT BID: BRIEFING, INTERACTION, AND DEBRIEFING

Any collaboration between you and a communication disorders professional should involve three steps: briefing, interaction, and debriefing (BID). The BID process will differ slightly between interviews and conferences and between assessments and intervention.

Briefing

Interviews or Conferences

During the briefing step, the speech-language pathologist or audiologist and you should address questions in the following areas:

- **Format of the interview or conference**—Determine who the participants will be besides the client. Other participants may include the client's family or professionals from other disciplines.

- **Purpose of the interview or conference**—Determine what should be accomplished and to what purpose. The purpose may be to gather more information from the client or the client's family, to decide if assessment is necessary, to supplement existing information about the client, or to report the results of an assessment.

- **Critical pieces of information to review**—Decide what procedure to follow and which questions will be asked first.

- **Relevant terminology to preview and define**—Discuss what terms may come up during the interview or conference.

- **Critical pieces of information to report**—Discuss what information needs to be conveyed and how it can be done effectively. For example, the client or the client's family may be provided with information on specifics of the assessment, or the meeting may focus on future intervention and educational or job placement.

- **Type of interpreting necessary**—Determine if the interpreting should be consecutive or simultaneous. The method and process will depend on the number of participants and the client's level of comprehension of English.

Assessment or Intervention

During the briefing process, you and the communication disorders professional should discuss the following:

- **Purpose of the assessment or intervention**—Discuss the reason for the assessment, the client's relevant background, and his or her general areas of strength and areas of challenge. When discussing intervention methods, include the purpose of the session and the desired outcomes.

- **Procedure to follow**—Review specific assessment or intervention materials as well as the order in which they will be used.

- **Gesture use**—If standardized testing is administered, discuss the appropriateness of the use of gestures or body language that might clue the client.

- **Test items and protocols**—Become familiar with the test items and protocols used in the assessment as well as materials that will be used in the intervention.

- **Method of recording**—Review the protocols and how responses need to be recorded. For example, decide if the answers should be marked as correct or incorrect or transcribed verbatim.

- **Basals and ceilings**—The communication disorders professional should guide you on which test items should be administered first, including how to establish a basal and when to stop administering the test items (i.e., ceiling).

- **Client roadblocks**—Discuss strategies to follow in case the client is uncooperative or responds differently than anticipated. That is, decide how to proceed if items are too easy or too difficult. It is not unusual to face situations where the process turns out to be different than expected, and the team needs to change strategies accordingly.

Interaction

Interaction is the step of the process that engages the client or family members in the interview, conference, assessment, or intervention activities. You should not be left alone during an assessment or intervention session, even when you have had prior experience. You must remember that the communication disorders professional is ultimately responsible for the process. The communication disorders professional may want to videotape or audiotape an interaction to facilitate reviewing the client's responses when analyzing the language sample.

Debriefing

Do not leave immediately after an interview, a conference, an assessment, or an intervention. It is important that you and the communication disorders professional have time to review the interaction together.

Interviews or Conferences

During the debriefing, you and the communication disorders professional should:

• Discuss whether the interview or conference was productive and why.

• Make notations about areas that went well and areas that should be emphasized next time the team collaborates.

• Decide whether a follow up is necessary and determine the role you will play in this follow up.

Assessment or Intervention

During the debriefing, you and the communication disorders professional should:

• Review the client's responses and analyze the client's language sample and any observed difficulties.

• Discuss areas that went well in your collaboration and others that may necessitate more emphasis in the future.

• Decide if a follow-up conference is needed.

Notes

_____

_____

_____

_____

_____

_____

_____

_____

_____

_____

_____

WHAT YOU SHOULD KNOW ABOUT RIOT: REVIEW, INTERVIEW, OBSERVE, AND TEST

Close collaboration between you and the communication disorders professional is necessary when assessing clients with speech, language, or hearing disorders. To ensure that a thorough workup is carried out, the team should follow the review, interview, observe, and test (RIOT) process.

Use of the RIOT process includes methods to ensure that CLD clients are assessed in an unbiased manner. Critical pieces of information about the client's background and observations gathered from various settings are considered in interpreting the test results. Not all pieces of information may be available, but the team should make an effort to gather as much relevant data as possible.

- **Review** school, job, and medical records and reports. These may include teachers' and employers' comments; linguistic, cultural, social, and family background; and previous therapy or testing results.

- **Interview** family members, employers, teachers, peers, and other informants. Document parents' or family members' perceptions of the client's skills, aptitudes, and challenges. During the interview, the communication disorders professional may obtain helpful information to decide if a more thorough assessment is necessary or to determine what additional areas should be assessed. Answers to questions related to the client's hobbies, reactions to his or her communication skills, and performance at school or on the job will assist in gathering a more thorough picture of the client.

- **Observe** the client in several contexts during the assessment to help interpret results and plan intervention. The number of observations might be limited in certain cases, such as when a client is hospitalized and needs to be assessed shortly after admission. Your perceptions can be very helpful in providing important information by comparing the client's behavior and language to a peer group that has similar linguistic and environmental backgrounds. Observations of the client's daily activities can also help the communication disorders professional design an appropriate intervention.

- **Test** by administering formal tests and informal procedures, including language samples and portfolios.

WHAT YOU SHOULD KNOW ABOUT STANDARDIZED TESTS

Use

The Individuals with Disabilities Education Act (IDEA) (1997) is a federal law that requires a child assessed for special education to be evaluated in the primary language "unless it is clearly not feasible to do so" (§ 614 [a] [3] [A] [ii]). The selection and administration of tests should not be discriminatory on a racial or cultural basis.

The use of standardized tests assists in comparing individuals to a normal population. The scores used for these comparisons are called *norms*. The tests include specific items that need to be administered following consistent directions for use. Only a limited number of tests have been developed using norms from a group of individuals whose primary language is other than English, and most of these have been developed for Spanish-speaking groups.

Standardized tests are helpful in determining how well a client performs in a particular area compared to other clients of the same age or grade level. In designing test items, the authors have a specific purpose in mind that is based on a theoretical or empirical framework. To develop norms, these test items are administered to a statistically representative, but often relatively small (often no more than 200 per age or grade level), sample of subjects. Groups differing in social or cultural background may be included in the sample, but the interpretation of the client's performance must take into account the differences between the client and the normed population. That is, a client whose background is different from that of the norm group may score lower on the test despite having adequate speech-language or hearing abilities just because the client has not had the same cultural experiences.

Language Differences

Language differences are especially critical in tests of speech and language skills. When words are translated, they may be shorter or longer than the original version, which may make the task easier or harder. Tests of grammatical usage may vary in difficulty, depending on how a grammatical feature (e.g., verb tense, feminine article, or noun-verb agreement) occurs in the other language, if it occurs at all. Even tests of vocabulary can be very different when translated because some words or concepts are less common in another culture or may have multiple meanings that do not occur in the other language.

Reliability and Validity

Standardized tests must be valid and reliable to draw useful conclusions from their results. *Validity* means that the test truly measures what it purports to measure (e.g., language comprehension or intelligence). *Reliability* means that the results will be consistent when administered in the same way to the same type of people.

Even when tests are normed on a particular bilingual population, their validity and reliability are compromised because each bilingual speaker's language proficiency in each language varies a great deal based on individual experience and differs from the sample population used in the norming of the test. Even more discrepancies can be found when an interpreter is involved in the testing process because no standardized tests have been normed using the assistance of an interpreter.

Notes

_____

_____

_____

_____

_____

_____

_____

_____

_____

_____

_____

_____

CASE STUDIES TO PRACTICE INTERVIEWING AND CONFERENCING SKILLS

Interviews

1. Interviews should include three people on each team. One person plays the role of the interpreter who speaks the client's language, the second person is the client's family member speaking the same language, and the third person is the communication disorders professional. One or more other people may be observers/evaluators.

2. Read Cases 2.1, 2.2, and 2.3 and become familiar with the Interview of the Child's Family Member (see page 29) or the Adult Interview (see page 33), as appropriate. Choose one of these case studies to role-play.

3. Based on information in the case, the person role-playing the family member should prepare some responses to interview questions.

4. The interpreter should practice vocabulary and phrases that will likely be used during the interview.

5. Role players carry out a briefing, interaction, and debriefing process following Collaborating during Interviews and Conferences: A Checklist (see page 26).

6. Observers/evaluators observe the role-play and use the checklist to note the performance of the role players.

7. Role players and observers/evaluators discuss the process and how well it matched the items in the checklist.

Conferences

1. Conferences should include three people on each team. One person plays the role of the interpreter who speaks the client's language, the second person is the client's family member speaking the same language, and the third person is the communication disorders professional. One or more other people may be observers/evaluators.

2. Team members read Cases 2.1, 2.2, and 2.3; choose one; and practice the information to be shared at the conference.

3. The interpreter should practice vocabulary and phrases that will likely be used during the conference.

4. Team members use the information from "Conferences: Sharing Information" (see page 35) and Collaborating during Interviews and Conferences: A Checklist (see page 26) to prepare a procedure for role-playing.

5. Team members role-play the briefing, interaction, and debriefing while observers/evaluators use the checklist to note the performance of the role players.

6. Role players and observers/evaluators discuss the process and how well it matched the items in the checklist.

CASE 2.1: PAUL, A 9-YEAR-OLD EXPERIENCING LEARNING PROBLEMS

Team Members: parent, interpreter, fourth-grade teacher, psychologist, English as a second language (ESL) teacher, speech-language pathologist, learning disabilities teacher, and principal

Paul is a 9-year-old predominantly (*) speaking child in fourth grade. His progress in acquiring English and academic skills has been slow compared to other students of similar linguistic and cultural backgrounds. Paul came from (*) and has been in the United States for two years. He attended first grade in (*) prior to emigrating to the United States. The school staff has limited information on his background. His parents have limited fluency in English. Paul has two siblings who have graduated from high school and still reside in (*).

Paul completed second and third grade in exclusively English-speaking classes. This is his third year of daily 30-minute ESL lessons and additional academic assistance from a bilingual tutor twice a week for a total of one hour. Paul's fourth grade teacher has modified assignments and paired him with another student who speaks some (*), but Paul has difficulty keeping up with his classmates. Math seems to be Paul's strongest subject. When Paul entered second grade, his English proficiency according to the Bilingual Syntax Measure–Level II (BSM-1) was rated at Level 1 (No Proficiency). A reassessment was done a month prior to this referral, and his English proficiency was at Level 3 (Survival Proficiency).

Paul has difficulty paying attention. Following directions in his native language is a challenge, as reported by his parents and his tutor. The school psychologist's observation of Paul in the classroom and on the playground corroborated this difficulty with attention and following directions. Paul interacted with another student who speaks the same native language, but very limited verbal interaction was observed between the two youngsters. Informal tasks indicated Paul has difficulty understanding what is expected of him even when repetitions and demonstrations are offered. He also has difficulty retaining new words and concepts. The psychologist attempted to teach Paul some new vocabulary words related to his favorite subject (wild animals), but Paul had difficulty remembering them. No health or developmental information is currently available. Paul passed the school hearing and vision screenings done two months earlier.

Use any language or country as appropriate.

CASE 2.2: GRACE, A 56-YEAR-OLD STROKE PATIENT

Team Members: Grace, Grace's husband, interpreter, and speech-language pathologist

Grace is a 56-year-old predominantly (*) speaking female who sustained a stroke that left her with a right hemiplegia. Grace's leg strength and control is slowly returning to normal, but not her arm or her hand. Her electroencephalography revealed a focal lesion in the left parietal-temporal region. She cannot see in the right field. She has difficulty processing what is said to her, and her expressive language is very difficult to understand. Sounds are often transposed in words (e.g., Grace says "tarp" instead of "part") or in sentences (e.g., "cake a tup" instead of "take a cup"). These problems are noted when Grace is asked to repeat words or phrases and when she speaks spontaneously.

Use any language or country as appropriate

CASE 2.3: JOHN, AN 11-YEAR-OLD STUDENT WITH A LANGUAGE-LEARNING DISORDER

Team Members: John's mother and father, interpreter, fifth-grade teacher, speech-language pathologist, psychologist, learning disabilities teacher, and principal

John is an 11-year-old boy enrolled in fifth grade whose primary language is (*). He emigrated to the United States from (*) when he was 4 years old. His school attendance has been regular, and he has not been back to his country of origin. He has attended school in the United States since kindergarten. He speaks his first language at home with his parents and family friends. He typically speaks English with his siblings and classmates.

Academic performance: John reads in English at the third-grade level, but relies on picture clues to understand what he reads. He can read pattern books easily, but he has more difficulty with texts that have unfamiliar contexts. He has problems understanding written instructions and his performance in social studies and in solving math story problems is very low. He does not always correct himself when he reads. John never learned how to read in his native language.

John writes simple sentences, but he makes many errors. He expresses main ideas in his writing, but has difficulty elaborating on a topic. Some of his spelling errors are phonetic, but others have no particular pattern. He does not follow punctuation rules consistently. His letter formation is good, but he writes slowly and takes a great deal of time to complete written assignments. He is beginning to learn computer keyboarding, but he has shown more difficulty than his classmates in remembering keys for the letters.

Use any language or country as appropriate

Continued on next page

Case 2.3—*Continued*

Social/Emotional skills: John is well liked by his peers. He seems to pay attention in class and is not disruptive or off task. John tries hard, but he has difficulty following oral and written directions. When he does not know how to do something, he hesitates asking even a buddy that has been assigned to help him. He has two friends he likes, but his verbal interactions with them seem limited.

John likes to draw, create items with clay, and paint. He helps his father on weekends by putting items on the shelves in the clothing store where his father is the manager. His father reports that he is very responsible and finishes what he is assigned to complete.

Cognitive skills: John's cognitive skills were assessed by a monolingual psychologist assisted by the interpreter who rephrased information that John did not understand. Visual-motor tasks and non-verbal cognitive tasks showed average performance for tasks that did not require a verbal response. Difficulty was noted in John's verbal interaction with the interpreter. His answers were brief, and he had difficulty narrating a story.

Speech and language/communication: Difficulty with oral expression was observed by the interpreter and the speech-language pathologist when they assessed John's communication skills in his primary language. A language sample using various topics indicated that John communicated and answered basic questions during conversation in his native language, but his comments were limited. He used language for various purposes, but had problems providing explanations, hypothesizing, or predicting situations. His syntax was adequate in his primary language as judged by the interpreter. This observation was also confirmed by his parents and the tutor that had worked with him during the two months prior to the formal testing. John had difficulty remembering directions with more than two steps. Repetition and additional visual clues seemed to improve his recall in English and his native language.

In English, John followed instructions, but needed many visual cues and concrete examples to understand all the information presented by the teacher. He could get by in English, but his proficiency was basic. His performance on standardized tests indicated difficulty in remembering directions, in providing synonyms, and with word associations. He had particular difficulty making up sentences using specific words.

Recommendations: John's language and learning difficulties did not appear to be connected to learning a second language. Based on observations, informal assessments, and performance on the standardized tests, the team recommended that he had a language learning disability that required special education.

John will participate in the classroom for most of his school day except for two hours a day when he will receive additional assistance in reading, math, language, and writing in the learning disabilities resource room. The resource specialist will also work with John in the classroom for three 45-minute sessions per week. The speech-language pathologist will work with John in a small group for 30 minutes one time per week and in the classroom for 30 minutes once per week.

Case 2.3—*Continued*

Objectives:

- John will verbalize instructions before carrying them out each time he is asked with 90% accuracy.

- John will use a tape recorder to dictate three ideas he remembers from each social studies and science lesson.

- John will use semantic maps to organize content to write five essays, each at least two paragraphs long.

- John will use the computer for written assignments one or more paragraphs in length.

- John will make entries in an interactive journal at least twice a week to exchange ideas with his teacher about books he is reading.

- John will complete fifth-grade math assignments and tests with 75% accuracy.

- John will tutor a second grader in reading and math two times per week.

ASSESSMENT OF CULTURALLY/LINGUISTICALLY DIVERSE (CLD) CLIENTS

In this session, you will learn:

- Strategies for working with clients and families during assessment

- Guidelines for assessment of speech-language disorders

- How to follow the briefing, interaction, and debriefing (BID) procedures when tests are available in a client's first language

- How to follow the briefing, interaction, and debriefing (BID) procedures when tests are not available in a client's first language

- Guidelines for eliciting a language sample

- Guidelines for assessment in audiology

- How to follow the briefing, interaction, and debriefing (BID) procedures during audiological assessments

INTRODUCTION

This session provides more detailed guidance in the process involved in assessing clients' communication skills and needs. You will learn the hands-on skills needed to communicate effectively with clients and their families as they communicate with you throughout the assessment process. Your direct communication with clients and families places you in an important role for helping them feel comfortable, making sure they understand and are involved in the assessment process, and making sure their needs are met. You will learn how to handle these situations confidently, in collaboration with the communication disorders professional. You will learn how to follow the BID process during speech-language and audiology assessments and how to prepare in advance for the specific assessment tasks that will be conducted.

SELF-ASSESSMENT ITEMS

1. What would you do if a client approached you with a question that you felt you could answer regarding a conference that took place with the communication disorders professional?

2. Describe how you might use the checklist in Figure 3.1 (see pages 54–55).

3. What would you do if a speech-language pathologist did not make the test manual available to you prior to your translation and administration of a test? How would you explain your actions to the speech-language pathologist?

4. What would you do if you began administering a test in a client's first language and the client gave responses using English?

5. Think of a test question or task that would be culturally unfair.

6. Describe three strategies you could use to learn and practice skills for eliciting a valid language sample from a child.

7. Audiologists use specialized equipment and terminology. How much of the procedures and equipment do you need to understand? What strategies can you use to become more familiar with terms that will be used during conferences?

SUGGESTED READINGS AND RESOURCES

Baker, C., and Jones, S.P. (1998). *Encyclopedia of bilingualism and bilingual education.* Clevedon, England: Multilingual Matters.

This is a colorful, illustrated encyclopedia that addresses issues concerning the acquisition and development of a second language. It includes descriptions of various bilingual programs in the United States and around the globe. The information is well-written, informative, and easy to understand.

Goldstein, B. (2000). *Cultural and linguistic diversity resource guide for speech-language pathologists.* San Diego, CA: Singular.

This guide includes information on aspects of language development and assessment of various linguistic and cultural groups. The information is presented in tables and outlines that are easy to follow.

Langdon, H.W., and Saenz, T.I. (Eds.). (1996). *Language assessment and intervention with multicultural students: A guide for speech-language-hearing professionals.* Oceanside, CA: Academic Communication Associates.

A well-referenced resource on various aspects of bilingualism and bilingual assessment in communication disorders.

Lubinski, R. (2001). Environmental systems approach to adult aphasia. In Chapey, R. (Ed.), *Language intervention strategies in aphasia and related neurogenic communication disorders* (pp.269–296). Philadelphia: Lippincott.

This chapter includes several sociological, personal, and functional considerations for bilingual adult aphasic patients. It includes helpful charts and questionnaires that can be used to interview the client and the client's family members.

PROCEDURES FOR WORKING WITH CLIENTS AND FAMILIES DURING ASSESSMENT

The following scenarios are discussed to help you understand the various situations that may arise during your interactions with clients and their families. You may find it helpful to review these situations and strategies when seeking resolutions to difficulties.

Arranging the Assessment Environment

Ideally, you should observe or interact with the client before the actual testing time to establish rapport. However, prior interaction with a client may not be feasible in some instances, like in cases where clients are admitted to a hospital because they have sustained some form of traumatic injury. The client should be told that he or she will be working with two people in the same room, and each person's role should be explained. This will help prepare the client to receive instructions from both the interpreter and the communication disorders professional.

The communication disorders professional must be present during the testing session, even if you have been trained to administer tests that are available in or have been translated to the client's first language. The communication disorders professional needs to be present to follow along with the testing, to observe the interaction between you and the client, to observe how the client reacts and responds, and to answer questions or provide further directions depending on how the assessment proceeds.

You should be seated directly facing the client with the communication disorders professional sitting to the side to observe both you and the client. It is best if you administer the items directly in the client's language without the communication disorders professional saying the information in English first. This is less distracting for the client and more aligned with standardized test procedures.

Respecting the Role of the Speech-Language Pathologist or Audiologist

You and the communication disorders professional need to work together and maintain the authority of the speech-language pathologist or audiologist before, during, and after the assessment process. You may need to state that the communication disorders professional is ultimately responsible for the diagnosis of the client and for planning the intervention. If the client or a family member has a concern, convey it so that the communication disorders professional can respond.

Checking That Clients and Their Families Understand Their Legal Rights

Clients and family members must be given all necessary information regarding their legal rights. You and the communication disorders professional need to spend time explaining these rights, even though the laws may have been translated into the client's first language and provided in written form. This includes rights when undergoing medical procedures, such as in a videoendoscopy, or during placement in a special education program. It is your duty to interpret documents containing these laws and rights using language that is understood by the client or the client's family. On some individualized education program (IEP) forms, client's parents are asked to indicate that they have received and understand their rights. Asking clients or family members to rephrase what they heard is a helpful way to ensure that they understand the information.

Ensuring that Parents or Family Members Are Involved in the Assessment Process

From the beginning, parents need to understand that they are full participants in their child's education, both general and special education. The Individuals with Disabilities Education Act (IDEA) (1997) requires that parents actively participate in the process of assessment, program planning, and placement in a program for children with special education needs. Therefore, you and the communication disorders professional need to ask parents directly for their opinions and seek their perceptions of the problem. In many instances, parents and other family members may not be comfortable offering their opinions for various reasons, including unfamiliarity with the process followed in the U.S. school system or feeling intimidated due to limited formal education. They may also have unquestioning trust in the expertise of professionals. In any event, you and the communication disorders professional need to ensure that the process allows clients and their families to be heard. This process may take time, but it ultimately helps protect and assist the client.

Handling a Client or Family Member Who Seeks Advice from You

Typically, a client or a family member of the client may feel comfortable sharing personal information with you before, during, or after a meeting. You should listen, but be honest and remind the individual that you may need to share this confidential information with another professional who can assist or solve the concern or dilemma. You should not provide advice or guidance that goes beyond your responsibility. For example, do not provide advice about counseling or discuss very personal matters. On the other hand, you may assist a client by contacting a person at a given agency on behalf of the client or contacting the client's employer to explain that the client's absence is due to a speech-language or audiological assessment or an intervention session. Keep the communication disorders professional informed about your activities, and seek his or her guidance when uncertain whether to assist the client or family member.

Following Up to Address Clients' or Families' Further Questions

A follow-up telephone call will allow clients and their families time to reflect on the meeting so that they may voice their questions or concerns. The call allows you to confirm that the client and his or her family understood the content of the meeting. In turn, the family can indicate whether they agree with the recommendations or whether they need more contact with the speech-language pathologist or the audiologist to clarify something. You should not respond to any questions before consulting back with the communication disorders professional. The best practice is for you to place the follow-up call only if you also participated in the previous meetings and only with the permission and guidance of the communication disorders professional.

Notes

GUIDELINES FOR ASSESSMENT OF SPEECH-LANGUAGE DISORDERS

The following guidelines will help you prepare for and successfully participate in speech-language assessment. Figure 3.1 includes a checklist that will assist you and the communication disorders professional in following the assessment process with greater success.

Figure 3.1 **Collaboration with an Interpreter in Assessment and Intervention: A Checklist**		
Briefing		
Purpose of the assessment or intervention is explained	Y	N
Procedures to be followed are reviewed	Y	N
Use of gestures, voice patterns, and other body language that might cue the client are discussed	Y	N
The interpreter is reminded to write down all relevant information and keep notes	Y	N
The communication disorders professional has test protocols to follow during the assessment	Y	N
There is evidence that the interpreter has interacted with the client prior to the session (variable)	Y	N
There is evidence that the communication disorders professional has interacted with the client prior to the session	Y	N
Comments: _____		
_____		
_____		
Interaction		
Communication disorders professional is present	Y	N
Interpreter asks questions immediately as needed	Y	N
Communication disorders professional takes notes	Y	N
Note Relevant Client Behaviors		
Displays general behavior problems such as perseveration, short attention span, distractibility	Y	N
Needs repetition and cuing	Y	N

Figure 3.1—*Continued*

Uses more gestures than words to express ideas	Y	N
Has difficulty with language skills such as pauses, hesitations, response delays, reauditorization, short answers	Y	N
Benefits from various strategies such as repetition, modeling, breaking down information	Y	N

Comments on other behaviors observed: _____

_____

Note Relevant Interpreter Behaviors

Uses appropriate nonverbal communication	Y	N
Gives clear instructions	Y	N
Provides adequate amount of reinforcement	Y	N
Cues or prompts the client where appropriate	Y	N
Takes notes	Y	N
Asks for information from the communication disorders professional when needed	Y	N

Comments: _____

_____

Debriefing

Client's responses are reviewed	Y	N
Interpreter relates what the client should or should not have said in response to specific questions	Y	N
Any difficulties in the process are reviewed	Y	N
Language sample is documented, annotated, and reviewed	Y	N

Comments: _____

_____

_____

Materials used for assessment or intervention : _____

_____

Keep these guidelines in mind throughout the assessment process:

- **Test limitations**—Most standardized tests do not provide norms for conditions where an interpreter or translator is involved in administering the test. This is one reason why the results of interpreted tests need to be deciphered with caution.

- **Subtests**—A comprehensive test is generally composed of several subtests. If the test is normed, the manual may have specific rules on what test item should be used to begin (basal) and where to end the test (ceiling). Directions may change from subtest to subtest. These details are included in the test manual, and some tests may include these directions on the individual administration form. The speech-language pathologist is responsible for making certain you know where to begin and end any given subtest.

- **Demonstration items**—Most tests and subtests have demonstration items to ensure that the client understands the directions. Administer these items exactly according to the directions in the manual. The speech-language pathologist can show you where to find the directions and can answer any questions you might have.

- **Repetitions and wait times**—The directions for the test specify whether repetitions are allowed and how long to wait for the client to respond before going on with the administration of the next item. When in doubt, consult with the speech-language pathologist.

- **Cuing**—The manual may indicate how to cue the client to provide other responses if the response is inaccurate. For example, a phrase such as "tell me more" or "can you think of another word" might be used. Only the particular cues that are spelled out in the test directions should be used. Again, when in doubt, consult with the speech-language pathologist.

- **Observing client behaviors**—Observe the client's responses to the test items to gather a more comprehensive impression about his or her ease or difficulty in responding to the various tasks. Discuss your observations with the speech-language pathologist during the assessment (if appropriate) or after, as part of the debriefing.

- **Deviations from directions**—Be certain to inform the speech-language pathologist about instances when you varied from the manual directions, and discuss how this may have affected the client's responses. Expect to be asked for a rationale as to why you deviated from the instructions. Ideally, make the speech-language pathologist aware of the alteration at the time it is occurring. If this is not feasible, discuss the deviations during the debriefing part of the assessment process.

- **Item readministration**—Once the administration of a given test is completed, the speech-language pathologist may ask you to readminister some of the items under modified conditions. Modified conditions may include repeating the instructions, repeating the target items, providing more examples, giving the client more time to respond, or providing a second chance to respond.

- **New scores**—New scores may be obtained through readministration, but should not be used as comparisons with the performance of the normed population. Documenting the modified conditions that were helpful in enhancing the client's performance may assist in planning intervention. This is called *dynamic assessment*. You will likely be called on to explain the modified conditions that were helpful and the "new scores" to clients and/or family members during the conference that follows assessment.

- **Raw scores**—When the total number of correct items is computed, a raw score is obtained. The raw score is converted by the speech-language pathologist to one or more statistical measures to compare the client's performance with a normal population. These scoring systems often use numerical scales called *standard scores* or *percentiles*. Each scale has reference points that indicate an average range and where the individual's performance falls within or outside that average range. Again, you will likely be called on to explain raw scores and numerical scales to clients and/or family members during the conference that follows assessment. Thus, you will need to make certain you have a complete understanding of the scoring system(s) for the test(s) you have administered.

Notes

_____

_____

_____

_____

_____

_____

_____

_____

_____

_____

_____

BID PROCEDURES WHEN TESTS ARE AVAILABLE IN THE FIRST LANGUAGE

As discussed in Session 2 (see "What You Should Know about BID: Briefing, Interaction, and Debriefing," page 37), the briefing, interaction, and debriefing (BID) process should be implemented during all of your collaborations with a speech language pathologist. In the following sections, you will learn how to apply the BID process when tests are available in a client's first language.

Briefing

Determine an agreeable time and location for assessment. To ensure that the process runs smoothly, you and the speech-language pathologist should work together as much as needed prior to the scheduled assessment session. The speech-language pathologist should meet with you to discuss the client's background information and to brief you on the test(s) and procedures that will be used. This information includes the reason for referral, the results of other testing, and pertinent background data that may include medical, developmental, social, educational, occupational, and language-use patterns at home or in the learning or occupational settings. You should take notes, ask questions, and review the background information presented by the speech-language pathologist and the family members when applicable. Keep in mind that if the client has been recently admitted to the hospital, there might not be much time for planning.

Next, the speech-language pathologist should explain the test items that you will administer, including their purpose, procedures, and manner of recording responses. You must become familiar with the test items to be certain that procedures are clear. Ask for clarification prior to and even during the assessment process when necessary. Keep a list of the tests with notes about administration handy during the session.

You and the speech-language pathologist should discuss strategies to follow in case the client does not cooperate or performs below or above expectations. More stretch breaks, shifting the test items, or postponing the session may be necessary. Also talk about the use of recording devices, such as a tape recorder or video camera, which may aid in the debriefing process.

Interaction

During testing, the speech-language pathologist should follow along on another copy of the test protocol to gain a general sense of the information being collected. The speech-language pathologist may write down observations about the body language of the client and the interpreter or make notations when the interpreter appeared to use too many words while providing instructions, misused reinforcement, or seemed to give too many or inappropriate hints or clues. These notes help the speech-language pathologist understand the client's performance more fully and will help him or her provide valuable feedback to you.

You should record all responses, take notes, and immediately ask for clarification when questions arise. Be honest and observant when unsure of what to do next. For example, ask the speech-language pathologist what to do when the client gives an answer that might be acceptable, but is not included in the list of possible answers.

You may interrupt the testing process from time to time to inform the speech-language pathologist about the client's progress. Make interruptions at appropriate times to minimize disrupting the client's concentration. These interruptions help the speech-language pathologist stay informed about the entire procedure. When interrupting, make sure the client understands what is happening.

You and the speech-language pathologist must keep in mind that a client may not respond in the first language because of language loss. Therefore, when in doubt, read-minister the items in English to gain a more thorough picture of the client's communication skills.

It is not unusual for a bilingual client to code switch (i.e., to use two languages in the same response or to respond to a question using the alternate language). This type of response should be documented and analyzed at the end of the assessment by the speech-language pathologist. Assessment should take place using one language first, beginning with the most dominant language (to be determined by asking the client or a family member). If the client does not respond in the first language, readminister the item in the other language after the test or subtest is completed in the first language.

Figure 3.2 (see page 60) includes questions to facilitate recording observations of the client during testing. The speech-language pathologist may ask you to watch for some of these behaviors or may ask you to modify some tasks during the session so that these behaviors can be examined.

Debriefing

You and the speech-language pathologist should compare the client's responses to the target responses, noting which were correct and what types of errors were made by the client. Provide the speech-language pathologist with relevant cultural and linguistic information that may have influenced the client's performance on specific items, such as the lack of appropriate terms in the target language or likely unfamiliarity with particular objects or activities. Discuss deviations from the standard administration, your impressions, and any difficulties related to the interpreting process.

Figure 3.2
Observations of the Client during Testing

- Can the client follow oral and written directions as expected?

- Is the client easily distracted by noise or visual stimuli? How sustained is the client's attention?

- Does the client perform with greater ease when the input is shorter, repeated, or rephrased?

- Does the client need more time to respond?

- Does the client perform better when visual cues are provided?

- Does auditory cuing aid in expression or recall of information? (For example, say the first sound or syllable of a word, as in "na" to elicit "narrow.")

- Are pictures helpful in enhancing the client's performance?

- Does the client's performance improve with more practice?

- Can the client respond with greater ease when examples are provided?

- Can the client retain newly acquired information? (For example, provide an answer to a question at the beginning of the session and probe to determine if the client can recall it in the middle or the end of the session.)

Notes

_____
_____
_____
_____
_____
_____
_____
_____
_____
_____
_____
_____

BID PROCEDURES WHEN TESTS ARE NOT AVAILABLE IN THE FIRST LANGUAGE

The purpose of assessment is to determine if a client has a communication problem, to evaluate the degree of difficulty a client has in communicating, and to plan intervention strategies. When there are not any normed tests in the client's first language, you and the speech-language pathologist must make an extra effort to prepare materials ahead of time and to focus more on observations of the client's performance. The speech-language pathologist may ask you to translate materials into the target language and then translate them back into English to ensure that the translation is precise (this process is called *back translation*). Consider the following steps in the BID process when tests are not available in a client's first language.

Briefing

You will translate materials and judge if items are culturally fair. For example, it may be unfair to ask clients who have been in the country for a short time to describe some U.S. holidays. Write down the translations for ease of administration. Translations and adaptations of tests should be used cautiously. A word in one language may be more difficult or more easy to understand in another language.

Typical materials that might be translated for a school-aged client include following oral directions of increasing complexity, naming various items using pictures, naming members of various categories (e.g., foods, clothing, animals, and occupations) or stating the category an item belongs to, answering questions based on paragraphs read in the target language, and participating in a conversation. If the client is literate in the first language, he or she might be asked to read paragraphs of increasing complexity and then answer comprehension questions or write an essay. Similar methods may be used when the assessment involves an older client who has been admitted to a hospital because of a stroke or traumatic injury.

Comparisons across languages help determine which tasks may be performed with greater ease in one language as compared to the other. For example, some clients may express themselves in one language better than the other depending on the topic (English for school or work or the first language for home-related activities). Comparisons across languages should be made in as many contexts as possible.

Gathering a language sample helps you observe many language features, including pragmatic (social communication) skills, use of correct grammatical structures, clarity of language expression, and intelligibility of speech. See "Guidelines for Eliciting Language Samples" (page 63) for more information.

The speech-language pathologist should select any questionnaires that will be administered to the client. Questionnaires can provide helpful information about what the client knows and is able to do. Review the questionnaires to ensure that they are appropriate.

You may prepare additional reading and writing activities in the client's first language. For example, the client may be asked to read some paragraphs of increasing difficulty and respond to questions regarding their content or vocabulary. Or the client may be asked to write an essay on a selected topic to assess ability to construct a narrative, use appropriate sentence structure, select accurate vocabulary, and apply spelling rules.

Interaction

The information provided in the "Interaction" section (see page 58) for following the BID process when tests are available in the client's first language is applicable when materials adapted to the client's language are used.

Debriefing

You and the speech-language pathologist should meet to review and analyze the client's responses. Compare the client's responses to what would be expected of a client who speaks the language as a bilingual speaker. The evaluation of the client's responses should take into account his or her linguistic and experiential background in each language. This is the speech-language pathologist's responsibility, but your input will be important.

The speech-language pathologist makes the final determination about the client's communication profile, but your input is important to substantiate the speech-language pathologist's observations. For example, the interpreter may indicate that the client used certain grammatical forms incorrectly several times. But, it is up to the speech-language pathologist to decide the impact and importance of this aspect in judging the client's overall communication skills.

Notes

_____

_____

_____

_____

_____

_____

_____

_____

_____

_____

GUIDELINES FOR ELICITING LANGUAGE SAMPLES

A language sample is a collection of the client's consecutive utterances (words, phrases, or sentences) during an interaction. The interaction should be structured to elicit a sample that is as close to the client's typical conversation as possible. Alternatively, the speech-language pathologist may have you collect a narrative sample (e.g., "tell a story" or "tell me the story you just heard") instead of or in addition to a sample of conversation.

A language sample can provide useful information about a client's communication skills, but eliciting and transcribing a representative sample requires skill, practice, and time. For example, more language is elicited from the client with questions like "tell me about..." or "how do you...?" compared to "where did you...?" or "do you...?" The first type of question is open-ended and usually requires full sentences to provide a complete answer. The second type of question can be answered with one word or a simple yes or no.

You may be asked to collect a language sample during an interaction in the client's first language. You will need to practice language sampling prior to performing this task with a client. A client may be shy or reluctant to speak at first. Clients may also not cooperate or may have very poor expressive language skills. Use a variety of comments and activities to encourage the client to verbalize. Periods of silence may follow your comments or questions before the client responds, and you need to be quiet and patient to enable the client to respond when ready.

Ask the speech-language pathologist to provide you with one or more practice opportunities in collecting and transcribing a language sample. The speech-language pathologist should observe your techniques and instruct you in how to transcribe the sample accurately. You should analyze the transcript together to identify techniques that were effective or ineffective in eliciting a valid language sample.

Collecting a Language Sample

Vary the context of the conversation to obtain a comprehensive sample. Discuss possible topics of conversation with the speech-language pathologist ahead of time. You should provide feedback to the speech-language pathologist on topics that might be sensitive or difficult to discuss because of cultural differences.

For a preschool-aged client, consider topics and settings related to playing with favorite toys and games, describing a favorite TV program, or discussing a hypothetical situation (e.g., what to do when the client cannot find a favorite toy or has a hard time falling asleep). For the school-aged client, include topics related to school or activities with friends.

To collect a narrative sample from a preschool or elementary school client, use a wordless book where the client has to make up the story to go along with the pictures. For the adolescent or adult client, use topics such as favorite pastimes and hobbies or how to resolve a difficult situation. Make certain that the sample is audiotaped or videotaped. (Remember that most computers can be used for recording samples now, if the microphone is close enough to the client to pick up the sound.)

Once the sample is completed, listen to the recording and write down what the client said word for word. This process is referred to as a *sample transcription*. Include notes about speech-sound and grammatical errors that you noticed in the first language.

Assessing a Language Sample

Remind the speech-language pathologist that cultural differences must be respected when evaluating narratives. For example, a narrative is the organization used when telling a story, but narratives may vary between cultures. In addition recounts (talking about what happened) and eventcasts (talking about what will happen) may not be as frequent among certain cultural groups. Keeping in mind these cultural differences, provide input to the speech-language pathologist when assessing the areas summarized in the next sections.

Pragmatic Skills

Be prepared to comment on the following questions:

- Did the client respond to questions and comments appropriately? Did the client maintain the topic at hand?

- Were ideas sequenced logically so as not to interfere with communication?

- Could the client use language to describe, ask for information, explain, retell, and inform?

- Did the client use more gestures than needed (i.e., did the client use gestures instead of using specific words)?

Form and Content

Answer the following questions for the speech-language pathologist:

- Did the client use sentences that were grammatically correct? (Be prepared to explain incorrect grammatical features you noted.)

- Did the client use appropriate vocabulary? (Be prepared to cite examples of inappropriate vocabulary.)

- Did the client pronounce words correctly? (Be prepared to explain any errors.)

- How many of the client's words or statements were unintelligible?

Manner of Language Expression

Finally, be prepared to answer these questions:

- Was there a time delay between the interpreter's questions and comments and the client's responses?

- Were there pauses and hesitations when the client seemed to search for words?

- Was voice quality adequate (i.e., did the voice call attention to itself because of hoarseness, harshness, or breathiness)?

- Were there any signs of stuttering? If yes, how often did they occur?

Notes

_____

_____

_____

_____

_____

_____

_____

_____

_____

_____

_____

_____

GUIDELINES FOR ASSESSMENT IN AUDIOLOGY

Figure 3.3 includes a checklist to assist you and the audiologist in following the BID process. Certain items may apply more to situations when hearing is tested, others when hearing aids are fitted and tested.

Figure 3.3 The BID Process in Audiology		
Briefing		
Purpose of the session is explained	Y	N
Procedure to be followed is reviewed	Y	N
Client's participation and responsibility is explained	Y	N
Audiologist explains the tests that will be administered and what information is sought	Y	N
Audiologist explains the properties of a hearing device, its care, and management	Y	N
Audiologist and interpreter plan ahead in case the client does not understand directions or is uncooperative	Y	N
Audiologist prepares the interpreter for questions that the client might have regarding testing or hearing aid fitting	Y	N
Comments: _____		
_____		
Interaction		
Conferences		
Interpreter uses "I" instead of "Mr. X says"	Y	N
Interpreter transmits all that client and audiologist say	Y	N
Team maintains eye contact with the client or family member (if culturally appropriate)	Y	N
Team's language is appropriate to the client or family member	Y	N
Interpreter maintains support role and does not usurp the responsibility of the audiologist	Y	N

Figure 3.3—*Continued*

Team acts as a unit	Y	N
Attention is paid to nonverbal cues	Y	N
Interpreter interprets clearly and precisely	Y	N
Interpreter asks for clarification when necessary	Y	N

Testing/Hearing Aid Fitting

Directions are clearly interpreted	Y	N
Client's concerns are interpreted	Y	N
Interpreter accurately records client's responses to speech recognition and/or word recognition tests	Y	N

Comments: _____

_____

_____

_____

Debriefing

Was the testing or conference productive?	Y	N
Is follow up necessary?	Y	N

If yes, what type(s)? _____

_____

_____

_____

Areas that went well: _____

_____

Areas to emphasize in the future: _____

_____

Comments: _____

_____

_____

Source: Langdon and Cheng (2002)

The following information will help you prepare for and successfully participate in audiological assessment. You should be aware of general procedures and common terminology used by audiologists. The audiologist will orient you to the specific information needed.

Audiologists typically work in a clinic, private practice, or hospital. Educational audiologists provide services in schools. Audiologists use more instrumentation than speech-language pathologists. The two most common tasks of audiologists are (1) measuring hearing sensitivity and (2) hearing aid assessment and fitting.

Testing rather than assessment is a more appropriate term to use in audiological examinations because the audiologist conducts objective measures of the hearing acuity of the client. Testing can occur at any age. In fact, with the increased use of infant hearing screening, you are likely to assist families with newborns. You are also likely to assist many families with geriatric members. Tests typically performed by an audiologist include:

- **Pure-tone thresholds—**(Air and Bone Conduction Audiometry) measure hearing sensitivity. Frequencies (tones) are tested at varying decibel (loudness) levels. Headphones deliver air conduction signals to identify air conduction loss. A behind-the-ear vibrator delivers bone conduction signals to identify sensorineural loss. Results are recorded on an audiogram.

- **Speech reception threshold (SRT)—**measures the intensity (loudness) needed for the client to repeat 50% or more of spondaic test words (two-syllable words that have equal stress, for example *cowboy, sunset,* and *baseball*).

- **Word recognition test (WRT)—**measures the intensity (loudness) needed for the client to repeat words accurately.

- **Tympanometry—**measures movement of the tympanic membrane and corresponding middle-ear function. It is administered with a tympanometer. Results are charted on a tympanogram.

- **Otoacoustic emissions (OAE)—**measures cochlear function using sounds naturally emitted by the inner ear.

- **Auditory brainstem response (ABR)—**measures the brain's response to sound. It identifies newborn hearing loss or the site of a lesion along the auditory nerve. Results are recorded on a graph.

After performing one of these tests, the audiologist will evaluate the results. Most typical findings are that the client may have a:

- **Conductive hearing loss**—caused by damage to the outer or middle ear. Causes include accumulation of earwax (i.e., cerumen) or fluid in the middle ear (i.e., otitis media if the fluid is infected), tumors, physical damage, or otosclerosis (fixation of the small bones of the middle ear).

- **Sensorineural hearing loss**—caused by damage to the inner ear or the auditory nerve (VIII cranial nerve).

- **Mixed hearing loss**—a combination of both conductive and sensorineural loss.

Notes

BID DURING AUDIOLOGICAL ASSESSMENTS
Briefing

Preparation discussions might include the following:

- You and the audiologist meet to review the client's medical chart and plan the testing process. Questions related to onset or progress of a hearing loss, past use of a hearing aid or amplification device, or other medically related questions are discussed.

- The audiologist explains the level of client participation needed. In many cases when an interpreter is not available, the procedure can be explained by the audiologist directly through demonstration using a combination of verbal and non-verbal directions (J. McCullough, personal communication, April 2000). But you may be helpful in explaining that the client must raise his or her hand even when a given signal appears to be very faint. With younger clients, you may assist in training the child to throw a peg or block into a box or basket when hearing a sound. Obtaining a tympanogram typically will not require your help because the reading is done automatically, without the client's direct participation.

- You prepare to answer the client's or family's questions in case there are concerns regarding the procedures or the outcome of the testing.

- You and the audiologist form a plan in case the client does not understand his or her role or when the testing cannot be appropriately conducted because the client is uncooperative.

- Some tests require clients to repeat words that they hear. You may be asked to present the words or to record the accuracy of a client's responses. Study any word lists ahead of time, and make the audiologist aware of any words that require a phrase or sentence in the client's language.

Interaction

The following are the tasks that you should engage in when face-to-face with the client:

- Interpret clearly and accurately all that is said by all parties involved prior to the testing.

- Help the audiologist ensure that the client understands his or her role in all the testing procedures that are planned.

- Ensure that the client follows directions such as raising his or her hand or throwing a peg in a box to signal that a tone is heard.

- If a client is confused or responds inconsistently, reexplain the procedures. Help the audiologist recognize when the client is unsure and follow the audiologist's guidance in restating the directions.

- Present word lists or record the client's production of the words.

- After completing the testing, you and the audiologist should take a few minutes to discuss the results and plan how those results will be explained to the client or family member. The audiologist often discusses the results with the client or family immediately following the testing.

- The audiogram, the tympanogram, and other testing results are explained. The audiologist indicates if the client's hearing loss is conductive, sensorineural, or mixed because the course of intervention is different in each case. The audiologist explains the effects of the hearing loss on the client's performance in home, work, or school situations and makes recommendations to respond to the effects.

Debriefing

After the interaction, plan to engage in a debriefing conference with the audiologist. In this conference:

- You and the audiologist should meet to review the process, define tasks that were successfully accomplished, and identify areas that may need more attention in the future.

- Discuss if the client or family understood the results of the testing and the follow up that may need to take place, such as referral to an otolaryngologist, hearing aid fitting, implementing recommendations, or the need for a phone call.

Notes

_____
_____
_____
_____
_____
_____
_____
_____
_____
_____

TRANSLATION ACTIVITY

This activity provides an opportunity for you to practice preparing a translation and back translation of a test protocol. Obtain a test or subtest from a speech-language pathologist and perform a prepared translation. For those who do not have access to speech-language test forms, some sample instructions from Strong's (1998) *The Strong Narrative Assessment Procedure* are listed below. The sample instructions are appropriate for use with a child; be sure to obtain an adult test protocol also. For all tests, discuss with the communication disorders professional what elements are important to consider when translating.

Sample Test Items

Give the student standard instructions:

Please look at this book and listen to the story. I have to leave for a few minutes. When I come back, I'd like you to tell me the story. You won't have the pictures to look at when you retell the story to me.

After the student listens to the story and you return to the room, say:

I didn't get to hear that story. Please tell it to me as completely as you can.

After the student tells the story, say:

Your story was great! Thank you! Now I have 10 questions for you to answer. These are questions about the story. Here's the first one.

Source: Strong (1998)

CASE STUDIES TO PRACTICE ASSESSMENT PROCEDURES

Standardized Test

1. Use the manual from the Clinical Evaluation of Language Fundamentals–3 Spanish (CELF–3 Spanish) (Wiig, Secord, and Semel, 1997) or from the CELF–3 (Semel, Wiig, and Secord, 1996) to respond to the questions in Case 3.1.

2. Assign team members to role-play an assessment session. You will need an interpreter, a client, and a speech-language pathologist. One or more others may be assigned as observers/evaluators.

3. Role players prepare and practice their interactions, referring to the manual instructions, the test's individual administration form, and Collaboration with an Interpreter in Assessment and Intervention: A Checklist (see page 54).

4. Review the questions in Case 3.1 to get familiar with the subtest.

5. Team members role-play the BID procedures while observers/evaluators use the checklist to note the performance of the role players.

6. Role players and observers/evaluators discuss how well the BID procedures matched the checklist and how well the test administration procedures were followed.

Audiology Assessment

1. Assign team members to role-play an assessment session. You will need an interpreter, a client, a family member, and an audiologist. One or more others may be assigned as observers/evaluators.

2. Read Case 3.2 or 3.3. Make a list of important points to be shared with the client, and prepare for questions that the client might have.

3. Team members role-play the briefing, interaction, and debriefing procedures while observers/evaluators use The BID Process in Audiology (see page 66) as a checklist to note the performance of the role players.

4. Role players and observers/evaluators discuss how well the BID procedures matched the checklist.

CASE 3.1: A CLIENT WHOSE PRIMARY LANGUAGE IS SPANISH IS GIVEN A SUBTEST OF THE CELF–3 (SPANISH)

Directions: Study the administration procedures for the Listening to Paragraphs Subtest of the CELF–3 (Spanish) on manual page 102 or the CELF–3 (English) on manual page 78.

- What are the directions for administering the subtest?

- How do you record the answers?

- Do you transcribe the answers or circle those that are provided in the protocol?

- Are there practice items?

- What, if any, information are you able to repeat?

- Where do you begin the test and where do you end it?

- What pace of reading do you follow?

- What do you do if the client does not respond to a question or gives the wrong response?

- Practice administering the test to a client with the speech-language pathologist observing you.

- Discuss what went well and what should be adjusted during the next administration.

- Ask the speech-language pathologist how he or she would report the results.

CASE 3.2: ROSA, A 28-YEAR-OLD SPANISH SPEAKER COMPLAINING OF HEARING DIFFICULTIES

Rosa is a 28-year-old Spanish-speaking client complaining of difficulty in following conversations within background noise. Rosa's proficiency in English is still limited, but she understands some conversations and responds appropriately in familiar situations. She prefers Spanish to English. Rosa has trouble engaging in social interactions at parties, family gatherings, and any events where noise levels are high. She does not experience the same challenges in quiet situations. She has no history of ear infections or tinnitus. She has no current or past employment or recreational noise exposure and no history of hearing loss in her family.

Audiometric assessment indicated normal hearing in both ears. Rosa's SRT levels were 0 dB for the right ear and 5 dB for the left ear. Her WRT was 96% for the right ear and 100% for the left ear. Lists of words (McCullough, Wilson, Birck, and Anderson, 1994) were administered and the interpreter reported that Rosa's pronunciation of the words was accurate. Tympanograms for both ears were normal.

The audiologist will explain to Rosa that her hearing is normal, and that it is difficult to determine the reason for Rosa's concerns. There is no peripheral auditory dysfunction. One possible source of the problem may be anxiety in situations where listening conditions are more demanding. The audiologist could perform assessment of the central auditory processing if Rosa wants to search further for possible explanations. A recheck in a year or sooner if additional symptoms develop will be suggested.

From *Introduction to Audiology: A Review Manual* (pp.262–264), by F.N. Martin and J.G. Clark, 2001, Boston: Allyn and Bacon. © 2001 by Allyn and Bacon. Adapted with permission.

CASE 3.3: SERGEI, A 19-YEAR-OLD RUSSIAN SPEAKER WITH A HEARING COMPLAINT

Sergei is a Russian-speaking 19-year-old who recently emigrated to the United States from Moscow and who is about to enter college. His English is still limited, so he was evaluated in collaboration with a Russian-speaking interpreter. Sergei has always had a hearing difficulty that prevented him from hearing easily, but he was able to manage without any intervention. He has more difficulty now that he needs to interact in English. There is no history of hearing loss or impairment in Sergei's family. Sergei has never had ear infections and has never worn hearing aids. Sergei's speech is intelligible, but sibilants are slightly distorted and there is some monotonous tone and loudness quality to his speech.

Audiological data indicated a mild to moderate hearing loss in both ears with SRT levels of 45 dB (right ear) and 40 dB (left ear). WRT was at 86% in the right ear and 82% in the left ear. The Russian Picture Identification Task (RPIT) (Aleksandrovsky, McCullough, and Wilson, 1998) showed that Sergei had difficulty discriminating between four rhyming words. Tympanograms were normal.

The diagnosis was a sensorineural hearing loss, probably cochlear of unknown etiology. The audiologist counseled Sergei to consider a hearing aid fitting and tried to point out the advantages for Sergei's use of hearing aids. Sergei was advised to consult with a physician to verify the audiologist's findings. The possibility of an FM system was suggested as well.

From *Introduction to Audiology: A Review Manual* (pp.262–264), by F.N. Martin and J.G. Clark, 2001, Boston: Allyn and Bacon. © 2001 by Allyn and Bacon. Adapted with permission.

CASE 3.4: TOM, A 75-YEAR-OLD CHINESE SPEAKER WITH PROGRESSIVE BILATERAL HEARING LOSS

Tom is a 75-year-old who has experienced a gradual progressive bilateral hearing loss over the past 15 years. He has no history of ear infections or exposure to noise. His greatest difficulty was discriminating speech in the presence of background noise.

Results of assessment indicated mild to moderate hearing loss in both ears with an SRT of 15 dB in both ears. His WRT was at 88% in the right ear and 84% in the left ear.

The diagnosis in this case was mild to moderate cochlear hearing loss in both ears. The possible etiology was presbycusis. The audiologist discussed the use of hearing aids.

From *Introduction to Audiology: A Review Manual* (pp.262–264), by F.N. Martin and J.G. Clark, 2001, Boston: Allyn and Bacon. © 2001 by Allyn and Bacon. Adapted with permission.

SESSION 4

CHALLENGES IN THE INTERPRETING AND TRANSLATING PROCESS

In this session, you will learn:

- How to recognize linguistic interferences during interpreting and translating

- How to avoid common translation errors

- The process for selecting and fitting hearing aids

- The briefing, interaction, and debriefing (BID) process for hearing aids

INTRODUCTION

Now that you have had opportunities to practice your interpreting or translating skills with your collaborating communication disorders professional, this session will help you identify and correct common errors. You will learn about linguistic factors that can interfere with understanding a client and making yourself understood with a client. Taking time to assess your skills will raise you to a more skilled level of practice.

For interpreters working with an audiologist, a detailed description of hearing aid fitting is provided for this specialized area of practice. You will also learn about the BID process for hearing aids.

SELF-ASSESSMENT ITEMS

1. During a session, you notice that the client uses a dialect quite different from your own. How will this affect your interpreting?

2. What type of interpretation errors have you been most aware of in your own experience (i.e., omissions, additions, substitutions, transformations, or misinterpretations of nonverbal communication)? How could you avoid them?

3. What would you do during a conference with a client being fitted for a hearing aid if the client is nodding, but you feel he or she does not understand?

4. If both a second language and sign language are needed during a conference, think through how that would affect your role as interpreter of the second language.

SUGGESTED READINGS AND RESOURCES

Langdon, H.W. (2000). Diversity. In E. Pritchard-Dodge, *The survival guide for the school-based speech-language pathologist* (pp. 367–397). San Diego, CA: Singular.

This chapter provides step-by-step guidelines on how to fairly assess and work effectively with English language learners. It includes factors and questions to consider in assessment and provides tips on deciding the best language for intervention.

Roberts, P. (2001). Aphasia assessment and treatment for bilingual and culturally diverse patients. In R. Chapey (Ed.), *Language intervention strategies in aphasia and related neurogenic communication disorders* (pp. 208–232). Philadelphia: Lippincott.

This chapter reviews the challenges of assessment and treatment of adults with language-based deficits. The effect of culture, definition of bilingualism, and adequacy of assessment materials are addressed. Includes information on bilingual aphasia and recovery as well as various treatment options and choice of language for intervention. Assessment tools in various languages are listed in an appendix.

Roseberry-McKibbin, C. (2002). *Multicultural students with special needs: Practical strategies for assessment and intervention.* Oceanside, CA: Academic Communication Associates.

This book describes linguistic and cultural aspects for various groups (e.g., Latino and Asian), which should be considered in the assessment and intervention process. Helpful charts and maps are included.

LINGUISTIC CONSIDERATIONS DURING INTERPRETING AND TRANSLATING

Differences in Language Structures

Variations across languages are reflected at the sound, word, and sentence levels. Some languages use sounds that do not exist in other languages. Words with the same meaning but spoken in two different languages may be quite different in their length and speech sounds. Some messages require many more syllables or words in one language compared to another. In addition, words are located in different positions within a sentence depending on the language. For example, adjectives may be placed before or after a noun. Pronouns may have formal and informal forms that indicate the relationship between the speakers, or this distinction may not be marked at all in some languages. Rather than interpret word by word, the interpreter must understand the message from the first language and restate it accurately in the second language.

Dialectal Variations

Dialects are regional variations within a language. These variations may result in vocabulary differences (e.g., the same word may indicate different meanings or different words may be used for the same meaning). Many pronunciation differences occur between regional dialects. None of these differences should be judged as less correct than another. Interpreters must be aware of usages that are correct in a particular dialect in order to transmit messages accurately and to assist the communication disorders professional in distinguishing between language differences and disorders.

Cultural Differences

Many terms and idiomatic expressions are difficult to translate because they are bound to the culture of the people who speak the language. For example, the word *enfermito* in Spanish is used to mean "a child who is sick" as well as "a child who is experiencing learning difficulties." Humorous statements are often difficult to interpret because of their use of idioms and multiple-meaning words. You may need to clarify intended meanings of ambiguous statements to avoid miscommunications.

Cultures also differ in social beliefs and relationships. Family members' understandings of disabilities, child rearing practices, involvement in rehabilitation, and acceptance of recommendations from professionals may all be influenced by their cultural background.

Nonverbal Aspects

Approximately 65% of the meaning in a conversation is conveyed by nonverbal communication, which includes body movement, use of personal space, and perception of time. You must pay attention to the meaning of facial expressions and intonation to synthesize the verbal and nonverbal aspects of a message simultaneously. Since facial movements, gestures, and other nonverbal signals have different meanings across cultures, you must be careful not to assume their meanings. Your job as an interpreter or a translator includes being knowledgeable of the nonverbal communication behaviors in both the first and second languages since so much meaning is conveyed nonverbally.

Code Switching

Code switching is the use of two different languages in the same response or responding to a question using an alternate language. This phenomenon is common in competent bilingual individuals and may be noted in interpreted or translated contexts. You may need to code switch when there is no equivalent word or concept in the other language. In doing so, it may also be necessary to give an explanation of the concept since it is likely that the recipient of the message will not know the foreign term. Ask the communication disorders professional to provide this explanation. Code switching by the client should not be considered a sign of a disability without considering other diagnostic information collected by the communication disorders professional.

Language Loss

Language loss is a regression of skills in an individual's first language. It may occur for many reasons, such as the person's lack of practice, use of the language only in certain situations, or social or political reasons that may discourage the use of the language. Language loss by the client should not be considered a sign of a disability without further diagnostic information collected by the communication disorders professional. Your observations as an interpreter will assist the professional to document the extent of the language loss and possibly the reasons for the loss as well.

COMMON INTERPRETATION AND TRANSLATION ERRORS

Errors in interpretation or translation cannot be avoided. However, they may be minimized through more practice working with the communication disorders professional. There are five frequent errors that may occur in the process of interpreting or translating:

1. **Omissions**—You leave something out. It could be a word, a phrase, or an entire sentence. This could happen because you do not think the extra words are important (e.g., instead of saying "rather difficult," you might say "difficult"). In some cases, however, even a single word can make a difference, as in *mildly* vs. *moderately* delayed. Omissions can also occur because you are unable to keep up with the speaker's rate of speech. As an interpreter, you can request repetition and/or slowing the speech rate to assist your accuracy.

2. **Additions**—You add words, phrases, or sentences that were not said or written. This may happen because you elaborate or editorialize by adding your own thoughts. This should be avoided. At other times, you may need to add a word when a concept does not translate directly into the other language. This second type of addition is not considered an error as long as the same meaning is conveyed.

3. **Substitutions**—You use other words, phrases, or entire sentences in place of the actual words. Substitutions can occur because you do not remember the specific word, phrase, or grammatical construction. In other instances, you may confuse words that sound almost the same (e.g., *entendre* vs. *attendre* in French or *sold* vs. *cold* in English). Lack of understanding or ability to keep up with the speaker may cause incorrect usage of pronouns.

4. **Transformations**—You change the word order of the original statement. It may result in an error if the meaning is altered, as in saying, "Peter was hit by Paul" instead of "Paul was hit by Peter." However, if the sentence is delivered as "Paul hit Peter," the meaning would not be altered, even though a transformation occurred. This change would not be considered an error during a conference or interview, but may have implications during an assessment of language skills that is examining a client's understanding or use of that specific grammatical construction.

5. **Misinterpretations of nonverbal communication**—You omit information that is conveyed nonverbally or may misinterpret the nonverbal information conveyed by a person from another cultural background. For example, nodding may be interpreted as agreeing with what is said, instead of meaning that the person is just listening. In addition to paying attention to nonverbal communication, you and the communication disorders professional should pay attention to stress on words and intonation in sentences. For example, there is a difference in saying "your child performs much better on tasks that require visual attention" compared to "your child performs *much* better on tasks that require visual attention."

Notes

_____

_____

_____

_____

_____

_____

_____

_____

_____

_____

_____

_____

HEARING AID FITTING

Understanding and Selecting Hearing Aids

The purpose of fitting a hearing aid is to make sure that the device provides adequate amplification or acoustic gain. Hearing aids include a microphone, an amplifier, a receiver, and a battery. The microphone picks up sounds and sends them to the amplifier, where the sounds are made louder. The sound goes to the receiver, which delivers the sound to the wearer's ear. The battery provides the power for the electronic system.

Fitting the hearing aid requires making an impression of the ear canal using a plastic material that hardens after a few minutes. The impression is sent to a laboratory that uses it to make an ear mold to fit the canal and contain the electronic components of the hearing aid. It is very important that hearing aids be properly maintained and cared for. This includes checking the battery and cleaning the outer part of the hearing aid.

Audiological Procedures to Fit Hearing Aids

The American Speech-Language-Hearing Association (ASHA) guidelines (1998) indicate that hearing aid fitting must be conducted in six steps:

1. **Evaluation**—You may be asked to assist the audiologist in explaining test procedures or administering test items. The results of the testing will help the audiologist determine the degree and type of hearing loss and if the client is a candidate for a hearing aid. Alternatively, some clients may be candidates for cochlear implants—electronic devices that are surgically implanted in the inner ear. An audiologist may explain this option to a client, but the procedure will be decided and performed by a physician.

2. **Treatment planning**—The client's hearing needs in daily life activities are assessed. For example, what are the most common environments in which the individual will be working and interacting with others? Will it be a noisy place, and if so, what type of noise? You may be asked to interview the client or a family member to collect this information, which will help determine the type of amplification needed.

3. **Selection of the hearing aid**—The audiologist will make the selection depending on the degree of hearing loss and the hearing demands that occur in the

daily life activities of the client. You may also be asked to interpret while the audiologist explains about the type of hearing aid prescribed, its functions, and its uses.

For your background information, you might want to know that the size of hearing aid devices has changed dramatically in the last 20 years. Initially, body hearing aids were always used, and they were much larger than today's models. The miniaturization of electronic circuits and batteries has allowed smaller and smaller hearing aids to be produced. Significant hearing losses typically need a larger style of hearing aid for more power and louder amplification. Milder losses can be adequately served by smaller hearing aid styles. These smaller styles are referred to as behind the ear (BTE) and in-the-ear (ITE). Recent advances in miniaturization have resulted in ITE models known as in the canal (ITC), which fill the outer part of the ear canal, and completely in the canal (CIC), which fit farther inside the ear and are barely visible.

4. **Verification**—The audiologist verifies that the hearing aid includes basic electroacoustics, cosmetic appeal, comfortable fit, and electroacoustic performance.

5. **Orientation**—You may be asked to interpret while the audiologist counsels the client on the use and care of the hearing aids. Some of this step can be demonstrated nonverbally by the audiologist. This is the stage where the audiologist also describes the realistic expectations that the client should have for the performance of the hearing aids.

6. **Validation**—In a follow-up session, the audiologist verifies that the hearing aid is appropriate given the client's hearing loss and daily communication needs. Your assistance may be needed in receiving feedback from the client on hearing aid performance.

Notes

THE BID PROCESS FOR HEARING AIDS

Briefing

Ask about the procedures that will take place, such as interviewing the client about his or her daily routine and communication needs, preparing an impression of the ear mold, or reviewing the functioning and care of the prescribed hearing aid. Discuss possible questions that the client or family might have so you can be prepared to interpret information on those subjects.

Interaction

Interpret as the audiologist carries out the hearing aid fitting as described in the previous section (see page 85). Interpret all information clearly to ensure that the client understands the information presented and is able to ask questions if necessary.

Interpret the audiologist's suggestions for controlling the acoustics of the environment as well as the expectations of families, teachers, and co-workers of the client. For example, in addition to suggestions for a classroom FM system, a young client might need to have individual speech-language intervention and preferential seating in the classroom. Other tips for adequate management include preventing reverberation (i.e., prolongation or persistence of sound within a room), controlling noise level, and using optimal speaker/listener distance. In the case of profound deafness, the use of various communication systems will need to be reviewed (e.g., sign language or total communication).

Debriefing

You and the audiologist should review the interpreting process and determine what was effective. Plan any necessary follow up, such as contacting the client or family to ensure that proper adjustment to the hearing aid or cochlear implant is taking place and to confirm any sequel appointments.

CASE STUDIES TO PRACTICE ASSESSMENT PROCEDURES
Informal Assessment

1. You will need a client, an interpreter, and a speech-language pathologist.

2. The speech-language pathologist reviews the information included in the question-naire in Figure 4.1 and assembles all the materials that are needed to assess a school-age client.

3. Translate the questionnaire to the client's language, and then ask another speaker of the same language to back translate the information to verify the accuracy of the translation.

4. Before administering the questionnaire, discuss your role in assisting the speech-language pathologist in making observations about the following areas:

   - The client's ability to follow oral directions.

   - The client's need for more than the usual expected time to respond.

   - The need for repetition to enhance the client's performance.

   - The client's attention skills.

   - How verbal cuing would assist the client in recalling information or expressing himself or herself.

   - How to increase the client's amount of spoken language in case the client is shy or uncooperative.

5. During debriefing, discuss how the client's responses tell something about his or her experiences.

Hearing Aid Consultation

1. You will need a parent, an interpreter, and an audiologist. One or more others may be observers/evaluators.

2. Read the information in Case 4.1 that the audiologist needs to share with the parent.

3. The interpreter should become familiar with terminology that will be used during the interaction.

4. Role-play the entire BID process with observers/evaluators using The BID Process in Audiology (see page 66) as a checklist to note performance of the role players.

5. Role players and observers/evaluators discuss how clearly the information was conveyed and how well the BID procedures matched the checklist.

Figure 4.1
Cognitive-Ecological-Functional Questionnaire

Objects Needed: Five crayons or markers (red, yellow, blue, black, and white), one long, one broken, one bigger; a box; a picture with just a face; a picture of body parts; a blank piece of paper; two cups, one with some water; clay.

Questions to the client:

1. What is your name? _____

2. How old are you? _____

3. When is your birthday? _____

4. What grade are you in? ____ What is your teacher's name? _____

5. Where do you live?_____ What is your address? _____

6. Do you have brothers and sisters? _____

7. Who do you live with? _____

8. What does your mom do?_____

9. What does your dad do? _____

10. Do you have friends? _____ What are their names?_____

11. What is your favorite game?_____ Tell me about it!_____
    _____

12. What is your favorite food? _____

13. What is your favorite TV show? _____ Tell me about it: _____
    _____

14. What is your favorite story? _____ Tell me about it: _____
    _____

15. What is your favorite book? _____ Tell me about it: _____
    _____

Produce the crayons.

16. Which one is bigger? _____ Which one is broken? _____
    Which one is longer? _____
    What can you do with a pencil? _____

Continued on next page

Figure 4.1—*Continued*

17. What color is this one? _____
    [If unable to name, ask] Which one is red? _____
    yellow?   blue?   black?   white?

18. How many do I have here? two   three   five   one   four
    [If unable to count, ask] Give me: two   five   four   one

Make two groups, one with four crayons and one with three, and ask:

19. Which one has more crayons? _____

20. Put the crayons in front of the box.

21. Put the crayons on top of the box. *[Leave the box unopened]*

Produce the piece of paper.

22. Draw a house for me.

23. Draw a man for me.

Produce the picture of a face.

24. Look at this picture and tell me what is missing. _____

25. Can you draw the parts that are missing?

Produce the picture of a person.

26. Can you name the parts of the body? _____
    _____

27. Show me your left hand. Show me your right hand.

Show the two cups, one with water. Point to the cup with water.

28. What is this for? _____ What is in this cup? _____

Pour the water from one cup to the other.

29. Which one has more water? _____

Produce the clay.

30. I am going to make a ball. *[Make a ball]* I am going to make a snake.
    [Make a snake] Tell me how you make a snake. _____
    _____

From *Assessing Asian Language Performance* (pp. 171–172), by L.L. Cheng, 1991, Oceanside, CA: Academic Communication Associates. © 1991 by Academic Communication Associates. Adapted with permission.

CASE 4.1: TIFFANY, A 5-YEAR-OLD WITH A HEARING IMPAIRMENT

Team Members: parent, interpreter, and audiologist

Tiffany is a 5-year-old girl who speaks (*) and has just been identified as having a moderate sensorineural hearing loss. Her family speaks (*) primarily. Hearing aids have just been fitted. The audiologist is explaining to the parent how to care for the hearing aids. Tiffany is supposed to wear her hearing aids at the volume 4 level as specified in the audiological report. The parent should purchase a stethoscope to use when checking that the hearing aid is in running order. Connect the hearing aid to the stethoscope with the hearing aid set to the M position. Begin at a low volume setting, rotate the volume control wheel up and down, and then listen for a steady increase in loudness as the volume is raised. Listen for any crackling sounds or circuit noise. If there is no sound, check or replace the battery. Finally, squeeze and shake the hearing aid to check if the aid is cut off and check for cracks in the hearing aid case, ear mold, and tubing. Also check the ear mold for a buildup of wax or moisture, and clean out any that is found (Lang, 2000).

* Use any language as appropriate

Notes
_____
_____
_____
_____
_____
_____
_____
_____
_____
_____
_____
_____
_____

SESSION 5

EVALUATION AND OUTCOMES

In this session, you will learn:

- Methods to assess your oral and written skills in two languages

- Techniques for you and the communication disorders professional to provide feedback to each other regarding the interpreting and translating process

- Ways to gain feedback from the client or a family member regarding the interpreting and translating process

- A method for self-evaluating your performance following an interpreting or translating session

INTRODUCTION

This handbook and the training provided by your collaborating communication disorders professional are just the first step in your continuing education. This final session provides tools you can use to help identify ways to improve the collaboration process with other professionals and areas in which you need further study or practice.

You may use the assessment of oral and written language to develop practice activities or to anticipate questions that may be presented at an interview for an interpreter or translator position. The evaluations of collaborators' skills provides a vehicle for the communication disorders professional to give you feedback on performance during an individual session or over a period of time, and you can provide similar feedback on the effectiveness of the communication disorders professional in his or her collaboration with you. A form is provided for clients or family members to give written feedback on the interpreting services they receive. You can perform your own self-assessment with another form.

SELF-ASSESSMENT ITEMS

1. What materials could you bring to a job interview to demonstrate your proficiency in two languages?

2. Why is it important for the interpreter or translator to evaluate the role of the communication disorders professional?

3. What methods could be used to encourage consumers to be more honest or critical in their evaluations of the interpreting process?

4. After you complete a self-assessment of your performance, what activities could you undertake to improve your performance in each of the items in Figure 5.7 (see page 106)?

SUGGESTED READINGS AND RESOURCES

Langdon, H.W., and Cheng, L.L. (2002). *Collaborating with interpreters and translators: A guide for communication disorders professionals.* Eau Claire, WI: Thinking Publications.

This text is a companion to this manual. It provides an in-depth account of aspects of interpreting and translating for speech-language pathologists and audiologists.

WEBSITES

Two major websites are listed because each offers links to other sources that will be helpful to the interpreter and translator

National Clearinghouse for Bilingual Education (*www.ncbe.gwu.edu*)

American Speech-Language Hearing Association (*www.asha.org*)

ASSESSMENT OF YOUR ORAL AND WRITTEN PROFICIENCY IN TWO LANGUAGES

Selection and hiring of interpreter and translator candidates should be based on the candidate's oral and written language proficiency in English and the target second language. Some or all of the following components may be used for candidate assessment.

Oral Language Skills

The oral examination proposed is similar to that of the Foreign Service Institute, which is based on a scale of 1 to 5, with 3 being the minimum standard accepted to perform a given professional task. Ideally, native speakers of both English and the candidate's target language will interview the candidate. This oral interview may take place in one group session or different sessions for each language. A suggested collection of topics appears in Figure 5.1 (see page 96).

Notes

Figure 5.1 Suggested Topics for Oral Interviews	
ENGLISH	**TARGET LANGUAGE**
Provide a short summary of your experiences or training.	Provide a short summary of your experiences or training.
You have lost the test that the communication disorders professional lent you. Describe what you would do.	You forgot to call the parent to cancel the appointment and she took time off from work. You have to apologize and postpone the meeting.
You do not agree with what the speech-language pathologist tells the family regarding how important it is that they work at home with their child. In your culture, the professional is the expert who provides all the treatment. Explain this cultural difference to the speech-language pathologist.	You have to interpret to a client that he or she has a hearing loss that is progressively getting much worse and the cause is unknown. The client will have to see the otolaryngologist to determine the source of the problem.
What is your opinion on bilingualism and bilingual education in the United States and your country?	What is your opinion on bilingualism and bilingual education in the United States and your country?
A client refuses an assessment because he or she fears being labeled. What would you say and how would you explain to the communication disorders professional?	The speech-language pathologist just said that the client must attend weekly intervention sessions. If the client does not come, progress will be much slower. How would you explain this to the client?
What experience do you have working with school-age children?	I'm going to say some sentences in English, and I would like you to repeat them in your other language.
What experience do you have in a health-care setting?	Describe some of the differences that exist between dialects of your language.
Are you willing to participate in training sessions to learn more about interpreting and translating in this work setting?	What is the most difficult interpreting task you have experienced?

Figure 5.1—*Continued*

SCORE RESPONSES 1–5

1 = Very difficult to understand, makes many grammar and pronunciation errors

2 = Sometimes difficult to understand because of grammar and pronunciation errors

3 = Intelligible in most instances, although makes some occasional grammar and pronunciation errors that are not severe enough to interfere with communication

4 = Intelligible all the time, although makes some pronunciation errors that do not distract from intelligibility

5 = Native-like, although pronunciation may not be perfect

Notes

_____

_____

_____

_____

_____

_____

_____

_____

_____

_____

_____

_____

_____

Written Language Skills

Written language skills may be assessed by asking the candidate to translate prepared materials. Figure 5.2 is a letter addressed to a parent announcing a meeting. Schools have official meeting notices that must be sent to families, and these often need to be translated. Many school staff also use a less formal letter to confirm the meeting and to get a confirmation from family members that they will attend.

In addition, speech-language evaluation reports often need to be translated into the client's or family's first language. Figure 5.3 provides a translation task based on the history section of an evaluation report.

**Figure 5.2
Sample Letter**

Dear Mr. and Mrs. Jones:

Ms. Lee talked to you on the phone about our meeting to review the results of your son's evaluation. The meeting will be held at Einstein Elementary School on Tuesday, January 22, at 2 PM in Room 17. The meeting will last approximately one hour. You will meet with the classroom teacher, the nurse, the principal, and me. Ms. Lee will be interpreting the meeting. You may bring a friend or relative to this meeting if you wish. We will discuss the results of my evaluation and possible speech-language therapy. If you have any questions, please call Ms. Lee or me at 555-2216.

Please sign the bottom of this page and circle Yes or No if you plan to attend the meeting.

Sincerely,

Helen Price, MA, CCC-SLP

Speech-Language Pathologist

Yes, I will be at the meeting.

No, I cannot be at the meeting.

_____

Signature

Figure 5.3
Selection from a Speech-Language Evaluation Report

History

Paul is 14-year-old boy from Japan who has difficulty performing academically compared to his peers who were raised bilingually. He has received additional assistance from tutors, and teachers have modified his program to accommodate his learning needs. The evaluations performed by the school assessment team indicate that Paul has average intelligence. His reading and math skills are at about the fifth-grade level.

Paul is a cooperative, motivated young man who tries his best. His greatest challenge is his ability to comprehend what he reads in textbooks that are written in English. His math computational skills are adequate, but he has difficulty with word problems. He communicates fairly well in English in conversation, but has difficulty explaining ideas or concepts with greater detail. His teachers report that his vocabulary knowledge is lower than expected considering that he has been in U.S. schools for four years. His language skills in his native language are lower than those of his peers. Paul did experience problems in acquiring his native language, according to his mother. His parents also reported academic problems in his home country.

Notes

_____

_____

_____

_____

_____

_____

_____

_____

_____

_____

_____

_____

_____

_____

The rubrics in Table 5.1 may be used to score the assessment of written language skills. To pass the writing portion, the candidate should have ratings of 3 or better in all categories. To have uniform judgements of performance, the same person or group should score all samples. You may also use this rubric on practice translation tasks to help you work toward the standard expected of professional translators.

Table 5.1 **Rubric to Score Written Language Skills**

Area	Level 1: Poor	Level 2: Below Average	Level 3: Average	Level 4: Above Average	Level 5: Excellent
Meaning	1 or more incorrect meanings	Some meanings unclear	Some imprecision, but adequate meaning	All meanings accurate	All meanings precise
Grammar	3 or more errors that are distracting or confusing	1–2 errors that cause confusion	Some errors, but only mildly distracting	Some errors that do not affect meaning	No errors
Spelling	More than 5 errors	4–5 errors	2–3 errors	1 error	No errors
Punctuation	More than 3 errors	3 errors	2 errors	1 error	No errors

EVALUATION OF COLLABORATORS' SKILLS

Evaluation of both team members is important to ensure quality of service to the client. Figure 5.4 is your evaluation completed by the communication disorders professional. Figure 5.5 (see page 103) is the evaluation of the communication disorders professional completed by you.

These similar evaluation forms should be used during your orientation in a new setting to clarify role expectations. They may be used for feedback to team members as often as necessary for monitoring performance or when required by the employing agency.

Figure 5.4
Evaluation of Interpreter's or Translator's Skills

Key: (0) Not applicable (1) Always (2) Often (3) Sometimes (4) Rarely (5) Never

General Behaviors

1. Does the interpreter ask questions to find out
   what is planned for a given meeting? 0 1 2 3 4 5

2. Does the interpreter seek clarification
   when something is ambiguous? 0 1 2 3 4 5

3. Does the interpreter listen carefully to
   what is said by all parties? 0 1 2 3 4 5

4. Does the interpreter share insights about a
   given culture in a manner that facilitates
   the process? 0 1 2 3 4 5

5. Does the interpreter appear to be respectful
   of both cultures and seem well respected by
   the community and the families that need
   the interpreter's services? 0 1 2 3 4 5

6. Is the interpreter willing to acquire new
   skills to perform the job more effectively? 0 1 2 3 4 5

Continued on next page

Figure 5.4—*Continued*

7. Is there evidence that the interpreter
maintains neutrality and confidentiality
throughout the process?   0   1   2   3   4   5

8. Does the interpreter accept positive feedback
from parents and other parties involved
in the process?   0   1   2   3   4   5

9. Is the interpreter punctual?   0   1   2   3   4   5

Specific Translation Skills

1. Does the interpreter appear to convey a
given message clearly?   0   1   2   3   4   5

2. Does the interpreter retranslate something
when it is unclear to any participant?   0   1   2   3   4   5

3. Does the interpreter use different methods of
conveying the same information?   0   1   2   3   4   5

4. Does the interpreter appropriately use
different levels of formality?   0   1   2   3   4   5

5. Does the translator appropriately use back translation
to ensure that a given document has preserved
its original meaning?   0   1   2   3   4   5

From *Collaborating with Interpreters and Translators: A Guide for Communication Disorders Professionals* (pp. 147–148), by H.W. Langdon and L.L. Cheng, 2002, Eau Claire, WI: Thinking Publications. © 2002 Thinking Publications. Adapted with permission.

Figure 5.5
Evaluation of the Communication Disorders Professional's Skills

1. Does the communication disorders professional provide you with sufficient information before a given job?   0   1   2   3   4   5

Describe what could be done to improve the process: _____

_____

2. Does the communication disorders professional debrief with you after a session?   0   1   2   3   4   5

Describe what could be done to improve the process: _____

_____

3. Does the communication disorders professional provide clear messages that are not too difficult to interpret?   0   1   2   3   4   5

4. Does the communication disorders professional listen carefully to what is said by the client even though not fluent in the language?   0   1   2   3   4   5

5. Does the communication disorders professional seek your insights about a culture in a manner that facilitates the process and serves the client?   0   1   2   3   4   5

6. Is the communication disorders professional willing to use suggestions that you provide?   0   1   2   3   4   5

7. Does the communication disorders professional provide you with helpful suggestions?   0   1   2   3   4   5

8. Are there sufficient resources for you to acquire necessary information to perform the job adequately?   0   1   2   3   4   5

Comments: _____

_____

_____

EVALUATION BY THE CLIENT

You may want to request feedback from the client or family member to identify areas needing improvement or topics to pursue for your continuing education. Figure 5.6 provides a format for clients to use in providing feedback. Communication disorders professionals may also choose to use this form to collect information regarding each interpreter used in a program for the purposes of program improvement.

Notes

Figure 5.6
Client Evaluation of the Interpreter

Dear_____:

Today you participated in a session where the services of an interpreter, Mr./Ms._____, were used. Your responses and feedback will help us monitor the quality of services provided by this person. Thank you for your time.

Language: _____   Date: _____

Purpose of the session: *(Please circle)*

To gather information   To share assessment results   To share progress

How many times have you worked with this interpreter?   1 2 3 4 5$^+$

How many times have you worked with this communication
     disorders professional?   1 2 3 4 5$^+$

On a scale from 0–5 please rate the following:

(0) Not applicable (1) Very good (2) Good (3) Average (4) Below Average (5) Poor

1. How clearly did the communication disorders professional and the
        interpreter explain their roles to you?   0   1   2   3   4   5

2. How well did you understand this interpreter?   0   1   2   3   4   5

3. How accurately do you feel the interpreting
        was done?   0   1   2   3   4   5

4. How assured do you feel that the information will be
        kept confidential?   0   1   2   3   4   5

5. How well did you understand your rights regarding
        assessment, receiving a given procedure,
        or the therapy suggested?   0   1   2   3   4   5

6. If you brought a bilingual advocate to the meeting,
        how well do you feel the team included
        this person's input?   0   1   2   3   4   5

7. How well were your concerns or questions
        answered?   0   1   2   3   4   5

8. Did the interpreter make you feel at ease?   0   1   2   3   4   5

9. Please rate your satisfaction in working with
        an interpreter   0   1   2   3   4   5

Please provide any further comments: _____

_____

From Obtaining Feedback from Non-English Speakers, by N. Garber and L.A. Mauffette-Leenders, In *The Critical Link: Interpreters in the Community* (pp. 131–143), by S.E. Carr, R. Roberts, A. Dufour, and D. Steyn (Eds.), 1997, Philadelphia: Johns Benjamins. © 1997 by Johns Benjamins. Adapted with permission.

SELF-ASSESSMENT

You should assess your skills on an ongoing basis. Figure 5.7 provides a list of questions that can guide a self-assessment.

Figure 5.7
Self-Assessment

Date: _____

Context:

❑ Conference to interview client with speech-language pathologist/audiologist

❑ Conference to present assessment results for speech-language pathologist/audiologist

❑ Intervention session for speech-language pathologist/audiologist

On a scale from 0–5 rate yourself on the following items:

(0) Not applicable   (1) Always   (2) Often   (3) Sometimes   (4) Rarely   (5) Never

1. My interpretation or translation was accurate.   0   1   2   3   4   5

2. I kept the information confidential.   0   1   2   3   4   5

3. I avoided giving direct advice to the client
   without the involvement of the communication
   disorders professional.   0   1   2   3   4   5

4. The client understood his or her rights regarding
   assessment, knew why he or she was receiving
   a given procedure, or understood the therapy
   or intervention that was suggested.   0   1   2   3   4   5

5. I collaborated successfully with an advocate
   brought by the client.   0   1   2   3   4   5

6. Overall, my interpretation was clear.   0   1   2   3   4   5

7. Things that went well this time: _____

   _____

8. Two areas to improve next time:

   _____

   _____

GLOSSARY

If unfamiliar terms are encountered in the following entries, the terms may be found elsewhere in the Glossary. Several sources were used to compile the Glossary (Figueroa and Ruiz, 1983; Gillam, Marquardt, and Martin, 2000; Nicolosi, Harryman, and Kresheck, 1996); they are listed in the References.

Accent

Phonetic traits of an individual's speech.

Acoustic Gain

A ratio of the output power or input power (gain = output − input).

Acoustic Impedance

Measurable contraction of the tympanic membrane in response to a tone.

Adaptive Behavior

Effectiveness of the individual in adjusting to the natural and social demands of his or her environment.

Affective

Related to the emotions and feelings of a person.

Air Conduction

Transmission of sounds to the inner ear through the external auditory canal and the structure of the middle ear.

American Sign Language (ASL)

The language of the deaf community in the United States. ASL has its own system in all areas of language form, content, and use.

Aphasia

Weakness or loss of the ability to give or to receive a verbal or written message. It does not have any relationship to impairment of the vocal cords, vision, or hearing.

Aptitude Test

A test that measures capacity, abilities, or talents for learning something.

Articulation

The way in which sounds are produced during speech.

Audiogram

A chart that shows an individual's hearing capacity. Sensitivity to sound conducted in the air and by the ear bones can be shown on this chart.

Audiologist

A specialist who identifies and measures hearing loss. Also helps in the rehabilitation of those with hearing disabilities by recommending specific hearing aids or devices.

Audiometric Evaluation

An evaluation of an individual's hearing sensitivity and acuity.

Auditory Brainstem Response (ABR)

A test that helps determine the site of a lesion to the cochlea, the brainstem, or the auditory nerve (VIII cranial nerve).

Auditory Cuing

Any strategy, such as stress, pitch, or intonation, that may assist in enhancing communication.

Auditory Memory

The ability to recall information that is presented auditorially.

Auditory Processing

The ability to make full use of what is heard. Includes the ability to discriminate, analyze, and associate what is heard.

Augmentative and Alternative Communication (AAC)

Any approach to support, enhance, or supplement the communication of individuals who are not independent verbal communicators. May use approaches such as picture boards and computer-assisted devices.

Autism

Abnormality in interpersonal relationships exhibited in early childhood. Effect on language development is variable. Reactions include resistance to change and possible peculiar interest in or attachments to animate or inanimate objects.

Back Translation

Translation of a document from a second language into the original language. For example, French to English and English back to French to check accuracy of the translation.

Basal

In testing, the lowest level at which testing is initiated on a given set of items.

Basic Interpersonal Communication Skills (BICS)

Term introduced by Cummins (1984) defining the level of an individual's language ability as it relates to communicating in daily situations or situations that are highly contextualized.

Behavior Modification

A process based on the belief that every behavior is learned and, consequently, must be unlearned. One must decide specifically which behaviors should be changed and how to make the changes in a definite way.

Behind the Ear (BTE)

A certain type of hearing aid that is worn behind the ear.

Body Language

Nonverbal features of communication, including gestures, facial expressions, and body language.

Bone Conduction

Transmission of sound to the inner ear through vibration applied to the bones of the skull. Allows determination of the cochlea's hearing sensitivity while bypassing any middle ear abnormalities.

Ceiling

In testing, the highest level at which an individual gave a response.

Central Auditory Processing Disorder (CAPD)

Difficulty in discriminating speech in the presence of background noise and frequently in the absence of loss of hearing sensitivity.

Cerumen

Earwax.

Cleft Lip or Palate

A space or opening that may occur in the lip and/or hard palate. It is a congenital condition.

Cochlea

The coiled tube in the inner ear that houses the sensory cells for hearing.

Cochlear Implant

An electronic device that is implanted in the cochlea to stimulate hearing.

Code Switching

Alternating use of two languages at the word, phrase, and sentence level with a complete break between languages in phonology.

Cognitive Ability

The act or process of knowing. To think in a logical and analytical form (used interchangeably with *intelligence*).

Cognitive Academic Language Proficiency (CALP)

Term introduced by Cummins (1984) differentiating the level of an individual's language ability as it relates to performing on tasks that are academic in nature.

Completely in the Canal (CIC)

A certain type of hearing aid that fits inside the ear and is barely visible.

Conductive Hearing Loss

A loss of hearing sensitivity caused by damage to the outer and/or middle ear.

Congenital

A disorder that occurs at birth or early in the developmental period.

Craneofacial Anomalies

Malformation of the cranium (skull) and facial areas.

Criterion-Referenced Test

A test that assesses the ability to perform a certain skill. For example, ability to read paragraphs of certain lengths and complexities, ability to comprehend directions, or ability to write definitions of specific words.

Cuing

Any strategy that will enhance a correct response (visual or auditory).

Decibel

Measure of the intensity of a sound, abbreviated as dB.

Dialectal Variations

Variations in the pronunciation, word usage, and even grammar and syntax within a given language.

Disfluencies

An interruption of the flow of speech sounds marked by repetitions, prolongations, or hesitations.

Distractibility

Difficulty paying attention.

Dominance

The language that is predominantly used or is most easily used by an individual exposed to two languages.

Dynamic Assessment

Assessment of an individual's skills using various methods to enhance his or her performance through repetition of information presented, demonstration of examples, or simplification of the information.

Dysarthria

A motor speech disorder due to impairment originating in the central or peripheral nervous system.

Dysphagia

Difficulty swallowing; may include inflammation, compression, paralysis, weakness, or hypertonicity of the esophagus.

Endoscopy

Refers to the examination of the interior of a canal or hollow space.

Ear Mold

A fitting usually made of plastic and fitting in the auricle of the ear. Designed to conduct amplified sound waves from the receiver of a hearing aid.

Eventcast

Refers to the use of language to describe events or information.

Expressive Language

Communication through the use of oral or written words.

Fine-Motor Coordination

The ability to use minor muscular groups, such as for writing or cutting.

Fluency

Absence of hesitations or repetitions during speech.

FM System

One of several possible assistive listening devices to increase reception of information presented auditorially.

Free Appropriate Public Education (FAPE)

A right of all children in the United States by federal law.

Frequency

Number of repetitions of compressions and rarefactions of a sound wave that occur at the same rate over a period of time. Expressed in Hertz (Hz). For example, a vibration of 125 Hz consists of 125 cycles per second.

Grammar

Principles or rules for speaking or writing according to the form and usage of a language.

Gross-Motor Coordination

The ability to use major muscular groups, such as for jumping or running.

Hearing Aid

An electronic amplifying device to bring sound more effectively into the listener's ear. Consists of a microphone, amplifier, and receiver.

Idiom

An utterance that has a hidden meaning (e.g., *out to lunch*).

Idiomatic Expression

A part of speech that includes an idiom.

Individualized Education Program (IEP)

An individual educational plan written to meet the special education needs of students 3–21 years of age.

Individual Family Service Plan (IFSP)

An individual educational plan written to meet the developmental needs of a child ages 0–3.

Individuals with Disabilities Education Act (IDEA)

Federal law passed in 1997 to ensure educational access and fair assessments and intervention for students experiencing a variety of learning difficulties.

Intelligibility

Ability to be comprehensible while communicating with someone orally.

Intelligence

Aggregate capacity to act purposefully, think rationally and deal effectively with the environment, especially in relation to the extent of perceived effectiveness in meeting challenges. Used interchangeably with cognitive ability.

Interpreting

Transmitting a message from one language to another orally.

In the Canal (ITC)

A specific type of hearing aid that fills the outer part of the ear canal

In the Ear (ITE)

A specific type of hearing aid that is worn in the ear.

Jargon Language

Verbal behavior of children, beginning at about 9 months and ceasing at about 18 months. It includes a variety of syllables that are inflected that approximate meaningful connected speech in advanced stages; some true words may be heard.

Language

Any accepted structured symbolic system for interpersonal communication composed of sounds arranged in ordered sequence to form words. Includes rules for combining words into sequences that express thoughts, intentions, experiences, and feelings. Composed of phonologic, morphologic, syntactic, and semantic components.

Language Loss

A regression of skills in an individual's first language as a result of lack of opportunity to use the language or forgetting some of it. Is frequent in individuals who use more than one language at a time. A loss that is very rapid may indicate a language disorder.

Language Sampling

A manually gathered or taped sample of an individual's consecutive utterances during an interaction (e.g., telling a story) or a conversation on various topics.

Laryngectomy

Surgical procedure where all or part of the larynx is removed.

Learning Disability

A significant difficulty with the acquisition and use of one or more of the following abilities: listening, speaking, reading, writing, mathematical computation or mathematical problem solving.

Lexicon

Vocabulary of a language.

Mixed Hearing Loss

A combined conductive and sensorineural hearing loss.

Modality

The way to acquire or receive sensations. Sight, sound, touch, smell, and taste are the common senses.

Morphology

The study of the smallest speech unit that has a differential function. For example, -s for plural and -ed for past.

Multiple-Meaning Word

A word that can have more than one meaning (e.g., *orange* or *glasses*).

Neurologic Examination

Tests to determine if an illness exists or if there is damage to the nervous system.

Nodules

Caused by inflammation to the vocal folds resulting in generally benign callouslike growth. The nodules are generally paired and located in the midpoint of the vocal folds.

Nonverbal Communication

See *paralinguistic*.

Norm

A set standard or pattern derived from a representative sampling of median achievement of a large group. It offers a range of values against which individual comparisons can be made.

Normal Curve

A graph (curve) that represents the distribution of performance of a sample that has been normed.

Observations

Recording behavior or performance.

Occupational Therapist

A specialist who helps patients develop useful physical and mental attitudes toward all the areas of daily life.

Oral Manometer

An instrument that measures the air blown into a tube to measure the amount of oral pressure that is exerted during respiration.

Oral Peripheral Examination

A speech-language pathologist examines the structures (and their functions) responsible in the production of speech.

Organic Disorder

Disorder with a known physical cause.

Otitis Media

Infection of the fluid in the middle ear.

Otoacoustic Emissions

Sounds generated within the normal cochlea.

Otosclerosis

A hearing problem caused by the fixation of the ossicles.

Paralinguistic

Includes all nonverbal features used in communication. For example, gestures, facial expression, body posture, speech volume, and intonation.

Percentile

Converted score compared to a ranking based on a normed population. For example, 90th percentile means that only 10% of the population sampled scored higher.

Perception

The process of interpreting sensory information. It consists of the exact mental association of the present stimuli with memories from past experiences.

Performance Score

What a person can do without needing to speak or verbalize.

Perseveration

Continuing to behave or to answer in a certain way when it is not appropriate. Difficulty in changing from one action, thought pattern, or assignment to another.

Phonology

The study of the sound system of a language, including pause and stress.

Physical Therapist

A specialist who helps patients in the treatment of disorders of bones, joints, muscles, and nerves by means of heat, light, massage, and exercise.

Pitch

Acuteness or gravity of a tone, dependent on the frequency of the vibrations producing it and their intensity and overtone structure.

Polyp

Bulging growth generally appearing on one of the vocal folds and located in the anterior middle portion of the vocal fold.

Pragmatics

The study of speaker-listener intentions and relations and all elements in the environment surrounding the message.

Presbycusis

A common condition causing hearing loss that is associated with aging.

Proficiency

Referring to the degree to which an individual is fluent in a given language.

Prostheses

Artificial substitutes for a missing body part.

Protocol

In testing, the sheet that is used to record an individual's responses.

Psychologist

A specialist who studies an individual's thinking and behavior processes.

Psychomotor

Refers to the reaction of the muscles, including development of the small muscles (e.g., cutting something) and the large muscles (e.g., walking and jumping).

Radiographic Study

An x-ray of a given body part, like the chest, neck, or skull.

Raw Score

In testing, the score that is obtained by subtracting total missed items from the ceiling.

Receptive Language

Ability to understand spoken (oral) or written communication.

Recounts

Retelling a story or event.

Reinforcement

A procedure where a certain stimulus is offered to elicit a response. For example, a student is given verbal or tangible praise when responding to a question or request.

Reliability

Means "consistency." It refers to the consistency of scores obtained by the same people when retested with the identical test or with an equivalent form of the test. Should include interscorer-interexaminer and internal consistency measures

Resonance Disorders

Abnormalities in the use of the nasal cavity when speaking. Resonance can be hypernasal (excessive nasality) or denasal (insufficient nasality).

Reverberation

Persistence of a sound in a given space as a result of multiple reflections after the sound has ceased.

Sample Transcription

Writing down what an individual said verbatim.

Scaffolding

Any strategy used to facilitate an individual's comprehension and/or response to a task.

Self-Concept

The idea that a person has about himself or herself.

Self-Help Skills

Refers to actions such as dressing oneself, eating, and other activities for functioning in the family, in the school, or in the community.

Semantics

Study of the meaning in language. Includes the relationships between language, thought, and behavior.

Sensorineural Hearing Loss

A hearing loss that stems from damage to any part of the inner ear and/or auditory nerve.

Social Maturity

The ability to take the social and personal responsibilities that are expected for people of similar age.

Special Education

Special instruction for children who have learning difficulties. These children must have an individualized education program (IEP).

Speech

Medium of oral communication that uses a linguistic code (language).

Speech Discrimination

Ability to compare sounds with other sounds, nonsense syllables, and monosyllabic or multisyllabic words.

Speech Reading or Lip Reading

Using visual cues to determine what is being said.

Speech-Language Pathologist

A specialist who works with children and adults in assessment and intervention for problems in speech and language.

Speech Reception Threshold (SRT)

The level at which the client can repeat correctly 50% of two-syllable words referred to as spondees, like *baseball*, *doormat*, *birthday*, or *cowboy*.

Standard Score

Derived score obtained by comparing a score to that of a normed population.

Standardized Test

A test consisting of specific items that must be administered and scored using a consistent method to compare the results to a normed population. Must have data on reliability and validity.

Stroboscopy

A method by which an instrument enables one to examine the vibration of the vocal folds.

Stuttering

Disruption in the normal fluency and time patterning of speech.

Syntax

Order of words forming a sentence. The order varies across languages.

Threshold

The lowest intensity necessary to produce an awareness of a stimulus. In the context of audiology, means the perception of a signal, tone, or word.

Tinnitus

Ringing or roaring perceived in the absence of any other noise.

Total Communication

The use of any method, including finger spelling, singing, speech, or speech reading, to enhance face-to-face communication.

Translating

Transmitting a message from one language to another in writing.

Traumatic Brain Injury (TBI)

An acquired injury to the brain caused by an external force resulting in total or partial functional disability and/or psychosocial impairment that adversely affects an individual's performance. Impairments can be in one or more areas, such as cognition, language, speech, memory, attention, reasoning, abstract thinking, judgment, problem-solving, physical functioning, and information processing.

Tympanic Membrane

The thin concave membrane that separates the external and the middle ear.

Tympanogram

A graph obtained from tympanometry indicating the function of the middle ear.

Tympanometry

Measure of the resistance of the tympanic membrane to various pressure changes.

Validity

The validity of a test verifies what the test measures and how well it does it.

Verbal Performance

The ability to solve problems through the use of language.

Videoendoscopy

The results of an endoscopy that are recorded on video.

Vocal Cords or Folds

Membranous cords located in the larynx composed of folds. The vocal folds vibrate when air is pushed through the larynx.

Vocal Stress

Difficulty in using voice at a normal pitch/loudness.

Voice Quality

A description of the voice that is produced by the vibration of the focal folds. Quality may be described as hoarse, breathy, or harsh.

Word Attack Skills

The ability to analyze words, recognizing word endings, prefixes, and root words.

Word Recognition Test (WRT)

A test to determine the intensity at which a given word may be heard.

REFERENCES

Aleksandrovsky, I.V., McCullough, J.K., and Wilson, R.H. (1998). Development of suprathreshold word recognition test for Russian-speaking patients. *Journal of American Academy of Audiology, 9,* 417–425.

American Speech-Language-Hearing Association. (1998). Guidelines for hearing aid fitting for adults. *American Journal of Audiology, 7*(1), 5–13.

Cheng, L.L. (1991). *Assessing Asian language performance.* Oceanside, CA: Academic Communication Associates.

Cummins, J. (1984). *Bilingualism and special education.* Clevedon, England: Multilingual Matters.

Figueroa, R.A., and Ruiz, N.T. (1983). *The bilingual special education dictionary.* Oakland, CA: The National Hispanic University.

Garber, N., and Mauffette-Leenders, L.A. (1997). Obtaining feedback from non-English speakers. In S.E. Carr, R. Roberts, A. Dufour, and D. Steyn (Eds.), *The critical link: Interpreters in the community* (pp.131–143). Philadelphia: Johns Benjamins.

Gillam, R.B., Marquardt, T.P., and Martin, F.N. (2000). *Communication sciences and disorders: From science to clinical practice.* San Diego, CA: Singular.

Individuals with Disabilities Education Act (IDEA) Amendments, 20 U.S.C. § 1400 *et. seq.* (1997).

Lang, J. (2000). Hearing impairment. In E. Pritchard-Dodge (Ed.), *The survival guide for the school-based speech-language pathologist* (pp.241–262). San Diego, CA: Singular.

Langdon, H.W., and Cheng, L.L. (2002).*Collaborating with interpreters and translators: A guide for communication disorders professionals.* Eau Claire, WI: Thinking Publications.

Lustig, M.W., and Koester, J. (1999). *Intercultural competence: Interpersonal communication across cultures.* New York: Longman.

Martin, F.N., and Clark, J.G. (2001). *Introduction to audiology: A review manual.* Boston: Allyn and Bacon.

McCullough, J., Wilson, R.H., Birck, J.D., and Anderson, L.G. (1994). A multimedia approach for estimating speech recognition of multilingual clients. *American Journal of Audiology, 1*(3), 19–24.

Nicolosi, L., Harryman, E., and Kresheck, J. (1996). *Terminology of communication disorders: Speech-language-hearing.* Baltimore: Williams and Wilkins.

Semel, E., Wiig, E., and Secord, W. (1996). Clinical Evaluation of Language Fundamentals–3 (CELF–3). San Antonio, TX: Psychological Corporation.

Strong, C.J. (1998). *The Strong narrative assessment procedure.* Eau Claire, WI: Thinking Publications.

Wiig, E., Secord, W., and Semel, E. (1997). Clinical Evaluation of Language Fundamentals–3 (CELF–3), Spanish Version. San Antonio, TX: Psychological Corporation.

Wisconsin Department of Public Instruction. (2002). *Special education rights for parents and children.* Retrieved January 14, 2002, http://www.dpi.state.wi.us/een/pcrights.html